Applications of Public Choice Theory to Public Policy

Economy, Polity, and Society

Series Editors

Virgil Henry Storr and Jayme S. Lemke, Mercatus Center

The foundations of political economy—from Adam Smith to the Austrian school of economics, to contemporary research in public choice and institutional analysis—are sturdy and well established, but far from calcified. On the contrary, the boundaries of the research built on this foundation are ever expanding. One approach to political economy that has gained considerable traction in recent years combines the insights and methods of three distinct but related subfields within economics and political science: the Austrian, Virginia and Bloomington schools of political economy. The vision of this book series is to capitalize on the intellectual gains from the interactions between these approaches in order to both feed the growing interest in this approach and advance social scientists' understanding of economy, polity, and society.

This series seeks to publish works that combine the Austrian school's insights on knowledge, the Virginia school's insights into incentives in non-market contexts, and the Bloomington school's multiple methods, real-world approach to institutional design as a powerful tool for understanding social behaviour in a diversity of contexts.

Titles in the series

Applications of Public Choice Theory to Public Policy, edited by Brian Meehan, Jayme S. Lemke, and Paul Dragos Aligica

Institutions and Incentives in Public Policy: An Analytical Assessment of Non-Market Decision-Making, edited by Rosolino Candela, Rosemarie Fike, and Roberta Herzberg

Market Process and Market Order: From Human Action, But Not of Human Design, edited by Rosolino A. Candela, Kristen R. Collins, and Christopher J. Coyne

Toward a Hayekian Theory of Social Change, edited by Peter J. Boettke, Erwin Dekker, and Chad Van Schoelandt

Knowledge and Entrepreneurship in Public Policy, edited by Christopher J. Coyne, Abigail R. Hall, and Eileen Norcross

Nudging Public Policy: Examining the Benefits and Limitations of Paternalistic Public Policies, edited by Rosemarie Fike, Stefanie Haeffele, And Arielle John

Economics and the Public Good: The End of Desire in Aristotle's Politics and Ethics, by John Antonio Pascarella

Applications of Public Choice Theory to Public Policy

Brian Meehan, Jayme S. Lemke,
and Paul Dragos Aligica

BLOOMSBURY ACADEMIC
NEW YORK • LONDON • OXFORD • NEW DELHI • SYDNEY

BLOOMSBURY ACADEMIC
Bloomsbury Publishing Inc, 1359 Broadway, New York, NY 10018, USA
Bloomsbury Publishing Plc, 50 Bedford Square, London, WC1B 3DP, UK
Bloomsbury Publishing Ireland, 29 Earlsfort Terrace, Dublin 2, D02 AY28, Ireland

First published in the United States of America 2025
This edition published 2025

Library of Congress Cataloging-in-Publication Data

Names: Meehan, Brian, 1986- editor | Lemke, Jayme S. editor | Aligică, Paul Dragoş editor
Title: Applications of public choice theory to public policy / edited by Brian Meehan, Jayme S. Lemke, and Paul Dragos Aligica.
Description: New York : Bloomsbury Academic, 2025. | Series: Economy, polity, and society | Includes bibliographical references and index. | Summary: "This volume uses empirical and theoretical evidence to explore applications of public choice theory to policy. Case studies from around the word are employed to illustrate this theoretical approach in different institutional environments"— Provided by publisher.
Identifiers: LCCN 2025014668 (print) | LCCN 2025014669 (ebook) | ISBN 9781666956351 hardback | ISBN 9781666956375 paperback | ISBN 9781666956368 ebook | ISBN 9798765154212 adobe pdf
Subjects: LCSH: Evidence-based policy | Rational choice theory
Classification: LCC H97.5.A66 2025 (print) | LCC H97.5 (ebook)
LC record available at https://lccn.loc.gov/2025014668
LC ebook record available at https://lccn.loc.gov/2025014669

ISBN: HB: 978-1-6669-5635-1
ePDF: 979-8-7651-5421-2
eBook: 978-1-6669-5636-8

Series: ECONOMY, POLITY, AND SOCIETY

Typeset by Deanta Global Publishing Services, Chennai, India

For product safety related questions contact productsafety@bloomsbury.com.

To find out more about our authors and books visit www.bloomsbury.com and sign up for our newsletters.

Contents

List of Tables and Figures

Figures

Tables

Introduction

Brian Meehan, Jayme S. Lemke, and Paul Dragos Aligica

The contributors to this book utilize the public choice approach to interpret, analyze, and, at times, even predict policy outcomes from a variety of contexts around the world. As you will see, the volume emphasizes how much can be learned from studying real people in the process of navigating political processes and institutional change. In this introduction and in the opening chapter, we directly address what the public choice approach is, its relationship to policy analysis, and how both can be improved through the incorporation of a diversity of theoretical and empirical strategies. After establishing these strategies, the rest of the contributors to the volume put them into practice to address issues such as educational reform in Ghana, policy responses to the Covid-19 pandemic, antitrust policy, the political role of supreme courts in the United States and in Latin America, the impact of taking a precautionary approach to energy policy, regulatory burdens as a form of time tax, and the looming uncertainty over how artificial intelligence will be governed as it continues to have an ever greater impact on our lives. So, before we go any further—what is public choice?

A Very Brief Introduction to Public Choice Theory

Although economic and political considerations are often treated separately in both academic and popular discourse, economic and political activity are, in reality, deeply intertwined. Political and legal systems have a significant influence on what types of economic activity are allowed or disallowed, encouraged or discouraged. Regulatory processes and legal codes can impact what types of entrepreneurial ventures will be feasible. Similarly, the processes of entrepreneurship, innovation, and exchange that make up the economy have a significant impact on how people will choose to interact with each other through collective choice processes. How people provide for themselves and pursue the projects of their lives will affect the types of political arrangements they find most desirable and most productive.

Although the interconnected nature of political and economic processes was recognized by classical thinkers in political economy from Adam Smith to Karl Marx, the conscious recognition of political and economic entanglement was often forgotten in the excitement generated by the projects of scientific management and central planning during the first half of the twentieth century. Economist Peter Boettke has referred to this trend as modern economics' "flight from reality" (Boettke 1997). In response, a variety of scholars from across disciplines and ideological perspectives began to work on a project that would come to be described as the field of public choice. Although many figures were important to these early developments—including Anthony Downs, Duncan Black, Gordon Tullock, William Riker, Mancur Olson, and Vincent Ostrom—two figures were particularly essential to the development of the ideas built on in this volume (Mueller 1976; Holcombe 2016). The first, James M. Buchanan, is the economist credited with developing both public choice economics and constitutional political economy (Buchanan 1987; 1999). He received the Nobel Prize in Economics in 1986 in recognition of his founding role in public choice economics. The second is Elinor Ostrom, the political scientist who won both the Johan Skytte Prize in 1999 (the top award in the field of Political Science) and the Nobel Prize in Economics in 2009 for her contributions to the study of collective action and institutional analysis (Ostrom 1998; 2010a; 2010b).

Public choice can be defined as the application of economic reasoning to the study of institutions and processes pertaining to non-market settings. In this context, economic principles such as utility maximization, cost-benefit analysis, and competitive behavior are used to analyze how decisions are made in sectors where the allocation of resources is not determined solely by market forces and the monetary price system. This approach helps our understanding of how individuals and groups within the non-market sector make choices, considering that, unlike traditional market transactions, these decisions often involve collective actions and public goods that affect broad groups of people.

A version of this definition emphasizes one specific aspect, which has to do with the incentive-based economic analysis of political institutions and collective decision-making systems. It examines how the behavior of political agents (e.g., politicians, government officials, and voters) is influenced by incentives and how these incentives can lead to outcomes that may not necessarily align with the general welfare or optimal public resource allocation. In doing so, public choice analysis often stresses that in addition to "market failure," there is also something called "government failure." When it comes to public policy relevance, government failure may be even more important than market failure since many arguments exist that claim market failure could be fixed by the intervention of the government. Thus, this public choice perspective highlights the importance of designing governance structures and policies in a way that aligns individual incentives with the overall social good, potentially mitigating issues like corruption, inefficiency, and policy failure.

Finally, public choice serves as a basic theoretical framework for constitutional political economy, which studies the legal and institutional structures within which political processes and economic decisions intersect (Buchanan 1987). This facet of public choice focuses on the rules of the game—namely, the constitution and other fundamental rules that dictate the boundary conditions for political and economic interaction. In this version or approach to public choice, the emphasis is on rules and rule-guided behavior. It analyzes how different constitutional rules can affect the behavior of political actors and policy outcomes, aiming to identify the constitutional arrangements that can promote efficient and fair outcomes in collective decision-making processes.

Although precursor ideas can be found in earlier works of moral philosophy, public choice began to take shape as a distinct sub-discipline in the 1950s as economists began to explore the relevance of their analytical toolkit to the study of political institutions (Black, Downs, Buchanan, Tullock, etc.) and political scientists near-simultaneously began to consider the relevance of economic theories and frameworks for their subject matter (Riker, Elinor Ostrom, and Vincent Ostrom). In part because of the diverse backgrounds of public choice scholars, public choice has remained a uniquely interdisciplinary group within the social sciences. Scholars working in the field of public choice have formal training in economics, philosophy, political science, political theory, history, and many other disciplines and continue to successfully engage in discourse on political institutions and political incentives.

Although scholars of public choice employ diverse approaches, they share a commitment to three core theoretical suppositions: behavioral symmetry, methodological individualism, and the rationality of action. Behavioral symmetry is perhaps the most radical of public choice's bases, as it directly challenges the tendency to consider politics and economics as fundamentally different realms of human activity, participated in by fundamentally different groups of people. Instead, public choice adopts the perspective that whatever assumptions are made of people in the political sphere should also be applied to activity outside of the political sphere, and vice versa (Buchanan [1979] 1999). However foolish or wise, narrow or open-minded, greedy or self-sacrificing you perceive humans to be, the same set of assumptions about human cognition, behavior, and choice should be applied to all domains of life.

Methodological individualism, more common across the social sciences yet still integral to the public choice approach, refers to the proposition that action originates in the cognitive processes of individuals (Buchanan 1954; [1979] 1999). As such, the perceptions and interests of the individuals involved in collective choice-making processes are the media through which plans are translated into action. Organizations cannot be presumed to act as cohesive, mind-melded units. Instead, questions of internal organization, conflict, and the rules that manage and mediate these conflicts are of critical importance. Public choice does not assume a government is "for the people" because its spokesperson says so; public choice looks at whether the rule-systems and other institutions in place are likely or unlikely to align the actions of political representatives with the interest of the people.

Public choice also adopts some version of rationality in its theorizing, although the exact version of rationality employed varies widely across the discipline. The Virginia School of public choice, typified by the first Nobel Prize winner in the field, James Buchanan, typically employs some version of the loose form of rationality that says individuals will only take an action when it is in their benefit to do so—whether that benefit is financial, experiential, relational, spiritual, etc. The Rochester School uses the most formal version of rationality, emphasizing the modeling of voting behavior and the formal propositions that make it logically consistent. Most recently, Elinor Ostrom and other members of the branch of public choice known as the Bloomington School of Institutional Analysis have advocated for the development of "second-generation models of rationality" (Ostrom 1998, 3) that are boundedly rational, recognize the limits of human will and cognition, and are adaptable according to the decision-making context. Regardless of the precise model adopted, the use of the concept of the rational actor has been and is important for the study of incentives and their inevitable counterpart—unintended consequences.

What emerged from this framework, which recognized the boundedly rational and imperfectly human nature of political actors, was an intellectual paradigm capable of recognizing the ways that politics *is* exchange (Buchanan [1979] 1999; Munger 2018). When people choose to challenge existing political institutions or work together to create new ones, they are engaging in a form of exchange behavior that is not so different from people engaging in trade and other market activities in order to accomplish objectives they would never be able to achieve in isolation. If collective projects are to succeed, those participating in them will need to find ways to cooperate that don't require superhuman sacrifice and intelligence. In order to understand how such a thing could be possible in the domain of practical politics, it will be important to bring a public choice perspective to questions of public administration and public policy.

Connections between Public Choice and Public Policy

Public choice theory, with its diverse approaches and applications, maintains an intrinsic connection with public policy analysis and assessment. Each definition or potential approach to the complex domain of public choice theorizing and reasoning highlights how different aspects of that domain are essential in understanding and shaping public policy environments. In this respect, we could go a step further and pinpoint, in much more specific ways, the linkages connecting public choice analysis to policy analysis.

For instance, when it comes to the notion of economic reasoning applied to non-market settings, there is a direct connection to public policy analysis in terms of optimizing resource allocation where market mechanisms are absent or inefficient. Public policy often involves decisions about distributing public goods and managing collective resources, areas where market signals like price mechanisms do not naturally guide decisions. Public choice theory helps policymakers understand the underlying economic behaviors and incentives that drive collective decision-making processes, thus enabling more efficient and effective policies that aim to maximize social welfare.

Similarly, when viewing public choice as an incentives-based analysis of the state and collective decision systems, the theory offers crucial insights into how to structure policy frameworks that align individual or group incentives with broader public interests. Misaligned incentives can lead to policy failures in the provision of public goods or to corruption. These misaligned incentives are prevalent in policy arrangements. For example, regulatory capture (Stigler 1971) is common in industries that allow entry barriers (qualifications for entry) to be determined, or significantly influenced, by individuals or firms actively operating in the regulated industry. Entities that are actively operating in the industry would prefer to face less competition, and one of the most effective ways to limit competition is to erect barriers to entry that reduce competition. This is often done in the name of promoting the "public good." Examples of regulatory capture include US occupational licensing requirements (Kleiner 2015; Meehan and Benson 2015), port authorities in the Philippines (Ponio et al. 2022), and others are found in this volume. By applying the principles of public choice, policymakers can design more efficient regulatory mechanisms (like proper checks and balances, incentive-compatible contracts, or performance-based rewards) that align the interests of public officials and policy implementers with those of the general public, thus enhancing the effectiveness and integrity of public policy initiatives.

Last but not least, viewing public choice as a theoretical apparatus for constitutional political economy underlines the importance of the constitutional framework in shaping effective public policies. This aspect of public choice examines how different constitutional arrangements can influence policy outcomes by structuring decision-making processes and defining the powers and limits of various political actors. A well-designed constitution, informed by public choice insights, can prevent concentrations of power and ensure that policy decisions are made transparently and accountably, thus reducing the risks of inefficiency and exploitation. This makes constitutional design a critical factor in long-term policy success and stability, ensuring that policies are not only developed but also implemented in a manner that truly reflects the democratic will and public interest.

In brief, public choice theory provides a robust set of tools and frameworks for analyzing, designing, and implementing public policies. In addition to the analytical angle and the intrinsic connections between the logic of public choice and public policy analysis and assessment, there is also a historical and genealogical connection between them, which deserves to be noted. Revisiting it gives us a deeper understanding of the relationship between the two domains and its evolution over time. During the formative years of public choice, the connection was particularly evident in the efforts to embed public choice insights within the field of public administration, an endeavor that was significantly driven by the works of Vincent and Elinor Ostrom. The Ostroms were instrumental during the 1960s and 1970s, introducing a paradigm shift in public administration that advocated for a shift to new principles, informed by public choice, aiming to fundamentally reshape the study and practice of public administration. This paradigm shift was not merely academic but was intended to address practical deficiencies in public administration and policymaking. Public administration and the emerging field of public policy analysis, having evolved distinctively within the broader discipline of political science, experienced a significant growth crisis that was exacerbated by their bureaucratic assumptions and underpinnings. This crisis was extensively documented and brilliantly analyzed by Vincent Ostrom ([1972] 2008) in his groundbreaking book *The Intellectual Crisis of American Public Administration.*

The Ostroms, recognizing the limitations imposed by traditional bureaucratization theories, posited public choice as a viable and necessary theoretical foundation for public administration. This was not only revolutionary but also timely, as it aligned with public policy as well as public administration's move toward a more independent and self-aware discipline in the latter part of the twentieth century. As noted, this period saw public administration distancing itself from political science and business administration, amid the rise of public policy studies as a distinct field focused on specialized policy issues.

The integration of public choice into the applied fields of public policy and public administration was thus supposed to provide a robust analytical framework that emphasized economic principles and decision-making processes, offering new methods to evaluate and enhance government and public agency performance. By framing public administration within public choice theory, the Ostroms wanted to facilitate a more analytical and efficiency-oriented approach to public sector management, stressing incentive structures and the alignment of public services with citizen needs. This was supposed to alter how public policies were formulated, evaluated, and implemented, ensuring that they were not only theoretically sound but also practically viable and responsive to the complexities of modern governance.

Initially, the Ostroms' attempt to integrate public choice perspectives into public administration and public policy was met with significant resistance and lack of acceptance within the established academic and policy communities. Despite their innovative and radical approach to addressing the complexities of public governance and management through the lens of public choice, Vincent and Elinor Ostrom found themselves somewhat estranged from the mainstream public administration discipline in the United States. As noted by many commentators, their relationship with American public administration was marked by distance and strain, primarily due to the interdisciplinary nature of their work and their readiness to shift theoretical and methodological approaches rapidly. This dynamic approach often clashed with the slower, more conservative trajectories typical of the discipline at the time.

Also, the intellectual environment during this period was not conducive to the type of paradigm shift the Ostroms were advocating. Their approach, which frequently challenged prevailing political forces and traditional public administration orthodoxies, was perceived as ideologically driven and somewhat confrontational. This perception only deepened the divide between the Ostroms and key figures within the American public administration community, many of whom took the critiques laid out in Vincent Ostrom's *The Intellectual Crisis* personally. Consequently, despite the relevance of their ideas, the Ostroms' contributions were seldom acknowledged by contemporary leaders in the "new public management" or "public governance" movements, who barely recognized their foundational influence.

Over time, however, the situation evolved favorably for the Ostroms' vision and for the public choice perspective. Their approach to public administration—emphasizing fragmentation, checks and balances, self-organizing networks, and competition for services—gained substantial traction. This led to significant policy and governance changes and a shift toward more differentiated, pluralistic, and decentralized government operations. These developments illustrate an ironic turn where the Ostroms' perspectives, initially marginalized, eventually found fertile ground, influencing profound transformations in public administration practices.

The story of Vincent and Elinor Ostrom's endeavor to integrate public choice into the framework of public administration and public policy is thus a journey from marginalization to mainstream acceptance and underlines a fundamental truth: public choice is intrinsically relevant to public policy, and that sooner or later, this reality will become salient and will influence the practice. This shift reflects a broader evolution in policy and administrative thought, recognizing that the principles underlying public choice are not merely theoretical constructs but may be operationalized as practical tools that can lead to better governance. As these ideas continue to be validated through successful application in diverse governance contexts, the intrinsic value of public choice theory becomes increasingly apparent.

Chapter Summaries

This volume, seen in this context, is a contribution to the ongoing effort to redefine and reaffirm the relevance of the public choice approach to the analysis of public policy and social issues. Each of the contributions in this volume is an attempt to engage from a perspective that is informed in one way or another, to various degrees, by public choice concepts, theories, or a general vision.

In Chapter 1, Brian Meehan emphasizes the strength of public choice in explaining public sector decision-making as it actually is. This chapter highlights the role of evidence-based narratives in elucidating actual political outcomes through the lens of public choice. These narratives demonstrate the power and predictive value of the public choice approach. For instance, the Baptist-Bootlegger theory of regulation is used to explain unusual interest group alliances and peculiar alcohol regulations across the United States. This theory is appealing on both theoretical and empirical grounds, and it also tells a memorable and entertaining story. This chapter advocates for the use of more empirically based and engaging theories. Public choice researchers can find policy or political outcomes that many may find peculiar and use theoretical and empirical tools to explain what is actually happening. The chapter expands on this by exploring the patchwork of occupational licensing rules throughout the United States and shedding light on public choice predictions regarding criminal justice reform, or the lack thereof. These evidence-based narratives serve to introduce and motivate the public choice case studies that form the core of this volume.

In Chapter 2, Brittany Giles-Jones documents how public choice theory can help explain and address inequities in disaster relief policy. The chapter focuses on the policy response to major hurricanes that have hit the state of Louisiana over the past 20+ years. Giles-Jones details the immediate impacts and the disaster relief policy responses for each of these storms. She explains how the incentives of regulators, embedded in the monocentric structure of disaster relief in the United States, have disproportionately negative impacts on minority groups. Pre-storm resources for preparedness and post-storm resources for recovery are often disproportionately allocated to those with political connections and do not reach vulnerable groups quickly. Giles-Jones highlights some improvements in US policy responses over time but contrasts the centralized, burdensome federal response with the more nimble polycentric disaster responses of Tribes and Tribal Nations in Louisiana. The chapter uses the various responses from different levels of government to illustrate how a more polycentric disaster relief approach could result in more tailored, equitable, and efficient responses to disasters.

In Chapter 3, Dallin Overstreet investigates the declining solvency of Unemployment Insurance (UI) trust funds in the United States through the lens of an endogenous polycentric system. Using a typical public choice approach, the analysis highlights the incentive structures influencing federal and state actors, leading to increased federal involvement and trust fund insolvency. By examining the interactions between federal and state actors, the analysis reveals how states exploit greater federal intervention during recessions, resulting in lower-than-necessary tax rates and greater trust fund insolvency. One of the broad analytical observations made by the chapter is that although other explanations, such as social policy retrenchment, partially explain the observed trends, the endogenous polycentric system approach offers a more comprehensive understanding of the UI system's complexities. On the applied side, the chapter highlights the need to clearly define roles and responsibilities in federal-state partnerships for efficient and effective social policy programs. The current UI system, characterized by a blend of centralized and decentralized elements, has deviated from its original design, leading to unintended consequences and inefficiencies. Thus, the chapter provides a foundation for research exploring policy reforms aimed at realigning incentives and fostering a more sustainable and responsive unemployment insurance system.

In Chapter 4, Malte Hendrickx presents the potential benefits of human challenge trials (HCTs) for combating infectious diseases. HCTs can accelerate the development of life-saving vaccines and other medical interventions, but they are not without risk. Hendrickx questions why these trials were not utilized to speed up vaccine development during the Covid-19 pandemic. The chapter argues that the reasons were structural rather than ethical. It begins by identifying which stages of the Covid-19 vaccine development process could have benefited from HCTs and provides a conservative estimate of the number of lives that could have been saved if HCTs had been employed shortly after authorities became aware of Covid-19. Hendrickx estimates that more than 5,500 lives could have been saved, as HCTs would have significantly accelerated vaccine development. The chapter then reviews the morally fraught history of HCTs and explains that common arguments against HCTs did not apply to the unique situation posed by the Covid-19 pandemic. Given that these arguments were not applicable, why were there no HCTs for Covid-19 vaccinations? The incentives of decision-makers in the vaccine development and approval process illustrate a lack of responsiveness to the novel situation the pandemic presented. The principal-agent problem faced by healthcare regulators led them to be significantly more risk-averse than would be rational for the informed public. The chapter suggests that unless current incentive structures are realigned, responses to future pandemics will likely remain inflexible and inadequate.

In Chapter 5, George Agyeah uses public choice theory to explore the complex case of educational reform in Ghana. Part of what makes Agyeah's chapter a unique and useful contribution to this important policy conversation is that it studies instances of both policy success *and* policy failure. Although there is much to learn from what has worked, there is also a good deal to learn from seeking to understand why particular programs have failed to meet students' needs. After studying a variety of policy reforms, Agyeah concludes that the rigidly hierarchical structure of the Ghanian education system has been the source of many failures in educational reform. Transplanting best practices from other nations and implementing them without regard to local context can easily create situations where the education being provided does not match the educational needs of the community. A more productive path forward requires investing in understanding how the varied history and institutions of different regions have shaped people's relationship with the educational system and what it will take to bring about successful reform. Agyeah's message is ultimately hopeful, highlighting the potential for shared governance structures to reintroduce local oversight and accountability into the education system, thereby better serving the needs of the students who are currently bearing the costs of educational failures.

In Chapter 6, Laura Montenovo studies how bunching—the accumulation of firms below a threshold—varies by industry based on the unionization level of the industry. High unionization rates within an industry may result in more employment protections that distort firm size, as unions push lawmakers for these enhanced protections. Enhanced or complicated employment rules may also create an environment where industry laborers rely on unions or union representation to engage in legal action for any violations of these rules. Higher union density also means that existing employment protections are enforced more vigorously than in less unionized industries. These employment protections are often designed to apply to larger firms, so the application and enforcement of the rules occur above a firm size threshold (a larger number of employees). This can create disincentives for firms to grow, causing them to bunch below the threshold to avoid the additional regulatory protections for workers, even if the smaller firms that emerge are less efficient. The chapter examines changes to employment protections in Italy to analyze these distortions and how they are related to union presence. The first finding is that the size distortion introduced by a law from 1970, which increased employment protections for firms with more than sixteen employees, is greater in industries characterized by high unionization than in less unionized ones. The second finding is that reforms aimed at liberalizing these protections, introduced in 2012 and 2015—which were opposed by unions within the country—impacted the bunching that existed due to the 1970 law. However, these reforms had less impact on industries with high unionization, as the size distortions that existed in these highly unionized industries before the liberalizations persisted after they were introduced. These findings are compared to other public choice literature that examines the impact of high levels of unionization on employment protections and industry structure.

In Chapter 7, Cory Jack explores the recent changes in US antitrust policy. Public choice theory is utilized to explain the rise of the current regulatory regime, headed by Federal Trade Commission (FTC) Chair Lina M. Khan, and to explore the potential long-term consequences of this change in leadership. Jack explains that Khan rose to her position by responding to political incentives, as the Biden Administration aimed to "reinvigorate" antitrust enforcement. Her rapid ascendancy to the FTC Chair position was partly due to her critiques of tech giants and their anti-competitive behavior. However, the case for this anti-competitive charge does not stem from the consumer welfare standards of antitrust from the recent past, which tend to focus on reductions in product quantity/quality and price increases as indicators of trade restraints. Instead, recent FTC lawsuits have expanded the role of the FTC into a more interventionist role, based on broader definitions of market power, and have shifted focus to the size of firms rather than typical consumer welfare standards. The chapter also uses public choice theory to explain how antitrust enforcement can be used as a protective measure against competition and posits that a more interventionist FTC could be captured by incumbent firms in an industry to limit competition.

In Chapter 8, Saige Hill addresses the extremely timely and relevant question of objectivity on the Supreme Court. In particular, she focuses on why objectivity is so difficult to achieve and how considerations from public choice theory might help us ameliorate some of the problems associated with the inevitability of personal bias seeping into the court system. Hill argues that despite its supposed objectivity, in practice, appointment to the Supreme Court is highly politicized, as are its rulings and choice of cases. This is all the more inevitable because of the Supreme Court's role as the final arbiter of the most contentious judicial disputes in the country—disputes which could potentially put a justice's duty in conflict with their other moral or ideological commitments. There are also possible financial and professional gains to be made through the adoption of particular political stances. As public choice theorists have observed in a variety of contexts, to ask a person to set aside all these potential biases may be practically and even cognitively impossible. In her conclusion, Hill presents some ideas inspired by public choice and political economy for how to limit the detrimental impact of bias on our judicial system, including changes to selection procedures, eligibility criteria, and the establishment of term limits.

The inquiry into the relevance of public choice theory for understanding judicial decision-making continues into Chapter 9 with Jean Vilbert's discussion of the judicialization of politics in Brazil. Vilbert argues that the focus of the judiciary has become increasingly political in Brazil, as it has in other parts of Europe, Latin America, and the United States. There are a variety of theories as to why the role of the judiciary may have shifted to become a more political one. Vilbert argues that in Brazil, the judiciary's powers of oversight were strengthened in the 1980s in hopes of avoiding future abuses of legislative authority. As a result, petitioners increasingly turned to the courts for the resolution of political conflicts, and consequently, the judiciary has played an increasingly significant role in legislative functions. This increased politicization can support democratic governance—as when interventions support human rights—but also has the potential to subvert democratic governance by overturning appropriately democratic legislative processes. Vilbert argues that public choice theory is a useful tool in understanding both the cause and the impact of the judicialization of politics. For instance, unlike in the United States, the judiciary essentially sets its own boundaries rather than being overseen by the legislative branch. This balance of powers—or perhaps more appropriately, imbalance—leads to a situation in which justices will have more scope to consider their personal interests when making decisions. Vilbert's conclusion is that there is a great deal of scope for future research on judicial politics and how it is shaped by the broader institutional context.

In Chapter 10, Gah-Kai Leung considers the complicated nature of personal interactions with administrative bureaucracies. In particular, Leung argues that public assistance programs often impose significant time costs on recipients, including not only compliance costs but also the costs associated with learning how to navigate the process and the psychological costs of any associated stress, frustration, or shame. Further, these costs can be so significant that they come to constitute a form of structural injustice that could be avoided if taken into serious consideration. Leung considers a variety of ways time taxes interact with justice, including possible regressive welfare effects, discrimination against individuals with lower human capital, fostering shame and a loss of self-respect among service users, and the violation of individuals' rights to direct their personal time. Time taxes can even functionally violate constitutional rights if they serve as publicly created obstacles to the exercise of those rights, such as in the instance of administrative requirements that make it difficult for individuals who have less experience navigating the system to be able to vote in public elections. In addition to calling our attention to an often-underappreciated facet of collective action, this chapter is also valuable for the way it demonstrates how public choice theory and normative political theory can be brought into productive conversation with each other, revealing insights that are important to the functioning of healthy political processes that would otherwise be missed.

In Chapter 11, Agostina Lorenzini explores the governance of Artificial Intelligence (AI) amid the emergence of large-scale inference technologies with applications that range from customer service chatbots and autonomous driving to facial recognition by government agencies. At the core of the discussion is concern about the ways one should encourage beneficial uses while limiting harmful ones. The investigation highlights the dangers of misuse of private data by large corporations and governments for manipulation and persecution, stressing that the real threat lies in human actions rather than in the potential of AI itself. As a general approach, the chapter uses the public choice perspective, broadly defined, to draw parallels with financial market regulations, considering both market-reinforcement and market-replacing approaches. The chapter claims that a regulatory framework for AI that grants property rights over data to individuals will give people more control over their data and its usage. The chapter emphasizes thus the importance of educating the public about their data's power and the implications of sharing it. It suggests that regulations should empower consumers with property rights over their data, allowing them to decide their level of participation in AI systems. This approach, argues Lorenzini, may be able to address privacy concerns without stifling innovation. Accordingly, the analysis advances a typical public choice reading of policy reforms aimed at realigning incentives for both efficiency and innovation objectives. By regulating the data collection process rather than imposing stringent bans, a balance can be achieved between protecting individual privacy and fostering technological advancement.

The results from these varied policy applications in different institutional environments lend support to the expanded use of public choice tools for explaining real-world events. Without analysis that thoroughly integrates real-world contexts with plausible explanations of human behavior rooted in an understanding of our epistemic and cognitive limitations, it can be all too easy to adopt misguided policy solutions that don't have much chance of success in a realistic world populated by imperfect, flawed, error-prone people. In applying public choice analysis to a diversity of global contexts, the contributors to this volume make a meaningful step towards better understanding our policy processes and ourselves.

References

Boettke, Peter J. 1997. "Where Did Economics Go Wrong? Modern Economics as a Flight from Reality." *Critical Review* 11 (1): 11–64.

Buchanan, James M. 1954. "Individual Choice in Voting and the Market." *Journal of Political Economy* 62 (4): 334–343.

———. 1987. "The Constitution of Economic Policy." *The American Economic Review* 77 (3): 243–250.

———. [1979] 1999. "Politics without Romance: A Sketch of Positive Public Choice Theory and Its Normative Implications." In *The Logical Foundations of Constitutional Liberty, Vol 1. The Collected Works of James M. Buchanan*, 45–59. Indianapolis, IN: Liberty Fund.

Holcombe, Randall G. 2016. *Advanced Introduction to Public Choice*. Cheltenham, UK: Edward Elgar Publishing.

Kleiner, Morris M. 2015. *Guild-Ridden Labor Markets: The Curious Case of Occupational Licensing*. Kalamazoo, MI: W.E. Upjohn Institute for Employment Research.

Meehan, Brian, and Bruce L. Benson. 2015. "The Occupations of Regulators Influence Occupational Regulation: Evidence from the US Private Security Industry." *Public Choice* 162: 97–117.

Mueller, Dennis C. 1976. "Public Choice: A Survey." *Journal of Economic Literature* 14 (2): 395–433.

Munger, Michael C. 2018. "30 Years after the Nobel: James Buchanan's Political Philosophy." *The Review of Austrian Economics* 31 (2): 151–167.

Ostrom, Elinor. 1998. "A Behavioral Approach to the Rational Choice Theory of Collective Action: Presidential Address, American Political Science Association, 1997." *The American Political Science Review* 92 (1): 1–22.

Ostrom, Elinor. 2010a. "Beyond Markets and States: Polycentric Governance of Complex Economic Systems." *American Economic Review* 100 (3): 641–672.

Ostrom, Elinor. 2010b. "A Long Polycentric Journey." *Annual Review of Political Science* 13 (1): 1–23.

Ostrom, Vincent. [1972] 2008. *The Intellectual Crisis in American Public Administration.* Tuscaloosa, AL: University of Alabama Press.

Ponio, Gideon, Yasmine Rashed, Edwin van Hassel, and Patrick Verhoeven. 2022. "Modelling Regulatory Capture in the Port Sector: A Case Study in the Philippines." *Case Studies on Transport Policy* 10 (2): 1005–1014.

Stigler, George J. 1971. "The Theory of Economic Regulation." *The Bell Journal of Economics and Management Science* 2 (1): 3–21.

1

The Importance of Evidence-Based Narratives in Public Choice Theory

Brian Meehan

When predicting the outcomes of collective action, public choice and public interest theories are often at odds. Many claim that public choice is too narrow or cynical about the effectiveness of regulation and legislation. This position was advanced by Kelman (1987, 93–94), who states:

> Cynical descriptive conclusions about behavior in government threaten to undermine the norm prescribing public spirit. The cynicism of journalists—and even the writings of professors—can decrease public spirit simply by describing what they claim to be its absence. Cynics are therefore in the business of making prophecies that threaten to become self-fulfilling. If the norm of public spirit dies, our society would look bleaker and our lives as individuals would be more impoverished. That is the tragedy of "public choice."

This "public spirit" Kelman speaks of may be what James Buchanan would call *politics with romance* (Buchanan 1999). It is the idea that we can suspend normal assumptions about human behavior because there is some romantic public spiritedness guiding those involved in political decision-making or bureaucratic action. It does seem appealing. If you have ever talked to a politician, they often like to claim they were called to lead or called to public service. They like to add this extra layer of "do good" that drives their actions. They are in it for the people, not themselves, and they will do what is best for the people. Again, this sounds appealing, and in fact many people may be motivated to help others through public sector action. Perhaps public choice scholars shortchange this motivating factor? Maybe, but public choice doesn't explicitly disallow individual motivations that are aligned with some preference for public spirit or public good. It just asks, given rational behavior, the institutional structures and rules that exist, and the potential individual payoffs of those involved, what type of policy should we expect? The usefulness of public choice comes from the same root that makes economics so useful—its explanatory power over actual outcomes.

Public choice arguments about motivations often struggle to resonate without the context, stories, and tangible outcomes that illustrate their validity. While the theoretical framework of public choice sheds light on the reality of decision-making within the public sector, it is through narratives and real-world examples that its power truly emerges. We require narratives that vividly depict how public choice theory aligns with actual political outcomes, showcasing its predictive prowess. In both my teaching and research, I've encountered many instances where public choice accurately anticipated outcomes, reinforcing its utility. The essence of my message is this: To appreciate the value of public choice, we must employ it to decipher real outcomes. Its predictive efficacy gains credibility when alternative models of behavior falter in explaining complex political and bureaucratic scenarios.

This is why, when teaching public choice concepts, one of the ideas that students typically understand and can relate to the most is Bruce Yandle's Baptist-Bootlegger theory of regulation (Yandle 1983). They do not seem to easily grasp purely theoretical discussions emphasizing concentrated benefits and dispersed costs, especially when those concepts are not followed by a direct example. In fact, students may view these discussions as cynical when regarding the actual workings of public policy formation. They often think the people that share their preferred political orientation are at least working for them or the public at large. For those of you who may not have heard of the Baptist-Bootlegger theory before, the overarching idea is that coalitions of people who might seem to be on opposite sides of a political issue can often be found working to support similar causes. It is usually a coalition that emphasizes morality on one side, and another group that can benefit from reductions in competition on the other. Regulation can often satisfy the motives of both groups. Being able to identify these coalitions can help explain the peculiar features of the regulation that you get. In the original Baptist-Bootlegger example, we have the moral cause of the Baptists to reduce the use and influence of alcohol on individuals, with the bootleggers, who produce illegal alcohol. County-level regulations of alcohol in the United States are a mix of restrictions on Sunday purchases, and more encompassing prohibitions on types of alcohol sold. But, outside of age limits, these restrictions are rarely on alcohol consumed. These restrictions on sales help reduce the proliferation of alcohol as the Baptists see it and reduce competition for the products of the bootleggers—but again, notice that consumption of alcohol is not prohibited.

The specific narrative example from the Baptist-Bootlegger theory provides grounds on which to understand a host of public choice insights. Given that I teach in the southeastern US, the majority of my students—though many are not yet twenty-one—possess at least a basic understanding of the diverse regulations governing alcohol sales. Many of them have experienced firsthand the various limitations imposed by cities or counties, such as restricted sales on Sundays, and have encountered even stricter regulations in certain areas. Many have probably asked why or questioned why Sunday morning restrictions are better for the public? Even at first blush, these rules don't do well with a public spirit or public interest theory of regulation. If we were worried about road safety or the health impact of alcohol overconsumption, wouldn't "public spirited" alcohol restrictions do more good on a Friday night rather than a Sunday morning? But public choice has an answer for this, a predictive model that would tell you to look deeper at the regulatory institutions, interested parties involved, and the incentives that these systems generate. It explains the similar motives coming from these coalitions that you might ordinarily regard as enemies—Baptists, that are generally against the use of alcohol, and Bootleggers, that produce illegal alcohol to be consumed. But, by working together to promote a policy goal, or at least working toward the same goal, they can achieve something they both want. It's about the relative payoffs for alcohol restrictions on Sunday, less alcohol consumption interfering with church and community on Sunday for Baptists, and a captive audience with less substitutes for the Bootleggers.

The rule-making process provides an avenue for this to occur; these rules are made at the county level in the United States. Support for local bureaucrats or politicians is not nearly as expensive as it might be for national politicians, and the rational ignorance of voters explains why elected officials and local bureaucrats supporting these policies are not thrown out of their positions right away. Baptists gain from these rules, Bootleggers gain from these rules, but the public at large does not. Restrictions on legal alcohol sales on Sunday make a lot of sense when you think about these groups and their respective incentives. It also explains why this odd phenomenon, that most people have run into before, persists.

You can point to these types of restrictions in counties across the United States on these maps, the places known for their large Baptist populations are often also known for their moonshining culture (see Figures 1.1 and 1.2); think Appalachia

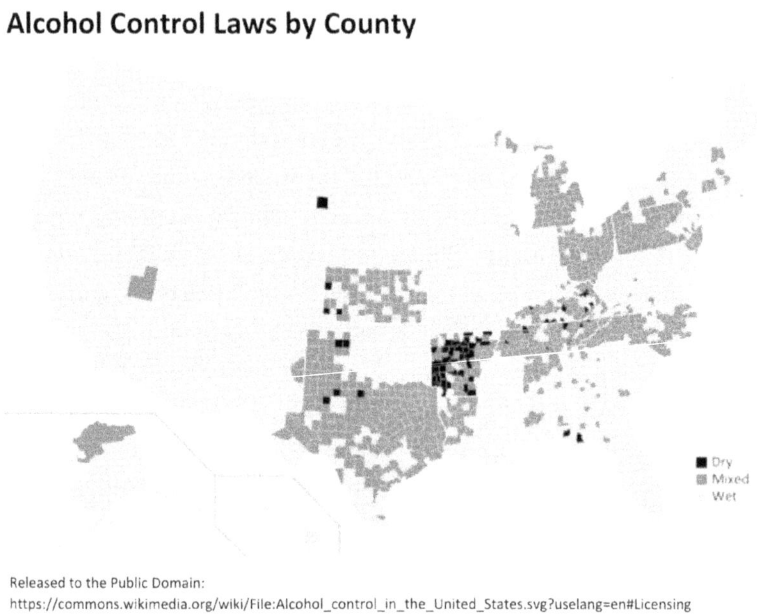

Figure 1.1 Alcohol control laws by county. Released to the public domain: http://commons.wikimedia.org/wiki/File:Alcohol_control_in_the_United_States.svg?uselang=en#Liscensing.

and the Bible belt in the southeastern US. Perhaps finding more evidence-based public choice explanations for odd policies is a way to promote the power of public choice, particularly when discussing policy. It is a way to enter an individuals' cognitive model for how rules and regulations are determined. I'm not claiming causal identification with these maps, but Yandle's idea has been empirically tested in other areas with different groups playing the roles of Baptists and Bootleggers: Jeremy Horpedahl does this with literal Baptists coalitions and liquor stores in counties with their neighbors being currently dry counties (Horpedahl 2021). The Baptists are motivated to reduce alcohol use by keeping the county dry and the neighboring liquor stores would prefer to keep their competition for liquor sales at a minimum, and so the dry county law persists when these coalitions are organized. Other examples include environmental groups and energy companies working to create barriers to new entry into energy markets (Yandle and Buck 2002) in the name of green environmental policy, as opposed to more economically efficient regulatory tools like carbon taxes or cap and trade programs.

As public choice scholars, we have the tools to explain policy outcomes that may puzzle most people, and I think this is where we can make some actual

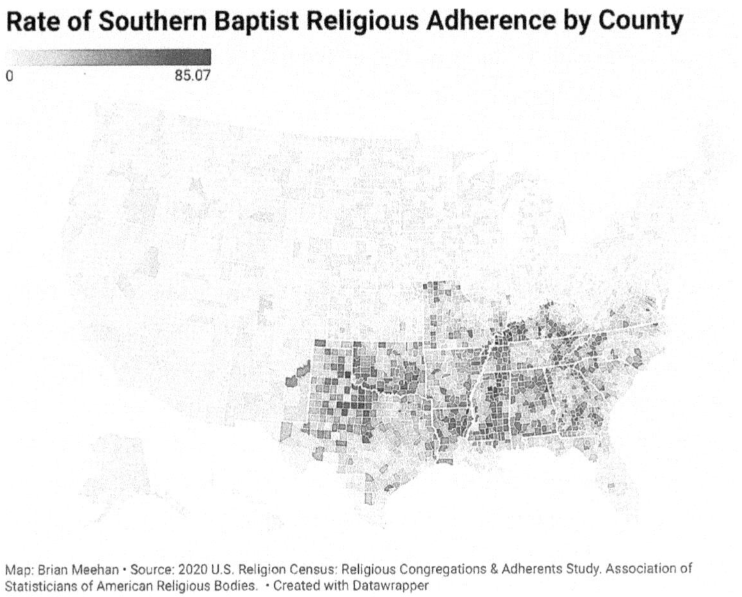

Figure 1.2 Rate of southern Baptist religious adherence by county. Map: Brian Meehan, from 2020 US Religion Census.

change in the reliance on policy to solve problems—by emphasizing the point that incentives matter and then providing concrete examples backed by actual evidence. The Baptist-Bootlegger theory explains a policy outcome that is often right in front of people; they can see it in a way that they might not be able to for other public choice concepts that don't have such a great story built into the name of the concept.

The Baptist-Bootlegger theory is a story that illustrates a complex phenomenon which has wide application. As stated by Craig and Dillon in an article written for the London School of Economics, one primary function of stories is to extend "the range of models available for reasoning" and "stories are a form of sense-making in the face of complexity and uncertainty" (Craig and Dillon 2021). The Baptist-Bootlegger theory of regulation is a story, backed up by actual outcomes, that explains a peculiar and persistent phenomenon. As public choice scholars, we should do more of this—more micro-level explanations of peculiar bureaucratic or regulatory outcomes. The usefulness of public choice is demonstrated with these memorable Baptist-Bootlegger-like stories, and it is equally important that we test the predictions of these models against actual outcomes. If we can demonstrate how useful the theory is at explaining these actual outcomes, students and scholars that might otherwise favor Kelman's reliance on public spirit might just incorporate some public choice in their continued understanding of political processes.

Occupational Licensing and Public Choice

Public choice scholars, at least in my own research areas of economics of crime and occupational licensing, have made some marginal policy progress using this approach, although we probably need to take a page out of Yandle's book and work on our catchy names for policy outcomes. One of the main tenets of public choice is the recognition that the incentives of public and private entities matter. Public policy predictions must take this into account. But, backing this up with actual examples and evidence can actually make people take notice, and it can make people take these models more seriously when looking at other collective action problems. I think this has happened for occupational licensing reform in the United States. If you are unfamiliar with US occupational licensing, think of it as a government permission slip that allows people to work in a given occupation. These permission slips are often accompanied by numerous requirements.

Much like the Baptist-Bootlegger phenomenon, there is usually a very vocal proponent for increasing these licensing requirements for entry into licensed occupations. Sometimes, new occupational licensing requirements are matched with grandfather clauses that create a two-tiered system of licensing—prior generations of licensees don't have to satisfy new requirements, while new entrants do. Public interest arguments for increasing licensing requirements include consumer safety and information problems in the marketplace. Yet, as my research, as well as the vast majority of research on these topics has found, increases in licensing requirements, including experience, training, testing, and licensing fees do not correlate with more safety or improved market performance (Knepper et al. 2022; Meehan and Benson 2017).

There is also such a hodge-podge of different occupational licensing rules in different US states that is difficult to explain when relying on public interest motives for regulation. What gives? Why, for example, does Louisiana need occupational licenses for florists while the other forty-nine states in the United States do not? Why do some states require years of experience to operate as an independently licensed private security guard when others require no experience at all? With just a few simple insights, a public choice economist can provide a narrative based on these empirical oddities. Occupational licensing can, in fact, serve as a barrier to entry for potential market entrants and increases in licensing requirements can limit entry and reduce competition. It is also the case that in many areas states allow these requirements to be determined by licensing boards that consist of already licensed industry members. Essentially, they are asking existing industry members to make rules about their potential competition. Most research findings in this area are consistent with public choice predictions: When you put licensed industry members in charge of establishing requirements for entry, they attempt to limit entry by increasing barriers to entry (see Kleiner 2015). The industry members are the bootleggers of this story, attempting to limit competition under the guise of safety and improved information. Consumer advocacy groups and safety proponents can act as the Baptists in this story. Importantly, legislators and the interested members of the public did not push back on this steady licensing creep until very recently. Special thanks here must go out to the Knee Regulatory Research Center, housed at West Virginia University. The Knee Center has connected many policymakers with the emerging research on this topic.

Recently, licensing reform has occurred in many states, including licensing rules for universal recognition of licenses in eighteen states (Deyo and Plemmons 2022), meaning if you get a license in one state you can practice that occupation in another state. This limits that hodge-podge pattern of licensing rules, increases mobility, and allows for competition across state borders. It also limits the effectiveness of licensing-imposed barriers to competition. Part of this reform is tied to pandemic-generated policies to allow more heath-related services to be provided remotely or across state borders. But without analyzing the odd patchwork of licensing rules and the public choice narrative that explains why it exists, I don't think the same level of progress could have been made. Policymakers would have gone right back to the old set of rules after the pandemic instead of being pushed to consider the impact of this increased competition and expanded access to goods and services that comes along with these licensing reciprocity rules.

Criminal Justice Reform and Public Choice

In a recent article, Torgler (2022) argues for an expanded use of public choice analysis in the field of Law and Economics. Legal outcomes are influenced by the incentives of law enforcement, judges, and others involved in the legal process—which is something that has been somewhat historically neglected in the Law and Economics literature until relatively recently. It seems like an obvious application; perhaps nowhere has the public interest motivation for collective action been more maligned than in the US criminal justice system. People on the left of the political spectrum, who otherwise have great faith in the public sector to achieve public interest goals, will stop short when discussing criminal justice. Policy and legal efforts to address public choice concerns in the U.S. criminal justice system have seen limited success. However, there is growing recognition of the perverse incentives faced by individual actors throughout the system. Blind faith in the system is not as popular as it once was. Bruce Benson and co-authors stated in 1994, "The economics of crime literature has generally ignored the incentives of the police bureaucrats who have considerable discretion in allocating their resources among a wide array of activities."

I have tried to use the tools of public choice in my own research when examining the institutional structures surrounding policing, crime, and security in the United States. Today much more scrutiny has been advanced to explain the behaviors of police that don't align neatly with public interest theory explanations of their actions. This recognition of these incentives comes as a backlash to police violence and abuses that can be explained using a bit of public choice. Police violence in the United States has been at the forefront of public discussion and media for a number of years. Exploring legal and contractual police liability generates an unfortunate set of consequences that are predictable from a public choice perspective.

For instance, Dharmapala and co-authors (2022) find that extensions of collective bargaining agreements stemming from a change in Florida law allowed some police departments to expand collective bargaining abilities, and instead of using these collective bargaining rights to write contracts that would allow police officers to satisfy the public interest or the public good, they instead pushed for liability protections and misconduct protections. Table 1.1 illustrates these liability and misconduct protections. Police departments that had these collectively bargained contracts were much more likely to have contractual protections for officers related to discipline for misconduct; they also tend to require the city to pay for any misconduct more often than non-collectively bargained police contracts. These collectively bargained contracts also tend to provide police with more access to evidence and information and are much more likely to automatically disqualify police complaints for a variety of reasons. If you expect the behavior of police and union negotiators to be self-interested

Table 1.1 Police Officer Protections in Eighty-One Large Cities with Union Contracts and Sixteen Large Cities with our Collective-Bargaining Agreements

	Percent with Protections	
	Union Contracts	**No Collective Bargaining Agreement**
Disqualifies Complaints	32.10%	0%
Restrictions/Delays Interrogations	61.73%	18.75%
Gives Officers Unfair Access to Information	50.62%	18.75%
Limits Oversight and Discipline	81.48%	6.25%
Requires City Pay for Misconduct	50.62%	6.25%
Erase Misconduct Records	53.09%	6.25%

Sources: Dharmapala et al. (2022): eighty-one cities with union contracts from Check the Police 2016. Other cities from state and municipal codes, policy and procedures manuals.

and self-preserving as opposed to having pure public good motivations, these outcomes make sense, but they also come with predictable behavioral responses on the back end. Sure enough, there was a 40 percent increase in the incidence of violent misconduct from these same police departments after these new collectively bargained contracts were negotiated. This enormous increase in the rate of violent misconduct dwarfed the misconduct rates at other police departments that didn't have these same collective bargaining rights. This is a narrative about a simple self-interested behavior by the public police, and the subsequent consequences that can be predicted using public choice but not with public interest theories of behavior.

In addition to these liability protections for police, the bureaucratic evolution of the US war on drugs also demonstrates the power of public choice to explain peculiar policies. Researchers, policymakers, and the public are finally coming to grips with the counterproductive incentive structures created by many US War on Drugs policies. Many of these issues have been illuminated by public choice economists for decades. In work coauthored by myself and Bruce Benson, we document how competing bureaucratic interests shaped and intensified these drug policies. One result of this competitive process was expansion in civil asset forfeiture programs. The public interest rationale for these programs is they deter drug crime and the distribution of drugs. But those public interest incentives are not the only incentives that were involved in crafting these policies. Civil asset forfeiture is when police confiscate assets including cash amounts of more than $500 and property that they suspect has been involved in the drug trade. The burden of evidence needed to make these forfeitures varies from state to state (see Table 1.2) but is often much lower than the "beyond a reasonable doubt" standard that we usually think of when it comes to burden of proof necessary to lead to a guilty verdict (Benson and Meehan 2018). These crimes also go down as crimes against property, so, in many cases, the people involved in these cases are never arrested or charged for a crime, but their assets are still seized.

A study by the *Washington Post* found that many police departments were dependent on these forfeiture funds, as they flow right back to the departments for their personal use. The *Post* found that forfeiture funds made up an average of 20 percent of the budgets of the departments studied. These civil asset forfeiture funds often flow right back to pay police officers and to provide various fringe benefits for departments, such as higher quality cars and even a margarita

Table 1.2 Standard of Proof in State Forfeiture Laws, 2011

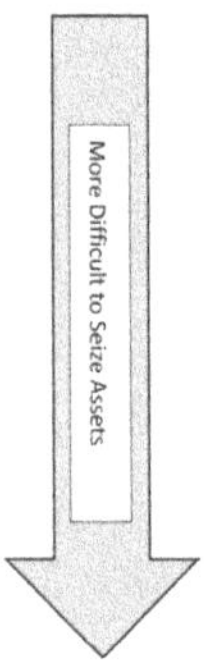

Standard of Proof	States
Prima facie/probably cause	Alabama, Alaska, Delaware, Illinois, Massachusetts, Missouri, Montana, Rhode Island, South Carolina, Wyoming
Probable cause and preponderance of the evidence	Georgia, North Dakota, South Dakota Washington
Preponderance of the evidence	Arizona, Arkansas, Hawaii, Idaho, Indiana, Iowa, Kansas, Louisiana, Maine, Maryland, Michigan, Mississippi, New Hampshire, New Jersey, Oklahoma, Pennsylvania, Tennessee, Texas, Virginia, West Virginia
Preponderance of the evidence and clear and convincing	Kentucky, New York, Oregon
Clear and convincing	Colorado, Connecticut, Florida, Minnesota, Nevada, New Mexico, Ohio, Utah, Vermont
Clear and convincing and beyond a reasonable doubt	California
Beyond a reasonable doubt	Nebraska, North Carolina, **Wisconsin

Source: Williams et al. (2011, table 2), Meehan and Benson (2017).
Notes: In states with two forfeiture standards, most commonly the higher one is for forfeiture of real property.
**State law effectively does not allow for civil forfeiture.

machine for the offices—which must be necessary for fighting crime during happy hour. From a public choice perspective, these outcomes are predictable. You can see how the incentives of such a program might cut against the public interest. This is particularly true when the burden of proof is low.

But here too, like with the occupational licensing example mentioned previously, recognition of these incentive problems has led to some action. The recent de-escalation of the war on drugs via legalization of marijuana has reduced opportunities for this theft in some states. Some states have also tried to earmark forfeiture funds such that they don't flow back to the police departments for personal use; in North Carolina, for example, they are earmarked for education purposes. But in a true story of revenge of the public choice incentives, the bureaucratic competition for resources has impacted that transition via a program ironically called Equitable Sharing. If the civil asset forfeiture law in a state earmarks the funds for non-police use, police departments can use the federal level department of justice procedures instead. The department of justice will sponsor the forfeiture, take a 20 percent handling fee, and then provide the other 80 percent back to the individual police departments so as to get around these rules. These rules have made it more difficult to reform police departments to focus on violent and property crime. Chris Coyne and Abigail Hall's book, *Tyranny Comes Home* (2018), also illuminates how the incentives of the US military industrial complex intertwine with domestic policing to produce more violent use of force by police. US policing and the criminal justice system as a whole are fruitful research grounds for public choice scholars.

Mischaracterizations of Public Choice

Moving to another sad incident of public choice neglect, in 2017, public choice and one of its founders, 1986 Nobel Prize–winning economist, James Buchanan, came under attack. Duke University historian Nancy MacLean wrote a book which painted the public choice approach as inherently anti-democratic and racist. One of MacLean's main examples for showing this was Buchanan's public choice writings on the potential merits of the school choice and education vouchers. MacLean sees these motivations as inherently excusing the practice of school segregation in the south by undermining public education policies advanced after the Brown v. Board of Education Supreme Court ruling. She makes the case that Buchanan's writings were influenced by Southern Agrarian poet Donald Davidson and pro-slavery writer John C. Calhoun. MacLean's book is a historical treatment, and many, including Phil Magness (2017a), Steve Horwitz (2017), and MacLean's own Duke colleague Michael Munger (2018), uncovered various historical inaccuracies in MacLean's portrait, including the fact that neither Davidson nor Calhoun are mentioned at all in the index of any of the twenty volumes of *The Collected Works of James Buchanan* (Magness 2017b). They have done tremendous work documenting these errors, but these errors have largely been ignored by the popular press and the external scholarly community.

MacLean's book also contains the claim that public choice theory is not backed by any empirical findings (Horwitz 2017), in spite of the fact that the discipline has a prestigious quarterly academic journal full of empirical work. This book was a finalist for the National Book Award for nonfiction in 2017, and The Nation named it the "Most Valuable Book of 2017" (Democracy in Chains 2024). Amazon reviews show it was lauded by the New York Review of Books, Oprah, and many others. But what Buchanan was actually trying to argue in his school choice writings is how a universal voucher system would allow families to choose among schools and could enhance school performance via the competitive market process. Perhaps, our next step as public choice scholars is to show how useful public choice is at predicting the actual outcomes on the policy issues she raises.

Let's meet MacLean head-on here and talk about education, about public schools and school choice in the United States. In the wake of the pandemic, many people seemed surprised about the responses of teachers' unions, school boards and many other parts of the education bureaucratic apparatus. After the Covid pandemic, several news outlets reported enormous declines in National Assessment of Educational Progress (NAEP) test scores in public schools in many states. Kathleen Porter-Magee posted on X (formerly Twitter), that if all of the Catholic schools were a state, they would be the best performing state in the country according to those same NAEP results (2022).

Obviously, the institutional environments for these schools are different; even among public schools, the institutional environments can be very different. There are different rules that cover public and private schools: We have differences in interested parties, we have differences in how decisions are made, and we also have differences in pandemic responses. Charter schools also had mediocre test performance using the same data. More recently Campos and Kearns (2024) found that Zones of Choice (school choice) in the public school system of Los

Angeles improved a host of student outcomes. Many people have found these results puzzling or have just assumed that the differential responses and outcomes might just come down to funding differences, as Nancy MacLean might argue. But, perhaps as public choice scholars, we could shed some light or investigate these different institutional arrangements and explain these outcomes. We could address some of MacLean's arguments around school choice and educational outcomes without having to invoke talk of John C. Calhoun or Donald Davidson at all.

I have talked mostly about US micro- or state-level studies on bureaucracy and regulation, but I want to point out that I have nothing against national-level studies on constitutional political economy—a vast and important component of public choice analysis that examines overarching constraints on public sector action via constitutions and rules for making the rules. If you do this work, or want to do this work, then great! It is not my comparative advantage, but it could be yours. But, when you are doing this type of work or any public choice work, don't forget the evidence; don't forget to connect the argument to real world stories. In economics, theory can become disconnected from practice if it isn't grounded in real-world context or empirical evidence—including experimental studies, which provide valuable insights into human behavior. In all cases, however, it's essential to consider the institutional constraints that shape those behaviors.

Conclusion

Elinor Ostrom was very good at using local stories and evidence to provide insight into larger theoretical issues. When I think about self-governance and collective action problems and the ways people get around these problems, I think of some of the stories from Ostrom's work and the evidence she provided to back her analysis up. A paper written in Land Economics by Ostrom and Edella Schlager (1992) illustrates this point. Instead of pontificating on hypothetical ways in which we could solve tragedy of the commons and other collective action problems, she went out and examined how groups of people handled these problems in reality, and backed her findings up with evidence. Lobster Fishermen in Maine deal with common pool resource problems; exclusion is difficult, and most would assume that, without strict regulation, a tragedy of the commons situation would occur and the lobster resource would be depleted as a race to fish ensues. In reality, what Schlegar and Ostrom found was quite different. Fishing communities had established a set of de facto property rights over fishing grounds and had developed other self-governance structures. Outsiders violating these rights were subject to punishment—gear destruction by community members—thus creating an enforcement mechanism and incentivizing people to obey the rules. A comparative institutional analysis with evidence follows in the paper. As these enforcement efforts were easy to administer in Northern Maine where the shoreline is easier to monitor, the southern part of the state abandoned these de facto property rights, as their coastline was more difficult to monitor, and boat technology made the range of lobster fishers wider. The groups in the North that maintained these de facto rules avoided the tragedy of the commons, saw more robust lobster numbers, and had higher and more consistent incomes, while avoiding the race to fish and the depletion of the resource. Meanwhile the lobster fishers in Southern Maine were unable to enforce these de facto rights and saw lower harvests, depleted stocks, and a race to fish.

Sometimes existing institutions and policy consequences can be explained with very simple public choice insights, like occupational licensing differences across states, the prevalence of different alcohol rules across counties, differences in police misconduct across cities, educational outcomes in different institutional environments, and even lobster fishing results in Maine. My efforts here have attempted to shine light on these processes and make sense of the outcomes. My comparative advantage lies in finding these evidence-based examples of public choice in action. The comparative advantage of others might be different; perhaps you are a talented theorist, and you disagree with my appeal to find more evidence—opportunity costs for my approach do exist, after all. But I believe there is a lot more room for evidence-based narratives in public choice. More of this type of research should bring more acceptance by mainstream policy scholars and the general population to public choice ideas. And perhaps the real-world outcomes examined by public choice scholars will also generate some reflection and reformulation of the existing models. But, in any event, looking toward the real world is imperative if the public choice program is going to gain more ground in the minds of individuals looking to explain the complexity and intricacies of policy formation and policy outcomes. This volume aims to do just that, by providing examples and evidence from across the globe for the usefulness of public choice as an explanatory framework.

References

Benson, B. L. and B. Meehan. 2018. "Predatory Public Finance and the Evolution of the War on Drugs." In A. J. Hoffer and T. Nesbit (eds.), *For Your Own Good: Taxes, Paternalism, and Fiscal Discrimination in the Twenty-first Century* (Chapter 8, pp. 167–195). Mercatus Center at George Mason University.

Buchanan, James M. 1999. "Politics without Romance: A Sketch of Positive Public Choice Theory and Its Normative Implications." In *The Collected Works of James M. Buchanan, Volume 1: The Logical Foundations of Constitutional Liberty*, 45–59. Indianapolis, IN: Liberty Fund, Inc.

Campos, Christopher, and Caitlin Kearns. 2024. "The Impact of Public School Choice: Evidence from Los Angeles's Zones of Choice." *The Quarterly Journal of Economics* 139 (2): 1051–1093.

Craig, Claire, and Sarah Dillon. 2021. "Storylistening: Why Narrative Evidence Matters for Public Reasoning and How to Use It." London School of Economics Blog. https://blogs.lse.ac.uk/impactofsocialsciences/2021/10/13/storylistening-why-narrative-evidence-matters-for-public-reasoning-and-how-to-use-it/.

Deyo, Darwyyn, and Alicia Plemmons. 2022. "Have License, Will Travel: Measuring the Effects of Universal Licensing Recognition on Mobility." *Economics Letters* 219: 110800.

Democracy in Chains. 2024. Wikipedia. https://en.wikipedia.org/wiki/Democracy_in_Chains#:~:text=Democracy%20in%20Chains%20was%20a,of%202017%22%20by%20The%20Nation.

Dharmapala, Dhammika, Richard H. McAdams, and John Rappaport. 2022. "Collective Bargaining Rights and Police Misconduct: Evidence from Florida." *The Journal of Law, Economics, and Organization* 38 (1): 1–41.

Horpedahl, Jeremy. 2021. "Bootleggers, Baptists and Ballots: Coalitions in Arkansas' alcohol-legalization elections." *Public Choice* 188 (1): 203–219.

Horwitz, S. 2017. "Democracy in Chains: The Deep History of the Radical Right's Stealth Plan for America" (Book review). *Cato Journal* 37(3), 593–608.

Kelman, Steven. 1987. "Public Choice and Public Spirit." *The Public Interest* 87: 80–94.

Kleiner, Morris M. 2015. *Guild-Ridden Labor Markets: The Curious Case of Occupational Licensing.* Kalamazoo, MI: W.E. Upjohn Institute for Employment Research.

Knepper, Lisa, Darwyyn Deyo, Kyle Sweetland, Jason Tiezzi, and Alec Mena. 2022. *License to Work: A National Study of Burdens from Occupational Licensing*. 3rd ed. Arlington, VA: Institute for Justice.

Magness, Phillip W. 2017a. "How Nancy MacLean Went a Whistlin' Dixie." https://philmagness.com/2017/06/how-nancy-maclean-went-a-whistlin-dixie/.

Magness, Phillip W. 2017b. *Nancy MacLean's Calhounite Imagination.* https://philmagness.com/2017/06/nancy-macleans-calhounite-imagination/.

Meehan, Brian, and Bruce L Benson. 2017. “Does Private Security Affect Crime?: A Test Using State Regulations as Instruments.” *Applied Economics* 49 (48): 4911–4924.

Munger, Michael C. 2018. “On the Origins and Goals of Public Choice: Constitutional Conspiracy?” *The Independent Review* 22 (3): 359–382.

Porter-Magee, Kathleen. 2022. “If Catholic Schools Were a State, They'd Be the Highest Performing in the Nation on All Four NAEP Tests.” October 24. https://twitter.com/kportermagee/status/1584660501656543232.

Schlager, Edella, and Elinor Ostrom. 1992. “Property-Rights Regimes and Natural Resources: A Conceptual Analysis.” *Land Economics* 68 (3): 249–262.

Torgler, Benno. 2022. “The Power of Public Choice in Law and Economics.” *Journal of Economic Surveys* 36 (5): 1410–1453.

Williams, Marian R., Jefferson E. Holcomb, Tomislav V. Kovandzic, and Scott Bullock. 2011. *Policing for Profit: The Abuse of Civil Asset Forfeiture*. Arlington, VA: Institute for Justice.

Yandle, Bruce. 1983. “Bootleggers and Baptists: The Education of a Regulatory Economist.” *Regulation* 7 (3): 12–16.

Yandle, Bruce, and Stuart Buck. 2002. “Bootleggers, Baptists, and the Global Warming Battle.” *The Harvard Environmental Law Review* 26 (1): 177.

2

Using Public Choice to Understand Historical Inequity in Disaster Planning and Response

Brittany K. Giles-Jones

During times of natural, man-made, and public health disasters, Communities of Color, Tribes, and Tribal Nations are often identified as socially vulnerable[1] or Economically Disadvantaged Rural Communities (EDRC)[2] and are among the most detrimentally impacted (FEMA 2023). In this chapter, I dissect the hurricane planning, response, and long-term recovery efforts in Louisiana between 2000 and 2022 to better understand the commonalities that make communities vulnerable and the areas of planning and response that are most lacking (NOAA 2016a). Focused on the perspective, experiences, and policies that impact Tribes and Tribal Nations, I aim to understand the depth and similarities of the long-term impacts of recovery efforts on personal and community health and well-being in these communities. This chapter focuses on connecting public choice and disaster policy, exploring implications that create points of failure that make these communities vulnerable, and understanding how some communities are better prepared to cope with disasters.

The goal of this chapter is to highlight the gaps, areas of improvement, and historical inequities in domestic disaster planning, along with trends within disaster historiography which, without strategic rectification, will continue to strain socially vulnerable communities' ability to respond to and recover from all disasters. Understanding the impacts of disaster history and event reporting can help shift planning and response efforts to better serve the whole community[3] and positively impact emergency and disaster management research.

While focused on the lived experience of Tribe and Tribal Nation members, the events studied aim to provide a multicultural understanding of how these events impact populations of various ethnicities, backgrounds, races, and lived experiences. Additionally, I will consider cross-disaster impacts and work to understand how disaster policy and decision-making following hurricanes created disadvantages that can become apparent or be exacerbated during other disasters.

Utilizing a transdisciplinary approach, the purpose of this chapter is to provide research that will help ensure a cycle of documented best practices related to disaster preparedness and recovery strategies that can be utilized by both practitioners (government officials along with public health and emergency management professionals) and academics (scholars and researchers). The goal is to discover techniques that can be implemented in various areas to increase mitigation in the entire community. This research can be used to simultaneously advance the capabilities, abilities, possibilities, and realities of regularly impacted communities, specifically the socially vulnerable and EDRC populations, while advancing the field of emergency management as a whole.

Exploring public choice theory allows for consideration of the same principles that are prevalent in the marketplace when analyzing the actions driving collective decision-making. These considerations can help us understand political and community impacts and primary motivations. Utilizing the teachings of James Buchanan as the foundation for understanding public choice theory and looking at disaster response and planning through this viewpoint can help deepen analysis of governmental and similar authorities' actions and to create links between disaster events while uncovering repeated and unique inequities.

Furthermore, there is significant evidence of the benefits of understanding disasters through an interdisciplinary and mixed-methods approach. Much like the research methods utilized to develop this chapter, Virgil Henry Storr and Emily Chamlee-Wright stress that the ability to understand the magnitude and impacts of disasters relies on combining theories and empirical strategies of multiple stakeholder types, including those in governmental, voluntary, private, and public sectors (Chamlee-Wright 2010; Chamlee-Wright et al. 2010).

Analyzing these foundations of inequity through the lens of public choice decisions and implications, while simultaneously considering the procedures and policies that set the basis for planning and response actions, can uncover truths about the realities of disaster planning and response, reveal similarities between events, and allow for stable best practices to be recommended.

Introducing polycentricity in disaster response efforts, event analysis, and future disaster planning can significantly elevate the success rate of implemented strategies and initiatives, which can limit the reality of significant loss of life and infrastructure (Coyne and Lemke 2011). A major factor in the coordination needed for successful cultural, economic, political, and social recovery and polycentricity requires multi-level collaboration and comparison, which considers and accommodates the needs of federal and local governments, the residents they serve, and private partnering organizations.

While significant differences can be noted within resource allocation, fund availability, willingness, and execution from the standpoint of researchers and practitioners, it is just as important to document commonalities in the experience of the disaster survivors. Through the investigation of hurricanes over the span of two decades, 2000–2022, I strive to understand the experiences and feelings of discrimination, de-prioritization, economic insecurity, and a lack of mutual respect and cultural competency demonstrated by disaster-response authorities. Additionally, I seek to understand the sustained community impacts on socially vulnerable, EDRC residents, and particularly the impacts on Tribes and Tribal Nations in Louisiana. Hurricanes historically have left recorded long-term impacts on the affected community. With the goal of investigating the public choice actions and consequences that resulted in long-term economic, community, and public health system impacts, this chapter aims to uncover best practices, lessons learned, and resources that can be provided to communities to increase mitigation and preparedness for future events.

Emergencies and disasters are often categorized by their type or remembered for their physical, financial, or direct political impacts; however, their social and cultural impacts are infrequently focused on. With each emergency or disaster event, the perception, expectation, and readiness of the responding community expand. Personal experiences shape how we understand, respond to, and cope with disasters. Throughout the United States alone, some disasters, such as blizzards, earthquakes, or tornadoes, may never be experienced by residents within their lifetimes. Alternatively, others are prone to consistent and repeat events of certain natural disaster types. There are some disasters that will forever change the United States's relationship with disaster planning and response due to their magnitude, impact, and shared experiences.

Hurricane recovery in Louisiana, particularly from Hurricane Katrina, is a prime example of the equal importance of physical and social recovery efforts. Additionally, the increased social response and coordination in the aftermath of the hurricane were critical to community survival and sustainability and far surpassed the expected capacity of residents. Understanding the complexities of social and cultural recovery helps us comprehend the crucial nature of coordinating both the cultural and political economy in disaster recovery and better recognize the internal resources and natural capabilities of each community.

Understanding Hurricanes and Tropical Storms

As defined by the National Oceanic and Atmospheric Administration, hurricanes are a type of tropical cyclone that has reached a sustained wind speed of seventy-four miles per hour (mph). While this chapter focuses on the impacts of hurricanes, it is important to acknowledge the magnitude and progression of tropical cyclones—rotating, warm-core, low-pressure storm systems without any fronts. Tropical cyclones form over tropical or subtropical waters and are categorized as tropical depressions, tropical storms, hurricanes, and major hurricanes, listed in order of maximum sustained wind progression. Tropical cyclones can escalate from a tropical depression to a major hurricane within hours to days. Therefore, there will be times throughout this chapter when it will be important to reference the progression of the researched hurricanes and impacts in other categories of tropical cyclones before escalating to a hurricane.[4] Specific to hurricanes, this research will analyze each hurricane's rating on the Saffir-Simpson Hurricane Wind Scale,[5] with the expectation of Category 5 hurricanes causing the greatest damage and Category 1 hurricanes causing the least amount of damage.

Understanding Louisiana's Climate and Storm Susceptibility

With a consistent subtropical climate, Louisiana is continually susceptible to frequent precipitation. While some areas of the state are prone to snowfall, most of the state experiences average winter temperatures of high 50s to mid-60s Fahrenheit (°F), with summers averaging between the mid-90s to low 100s °F. Some parts of Louisiana often experience summer temperatures of up to 105 °F. These weather conditions create an average of 60 days of thunderstorms each year across the state, which all have the potential to develop into full hurricanes. Since 2000, Louisiana has experienced over twenty tropical cyclones (NOLA Ready 2023). With recurring warm days and frequent thunderstorms, populations in Louisiana must have mitigation strategies and readily available response resources to prevent catastrophic outcomes and long-term negative impacts.

Hurricane Katrina

To date, Hurricane Katrina has been one of the deadliest hurricanes to hit the United States, killing an estimated 1,833 people, leaving millions homeless, and causing over 160 billion dollars in damages. There are significant mitigation and response lessons that can be learned from this disaster. These lessons have improved upon the response and recovery capabilities lacking during the event. Furthermore, Hurricane Katrina uncovered underlying inequities in mitigation and post-disaster planning, which worsened the outcomes, recovery capabilities, and realities of the event (Quinn 2006).

Starting as a tropical depression forming over the Bahamas on August 23, 2005, the event escalated into a tropical storm and made landfall in Florida on August 25, 2005. Hurricane Katrina continued to travel along the Gulf of Mexico, escalating to a Category 5 before decreasing to a Category 3 by the time the storm hit New Orleans, Louisiana, on August 29, 2005, and submerged 80 percent of the city by August 31. This area is known for having an extremely high population of people of color in comparison to much of the United States: 57 percent of the city's population identifies as Black or African American, and almost 15 percent identify as American Indian or Alaska Native, Asian, Native Hawaiian or Pacific Islander, Hispanic or Latino, and multiracial (Census 2023). New Orleans is an area that is particularly known for its Creole, Black American Jazz, and other Afro-American and Afro-Caribbean cultural aesthetic elements. Inevitable impacts were displayed in immediate recovery techniques and strategies of evacuation, sheltering, feeding, and medical care. However, despite recovery and response shortages and outcomes that have the potential to happen during any disaster, residents felt their mistreatment, lack of care, and disregard for recovery were heightened because of the significant number of residents of color (Aten et al. 2010). During Hurricane Katrina, communities of color made up nearly 80 percent of the population in flooded neighborhoods. As much as 28 percent of the city population in New Orleans was living below the poverty line before the storm, and the 105,000-plus residents who did not have access to a car—two-thirds of whom were African American—faced severely limited evacuation options. Lastly, nearly half of the population harmed by the broken levees in Hurricane Katrina were African American. Over the fifteen years post disaster, several communities increased disaster mitigation efforts, while others, primarily those of color, are still looking for access to long-term housing that will be affordable, with consideration for enhanced storm mitigation, sustainability, and preparedness needs (Fussell and Harris 2014). The population looking for housing solutions includes both those who were completely displaced and those seeking disaster-recovery housing repair funding for damaged properties (Davis et al. 2020).

During both the hurricane and long-term recovery, social coordination and strategic community planning have been prevalent. Strong community organizations with a broad capacity for response and recovery demonstrated how reliance on these systems can leave communities in a position of self-governance and in alignment with polycentric governance, which can increase resilience (Grube and Storr 2013).

While there have been numerous critiques and mixed feelings about the response to Hurricane Katrina, there are major factors in mitigation planning and emergency system funding for future disasters that have been implemented due to lessons learned. To address any feelings of lack of information dissemination, local authorities worked together with the National Weather Service (NWS) in preceding years, and directly in response to the outcome of Hurricane Katrina, to enhance knowledge and emergency message-sharing capabilities for future similar events and further expanded message-sharing capabilities for all disaster types across the targeted areas. The success of this effort was also made possible by residents changing their way of thinking about evacuation, the severity of storm impacts, and emergency messaging, and their willingness to take warnings more seriously in future disasters.

Hurricane Rita

One of the greatest lessons learned during Hurricane Katrina was the importance of infrastructure strength and sustainability. These breaches severely exacerbated damages, impacts, and loss of life, though officials utilized this experience to strengthen levee systems to mitigate against potential levee breaches in the future. Less than two months after Hurricane Katrina, on September 24, 2005, Hurricane Rita struck Southwest Louisiana at a Category 3[6] level, after reaching Category 5[7] four days prior, with sustained winds of 180 mph. Hurricane Rita offers a prime example of the importance of cross-jurisdictional collaboration in response and mitigation efforts across states.

Hurricane Rita was the strongest hurricane to specifically strike a combination of Southern Texas and Southwest Louisiana in over fifty years, and the response software and strategies elevated and executed because of Hurricane Katrina were evident within the response to this new disaster. Recorded as one of the strongest hurricanes ever in the Gulf of Mexico, and fourth strongest in the Atlantic Basin, the hurricane was noted to be responsible for 100 indirect fatalities, but only seven direct fatalities (NOAA 2023b). The vast difference in death rates between Hurricanes Katrina and Rita illustrates the strength of the policies, procedures, and resources that were implemented due to analyses of public reactions and experiences suggesting information and communication failures during previous disasters. However, the stark difference in death rates also raises questions about evacuation practices and unaddressed long-term needs.

In Louisiana, the National Weather Service (NWS), local emergency management agencies, and local officials assessed the public experience and the gaps in response capabilities, implementing community outreach events that would be beneficial in expanding responsiveness and preparedness for multiple disaster types. The mitigation efforts established by the NWS in Lake Charles, Louisiana, included increasing coordination with local, state, and federal officials and the creation of strategies to distribute information more effectively and efficiently to the public, emergency managers, and disaster event responders. Mitigation and preparedness techniques were elevated by utilizing public interest and prioritizing disaster policies and funding to positively impact future event outcomes and to focus on community partnerships and coordinate with officials as equally as pre-established internal community organizations and national Voluntary Organizations Active in Disasters (VOADs). While there were many successes demonstrated throughout Hurricane Rita, public-facing pre-disaster workshops, events, tours, and drills were executed to continue mitigation and better inform the public and prepare for a variety of catastrophic weather events.

More than a week before Hurricane Rita made landfall, the NWS began conference calls with the Southwest Louisiana Shelter Task Force, Texas Department of Emergency Management, and local Emergency Managers from Southwestern Louisiana and Southeast Texas. This cross-jurisdictional coordination allows for mass situational awareness and enhances the ability to relay the shifting realities of the hurricane to better prepare the communities in its path. Additionally, the prioritization of funding to enhance communication systems and public knowledge in response to the loss of life, infrastructure, and community experienced in prior events strengthened community response resources and interest.

During Hurricane Rita, aircraft tours, school tours, open house events, civic club luncheons, emergency management and responder drills, and workshops were just a few of the ways mitigation funding was spent to enhance the response capabilities of the whole community. While the NWS, local emergency management agencies, and government authorities must be credited for analyzing past event experiences and reports and successfully creating procedures and opportunities for the whole community to increase readiness, the public holds sole responsibility and credit for choosing to engage in preparedness activities. That increased public interest in hurricane preparedness directly contributed to a reduction in the loss of life during Hurricane Rita.

Demonstrating the importance of official community accessibility and resources, in combination with proactive decisions related to disaster planning and anticipated response needs, they created a culture of information distribution and communication, integrated comfortability among residents, which enabled the NWS Lake Charles to issue early warning messages, perform pre-hurricane equipment maintenance checks, and increase media coordination that saved countless lives during Hurricane Rita, which was not previously utilized during Hurricane Katrina.

Hurricane Gustav

Hurricane Gustav illustrates the constantly changing nature of hurricanes and other tropical storms. Beginning on August 25, 2008, Hurricane Gustav was the seventh tropical depression near the Caribbean in 2008. Almost immediately escalating to a tropical storm, Gustav officially reached hurricane status by August 26, 2008, with a sustained wind speed of 74 mph. Providing some hope of lower anticipated impacts, Gustav lost official hurricane status just before crossing over Southwestern Haiti. However, the reduced storm status quickly shifted to a Category 4 hurricane prior to making landfall in Cuba on August 30, 2008. By September 1, 2008, Hurricane Gustav made landfall in Southeast Louisiana, where it caused heavy rainfall across the region for three days (NOAA 2016b).

"We weren't sure how the events would play out with this storm, so we wanted to make sure we were prepared for everything," noted Bureau of Alcohol, Tobacco, Firearms, and Explosives Assistant Special Agent in Charge,

Jeff Stirling. While Hurricane Gustav caused the evacuation of over two million people along and near the Louisiana coast, it resulted in less than ten recorded deaths (Schwartz, 2008). Noting the potential similarity to the outcomes of Hurricane Katrina, the same building that was utilized three years prior as a Joint Field Office during the Hurricane Katrina response was transformed into an Emergency Support Function 13 (ESF-13)[8] group headquarters. Area officials coordinated with the federal government to ensure the area was prepared for a potentially catastrophic event less than five years after Hurricane Katrina. Acting on documented lessons learned from Hurricane Katrina, the US Federal Bureau of Investigation's (FBI) Critical Incident Response Group (CIRG) and Technical Response Unit mobilized in Louisiana a day before Hurricane Gustav made landfall (FBI archives 2008)[9].

While noticeably absent from the previous two disasters, one of the most insightful reports about the status of Tribes and Tribal Nations (also referred to as Indigenous People) was the pre and during-event updates from Brenda Dardar Robichaux, Principal Chief of the United Houma Nation (Principal Chief) through the *Indigenous Issue Today* blog site (2008). Demonstrating the importance of cultural considerations, interactive community response, the power in the utilization of technology, and overall positive public participation decisions, the Principal Chief was able to implement four identifiable strategies that prevented a catastrophic outcome for the Houma Nation, which had been projected to be one of the worst-impacted Tribes or Tribal Nations during Hurricane Gustav. Identified implemented strategies included *Pre-event Internal and External Donation Coordination*, which was demonstrated on August 29, 2008, when the Principal Chief published a call for internal and external community donations. The strategy of *Disclosing Pre-Disaster Realities* was utilized from August 29, 2008, to September 1, 2008, when the Principal Chief continually spoke about the reality of recovery from Hurricanes Katrina and Rita. The researched literature discloses many people within the Houma Nation were still living in FEMA trailers prior to Hurricane Gustav because of these two hurricanes and noted increased vulnerability and susceptibility to damage. Third, the Tribe strategized to *Establish Coordination with Emergency Management Officials*, and on August 29, 2008, it was noted that coordination with the local Office of Emergency Preparedness authorities was stabilized to ensure officials were aware of the community's needs. Lastly, *Sheltering* was one of the most significant strategies implemented and actions taken by the Principal Chief, who decided to adhere to public concern and personally shelter approximately twenty community members within their residence. Despite power outages and winds of 85 mph, the Principal Chief was able to personally house as many community members as possible, ensure the majority of others were evacuated, and maintain consistent communication with internal and external responding stakeholders.

This is directly in alignment with the core aspects of polycentric governance, which relies on the ability to analyze complex issues and potential strategies for solutions from a multi-authority perspective while considering impacts on vastly different populations. As displayed in Hurricane Gustav, polycentric governance goes beyond the traditional levels of decision-making to provide a multi-level perspective that encompasses the views of federal, state, local, and global authorities and creates cross-level links between them. Pivotal to the outcome of all the discussed disaster events, and highlighted within Hurricane Gustav, was the capacity for cross-sectional and plural-community consideration and coordination, which helped develop strategies to accommodate subcultures within the state during broader community planning, while also capturing the response and recovery abilities and limitations of private, voluntary, public, community, and faith-based organizations as critical partners. Lessons learned from Hurricanes Katrina and Rita highlighted the benefits and need for an omni-functional response, capitalizing on cross-jurisdictional federal and political resources while supporting units that were designed to handle specific disaster response responsibilities such as debris removal, resident services, funding assistance, and housing solutions.

With Hurricane Gustav, planning and response actions appeared to be as crucial as both public response and interest and the governmental official response decisions. Utilizing lessons learned from Hurricane Katrina and critically analyzing the response actions of citizens and responding authorities added to the creation of strategic evacuation plans and saved countless lives. After an in-depth review of the internal actions of the Houma Nation community members, it is clear that public choice action, from sheltering decisions to the elevation of public coordination, demonstrated community response and long-term recovery capabilities. During Hurricane Gustav, the Houma Nation extended its resources and cultural practices of community building and restoration to ensure emergency responders were provided for and infrastructure restoration could begin and be completed. Furthermore, the Houma Nation utilized its resources to ensure internal emergency sheltering, which can be an example for internal and collaborative aid in the future.

Hurricane Laura

Forming as a tropical wave off the west coast of Africa on August 16, 2020, the storm moved east to west across the tropics, bringing clouds and thunderstorms. As Hurricane Laura traveled westward, it continued to gain strength and encounter geographical areas in its path for the next 10 days. With sustained winds of 150 mph after reaching Category 4, Hurricane Laura made landfall on August 27, 2020, in Cameron, Louisiana (NOAA 2023a). Louisianan and Texan communities could still remember the devastation from Hurricane Katrina 15 years prior and were currently dealing with the challenges of Coronavirus Disease 2019 (Covid-19) maintenance and recovery, while preparing for the unknown outcome of Hurricane Laura (Richard et al. 2021). Increased mitigation and response efforts, implemented due to previous disaster experiences, were proven successful based on the initial review. The combined death toll from Laura in the United States and Hispaniola was forty-seven, which was significantly lower than the fatalities reported during Hurricane Katrina and Hurricane Rita. The most significant challenge that mitigation efforts faced during Hurricane Laura was the wind speeds, which broke 150-year records for Southwest Louisiana and threatened a catastrophe far beyond the scale of the one that actually occurred.

This avoidance of a catastrophic outcome was due partially to the analysis of best practices and utilizing them to implement federally supported public actions that would amplify response capabilities for the whole community. Prior to Hurricane Laura making landfall in the US emergency declarations in Louisiana and Texas were expanded to cover emergency protective repose actions taken by state, local, and Tribal officials. Understanding the significant impact that similar prior events had on local communities, federal support aimed to help alleviate the suffering and hardship caused by emergencies on the local population, and provide sufficient assistance related to emergency measures. In addition to expanding federal policy to ensure response capability, FEMA deployed Regional Incident Management and Urban Search and Rescue teams to both Louisiana and Texas to provide immediate assistance in locating missing people (FEMA.gov 2020).

Some of the most effective response and recovery actions were designed based on an understanding of previous public choice actions, and decisions were implemented to accommodate public habits and noted limitations. Before Hurricane Laura made landfall, FEMA stationed more than 500,000 meals, 800,000 liters of water, blue roof sheeting, infant toddler kits, and generators at the Roseland Staging Area and Camp Beauregard in Louisiana. Understanding the feelings of housing recovery neglect, as previously noted with the experience of the Houma Tribe, FEMA and its federal partners mobilized impact assessment teams to begin immediate recovery. Immediate recovery assistance included roofing, planning and response, and emergency power support flood-fighting.

There were several direct strategies that were implemented to increase community mitigation and response capabilities. However, public interest, contribution, and experience are equally as insightful as official planning efforts. The experience of the Coushatta Tribe in Louisiana questions the valuation and acknowledgment of tribal contributions to public infrastructure repair and recovery. In addition to offering assistance for public road repair, the Tribe provided shelter, water, and power to first responders. Despite gallant efforts to establish lines of coordination, Tribe Chairman David Sickey reported limited outreach from the federal government to the Tribe, prior to, during, or after Hurricane Laura.

Hurricane Ida

On August 27, 2021, on the sixteenth anniversary of Hurricane Katrina, Hurricane Ida made landfall near Port Fourchon, Louisiana, at Category 4 strength after originating as a tropical depression just a day prior near Kingston, Jamaica (NOAA 2023c). Producing significant flash flooding, wind, and storm surge, Hurricane Ida immediately impacted roadway access and worsened regional weather conditions, which created catastrophic flooding and produced thirty-five known tornadoes. Proven to be a resource in previous hurricane events, the NWS assembled a Service Assessment Team to evaluate the hurricane response performance prior to and during the hurricane. The hurricane was responsible for a recorded eighty-seven deaths along its overland path from Louisiana to New England, twenty-eight of which were indirect aftermath fatalities (Encyclopedia Britannica 2023).

A thorough Service Assessment was produced by the US Department of Commerce, compiling the findings of the Ida Assessment Team and uncovering best practices and offering recommendations in the following focus areas:

1. Operations,
2. Systems and Facilities,
3. Service Backup and Mutual Aid,

4. Impact-Based Decision Support Services,
5. Service Equity and Vulnerable Populations,
6. Training and Proficiency,
7. Transportation Services.

Most significant in understanding the ideology behind and the success of official planning and response actions is the focus on service equity and vulnerable communities, which directly reviews service delivery to underserved communities and assesses the ability to serve vulnerable populations (NOAA 2023). The *Hurricane Ida Service Assessment* consolidates reports, interviews, and findings to understand public actions and create recommendations for future events (Weather.gov 2023). The assessment team determined that public actions during the hurricane were a direct result of an emphasis on communication and accessibility. While the recorded fatalities during Hurricane Ida were significantly lower, the same practice of migration de-prioritization for communities of color and lack of consideration of community needs related to socially vulnerable populations was just as present as with Hurricane Katrina (White et al. 2007). While prioritizing outreach for certain communities, the NWS offices mentioned not fully knowing how to locate socially vulnerable populations, how to serve them once located, or how to understand community needs. In both disasters, the pre-conditions of the community and the ability to access and disseminate information, pre-established response resources, and recovery plans were essential in the immediate response capabilities and long-term recovery abilities of socially vulnerable residents.

One of the most impacted and neglected socially vulnerable populations is Tribes and Tribal Nations who were completely left out of the Hurricane Ida Service Assessment (Bowman 2021). The residents of Isle de Jean Charles are faced with long-term questions related to housing and relocation. Forced relocation or an uncertain future is the reality for generations of Charles Choctaw Nation and United Houma Nation members who are the main inhabitants of this area (Jacobo et al. 2023). Exasperated by the impacts of Hurricane Ida, the Isle de Jean Charles is a victim of a combination of migration planning de-prioritization, lack of disaster recovery support, and climate change, resulting in resident displacement and being the first community to be considered displaced by climate change by the federal government (Chavez and Lane 2022; Santana 2022).

Long a place of refuge for Native people pushed out of their homelands, the Southeastern Louisiana Bayou has been the home of thousands of Pointe-Au-Chien, United Houma Nation, Grand Caillou/Dulac Band of Biloxi-Chitimacha-Choctaw, and other Native American Tribal members since 1682. During Hurricane Ida, over 60 percent of community members experienced damage or total property loss. Nine months after the hurricane made landfall, many community members were still living in FEMA Trailers or travel campers next to the remains of their homes if they were not forced to relocate altogether. While some residents will be eligible for disaster recovery funding based on their Tribe or Tribal Nations' federal status, many of the Tribes and Tribal Nations are not recognized by federal or state governments, despite decades of seeking recognition. Heightening major recovery concerns for residents are economic and physical recovery capabilities: traditionally, Tribal residents living in this area have been self-sustaining and thrive from the land and proximity to water. However, in addition to permanently damaged land, the lack of federal or state recognition severely impacts recovery funding eligibility. After decades of public policy decision-making and implementation created infrastructure development discrimination and natural coastal erosion, Tribal members are facing a difficult and long road to hurricane recovery and community restoration.

Common Denominators Creating Historical Inequality for Tribes and Tribal Nations in Louisiana

As previously mentioned, due to a subtropical climate with winters averaging temperatures between the high-50s to mid-60s°F, and summer temperatures in the mid-90s to 100°F, the entire state of Louisiana is more susceptible to climate conditions that create hurricanes in comparison to other parts of the United States. With an average of 60 days of thunderstorms per year, communities across Louisiana are consistently at risk of the life-altering impacts of hurricanes and other tropical storms. However, within a state that is inherently vulnerable, there are some populations that are more susceptible to negative impacts from disasters. Among these communities are the Tribes and Tribal Nations. There were significant similarities between the decision factors that helped residents decide if they would remain at home throughout the event, relocate, or return home post hurricane. Such factors included economic promise or stability upon return, a habitable and safe home to return to, existing or returning cultural elements, and resource availability. These factors not only had important implications for returning Tribes, Tribal Nations, and residents of color but also for those of lower socioeconomic status and renters vs. homeowners (Lee et al. 2009).

Feelings of Pre-event Discrimination or De-prioritization

During Hurricane Katrina, residents of color expressed the feeling that evacuation prioritization was given to predominantly white or more affluent neighborhoods, even though economically disadvantaged communities and communities of color proved to be more prone to flooding and often experienced greater impacts (Randall 2019).

Years later, while coordination was established with Emergency Management Officials and the United Houma Nation during Hurricane Gustav, the establishment of that coordination did not happen until three days before the hurricane made landfall. This timeframe left limited opportunities to connect all points of contact, establish proper information distribution methods for community members, or give them opportunities to implement any pre-disaster best practices that might be distributed by emergency managers.

Utilizing tribal lessons learned from previous disasters, gallant efforts were made by tribal leaders to establish lines of coordination between the federal government and the Coushatta Tribe prior to Hurricane Laura, though there was reported to be limited outreach from the federal government to the Tribe, prior to, during, or after Hurricane Laura.

There were several direct strategies that can be identified that were implemented due to public choice analysis in an effort to increase whole community mitigation and response capabilities. However, public contribution and experience are equally as insightful as official planning efforts. The experience of the Coushatta Tribe in Louisiana questions the valuation and recognition of tribal contributions to public infrastructure repair and recovery: in addition to offering assistance for public road repair, it was the Tribe that provided shelter, water, and power to first responders. Despite extending tribal resources to ensure public infrastructure repair was completed and, in some locations, possible at all, as well as helping to maintain logistics which made immediate response and recovery operations possible, the Tribe did not experience the same generosity when seeking federal and state disaster recovery resources.

Lack of Disaster Funding or Economic Promise

Demonstrating the long-term housing impacts any catastrophic disaster can have, many Houma Nation community members were still living in FEMA trailers three years later, thanks to Hurricanes Katrina and Rita, when Hurricane Gustav made landfall, which increased vulnerability and susceptibility to damage. As the twentieth anniversary of Hurricane Katrina quickly approaches, several communities across Louisiana have increased mitigation and response capabilities. However, many residents, primarily Tribes, Tribal Nations, and those of color, are still looking for access to sustainable and affordable long-term housing, inclusive of disaster-recovery housing repair.

Lacking Mutal Respect, Cultural Competency, and Tribal-Specific Communication Systems

Tardy coordination between Emergency Management Officials, Tribes, and Tribal Nations excludes many community members from early warning messages and eliminates residents' ability to be as prepared as their cultural and ethnic counterparts (Allen 2007).

While there have been numerous noted accounts of federal and state strategies planning for the whole community, there is clear evidence that Tribes, Tribal Nations, and communities of color are historically and presently being omitted from a range of pre-disaster planning and outreach opportunities. More significant to the longevity of community sustainability are the ripple effects these inequities create within disaster recovery, funding eligibility, and resident return capabilities (Chavez 2021).

Vital to the ability to establish and maintain a positive recovery phase, cultural competency should consistently be applied throughout every phase of disaster planning, response, and recovery. Cultural considerations such as diet, religion, housing habits and needs, community resources, community self-sustainment history, health and access needs, and leadership culture should be considered among other disaster and community-specific needs.

Despite limited outreach from the federal government in relation to Hurricane Laura, the Coushatta Tribe acted as a disaster response resource by providing shelter, water, and power to first responders. Even without strong federal coordination or support, the tribe continued to assist with mitigation and recovery activities, which would benefit the whole community by assisting with public road and infrastructure recovery. Yet, the Tribe has received some of the least support, was not prioritized the same way as others, and is still working through long-term recovery (Bautista 2020).

One of the greatest cultural consideration blunders related to disaster event reporting took place in the aftermath reporting of Hurricane Ida, when the experiences and reality of Tribes and Tribal names were excluded from the *Hurricane Ida Service Assessment*. A document that will be utilized by researchers and practitioners to study event conditions and prepare for future events severely disadvantages Tribal access to resources and consideration when those groups are excluded from consideration.

Conclusion

It must be acknowledged that the frequency and severity of natural disasters and global events have changed significantly over the past decades with the advancement of technology, access, experience, and climate change. Additionally, all events are not equally captured or reported in all areas of the United States and therefore there are inevitable gaps in all disaster research. However, the goal is to use available resources and research to plan for these gaps and make considerations for underrepresented communities. Cultural habits, best practices, and experiences significantly impact how people understand disaster threats, severity, and personal response actions. Tribes, tribal nations, and communities of color often need targeted and culturally appropriate resources for the most robust and effective planning and response to occur.

Evidence presented in this chapter illustrates there is a myriad of reasons inequity is experienced within disaster planning and responses to various disasters. Economic impact and fund availability are often at the center of planning and response capabilities; however, prior experience and a ready planning or response authority can also majorly impact the outcome of natural disasters and global events. Through the study of Hurricanes Katrina, Rita, Gustav, Laura, and Ida, the goal of this chapter has been to uncover the tactics that enhance mitigation, preparedness, response, and recovery within communities while analyzing the policies that create inequality in emergency and disaster management.

Notes

1 *Social Vulnerability* is defined by the Federal Emergency Management Agency as the susceptibility of social groups to the adverse impacts of natural hazards, including disproportionate death, injury, loss, or disruption of livelihood. All communities across the United States are given a social vulnerability score and rating based upon criteria outlined in the National Risk Index. For more information on the definition of social vulnerability and to view the rankings throughout the country, please visit: https://hazards.fema.gov/nri/social-vulnerability
2 Economically Disadvantaged Rural Communities are referenced by the Federal Emergency Management Agency and defined by the US Code (42 U.S.C. § 5133(a)—*Small Impoverished Community*) as a community of 3,000 or fewer individuals that is economically disadvantaged, as determined by the state in which the community is located and based on criteria established by the President. For more information, visit: https://uscode.house.gov/view.xhtml?req=granuleid:USC-2007-title42-section5133&num=0&edition=2007
3 The term *Whole Community* is referenced throughout this document as a combination of a range of specific community types as defined by the Federal Emergency Management Agency. Further definition information can be found via: https://www.fema.gov/glossary/whole-community#:~:text=Whole%20Community%20includes%3A,Nonprofit%20groups
4 For further information about the definition of Tropical Cyclones, Depressions, Storms, as well as Hurricanes, please visit the National Oceanic and Atmospheric Administration website: https://oceanservice.noaa.gov/facts/hurricane.html
5 The Saffir-Simpson Hurricane Wind Scale utilizes a 1 to 5 rating system based on sustained wind levels to estimate hurricane severity and potential property damage. The National Hurricane Center and Central Pacific Hurricane Center recognize categories 3 through 5 as major storms. For more information regarding hurricane categories and ratings, please visit: https://www.nhc.noaa.gov/aboutsshws.php
6 Category 3 Hurricanes have sustained winds of 111,—129 mph.
7 Category 5 Hurricanes have sustained winds of 157 mph or higher.
8 The Emergency Support Function (ESF) structure provides a design for the coordination of Federal interagency support for a federal response to a disaster event (as classified by FEMA). Most frequently providing mechanisms for grouping functions consistently used to provide federal support to states, ESFs are intended to provide a structure for Presidentially Declared Disasters, emergencies under the Stafford Act, and Non-Stafford Act incidents. For more information on ESFs, please visit: https://www.fema.gov/pdf/emergency/nrf/nrf-annexes-all.pdf.

9 For further information about direct FBI coordination in Hurricane Gustav, please visit the digital FBI archives via: https://archives.fbi.gov/archives/news/stories/2008/september/gustav090508

References

Allen, Troy D. 2007. "Katrina: Race, Class, and Poverty: Reflections and Analysis." *Journal of Black Studies* 37 (4): 466–468.

Aten, Jamie D., Sharon Topping, Ryan M. Denney, and Tania G. Bayne. 2010. "Collaborating with African American Churches to Overcome Minority Disaster Mental Health Disparities: What Mental Health Professionals Can Learn from Hurricane Katrina." *Professional Psychology: Research and Practice* 41 (2): 167.

Bautista, Lillian. 2020. "Coushatta Tribe Begins Long Road to Recovery after Hurricane Laura." *The Hill*. September 17. https://thehill.com/homenews/state-watch/516979-coushatta-tribe-begins-long-road-to-recovery-after-hurricane-laura/.

Bowman, Emma. 2021. "Pushed to the Edge, Tribe Members in Coastal Louisiana Wonder Where to Go after Ida." *National Public Radio*. October 2. https://www.npr.org/2021/10/02/1040259898/hurricane-ida-louisiana-houma-tribe.

Chamlee-Wright, Emily. 2010. "The Cultural and Political Economy of Recovery: Social Learning in A Post-Disaster Environment." UK: Routledge.

Chamlee-Wright, Emily, and Virgil Henry Storr, eds. 2010. *The Political Economy of Hurricane Katrina and Community Rebound*. Cheltenham, UK: Edward Elgar Publishing eBooks.

Chavez, Roby. 2021. "Why Some Indigenous Tribes Are Being Left Behind in Louisiana's Ida Recovery." *PBS. Public Broadcasting Service*. October 20. https://www.pbs.org/newshour/nation/why-some-indigenous-tribes-are-being-left-behind-in-louisianas-ida-recovery.

Chavez, Roby, and Sam Lane. 2022. "Climate Change's Uneven Impact on Communities of Color Compounded by Uneven Flow of Aid." *PBS NewsHour*. August 26, 2022. https://www.pbs.org/newshour/show/climate-changes-uneven-impact-on-communities-of-color-compounded-by-uneven-flow-of-aid.

Coyne, Christopher, and Jayme Lemke. 2011. "Polycentricity in Disaster Relief." *Studies in Emergent Order* 4: 40–57.

Davis, Shelina, Knesha Rose-Davison, and Dean G. Smith. 2020. "Hurricane Katrina at 15: Introduction to the Special Section." *American Journal of Public Health* 110 (10): 1461–1462.

Encyclopedia Britannica. 2023. "New England." *Encyclopedia Britannica*. October 4. https://www.britannica.com/place/New-England.

Federal Bureau of Investigations. 2008. "FBI Joins Response to Gustav." In *FBI Part of Joint Federal Response to Gustav*. Federal Bureau of Investigations. September 5. https://archives.fbi.gov/archives/news/stories/2008/september/gustav090508.

Federal Emergency Management Agency. 2023. "Social Vulnerability." *Vulnerability | National Risk Index*. The Federal Emergency Management Agency. https://hazards.fema.gov/nri/social-vulnerability.

FEMA. 2020. "Hurricane Laura Federal Response Update." *FEMA.Gov*. August 27. https://www.fema.gov/press-release/20200827/hurricane-laura-federal-response-update.

Fussell, Elizabeth, and Elizabeth Harris. 2014. "Homeownership and Housing Displacement after Hurricane Katrina among Low-Income African-American Mothers in New Orleans." *Social Science Quarterly* 95 (4): 1086–1100.

Grube, Laura E., and Virgil Henry Storr. 2013. "The Capacity for Self-Governance and Post-Disaster Resiliency." *The Review of Austrian Economics* 27 (3): 301–324.

Indigenous Issues Today. 2008. "Hurricane Gustav and Indigenous Peoples along the Gulf Coast." In *Hurricane Gustav and Indigenous Peoples Along the Gulf Coast*. Indigenous Issues Today. September 2. https://indigenousissuestoday.blogspot.com/2008/09/hurricane-gustav-and-indigenous-peoples.html.

Jacobo, Julia, Dominick Proto, and Ginger Zee. 2023. "How Sea Level Rise Drove the Native Community of Isle de Jean Charles from Their Homes." *ABC News Network*. April 20. https://abcnews.go.com/US/sea-level-rise-drove-native-community-isle-de/story?id=98479346.

Lee, Eun-Kyoung Othelia, Ce Shen, and Thanh V. Tran. 2009. "Coping with Hurricane Katrina: Psychological Distress and Resilience among African American Evacuees." *Journal of Black Psychology* 35 (1): 5–23.

National Weather Service. 2023. *Service Assessment: August-September 2021 Hurricane Ida*. U.S. Department of Commerce. https://www.weather.gov/media/publications/assessments/Hurricane_Ida_Service_Assessment.pdf

New Orleans, City of 2023. "Hazards." In *Tropical Cyclones - NOLA Ready*. The City of New Orleans. Accessed October 8. https://ready.nola.gov/hazard-mitigation/hazards/tropical-cyclones/.

NOAA National Centers for Environmental Information. 2023. "In Harm's Way: Hurricane Ida's Impact on Socially Vulnerable." *ArcGIS StoryMaps*. Esri. April 3. https://storymaps.arcgis.com/stories/780e11bd19cc4dfca54ac8fb1d5e926f.

Quinn, Sandra C. 2006. "Hurricane Katrina: A Social and Public Health Disaster." *American Journal of Public Health* 96 (2): 204–204.

Randall, K. 2019. "What We Learned from Hurricanes Katrina and Rita - Texas A&M Today." *Texas A&M Today*. June 10. https://today.tamu.edu/2015/08/18/what-we-learned-from-hurricanes-katrina-and-rita/.

Richard J., Robbie Berg, David P. Roberts, and Philippe P. Papin. 2021. "Hurricane Laura." *National Hurricane Center Tropical Cyclone Report*. United States National

Oceanic and Atmospheric Association. May 26. https://www.nhc.noaa.gov/data/tcr/AL132020_Laura.pdf.

Santana, Rebecca. 2022. "In Louisiana, Native Americans Struggle to Recover from Ida." *AP News*. June 15. https://apnews.com/article/climate-trending-news-federal-emergency-management-agency-louisiana-us-91573cf1603876d6fe391045351b21c1.

Schwartz, John. 2008. "Gustav Was No Katrina, but Next Time ..." *The New York Times*. September 6. https://www.nytimes.com/2008/09/07/weekinreview/07schwartz.html.

United States Census Bureau QuickFacts. 2023. "U.S. Census Bureau QuickFacts: New Orleans City, Louisiana." *Census Bureau QuickFacts*. https://www.census.gov/quickfacts/fact/table/neworleanscitylouisiana/PST045223.

US Department of Commerce, NOAA. 2016a. "Tropical Weather." *National Weather Service*. NOAA's National Weather Service. September 12. https://www.weather.gov/lch/nwsem.

US Department of Commerce, NOAA. 2016b. "Hurricane Gustav - September 1, 2008." *National Weather Service*. NOAA's National Weather Service. December 2. https://www.weather.gov/mob/gustav.

US Department of Commerce, NOAA. 2023a. "Hurricane Laura 2020." *National Weather Service*. NOAA's National Weather Service. June 22. https://www.weather.gov/lch/2020Laura.

US Department of Commerce, NOAA. 2023b. "Hurricane Rita 2005." *National Weather Service*. NOAA's National Weather Service. June 22. https://www.weather.gov/lch/rita_main.

US Department of Commerce, NOAA. 2023c. "2021 Hurricane Ida Service Assessment." *Weather.Gov*. United States Department of Commerce. April. https://www.weather.gov/media/publications/assessments/Hurricane_Ida_Service_Assessment.pdf.

White, Ismail K., Tasha S. Philpot, Kristin Wylie, and Ernest McGowen. 2007. "Feeling the Pain of My People: Hurricane Katrina, Racial Inequality, and the Psyche of Black America." *Journal of Black Studies* 37 (4): 523–538.

3

Unemployment Insurance Trust Funds Under Pressure

Incentives, Interventions, and Insolvency

Dallin Overstreet

Unemployment insurance (UI) is a social safety net program that provides temporary income support to workers who lose their jobs through no fault of their own. In the United States, UI is jointly administered by federal and state governments, with each level having different roles and responsibilities. While the federal government sets minimum standards and provides funding and guidance to states, states have considerable discretion in determining tax rates, benefit levels, eligibility criteria, and administrative procedures for their UI programs. This decentralized structure of UI creates a complex interplay of incentives and behaviors among different actors at federal and state levels, which may affect the solvency and adequacy of UI programs.

The main goal of this chapter is to analyze how the funding and provision of UI programs across states are influenced by public choice considerations like the incentives of politicians and bureaucrats at the federal and state levels. It poses two research questions: (1) How do the incentives embedded in the UI system at each level of governance shape the overall dynamics of the system? and (2) How does federal intervention during recessions affect the solvency of state UI trust funds? The chapter argues that federal intervention during recessions creates a moral hazard problem, incentivizing states to underfund their UI trust funds, while also serving the political interests of both federal and state politicians, as well as the administrative interests of state bureaucrats who run the program.

To support these arguments, this chapter draws on public choice theory as a framework for understanding how self-interested actors make decisions in political settings. The chapter reviews the relevant literature on UI, public choice theory, and polycentric governance. I then present an empirical analysis of UI trust fund balances from the inception of the program to 2022. Finally, I discuss the implications of the findings for policy and future research.

This chapter contributes to the literature on UI by providing a comprehensive analysis of how federal-state interactions affect UI outcomes across states over time. It also adds to the literature on public choice theory by applying it to a specific policy domain that involves multiple levels of government. Moreover, it challenges some assumptions of polycentric governance by showing its potential drawbacks for social welfare provision. By doing so, this chapter aims to shed light on one of the most important social safety net programs in the US economy.

Unemployment Insurance in the United States

The US unemployment insurance (UI) system is a joint federal-state program that provides temporary income support to workers who lose their jobs through no fault of their own (U.S. Department of Labor n.d.). While the federal government sets certain baseline requirements that states must meet, like minimum taxable wage bases or speed and accuracy of benefit payments, states are largely left to operate on their own. States set their own eligibility requirements, payment amounts, maximum durations of claims, and several tax considerations (Center on Budget and Policy Priorities 2014).

The UI system is financed by taxes levied on employers at both federal and state levels. Federal taxes are used to fund administrative costs at both the federal and state levels, extended benefits during recessions, and loans to insolvent state trust funds. State taxes are deposited directly into state UI trust funds that pay for regular UI benefits and interest on federal loans. Thus, while states are the sole managers of their state trust funds, they are reliant on the federal government for their administrative budgets to administer the program, as well as for any additional funds needed due to insolvency (Center on Budget and Policy Priorities 2014).

The solvency of state UI trust funds is a key indicator of the financial health and adequacy of the UI system (Brookings Institution 2020). A solvent trust fund means that a state has enough reserves to pay for UI benefits without borrowing from the federal government or other sources. A solvent trust fund also allows a state to maintain lower tax rates on employers and higher benefit levels for claimants. However, many states have faced chronic or cyclical insolvency problems in their UI trust funds, especially during recessions when benefit payments increase and tax revenues decrease.

States that face insolvency in their UI trust funds due to insufficient reserves can borrow from the federal government to pay UI benefits. However, federal loans come with clear stipulations and criteria that states must meet (U.S. Congressional Research Service 2023). States may receive interest-free loans during the fiscal year if they agree to fully repay the loans by September 30th and meet specified solvency and tax effort requirements. To receive loans after September 30th, states must request loan advances from the Federal Unemployment Account within the Federal Unemployment Trust Fund. These post-September 30th loans accrue interest that states must repay unless temporarily waived, as occurred in 2020–2021. States that do not repay their loans by November 10, after the second consecutive January 1 with an outstanding loan balance, will face higher Federal Unemployment Tax Act (FUTA) rates for employers until the loan is repaid. The FUTA tax credit reduction starts at 0.3 percent and increases by 0.3 percent annually so long as the loan remains unpaid. Additional tax add-ons may also apply after the second and fifth years of an unpaid loan. While federal loans provide needed funding when state reserves are insufficient, the stipulations around repayment, interest charges, and higher FUTA rates attempt to create accountability for states to repay their UI debts and incentivize them to maintain adequate trust fund solvency.

The general inability to adequately fund state UI trust funds has been studied by many scholars, with several explanations existing. One concept to note is that of retrenchment in the US social welfare policy literature. Hacker (2004) describes retrenchment as policy changes that cut social expenditure, restructure welfare state programs to conform to the residual welfare state model more closely, or that alter the environment politically in ways that may increase the probability of these two outcomes in the future. As circumstances have changed economically and politically, many states have not responded with changes to their UI programs. Because of this, the protections created by the UI program have slowly eroded over time due to the lack of adjustment on the part of many states. Scholars have used the retrenchment framework to understand the slow erosion of UI benefits (i.e., the level of UI benefits has not grown sufficiently over time), but fewer have applied it to the financing of the program itself (Anderson 2001; Davidsson and Marx 2013).

Another explanation for trust fund insolvency may be the shift in how states choose to tax employers. The United States' UI system was designed to be forward-funded, meaning that states are supposed to accumulate reserves in their UI trust funds during periods of economic growth and then use those funds to provide payments to unemployed workers during economic downturns and recessions (Goss and Knudsen 1999). Employers who have more experience with unemployment (or who tend to lay off more employees) face higher state UI tax rates while employers that experience less unemployment pay lower taxes. Scholars have found that for the first four decades of the program's existence, most states operated under this forward-funded framework. However, over the past 40 years, many states have instead adopted a pay-as-you-go approach, keeping UI taxes artificially low when the economy is healthy instead of preparing for a potential recession by building adequate trust fund reserves (Stone and Chen 2014). In theory, an optimal UI program would tax the exact amount needed to cover expenditures during an economic downturn. Taxing too much puts an unnecessary burden on the economy and is politically unpopular, while taxing too little during economic expansions leads to insolvent trust funds incapable of smoothing consumption during a recession and increases reliance on federal funds.

The solvency of state UI trust funds, however, depends on various factors, such as economic conditions, benefit generosity, tax structure, administrative efficiency, and policy choices, and cannot be attributed to one sole explanation. Several studies have examined how these factors affect the solvency of state UI trust funds over time and across states. Long periods of high unemployment rates have had devastating effects on trust fund solvency (Vroman 2012). For example, during the Great Recession and subsequent years, thirty-five state UI programs depleted their UI trust funds, necessitating federal involvement through financial loans to the programs (Weiner 2012). Since this time, states have struggled to climb back to the levels of solvency recommended by the Department of Labor (DOL), especially with the immense strain created by the Covid-19 pandemic on the UI system (Lachowska and Vroman 2020; Rhodes 2021). Similarly, Vroman (2010) analyzed the causes and consequences of state UI trust fund insolvency during the Great Recession of 2007–2009. He found that states with low tax rates, high taxable wage bases, high replacement rates, long potential duration of benefits, and low minimum reserve ratios were more likely to become insolvent during the recession. He also estimated that insolvent states would face higher interest payments and FUTA credit reductions in the future. However, the general insolvency of state trust funds is not a recent phenomenon: it has been plaguing UI systems for decades. State trust funds have shown a decline in solvency measures since 1947, with clear dips in solvency when unemployment levels increase (Goss and Knudsen 1999).

An additional but somewhat neglected explanation of trust fund insolvency is the federal government's involvement in the funding of benefit payments provided to eligible claimants and the incentives it creates. Wandner (2018) reviewed how federal legislation affected the solvency of state UI trust funds since 2008. He discussed how various provisions in the American Recovery and Reinvestment Act (ARRA), Unemployment Compensation Extension Act (UCEA), Tax Relief Act (TRA), Middle Class Tax Relief Act (MCTRA), American Taxpayer Relief Act (ATRA), Coronavirus Aid, Relief, and Economic Security (CARES) Act, and American Rescue Plan (ARP) Act provided financial relief or incentives to states with insolvent or low-solvency UI trust funds. Indeed, Smith and Wenger (2013) found that states with highly solvent trust funds tend to have both higher average and maximum weekly UI benefit amounts. This could imply that states with less solvent trust funds may not have a strong desire to fund UI as a safety net program, instead depending on federal loans to bail them out when needed. Thus, failure to tax sufficiently during economic booms due to political constraints could be an explanation for insolvent trust funds.

The interaction between federal and state policy is of particular interest to this chapter. As noted, states are responsible for managing their own UI trust funds and, for the most part, the administration of their UI programs. However, increased federal involvement in the program may be slowly eroding the financial integrity of the system over time, leading to the insolvency of state trust funds and increased reliance on federal funds. Although the federal government may be attempting to prop up the system with additional funds during recessions, it may actually be creating new incentives for state-level actors to contribute to the overall insolvency of the system.

Endogenous Systems and Polycentricity

While the aforementioned scholars have rightly focused on aspects of the program that have led to insolvency, a lack of focus on the institutional structure of the UI system and the incentives it creates has left scholars asking why taxes have not increased to account for insolvency, and why states have shifted to the pay-as-you-go tax scheme. Thus, an examination of the rules of the game of the UI system is necessary.

The United States' UI system can be viewed as an endogenous polycentric system. An endogenous polycentric system is a system of governance where multiple authorities with overlapping domains of responsibility interact in complex and ever-changing ways, and out of these seemingly uncoordinated processes of mutual adjustment emerges a persistent system of social ordering. Within this system, actors at the various levels of governance respond to incentives, driving the system towards some unspecified destination, seemingly guided by an invisible hand (Hayek 1945). However, this invisible hand may not always lead to optimal or desirable outcomes for the system as a whole or for its individual components. The endogenous polycentric system may also face various challenges and dysfunctions that undermine its sustainability or performance. Therefore, understanding the dynamics and mechanisms of this system can help identify potential areas for improvement or reform.

Endogenous Systems

An endogenous system is a system that is influenced by factors within itself, rather than by external factors (Sterman 2002). An endogenous system can be contrasted with an exogenous system, which is determined by factors outside of itself (Klir and Simon 1991). Endogenous systems can be seen as complex adaptive systems that evolve and adapt to changing conditions within their boundaries, with emergent properties that are not predictable or deducible from their components (Holland 1995). In contrast, exogenous systems are more static and rigid in structure and function, with more deterministic properties that are derived from their rules and parameters.

One of the characteristics of an endogenous system is that it can exhibit feedback loops (Senge 1990). Feedback loops are processes where the output of a system affects its input, creating a circular or cyclical relationship. Feedback loops can be positive or negative, depending on whether they increase or decrease the magnitude of the initial change in a system. Positive loops amplify the initial change in a system, leading to exponential growth or decline, while negative loops counteract the initial change in a system, leading to equilibrium or oscillation. Feedback loops are important for understanding how endogenous systems behave and respond to changes over time (Diehl and Sterman 1995).

Another characteristic of an endogenous system is that it can have multiple levels of organization and interaction (Sterman 2002). Endogenous systems can be composed of smaller subsystems that have their own dynamics and feedback loops, as well as be part of larger supersystems that influence and constrain them. For example, the human body is an endogenous system that consists of various organs and tissues that function independently and interdependently, while also being affected by external factors, such as the environment and society. The levels of organization and interaction in endogenous systems can create complex patterns of behavior and outcomes that are not easily explained by simple linear models of causal relationships (Holland 1995). Endogenous systems can also exhibit self-organization, where order and structure emerge spontaneously from the interactions among the system's components, without any external intervention or design (Kauffman 1993).

Endogenous system thinking has been applied in various fields and in many policy-relevant areas (Meadows 2008). This style of analysis has been used to analyze the dynamics of policy change and implementation in complex settings, like health care reform, climate change adaptation, and urban planning (Sabatier and Weible 2019). Similarly, it has been used to design and evaluate interventions that aim to improve system performance and outcomes, such as health system strengthening, disaster risk reduction, and community development (Plowman et al. 2007). It has also been used to foster collaboration and learning among diverse stakeholders who are involved in or affected by a complex system problem, such as water governance, food security, and social justice (Pahl-Wostl et al. 2007). By applying endogenous systems thinking, we can better understand the root causes, interdependencies, feedback, trade-offs, leverage points, unintended consequences, and potential scenarios of a complex system problem. We can design more effective and sustainable interventions that take into account the diversity, adaptability, resilience, and emergence of endogenous systems.

Polycentric Governance

To an individual acquainted with the fields of public choice and polycentric governance, some of these distinguishing characteristics of endogenous systems may sound quite familiar. Polycentric governance is a term that refers to a complex form of governance with multiple centers of decision-making, each of which operates with some degree of autonomy and takes into account the actions and preferences of others (Carlisle and Gruby 2019). It can involve formal organizations and informal groupings of various actors, such as governments, businesses, civil society, and communities (Ostrom 2010a). Polycentric governance can be seen as a way to balance centralized and decentralized decision-making, foster collaboration and learning among diverse stakeholders, and provide institutional fit for complex systems.

Polycentric governance can be seen as an example of an endogenous system, as it is influenced by factors within itself, rather than by external factors (Thiel et al. 2019). This can involve feedback loops and multiple levels of organization and interaction. For example, polycentric governance can have positive or negative feedback loops that affect the performance and outcomes of different authorities and their interactions. Polycentric governance can also have various levels of organization and interaction, such as local, regional, national, and global levels, that create complex patterns of behavior and outcomes that are not easily explained or predicted by simple linear models of causal relationships. Polycentric governance can also exhibit self-organization, where order and structure emerge spontaneously from the interactions among the authorities involved, without any external intervention or design (Oberlack et al. 2018).

Polycentric governance can be seen as a way to address collective action problems and manage common resources (Ostrom 2009). Similar to endogenous systems thinking, it has been applied in many policy-relevant areas but is probably most famously used by Elinor Ostrom. Ostrom used the concept of polycentric governance in governing the commons to challenge the conventional wisdom that common-pool resources are doomed to be overexploited and require centralized regulation (Ostrom 1990). She argued that polycentric governance can enable local communities to self-organize and craft their own rules and institutions for managing their shared resources, while also interacting with other actors at different levels of governance. She showed that polycentric governance can provide several advantages for governing the commons, such as: enhancing adaptive capacity by allowing experimentation, learning, and innovation among multiple decision centers; providing institutional fit by matching the scale and diversity of natural resource systems with appropriate governance arrangements; and mitigating risk by creating redundancy and diversity among governance actors and institutions (Ostrom 2010b). However, Ostrom recognized that polycentric governance is not a panacea for all problems, and that it may face various challenges or limitations, such as: coordination problems among multiple decision centers with overlapping or conflicting interests or goals; transaction costs of information sharing, monitoring, enforcement, and conflict resolution among diverse actors; and power imbalances or inequalities among different actors or groups within the system (Ostrom 2014).

UI as an Endogenous Polycentric System of Governance

The United States' UI system was originally designed with distinct responsibilities for federal and state-level governance to ensure a well-balanced and functional framework. The decentralized nature of the system was intended to allow for well-tailored responses to economic downturns depending on the circumstances present in each state. However, the evolving incentives faced by political actors at both levels have contributed to increased federal involvement, culminating in the insolvency of state trust funds. In this section, we delve deeper into the incentives faced by federal and state-level politicians and how their interplay has reshaped the UI system's functionality.

Public Choice Considerations

The public choice approach to public finance and fiscal policy offers a useful framework for understanding the behavior of the federal and state actors in the UI system. Public choice theory applies economic tools and principles to the study of political science and government decision-making. It assumes that political actors are self-interested and rational agents who respond to incentives and constraints (Buchanan and Tollison 1984). Public choice theory analyzes how political institutions, rules, and processes affect the allocation of resources and the distribution of benefits and costs in society. It also examines how political outcomes deviate from the public interest due to factors such as information asymmetry, collective action problems, rent-seeking, moral hazard, and expressive voting (Buchanan and Tullock 2003).

Two influential scholars in the public choice tradition are James Buchanan and Richard Wagner, who have made significant contributions to public finance and fiscal policy. One of the key contributions of Buchanan and Wagner is their critique of the Keynesian paradigm of macroeconomic policy. In their book *Democracy in Deficit: The Political Legacy of Lord Keynes* (2000), originally published in 1977, they argue that Keynesian economics creates a bias toward deficit spending and debt accumulation in democratic governments. They challenge the assumption that governments can fine-tune the economy by adjusting fiscal policy according to the needs of the situation. They show that fiscal policy is determined by self-interested politicians who face electoral incentives and institutional constraints. They claim that politicians have strong incentives to increase spending and lower taxes during recessions, but weak incentives to reduce spending and raise taxes during expansions. They also claim that Keynesian economics neglects the long-term consequences of deficit spending and debt accumulation, such as crowding out private investment, distorting intergenerational equity, and creating inflationary pressures. They propose some alternative budgetary rules and institutional reforms to limit the scope of discretionary fiscal policy and restore fiscal responsibility.

Another key contribution of Buchanan is his analysis of public debt and its incidence. Wagner (2014b) challenged the orthodox view that the burden of public debt is borne by the current generation. He argues that public debt creates moral hazard, meaning that politicians take more risks because another party bears the cost of those risks. He shows how moral hazard incentivizes politicians to shift the burden of debt to future generations, and that this has important implications for fiscal policy and democratic governance. He applies public choice theory to analyze the incentives and constraints faced by politicians and taxpayers in relation to public debt. He shows how moral hazard affects the allocation of resources over time, the distribution of income across generations, and the intertemporal choices of individuals. He suggests that a constitutional balanced-budget amendment could reduce moral hazard and ensure intergenerational equity.

A third key contribution comes from Wagner in his exploration of fiscal sociology and its implications for public finance. Wagner (2014) develops a fiscal sociology approach to public finance, drawing on the insights of Buchanan and other scholars. He argues that public finance is not merely a technical or normative discipline, but also a social science that studies the interactions between fiscal institutions and social processes. He examines how fiscal institutions shape and are shaped by social norms, values, beliefs, and preferences. He also analyzes how fiscal institutions affect economic performance, social order, and political legitimacy. He shows how different types of fiscal systems reflect different types of social orders, such as hierarchical, individualistic, or cooperative, and how different types of fiscal systems generate different types of problems or challenges, such as coordination, cooperation, or conflict.

These contributions by Buchanan and Wagner help to frame the major arguments of this paper and to understand the behavior of federal and state politicians within the UI system. Efficient fiscal policy is difficult to implement and maintain due to the self-interested nature of politicians and the institutional structures within which they operate, which tend to drive government to run deficits. Moral hazard is also seen as a real issue in polycentric financial systems, with politicians relying on lenders of last resort to cover excess spending, especially by pushing for the financial implications of debt to be handled in the future rather than now. Lastly, they show the structure of fiscal systems create different incentives and coordination issues that drive the system. These arguments will now be applied to the UI system and the actors involved in it.

Duties and Incentives of Federal and State Actors within a Polycentric Framework

In the United States' UI system, the original allocation of responsibilities was such that the federal government's primary role was to establish the legal infrastructure and guidelines for administering the UI program, while the onus of funding and managing the UI system was on the states. However, the inherent ability of the federal government to intervene during recessions, acting as a lender of last resort or providing supplementary benefits, has resulted in it gaining substantial control over the UI system. Consequently, federal politicians and bureaucrats navigate a complex set of incentives that influence their actions during different economic phases. The UI system's polycentric governance structure engenders different types of relationships between the federal and state actors, namely cooperation, competition, and conflict, each of which plays a critical role in shaping the system's evolution and functionality.

Cooperation is clearly visible during recessions, when federal politicians have a potent incentive to increase benefits and extend their duration, as voters favor decisive countermeasures to mitigate the downturn's impact. This joint effort between federal politicians and the public during times of need enables the politicians to portray an image of empathy and proficiency, thereby enhancing their political standing and re-election prospects. Expanding federal benefits can help them secure larger budget allocations for the UI program, further cementing their influence. However, this cooperation has also contributed to a shift in the balance of power, with federal actors gaining increased control over the UI system.

In contrast, during economic expansions, federal politicians face minimal incentives to meddle in the UI system. With lower unemployment rates and less demand for government assistance, voters exhibit reduced concern for government intervention, at least regarding unemployment insurance. The preference of employers and voters for lower taxes can incite competition among federal politicians, who may even experience backlash for any interference in state affairs that is perceived as overreach. Consequently, federal actors are more likely to defer to the states during expansions, as involvement could lead to unfavorable political outcomes.

Meanwhile, state politicians, tasked with determining the taxable wage bases, tax rates, eligibility requirements, and benefit amounts for eligible claimants, might engage in competition with each other to maintain lower tax rates during expansions, aiming to attract businesses and stimulate economic growth. This competition, however, can lead to underfunded trust funds and reduced capacity to handle increased benefit demands during recessions.

During economic downturns, state politicians face increased pressure to provide relief for their constituents. In response, they may expand UI benefits or loosen eligibility criteria, even if it involves soliciting assistance from the federal government. This cooperative effort with the federal government can demonstrate their responsiveness to the needs of their constituents, potentially improving their political standing. However, this reliance on federal assistance may also be viewed as a lack of foresight and financial prudence, giving rise to conflicts.

These relationships—cooperation, competition, and conflict—form an intricate web of interactions that shape the dynamics of the UI system. They contribute to the incentives faced by federal and state actors, the decisions these actors make, and ultimately, the issues of increased federal involvement and trust fund insolvency that the UI system faces today.

Moral Hazard and the Path to Insolvency

The intricate interaction of incentives among federal and state politicians has induced significant transformation in the governance of the UI system, causing it to deviate from its initial design. Rooted in the polycentric character of the UI system, where authority is divided between federal and state entities, the endogenous incentives within the system have gradually propelled the program towards insolvency, particularly evident in the precarious state of the trust funds.

This concept resonates with Hayek (1945) and Wagner's (2014) postulations, which contended that human societies function as complex systems. Hence, political decision-making is an intrinsic, rather than external, process within these systems: It comes with its own set of costs and trade-offs that cannot be disregarded. Hayek's notion of spontaneous order offers insight into how inherent incentives in the UI system operated as a silent driving force, gradually reshaping the system's regulations and the conduct of its stakeholders. This evolution has led the UI system to its current state, teetering on the edge of insolvency. Similarly, Wagner's entangled political economy theory asserts that politicians and voters are not isolated entities, but integral parts of the same endogenous system. The political landscape is not an external factor to the economic system, as politicians and voters operate within the same systemic framework as other economic agents.

Over the years, a detrimental feedback loop has eroded the originally balanced distribution of responsibilities within the UI system. State politicians have increasingly leaned on federal intervention during economic recessions, comforted by the knowledge that the federal government will offer additional funding as needed. This moral hazard encourages states to underfund their UI programs during economic booms, thereby contributing to the insolvency of state trust funds over time. This phenomenon bears a striking resemblance to the theories proposed by Buchanan and Wagner, and results in an insolvent and inefficient UI system that is neither entirely polycentric nor monocentric.

Empirical Evidence

The growing impact of incentives on the UI system, as discussed earlier, can be observed through programmatic data provided by the Department of Labor (DOL). This section presents a series of descriptive statistics to illustrate the role of these incentives in the worsening solvency of state UI programs and the increasing level of federal intervention over time. The data demonstrate that the incentives created by the UI system's structure have contributed to the observed changes in state tax rates and trust fund balances.

State UI Activity

State trust fund balances are directly funded through State Unemployment Tax Act (SUTA) taxes imposed on employers within their respective states. These taxes are determined at the state level, resulting in variations across states. As the incentives created by the structure of the UI system encourage states to maintain low tax rates during economic expansions, the solvency of state trust funds is negatively impacted. In turn, this affects the ability of state governments to provide adequate unemployment benefits during economic downturns.

Figure 3.1 illustrates the changes in state UI tax revenues between 1970 and 2021. During this period, total tax revenues increased from approximately $2.5 billion to $38.6 billion. Although this growth may initially suggest sound financial management by the states, examining the effective tax rate as a percentage of total wages reveals a different picture. The decline in effective tax rates over time, as states attempt to gain favor with employers and constituents, exacerbates the solvency issue, as insufficient tax revenue is collected to support UI programs during economic downturns. This decline in tax rates can be linked to the strategic behavior of state politicians, who respond to the incentives created by the UI system.

The effective tax rate exhibits a strong correlation with the business cycle, increasing during economic expansions and decreasing during recessions. However, a noticeable difference exists between the average effective tax rates from 1970–1995 and 1996–2021. While the earlier period witnessed an average effective tax rate of 1 percent of total wages, the latter period recorded a lower average of 0.67 percent. This reduction corresponds to the argument that the evolving incentives within the UI system have driven states towards maintaining lower tax rates, ultimately jeopardizing trust fund solvency. Consequently, this leaves the state trust funds more vulnerable to economic shocks and dependent on federal intervention.

State trust fund balances display a similar trend. Although the aggregate reserves held by states have grown since 1940, the increase is not substantial,

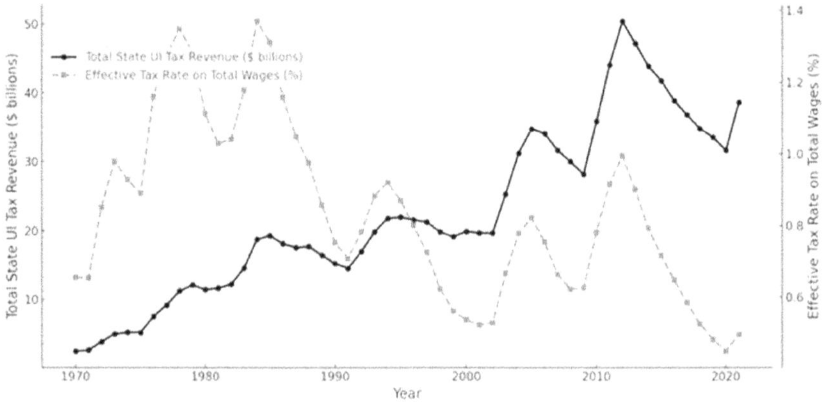

Figure 3.1 State UI average tax rate and revenue. Created by author, using data from US Department of Labor, Employment and Training Administration, "ETA Handbook 394," https://oui.doleta.gov/unemploy/DataDownloads.asp.

reflecting the impact of the incentives on trust fund solvency. When comparing trust fund reserves to total wages paid by US employers, the proportion of reserves relative to wages has declined since the 1940s. Figure 2 indicates that trust fund reserves as a percentage of total wages in the United States peaked in 1945 at approximately 10.37 percent. Since then, rates have steadily decreased, reaching just 1 percent before the Covid-19 pandemic and -0.01% in 2021. This decline illustrates the consequences of the interplay between federal and state actors, as their responses to the UI system's incentives contribute to the erosion of trust fund solvency.

The DOL commonly utilizes a method of comparing tax revenue and trust fund balances to total wages paid in the United States as a means of assessing the solvency of state UI programs. This approach establishes a standardized benchmark for states to determine the minimum solvency levels they should aim to achieve. A prominent solvency indicator is the Average High-Cost Multiple (AHCM), which approximates the duration for which a state can maintain benefit payments under adverse economic conditions without collecting additional revenue.

The AHCM signifies the number of years a state can dispense benefits at a rate equivalent to the average amount paid out during its three highest-cost 12-month periods over the previous twenty years, without receiving any supplementary revenue. For example, a state with an AHCM of 1.5 could sustain benefit payments for one and a half years at the same rate as the average of its

Figure 3.2 "UI Trust Fund Balance ($ Amount versus % of Wages)." Created by author, using data from U.S. Department of Labor, Employment and Training Administration, "ETA Handbook 394," https://oui.doleta.gov/unemploy/DataDownloads.asp.

three most demanding 12-month periods in the past two decades, without any additional tax revenue. This solvency measure takes into consideration the state's prior experiences in funding the UI program, fluctuations in trust fund balances, and its economic conditions, such as the total wages paid within the state.

Figure 3.3 presents the average US state AHCM values from 1957 to 2021, illustrating a marked decline in the resiliency of the typical trust fund within the country. In 1957, when the AHCM was initially used as a measure of solvency, the average state had a value of 3.02, signifying that a state could disburse approximately three years' worth of benefits at the highest rate experienced in the past twenty years without additional revenue. Unfortunately, the average state has not registered an AHCM greater than one since 1990. Prior to the Covid-19 pandemic, states exhibited an average AHCM of roughly 0.8.

In summary, the evidence presented demonstrates the trend toward state UI insolvency, driven by the incentive structure embedded within the UI system. State trust funds are increasingly vulnerable to economic shocks, as the incentives encourage states to maintain low tax rates during economic expansions, subsequently undermining the solvency of state trust funds and hindering their ability to provide adequate unemployment benefits during downturns. The federal government's role, however, deviates from this pattern, as it consistently increases spending and intervenes in the program during recessions. As the average state AHCM continues to decline, it is clear that the states' response to the incentives within the UI system is leaving them more reliant on federal

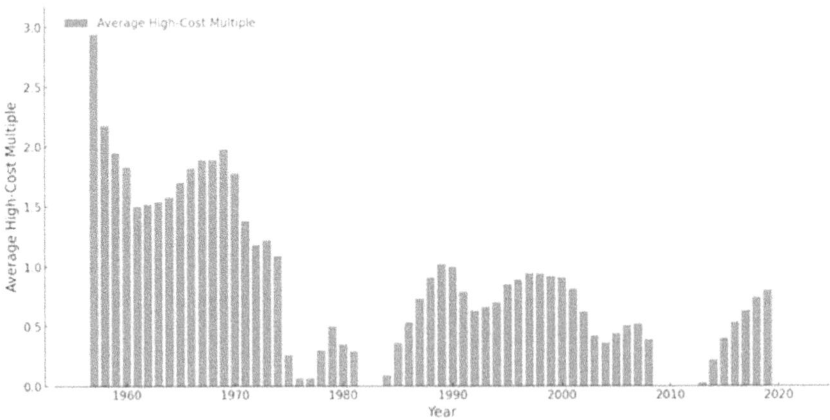

Figure 3.3 Average state UI trust fund solvency. Created by author, using data from US Department of Labor, Employment and Training Administration, "ETA Handbook 394," https://oui.doleta.gov/unemploy/DataDownloads.asp.

assistance. In the following section, I will present evidence illustrating the striking contrast between the behavior of state governments and the federal government in terms of increased spending and program intervention during economic crises.

Federal Involvement in UI

In stark contrast to the trends in state UI activity, federal involvement in the UI program has escalated significantly since 1938. The divergence between state and federal actions is evident in the shift in the funding sources for state trust funds and the level of UI spending by each level of governance. As states have collected less revenue over time, leading to lower trust fund balances, the federal government has stepped in to fill the gap. This intervention has grown over time, creating a feedback loop in the system that results in greater federal action and reduced state UI activity.

Figure 3.4 illustrates the composition of state UI trust funds, with the distinction between state funds and federal loans. Given that the federal government acts as a lender of last resort for states during times of insolvency, total trust fund balances can be conceptualized as a proportion of state funds versus federal loans. From 1938 to 1974, federal loans constituted a small portion

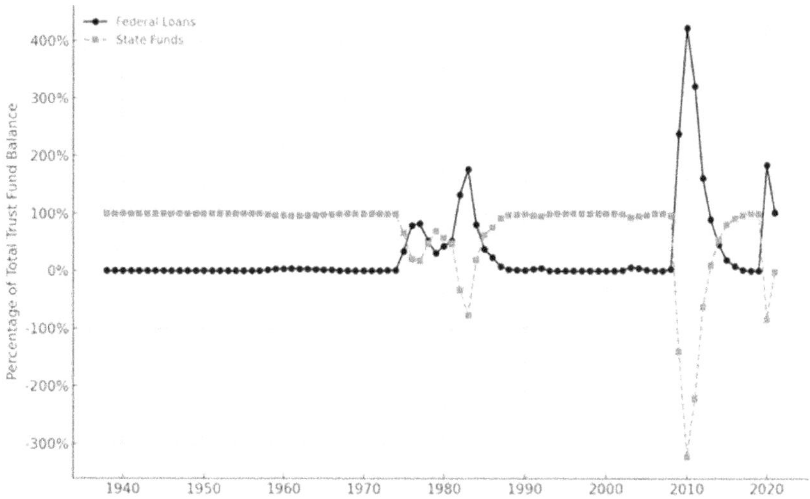

Figure 3.4 Composition of state trust fund balances. Created by author, using data from US Department of Labor, Employment and Training Administration, "ETA Handbook 394," https://oui.doleta.gov/unemploy/DataDownloads.asp.

of the total state trust fund balances, peaking at 4 percent in 1961, and averaging approximately 0.79 percent per year throughout this period. However, from 1975 to 2021, states became increasingly reliant on federal loans to maintain solvency. During this latter period, state trust funds were, on average, composed of about 52.5 percent federal loans, with substantial negative state fund balances recorded in 1982–1983, 2009–2012, and 2020–2021. Consequently, in three out of the last five US recessionary periods, states have depended on the federal government to fulfill their legal obligations to provide unemployment compensation to eligible claimants. Moreover, in four out of the last six recessions, federal loans have constituted a larger percentage of state trust funds than state funds themselves.

The trend of increasing federal intervention is also evident in the spending patterns of federal and state governments. Figure 5 presents a comparison between federal and state UI spending as a percentage of total UI spending, providing a more granular perspective on the shifting financial responsibilities over time. Consistent with the evidence presented thus far, Figure 5 illustrates robust state support in the early stages of the program, which gradually diminishes as federal intervention increases.

In Figure 3.5, federal spending encompasses not only loans to state trust funds but also additional or extended benefits disbursed to eligible claimants. The chart reveals the various recessionary periods throughout US history and highlights the growing role of the federal government in providing financial assistance during these times. This increasing federal presence is evident as

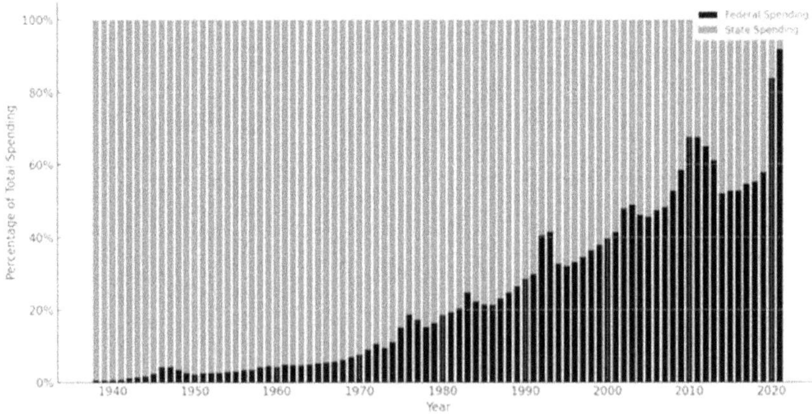

Figure 3.5 State vs federal UI spending. Created by author, using data from US Department of Labor, Employment and Training Administration, "ETA Handbook 394," https://oui.doleta.gov/unemploy/DataDownloads.asp.

the percentage of federal spending has risen with each successive economic downturn since 1938.

Furthermore, the additional benefits provided by the federal government have expanded over time to cover a broader range of unemployment situations. These include new federal programs propped up during recessions, such as Disaster Unemployment Assistance, various Extended Benefits programs, Pandemic Unemployment Assistance, and Federal Pandemic Unemployment Compensation. These programs have provided additional support during disasters that cause recessions, exceptionally long periods of unemployment, and during the Covid-19 Pandemic. For example, during the Covid-19 Pandemic, the federal government increased benefit payments for an extended period by $600 per claim, regardless of the state a claimant lived in or how much the claimant qualified for at the state level. Similarly, during the Great Recession, the federal government instituted several Extended Benefits programs designed to allow claimants to claim benefits far beyond the typical twent-six-week time span of eligibility at the state level. As a result, the federal government's influence in the UI program has grown not only in terms of financial support but also in the scope of assistance offered to eligible claimants. This trend underscores the evolving relationship between state and federal governments, as states have become more reliant on federal support during periods of economic stress. Furthermore, the increasing dependency on federal assistance highlights the potential consequences of the incentive structure within the UI system, which has driven states to underfund their trust funds and rely more heavily on federal intervention.

Finally, as noted in the previous section, state UI trust fund balances and tax rates as a percentage of total wages paid by employers have decreased dramatically over time. Figure 3.6 shows this same trend for state UI spending, with a somewhat different pattern of federal spending.

While state spending as a percentage of total wages obviously declines during this timeframe, federal spending appears to grow. This trend is clearer when shown starting from 1938 but is drowned out by the quantity of state UI spending early in the program's life. This uptick in federal spending as a percentage of total wages could help explain how replacement ratios, or the percentage of a worker's wages that are replaced by UI benefits, have remained relatively consistent over the same period.

In summary, this section demonstrates the increasing federal intervention in the UI system, driven by the incentive structure that has evolved since the

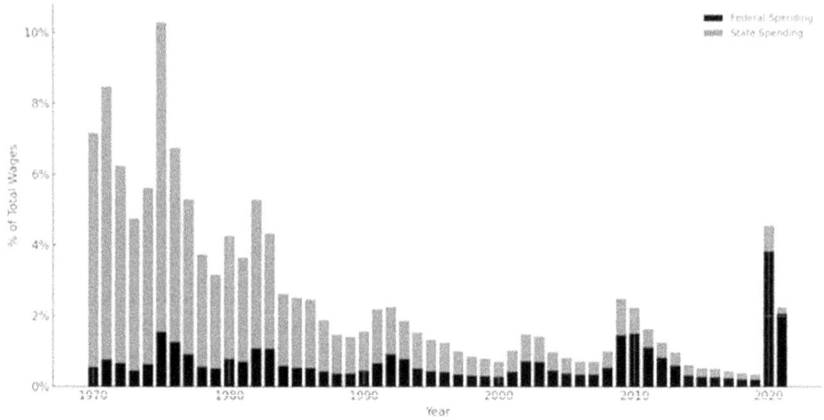

Figure 3.6 UI spending as a percentage of total wages. Created by author, using data from US Department of Labor, Employment and Training Administration, "ETA Handbook 394," https://oui.doleta.gov/unemploy/DataDownloads.asp.

program's inception. Over time, federal involvement has expanded, while state spending has experienced a dramatic decline. The original incentive structure of the UI program has fostered an inefficient system predisposed to insolvency due to the incentives embedded within it. The consequences of this structure include a growing reliance on federal assistance during economic downturns and an erosion of state trust fund solvency. As the role of the federal government continues to grow in response to the incentive structure, it is crucial to reevaluate the system to ensure the long-term sustainability of unemployment insurance programs in the United States.

Empirical Evidence Explained

While it is easy to point out correlations between two variables, it is much more difficult to prove causal relationships, especially in such an endogenous system filled with feedback mechanisms such as the one that has been described. In the previous sections, we have examined the impact of incentives embedded within the UI system on state trust fund insolvency and the increasing federal intervention in the program. This section aims to interpret the empirical results and explore the causal relationship between the incentive structure and the observed phenomenon of state UI trust fund insolvency.

The analysis has revealed significant trends in the behavior of state and federal governments in response to the incentives inherent in the UI system. Firstly, we observed that state UI trust funds have become increasingly insolvent over time, primarily due to states maintaining low tax rates during economic expansions. This behavior can be attributed to the strategic actions of state politicians who respond to the incentives created by the UI system. Secondly, we found that federal intervention in the UI program has consistently increased, particularly during periods of economic stress. This growing federal presence highlights the evolving relationship between state and federal governments and the increasing dependency of states on federal support to maintain their UI programs.

This analysis potentially identifies a causal relationship between the incentive structure in the UI system and the insolvency of state trust funds. The feedback mechanisms driving the system towards insolvency can be identified in the strategic behavior of state actors who, in response to political incentives, maintain low tax rates, thus jeopardizing trust fund solvency. The increasing federal intervention further exacerbates this issue, as it creates a cycle of dependency and reduced state involvement in the UI program. Political incentives play a crucial role in this causal relationship. State politicians are motivated to maintain low tax rates to gain favor with employers and constituents, while the federal government is incentivized to step in during economic downturns to provide additional support and maintain the stability of the UI system. These actions, driven by political incentives, contribute to the observed trends and patterns in state trust fund insolvency and federal intervention.

Efficiency Concerns

Although this chapter does not aim to establish whether a centralized or decentralized UI system is more effective in addressing the needs of unemployed workers in the United States, it is noteworthy that the present UI system endeavors to embody both centralization and decentralization simultaneously. The initial design of the UI program was predicated on a decentralized approach, enabling states to adapt and respond more effectively to local economic conditions than a centralized system would allow. Nonetheless, the contemporary system, characterized by states relinquishing partial control to the federal government, has resulted in an inefficient distribution of responsibilities. This inefficiency results in inadequate taxation and a loss of the initial efficiency benefits.

The efficiency implications of the current UI system are not trivial and emphasize the importance of clearly specifying rules and aligning incentives for better functioning federal-state programs. As states cede partial control to the federal government, the lines of responsibility become blurred, creating a system where states continue to tax, but not at levels sufficient to ensure trust fund solvency. This inefficiency can lead to increased costs and administrative burdens for both state and federal governments, as well as a reduced ability to effectively address the specific needs of local labor markets. To restore efficiency, it is crucial to reevaluate the division of responsibilities between state and federal governments and reestablish a clear delineation of roles.

As such, when designing federal-state programs, such as the UI system, it is essential to establish clear rules and align incentives to promote efficient functioning and avoid unintended consequences. In the case of the UI system, a more explicit specification of rules and better alignment of incentives might have prevented trust fund insolvency issues and maintained the program's initial efficiency benefits. Possible approaches to enhancing rule clarity and incentive alignment could include the establishment of federal minimum standards for tax rates, the implementation of automatic tax rate adjustments based on economic conditions, or the creation of incentives for states to maintain adequate trust fund balances.

Policymakers must recognize the importance of efficiency in the UI system and take steps to ensure that the program is both sustainable and responsive to the specific needs of state labor markets. This may involve reevaluating the incentive structure, strengthening trust fund solvency, and clarifying the division of responsibilities between state and federal governments, as well as establishing clear rules and aligning incentives for better functioning federal-state programs. Ultimately, these changes will contribute to a more effective and efficient UI system that can better serve the needs of workers, employers, and governments in times of economic uncertainty.

Competing Theories

While other general theories, such as social policy retrenchment, can partially explain the trend towards insolvency, they do not adequately explain why federal involvement has been increasing. The endogenous polycentric system approach described in this analysis helps to explain the incentives embedded in the United States' UI program at each level of governance, guiding the evolution of the program toward an unanticipated destination.

Social policy retrenchment refers to the process of reducing the scope and scale of social policies and programs provided by the government. This phenomenon often arises in response to financial pressures, such as budget deficits or economic downturns, as well as ideological shifts toward limited government intervention in social welfare. Retrenchment can manifest in various forms, including reductions in benefits, tightened eligibility criteria, and the implementation of cost-sharing measures between beneficiaries and the government. The concept of social policy retrenchment gained prominence in the late twentieth century, particularly during the era of neoliberal economic policies. These policies prioritized fiscal austerity, deregulation, and market-oriented reforms, leading to the restructuring of social welfare systems in many developed countries.

In the context of the United States, social policy retrenchment has been driven by several factors. First, the rise of conservative political ideologies, which favor limited government intervention, has led to a push for reduced social spending. Second, concerns about fiscal sustainability and budget deficits have prompted calls for austerity measures, including cuts to social programs. Finally, globalization and the consequent increase in economic competition have heightened concerns about the efficiency and competitiveness of the economy, leading to calls for reducing the burden of social welfare programs on public finances. As such, social policy retrenchment has become a key component in analyzing the changes in welfare state provisions over time.

Although social policy retrenchment offers a partial explanation for the decline in UI trust fund solvency, it does not adequately address the rising federal involvement in the UI system. Moreover, the overall UI system is not consistently witnessing a decrease in program generosity, particularly when taking into account its original purpose to stabilize consumption during recessions—periods when federal intervention typically augments benefit payments. To gain a more comprehensive understanding of the current state of the UI program, it is essential to thoroughly examine the incentives and interactions between federal and state actors within the framework of the endogenous polycentric system approach.

Conclusion

In conclusion, this paper has demonstrated that the decreasing solvency of UI trust funds in the United States can be attributed to the incentives embedded within the endogenous polycentric system that characterizes the United States' UI program. The analysis reveals that federal actors are motivated to increase their involvement in the program during recessions, providing an opportunity for state politicians to capitalize on this heightened participation. Consequently, states implement lower-than-necessary tax rates, which exacerbates the issue of trust fund insolvency over time.

While alternative explanations such as social policy retrenchment partially account for the decline in UI trust fund solvency, they do not provide a comprehensive understanding of the increasing federal involvement in the UI system. The endogenous polycentric system approach offers a more nuanced perspective, highlighting the intricate interplay between federal and state actors and their respective incentives.

This analysis underscores the importance of clearly defining roles and responsibilities in a federal-state partnership to ensure efficiency and effectiveness in social policy programs. The current UI program, with its blend of centralized and decentralized elements, has deviated from its original intention of being a state-responsive, adaptive system, leading to unintended consequences and inefficiencies.

Future research should explore potential policy reforms to realign incentives and promote a more sustainable UI program. By addressing the incentive structures within the endogenous polycentric system, policymakers can work toward developing a UI program that maintains its responsiveness to local needs while ensuring long-term solvency and efficiency.

References

Anderson, Karen M. 2001. "The Politics of Retrenchment in a Social Democratic Welfare State: Reform of Swedish Pensions and Unemployment Insurance." *Comparative Political Studies* 34 (9): 1063–1091.

Brookings Institution. 2020. "How Does Unemployment Insurance Work? And How Is It Changing during the Coronavirus Pandemic?" https://www.brookings.edu/blog/up-front/2020/07/20/how-does-unemployment-insurance-work-and-how-is-it-changing-during-the-coronavirus-pandemic/.

Buchanan, James M., and Robert D. Tollison. eds. 1984. *The Theory of Public Choice—II*. Ann Arbor, MI: University of Michigan Press.

Buchanan, James M., and Gordon Tullock. 2003. "What Is Public Choice Theory." In *Rationalizing Capitalist Democracy: The Cold War Origins of Rational Choice*

Liberalism, edited by S. M. Amadae, 133–155. Chicago, IL: University of Chicago Press.

Carlisle, Keith, and Rebecca L. Gruby. 2019. "Polycentric Systems of Governance: A Theoretical Model for the Commons." *Policy Studies Journal* 47 (4): 927–952.

Center on Budget and Policy Priorities. 2014. "Introduction to Unemployment Insurance." https://www.cbpp.org/research/introduction-to-unemployment-insurance.

Davidsson, Johan B., and Paul Marx. 2013. "Losing the Issue, Losing the Vote: Issue Competition and the Reform of Unemployment Insurance in Germany and Sweden." *Political Studies* 61 (3): 505–522.

Diehl, Ernst, and John D. Sterman. 1995. "Effects of Feedback Complexity on Dynamic Decision Making." *Organizational Behavior and Human Decision Processes* 62 (2): 198–215.

Goss, Ernest, and James Knudsen. 1999. "Evaluation of Solvency Standards for State Unemployment Insurance Trust Funds." *Public Budgeting and Finance* 19 (4): 3–20.

Hacker, Jacob S. 2004. "Privatizing Risk without Privatizing the Welfare State: The Hidden Politics of Social Policy Retrenchment in the United States." *American Political Science Review* 98 (2): 243–260.

Hayek, Friedrich A. 1945. "The Use of Knowledge in Society." *The American Economic Review* 35 (4): 519–530.

Holland, John H. 1995. *Hidden Order: How Adaptation Builds Complexity*. New York: Basic Books.

Kauffman, S.A. 1993. *The Origins of Order: Self-organization and Selection in Evolution*. New York: Oxford University Press.

Klir, George J., and Herbert A. Simon. 1991. *The Architecture of Complexity*. New York: Springer.

Lachowska, Marta, Wayne Vroman, and Stephen A. Woodbury. 2020. "Experience Rating and the Dynamics of Financing Unemployment Insurance." *National Tax Journal* 73 (3): 673–698.

Meadows, Donella H. 2008. *Thinking in Systems: A Primer*. White River Junction VT: Chelsea Green Publishing.

Oberlack, Christoph, Sébastien Boillat, Stefan Brönnimann, Jean-David Gerber, Andreas Heinimann, Chinwe Ifejika Speranza, Peter Messerli, Stephan Rist, and Urs Wiesmann. 2018. "Polycentric Governance in Telecoupled Resource Systems." *Ecology and Society* 23 (1): 16.

Ostrom, Elinor. 1990. *Governing the Commons: The Evolution of Institutions for Collective Action*. Cambridge, UK: Cambridge University Press.

Ostrom, Elinor. 2009. "Polycentric Systems as One Approach to Solving Collective-Action Problems." In *Climate Change and Sustainable Development: New Challenges for Poverty Reduction*, edited by Mohamed Salih, 17–35. Cheltenham, UK: Edward Elgar.

Ostrom, Elinor. 2010a. "Beyond Markets and States: Polycentric Governance of Complex Economic Systems." *American Economic Review* 100 (3): 641–672.

Ostrom, Elinor. 2010b. "Polycentric Systems for Coping with Collective Action and Global Environmental Change." *Global Environmental Change* 20 (4): 550–557.

Ostrom, Elinor. 2014. "Do Institutions for Collective Action Evolve?" *Journal of Bioeconomics* 16: 3–30.

Pahl-Wostl, Claudia, Marc Craps, Art Dewulf, Erik Mostert, David Tabara, Tharsi Taillieu. 2007. "Social Learning and Water Resources Management." *Ecology and Society* 12 (2): 5.

Plowman, Donde Ashmos, Stephanie Solansky, Tammy E. Beck, LaKami Baker, Mukta Kulkarni, and Deandra Villarreal Travis. 2007. "The Role of Leadership in Emergent, Self-Organization." *The Leadership Quarterly* 18 (4): 341–356.

Rhodes, Martin. 2021. "'Failing Forward': A Critique in Light of Covid-19." *Journal of European Public Policy* 28 (10): 1537–1554.

Sabatier, Paul A., and Christopher M. Weible. 2019. "The Advocacy Coalition Framework: Innovations and Clarifications." In *Theories of the Policy Process*, edited by Christopher Weible, 189–220. New York: Routledge.

Senge, Peter M. 1990. *The Fifth Discipline: The Art and Practice of the Learning Organization.* New York: Doubleday Publishing.

Smith, Daniel L., and Jeffrey B. Wenger. 2013. "State Unemployment Insurance Trust Solvency and Benefit Generosity." *Journal of Policy Analysis and Management* 32 (3): 536–553.

Sterman, John. 2002. *System Dynamics: Systems Thinking and Modeling for a Complex World.* New York: McGraw-Hill Education.

Stone, Chad, and William Chen. 2014. "Introduction to Unemployment Insurance." Center on Budget and Policy Priorities. https://www.cbpp.org/research/introduction-to-unemployment-insurance.

Thiel, A., R. Pacheco-Vega, and E. Baldwin. 2019. "Evolutionary Institutional Change and Performance in Polycentric Governance." In *Governing Complexity: Analyzing and Applying Polycentricity*, edited by Adreas Thiel, William A. Blomquist, and Dustin E. Garrick, 91–110. Cambridge, UK: Cambridge University Press.

U.S. Congressional Research Service. 2023. "The Unemployment Trust Fund (UTF): State Insolvency and Federal Loans to States (RS22954)." https://crsreports.congress.gov/product/pdf/RS/RS22954.

U.S. Department of Labor, n.d. "How Do I File for Unemployment Insurance?" https://www.dol.gov/general/topic/unemployment-insurance.

U.S. Department of Labor, Employment and Training Administration. "ETA Handbook 394." https://oui.doleta.gov/unemploy/DataDownloads.asp.

Vroman, Wayne. 2010. *Role of Unemployment Insurance as an Automatic Stabilizer during a Recession.* Darby, PA: DIANE Publishing.

Vroman, Wayne. 2012. "Financing Unemployment Insurance after the Great Recession." *Urban Institute Brief #7*. Washington, DC: Urban Institute.

Wagner, Richard E. 2014a. "Entangled Political Economy: A Keynote Address." In *Entangled Political Economy (Advances in Austrian Economics, 18)*, edited by Roger Koppl, and Steven Horwitz, 15–36. Leeds, UK: Emerald Group Publishing Limited.

Wagner, Richard E. 2014b. "James Buchanan's Public Debt Theory: A Rational Reconstruction." *Constitutional Political Economy* 25: 253–264.

Wandner, Stephen A. 2018. "Why the Unemployment Insurance Program Needs to Be Reformed." In *Unemployment Insurance Reform: Fixing a Broken System*, edited by Stephen Wandner, 1–22. Kalamazoo, MI: W. E. Upjohn Institute.

Weiner, Jennifer. 2012. "When the Tide Goes Out: Unemployment Insurance Trust Funds and the Great Recession." *New England Public Policy Center*. Research Report 12–1. https://www.bostonfed.org/publications/new-england-public-policy-center-research-report/2012/when-the-tide-goes-out-unemployment-insurance-trust-funds-and-the-great-recession-lessons-for-and-from-new-england.aspx.

4

Why Were There No Human Challenge Trials For Covid-19 Vaccine Development?

Malte Hendrickx

As of writing this, the Covid-19 pandemic has caused 6,879,677 confirmed deaths (WHO 2023).[1] However, this number is likely an underestimate, as many deaths related to Covid-19 are not officially recorded, and various countries either intentionally or unintentionally undercount the number of deaths caused by the virus (Karlinsky and Kobak 2021; Atanasov et al. 2023). The availability of effective Covid-19 vaccines has played a significant role in preventing an even higher death toll. These vaccines have proven to be highly effective in reducing both the risk of infection and mortality rates. Remarkably, these vaccines were developed within an unprecedented timeframe, with the first vaccinations becoming available approximately one year after the initial Covid-19 cases were detected in Wuhan.

To get a sense of this staggering speed, consider the timeline of the vaccine rollout. A cluster of Covid-19 patients was first identified around December 12, 2019 (CDC Museum n.d.). The first sequencing of the Covid-19 genome, which enabled researchers to work on a vaccine, happened on January 10, and preclinical studies commenced later that month. Phase 1 and 2 trials began in April and Phase 2 and 3 trials in July. Data from Phase 3 trials were submitted to regulators starting in August on a rolling basis to speed up the review. Sufficient data from trials to make conclusions regarding vaccine efficacy were available at the end of the year, and vaccines were approved for emergency use on December 11. Never has a vaccine been developed and authorized for use more quickly than the Covid-19 vaccine: A typical vaccine development process takes between five and ten years (Pronker et al. 2013).

Yet, this chapter argues that this process could and should have been sped up by several months. Put briefly, vaccine efficacy and safety were tested by vaccinating a subject population, and then the researchers waited multiple months to see if naturally occurring infections were reported at a lower rate than within a non-vaccinated control group. An alternative way of testing vaccine efficacy was available. Human Challenge Trials (HCT), in which subjects are vaccinated and then intentionally exposed to Covid-19, allow researchers to establish the efficacy of a vaccine more quickly by skipping the months-long period of waiting for natural infections to occur. I argue that using HCTs early on, on a conservative estimate, would have sped up vaccine development by 2–3 months, which would have saved thousands of lives. This leads us to the central question this chapter pursues: Why were HCTs not used?

From a technical perspective, HCTs were clearly an option. In fact, researchers at the Imperial College of London, in cooperation with the NHS and with approval by the WHO, ran an HCT for Covid-19 infections (rather than vaccines) in 2022 (Killingley et al. 2022). The young adults participating in the study were not immunized against Covid-19, nor did they have immunity from previous infections. Of course, this HCT happened much too late to affect the development of Covid-19 vaccines.

Why were there no early HCTs for the Covid-19 vaccines? I argue that contrary to widely held belief, ethical concerns were not the reason why HCTs were not employed. Rather, the failure to employ HCTs earlier during the pandemic is best understood through the lens of public choice theory: namely, it is explained by the incentive structure of healthcare regulators forming a *principal-agent* problem (Stiglitz 1989). In a principal-agent problem, a decision-maker (the agent) represents the interests of another group (the principal), making decisions in their stead. When the incentives of the agent diverge from those of the principal, the rational decision of the agent is not in the principal's best interest: a principal-agent problem arises (Arrow [1971] 1992). In the case of Covid-19 vaccines, healthcare regulators had incentives to be significantly more risk-averse than the population whose interests they represented. It was consequently rational for them to block HCT proposals by the research community, despite HCT approval being in the best interest of the population. I illustrate that without reforms, this problem is likely to arise again in the future, and sketch solutions to avert a recurrence of principal-agent problems in future pandemics.

The rest of the article proceeds as follows: I review literature on the development of Covid-19 vaccines to provide a conservative estimate of both how much earlier a vaccine could have been approved had HCTs been used (3 months) and how many lives doing so could have saved in the United States within the first 3 months of approval (5590). These estimates take a maximally conservative approach: They should be taken as establishing the lowest possible number of lives saved, rather than a comprehensive estimate. I thereby illustrate the stakes of not employing HCTs in Covid-19 vaccine development were not trivial. Historic literature on HCTs then distills the main ethical concerns that HCTs introduce. I then argue that these ethical concerns were not applicable to the case of the early Covid-19 HCT vaccine studies. My argument centers on the availability of a large pool of volunteers that were (1) non-marginalized, (2) low-risk, and (3) able and willing to provide informed consent to HTC. Having ruled out the most common ethical objections against HCT, I offer an alternative explanation, reviewing the usefulness of public choice analysis to understand public response to infectious diseases. By illustrating how and why the incentives of healthcare regulators diverged from that of the general population, I show that it was rational for healthcare regulators to be much more risk-averse than a rational member of the general public with regard to Covid-19 HCT. I argue that this is the real reason for why no HCTs were deployed in the development of Covid-19 vaccines. I end by drawing lessons from the case of Covid-19: unless institutional reforms are undertaken, it is likely that similar problems will reoccur and lead to an inadequate response during future pandemics, leading to significant loss of life.

The Counterfactual Impact of HCTs on Vaccine Rollout Timelines

Before answering the question of why no Covid-19 vaccine HCTs were used, we need to establish the counterfactual impact of such HCTs: after all, were the impact trivial or negative, that would settle why no HCTs were used. The counterfactual impact of such HCTs crucially depends on two questions: Firstly, how much earlier would a Covid-19 vaccine have been approved with HCTs? Secondly, how many lives would this earlier approval have saved? Let us address the former question first.

Vaccine development is typically grouped into four stages: Phase 1, Phase 2, Phase 3, and Phase 4 trials. Phase 1 establishes safe dosage ranges by gradually increasing dosages to healthy volunteers. Phase 2 tests for efficacy (i.e., capacity to produce beneficial effects) and side effects on healthy subjects. Phase 3 tests for efficacy, effectiveness, and side effects on a larger sample of healthy subjects. Phase 4 monitors the intervention after release. Phase 1 and Phase 4 are not candidates for benefiting from early HCT: Phase 1 testing is quick and requires no exposure to disease, whereas Phase 4 happens after approval of the vaccine has been given. It is thus Phase 2 and Phase 3 that could have potentially benefited from HCT approval. Let us review how much they could have benefited in a bit more detail.

HCTs require preparation. Nguyen et al. (2021) estimates preparation time for Covid-19-specific HCT at roughly 2 months: 2 weeks to isolate and screen volunteers for exclusionary health factors, 2 weeks after vaccination to wait for the immune response to develop, and 4 weeks post-trial to observe and resolve effects of the infection. Given that this preparation time exceeds the time a vaccine candidate is in Phase 1, it seems unlikely that the consequent Phase-2 trial could be replaced by a HCT. Rather, running a Phase 2 trial alongside a HCT is preferable, as Nguyen et al. (2021) and Eyal, Lipsitch, and Smith (2020) recommended. The crucial benefit of doing so is that the HCT trial data can replace Phase 3 data. Regular Phase 3 trials wait for natural infection to occur. They thus suffered from fluctuating incidence rates, which foreseeably delayed results (Heriot, Jamrozik, and Selgelid 2020). HCTs do not face this problem: exposure is guaranteed by the design of HCT. The duration of Phase 3 trials varied between vaccine candidates, with the quickest and most popular candidate vaccine (Pfizer/Biontech) spending 4 months in a Phase 3 trial until emergency use: This is the amount of time by which a HCT could have sped up the authorization of a Covid-19 vaccine. Let us subtract one month to allow a generous timeframe for reviewing the data a HCT could have gathered, as well as any unforeseen hiccups in running a trial.

Establishing a Lower Bound for the Impact of Covid-19 HCT: 5590 US Deaths Averted in the First 3 Months of Counterfactual Vaccine Approval

We saw that HCTs, if employed alongside a Phase 2 trial, could plausibly have sped up vaccine development by at least 3 months in bypassing the need for a Phase 3 trial. How many lives would have been saved by Covid-19 vaccines being approved 3 months earlier?

Gauging the exact impact of such a measure is impossible: It requires access to a counterfactual we do not have. Estimations have been attempted in the context of other countries: for example, Ferreira et al (2023) estimates that accelerating vaccine rollout in Brazil by 2 months would have averted around 47,000 deaths. In another study, Yamana et al (2023) estimate that the availability of the Covid-19 vaccine saved around 120,000 lives in the first six months of its rollout. Taking these studies to inform our priors, it seems credible that had vaccines been available three months earlier, they would have saved at least a five-digit number of lives. While not much in the arguments provided in this chapter rests on the exact number of deaths averted by an early Covid-19 HCT, let us try our hand at a maximally conservative estimation of lives saved: a maximally conservative estimate strengthens the argument of the HCT skeptic, who I will argue against.

There are many ways in which an earlier approval of Covid-19 vaccines could have saved lives. For example, earlier data on which vaccines seem promising would have allowed manufacturers to start producing vaccines significantly earlier (Levine et al 2005, Yeoh 2020, Khamsi 2020). Earlier vaccine rollout would have reduced the likelihood of new and dangerous Covid-19 variants emerging and spreading. For example, the Delta variant wreaked havoc after first emerging in October: a vaccine rollout in September would have presumably reduced the death toll of the Delta variant considerably. Also, consider that many countries experience seasonal differences in the impact of Covid-19, facing a strong increase in infections and fatalities in winter. Had vaccine distribution started in September, the "winter wave" of 2020 could have been broken significantly earlier. Fatalities reached all-time heights between January and March: it is unlikely this would have happened had populations already had access to vaccines in September. Lastly, early access to vaccines would have made non-pharmacological measures such as lockdowns obsolete much earlier, leading to positive effects both for individuals and the economy. An analysis by Hafner and colleagues estimates the annual economic damage of Covid-19 without vaccines at 3.4 trillion dollars: speeding up vaccine development by 3 months would then have reduced such losses by 850 billion dollars (Hafner et al 2022).

I will put aside all these ways in which an early vaccine rollout would have reduced the Covid-19 death toll and benefited society, in order to arrive at a minimal estimate. I will do so by only looking at the United States, roughly 5 percent of the global population, within the 3-month window following our counterfactual vaccine approval date of September 20. I thank German epidemiologist Emil Iftekhar for helping me in arriving at this lower-bound estimate.

To establish a lower bound, we used excess mortality and vaccination data for the United States provided by Our World in Data. To establish a counterfactual vaccine rollout, we used vaccination data of the first three months of actual vaccine rollout, starting on December 13 and moved it to a counterfactual vaccination rollout date, September 20 (12 weeks earlier). We interpolated missing values in the excess mortality data, calculated daily death numbers from cumulative excess mortality numbers, and smoothed the time series by calculating the 7-day rolling average. We estimated vaccine efficacy conservatively at 90 percent (Atanasov et al. 2023). For every day in the considered time period, the number of averted deaths was calculated as:

> Observed Excess Deaths * Vaccine Efficacy * Fraction of Fully Vaccinated Population

For the three-month time period considered, the number of deaths averted was 5,590. As can be seen in the Figure 4.1, the number of deaths averted increases as the share of fully vaccinated individuals increases. Naturally, modeling the effect of early Covid-19 vaccine approval for a longer timeframe would give us a higher number, but the aim is not to provide a dramatic result: rather, even on this maximally conservative estimate, 5,590 lives would have been saved.

Ignoring all indirect effects of vaccinations, 95 percent of the world population, the fact that prioritizing vulnerable members of the population greatly enhances vaccine efficacy, as well as limiting our analysis to 3 months, the counterfactual impact of HCTs would still have been preventing 5,590 deaths. To put this into context: Even at this lower bound, the number of human lives that early Covid-19 HCT could have saved is roughly twice as high as the death toll of the 9/11 terrorist attacks, the largest terrorist attack in human history. It is highly likely that the death toll that could have been averted is at least one or two orders of magnitude higher.

As I have argued, human challenge trials could realistically have sped up the development of Covid-19 vaccines by 3 months. On a highly conservative estimate, this would have prevented at least 5,590 deaths within 3 months in the United States alone. Why, then, were HCTs not employed? A brief history of HCTs provides us with ample evidence of moral reasons for which HCT may have been rejected.

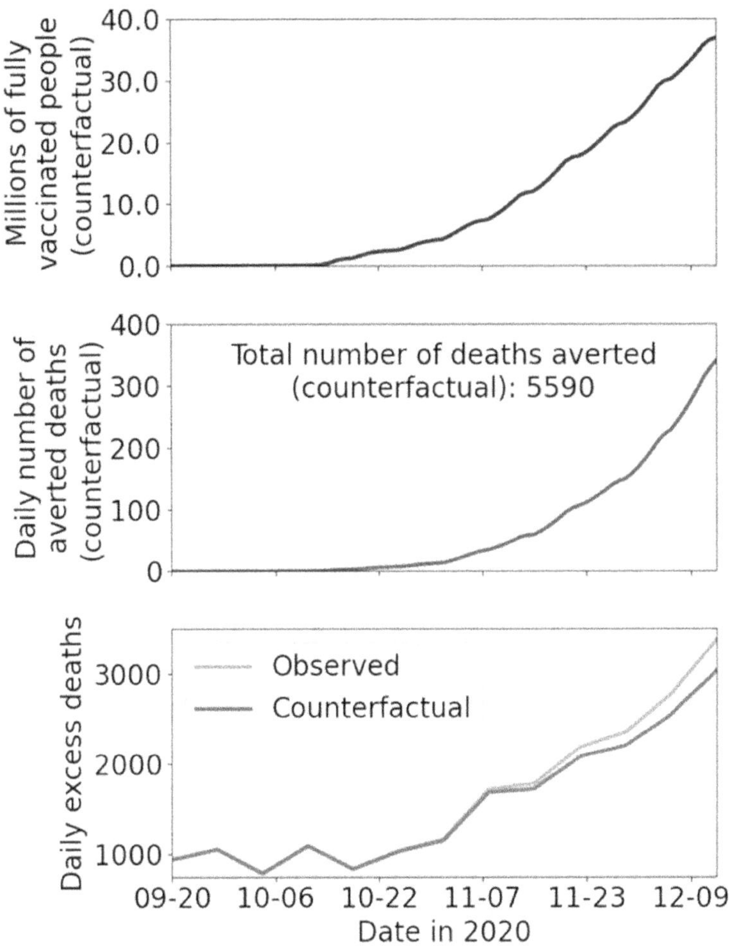

Figure 4.1 Modeling the effect of early Covid-19 vaccine approval. Created by author.

Moral Reasons against HCT

Human Challenge Trials—the experimental infection of humans to further medical research—became more frequent in western medicine during the eighteenth and nineteenth centuries. Far from having the rigid setup contemporary HCTs have (Levine 1998), early experiments by the likes of John Hunter, Edwards Jenner, Alexandre-Francois Ollivier, and René Desgenette frequently involved both self-experimentation and infection of those near to the researchers in question. Jenner famously took viral material from his milkmaid to inoculate his gardener's son and later intentionally exposed him to smallpox (Centers for Disease Control and Prevention n.d.). This procedure should strike us as quite unethical: It seems dubious that the nine-year-old son of an employee of the principal investigator could have refused the procedure.

Examples of such dubious power dynamics form a common theme in the history of early HCT research (Metzger et al. (2019) provide a concise and accessible overview). Let us review some uncontroversially unethical HCTs that Metzger discusses. Albert Neisser, a nineteenth-century doctor, used prostitutes and orphans as research subjects and refused to inform them about the dangers of his experiments. Nazi researcher Schilling ran experiments on prisoners and mentally handicapped people (Weindling et al. 2016), as did many other Nazi scientists. In Japan, the infamous Unit 731 performed experiments, including deliberate exposure of thousands of captives to diseases and toxins (Harris 2002).

Unethical experimentation was far from an exclusive wartime horror. After the war, John Cutler exposed inmates, soldiers, and mentally handicapped subjects to syphilis to establish the efficacy of a new drug (Hornblum 1997; Lerner 2007). Yet, the issue was largely discussed outside of the public eye, and no comprehensive reforms were undertaken to stop such atrocious experimental protocols.

In 1972, information about a shockingly unethical 40-year longitudinal study on syphilis leaked to the press. Hundreds of black men in Tuskegee, Alabama were enrolled in an experiment, lured by the false promise of free healthcare, yet the participants, 400 of whom suffered from syphilis, were denied treatment with penicillin so that researchers could observe the untreated course of a syphilis infection. While this study was not an HCT, as subjects were enrolled based on a previous infection, it created enough of a public outcry to lead to significant reforms in the ethical standards surrounding HCTs and other medical experiments (McCallum et al. 2006).

In all the above-mentioned examples, subjects did not consent to the procedures undertaken on them. In most, subjects were drawn from vulnerable populations such as low-income populations, racial minorities, children, and prisoners. Lastly, in many of the examples above, subjects were exposed to significant harm, the magnitude of which was not disclosed to them in full. These three factors were commonly singled out as different ways in which the experiments described were unjust and unethical. Ethical and regulatory limitations on experiments today focus on these criteria, most prominently laid out in the multilateral declaration of Helsinki (WMA declaration of Helsinki).

As a consequence of these reforms, HCTs have become part of the standard repertoire of vaccination research and are routinely used in medical research.

Of course, an HCT for Covid-19 is very different from the atrocities of fascist regimes in the Second World War or from the racially motivated crimes of the Tuskegee syphilis researchers. Yet, the ethical integrity of a Covid-19 trial, like any HCT, depends on clearing the same ethical standards these historic cases so egregiously failed to uphold. Can people give free, informed consent during the heyday of a poorly understood disease, such as Covid-19 undoubtedly was in 2020? Could Covid-19 HCT have avoided drawing from vulnerable populations yet retained a large enough sample size to establish conclusive results? Lastly, is the chaotic and random nature of the Covid-19 health risk an acceptable harm that can be disclosed to and accepted by a HCT participant? I will now argue that the answer to all three questions is, in the case of Covid-19, a loud and resounding yes.

Informed Consent by Non-Marginalized Low-Risk Volunteers: No Moral Reasons against Covid-19 HCT

We have seen the three central ethical worries about Human Challenge Trials: the exploitation of vulnerable populations, a lack of informed consent, and a subsequent cause of unjust harm. How, one may ask, could we establish whether a Covid-19 HCT would have met these standards, given no such Covid-19 HCT happened?

It is easy to see the ways in which an early Covid-19 HCT could have been ethically problematic. For example, HCTs could have drawn from involuntary subjects in testing the efficacy of the vaccine. HCTs could have exploited vulnerable populations directly or indirectly: for example, by directly recruiting from populations that are disadvantaged by the healthcare system or indirectly by tying participation to a financial compensation so that participation may strike economically vulnerable populations as being the only way out of poverty. Lastly, the researchers may have chosen to not disclose the potential harm of a Covid infection to participants, leading them to agree without fully realizing what risks such agreement incurs. In such cases, early Covid-19 HCT would have been unethical, and it would be well justified to not adopt them. I argue that there was no need for such unethical steps to recruit participants, because there was a large pool of low-risk, non-marginalized volunteers that were able to provide informed consent to the procedure.

In March 2020, the organization “1 Day Sooner” explicitly set out to gather a large pool of volunteer subjects for potential early Covid-19 vaccine HCT. The hope was to accelerate the process of a HCT by providing researchers with easy access to a sample of volunteers that matched the criteria for an ethical HCT. 1 Day Sooner quickly gathered a pool of 38,000 volunteers, far exceeding the numbers required for a large challenge trial (for comparison, the British HCT on Covid infections used thirty-six subjects). I will now argue that 1 Day Sooner succeeded at providing such a research pool, thereby eliminating the prominent and well-founded ethical worries regarding an early Covid-19 vaccine HCT. Despite this success, HCTs were not adopted: I will address why they were not adopted in the next section.

Volunteers for the 1 Day Sooner campaign mainly comprised young, healthy adults. This is only sensical: The risk of Covid-19-related health complications is greater with increasing age or comorbidities. Of course, even young adults run health risks. Ethical analyses on Covid-19 HCTs have deemed such HCTs as acceptable as long as they “have considerable potential to directly benefit participants, are designed to limit and minimize risks to participants, and are done with strict infection control measures to limit and reduce third-party risks” (Jamrozik and Selgelid 2020). Another analysis concludes:

> [T]hese studies are considered ethical if certain criteria are met. Participants in human challenge studies must be relatively young, in good health and must receive the highest quality medical care, with frequent monitoring. Tests should also be performed with great caution and specialized medical supervision (Calina et al. 2020).

None of the conditions mentioned here seem especially difficult to meet with a subject pool of volunteers and a competent team of researchers. It thus seems natural to conclude that a possible Covid-19 HCT could have passed the ethical criteria of low-risk experimentation by using a low-risk population.[2]

What about the exploitability of the volunteer population? For example, had we reason to believe the experiment was mainly drawing upon marginalized groups or that the volunteers were participating because of social pressure, we may consider their participation ethically objectionable (Franklin and Grady 2001; Evers et al. 2015). An analysis of the volunteers to the 1 Day Sooner volunteer pool shows such worries to be misguided (Rose et al. 2021). Volunteers were not only younger, but also wealthier and more likely to be educated than the general population. A higher proportion of the volunteer population identified as white and male than in the general population, alleviating concerns that the volunteers would mainly be drawn from disadvantaged populations. Furthermore, psychological questionnaires were used to establish motivations for volunteers: It was established that subjects did not show elevated risk-taking behavior in health-related domains, nor that they felt motivated by fame or respect by peers. Rather, the volunteer population showed elevated scores on measures of altruistic helping behavior, indicating ethically unproblematic motives. Lastly, researchers by no means would have had to draw participants randomly but could select a subject population in which any such worries are minimized. Given the availability and composition of the large volunteer pool, an early Covid-19 vaccine HCT could thus have easily drawn subjects from non-vulnerable populations.

Besides risk and vulnerability concerns, the third central ethical concern centers around *informed* consent. While it seems clear that volunteers give consent when signing up for studies (as opposed to non-volunteer populations), it may be doubted that such consent was *informed*. To give a simple example, if you consent to participating in a malaria HCT but are not aware that malaria can incur severe risks, your consent is not sufficient to render your participation ethically unproblematic unless I inform you of these risks before you give consent. But volunteers recruited by 1 Day Sooner were not in such a situation. First and foremost, their decision fell at a moment when our best knowledge regarding the health effects of Covid-19 was transmitted almost in real time, with any new research eagerly dissected by various media channels. Secondly, there is no reason to assume researchers need to hide risks or information from individual subjects to get a large enough research population, given the very large volunteer pool One Day Sooner provided. Lastly, the health screening involved in routine Human Challenge Trials would itself inform participants of the risk they individually face and allow researchers to select against participants with comorbidities the participants themselves were unaware of. Because of this, it is not only likely that volunteers are able to provide informed consent, but it also seems likely that the process itself would be able to provide them with more accurate information regarding the risk of a Covid infection than they would otherwise have, regardless of whether they end up consenting to being voluntarily exposed to the virus in the HCT or not. Informed consent thus would not have posed an ethical objection to a volunteer-based early Covid-19 HCT.

In the face of these misguided concerns, it seems negligent to ignore the large benefit early Covid-19 HCT would have had. We have seen above that even a maximally conservative estimate puts the numbers of lives saved in the thousands. I am not unique in identifying the problem of ignoring the deaths of thousands in order to avoid HCT. Chappell and Singer (2020) write:

> The longer we take to find it out, the more lives will be lost. If volunteers, fully informed about the risks, are willing to help fight the pandemic by aiding promising research, there are strong moral reasons to gratefully accept their help. To refuse it would implicitly subject others to still graver risks. (Chappell and Singer, 2020)

Reflecting on the ethical tragedy of an avoidable, months-long pandemic that could have been averted by enacting measures such as Covid-19 HCT, they note the importance of understanding why institutions failed to enact extraordinary measures during the pandemic: a project the next section will undertake.

> Possible risks from medical intervention are inflated in perceived moral significance, while objectively greater risks from the pandemic are comparatively neglected—even when these status quo risks involve thousands upon thousands of excess deaths that could have been prevented. There are presumably systemic reasons to do with institutional incentives that can help explain the causal provenance of this moral disaster. It will be important for social scientists to clarify the causal mechanisms that reinforce status quo bias in public health policy, and for changes in institutional design to set us on a better track next time around. (Chappell 2022)

Philosophers were not the only group calling for HCT early on. Overall, 177 researchers, including 15 Nobel Laureates, published an open letter urgently calling upon the FDA, the American government, and the WHO to approve HCTs in Covid-19 vaccine development (1DaySooner 2020). Surveys indicated broad approval for HCTs in the general population (Broockman et al. 2021).

To summarize this analysis: Common ethical objections were not applicable to early Covid-19 vaccine HCTs. A large pool of volunteers was recruited early on during the pandemic. These volunteers were at sufficiently low risk and stood to benefit both themselves and others by participation. They were not from marginalized groups, nor is there reason to believe that they were under psychological or social duress in making the decision to volunteer. Lastly, they were able to give informed consent to a Covid-19 vaccine HCT. Researchers and the public urgently called for an approval of HCTs. Given the moral importance of early access to vaccines during a global pandemic, a central question becomes understanding how and why institutions failed to allow for a Covid-19 vaccine

HCT. The next section suggests that a fruitful way of answering this question is found in the literature of public choice theory, which I will now introduce.

The Need to Apply Public Choice Theory to Infectious Diseases

When considering political choices, we often think about what a state, government or party does. However, states, governments, or parties do not make decisions—individuals do. Public choice theory analyzes political decisions as a result of individual decision-making, for example by elected officials or bureaucrats. Often, they argue, the incentives that decision-makers face offer a more realistic understanding of how and why a political outcome occurred than do stated political aims (Buchanan 1999). Public choice analyses have proven useful and informative on a wide range of topics. Often, such work illustrates a divergence of public interest and individual interest. For example, the public benefits from well-behaving convicts being released into society and into the workforce, but even if their recidivism rate is astonishingly low, every single convict that reoffends can be exploited by political opponents of elected officials to undermine their reelection. Elected officials thereby have a strong interest in not releasing convicts early, even if early release programs are in the public interest (Surprenant and Brennan 2019). When individual and public interests diverge, public choice teaches us that the individual interest typically wins. It is the elected official, not the public interest, that ends up deciding on a policy.

Despite wide-ranging applications of public choice theory, healthcare has so far eluded much scrutiny. Authors such as Anderson (1989) and Tollison and Wagner (1991) noted early on that few public choice analyses have focused on issues of public health. Roughly three decades later, Leeson and Thompson (2023) reaffirm the need for more public choice scholarship on matters of public health. Even fewer public choice theorists have analyzed matters of infectious diseases. Providing a public choice perspective on how governments and individuals handle infectious diseases seems even more pressing as the Covid-19 pandemic has highlighted the difficulty of aligning government and private interests for adequate pandemic responses (welcome exceptions are found in Daumann and Follert (2020), discussing the allocation of government programs during the covid pandemic, Storr et al. (2021), discussing the problem of knowing which services as essential for stay-home orders, and Coyne et al. (2021)).

For example, consider the following dilemma. To handle a pandemic well, one needs adequate information on how many infections and deaths occur in a country. Such information is important both to inform policy decisions and personal decisions by the population. For example, during an infection surge, it seems prudent to reduce contacts and risk, but when infections and deaths soar, the decision-maker may be blamed for mishandling the pandemic. Consequently, there is a perverse incentive for the decision-maker to underreport the number of infections and deaths, even if that worsens both political and individual decision-making. It is thus not surprising that many officials, particularly in authoritarian states that lack appropriate checks on political decision-making, are underreporting Covid-19 infections and deaths (Karlinsky and Kobak 2021).

For another example, consider the Covid-19 vaccine allocation, which was partially driven by individual rather than public interests. During the early stages of vaccine rollout, powerful individuals and interest groups alike tried to hasten their access to the vaccine, as political economists predicted (Goel, Nelson, and Goel 2021). In a particularly blatant example, a German major and his staff received covid vaccines well ahead of their assigned time and tried to hide this by forging documents (DW 2021). For another example, consider interest groups of all kinds advocating to have their members be classified as a priority group to be eligible for earlier vaccination. Insofar as some of these groups did not consist of high-risk individuals, such lobbying was not in the public interest, yet was often successful. For example, Californian teacher unions fought vigorously and successfully to be granted 1b prioritization status: this status was the same that, for example, people with severe disabilities that increased the risk of fatal Covid-19 infections were assigned. This was even though teachers, at the time, were largely not teaching at all or were teaching remotely, due to widespread school closures (County of San Diego 2021; Work in Progress 2022). The same holds true for, for example, for US farmer unions, despite farm work not holding any special status with regard to infection or mortality risk from Covid-19, and no danger of food shortages facing the United States. In short, both Covid-19 reporting, and Covid-19 vaccine rollout are two striking examples of how individual interests, rather than stated aims, can capture the political process and dominate decision-making. Both examples illustrate a clear benefit that public-choice analysis can bring to the study of pandemic decision-making by bringing into clearer focus the ways that the interests of individuals shape the political process.

Now, let us apply the method of public choice analysis to the case of Covid-19 vaccine HCT.

The Real Reason Why There Were No Human Challenge Trials for Covid-19 Vaccines: The Principal-Agent Problem

So far, I have proposed two claims about early Covid-19 HCTs: that they would have likely saved a considerable number of lives by speeding up approval and that they were not subject to the ethical concerns inherent to HCT research. Why, then, was no effort made to speed up Covid-19 vaccine development using HCTs? I propose that the reason is not to be found in the lofty heights of moral theorizing, but in a much more mundane place: in the incentive structure of individual decision makers.

Both the approval of HCTs and of Covid-19 vaccines themselves are decisions made by experts—in particular, by the Center of Disease Control and Prevention. There are good reasons to put decisions about the approval of medicine and experiments in the hands of experts. While the approval of a medicine or experiment may impart significant benefits or harm to the population, it is unreasonable for the population itself to make an informed decision on each medicine or experiment's costs and benefits. There are simply too many such decisions for the public to keep track of: as a result, the FDA regulates the consumption of products worth roughly $2.7 trillion a year (Food and Drug Administration, 2023). Additionally, such decisions require detailed knowledge of the subject matter at hand, which can hardly be expected of the general population. It is thus well justified to have many decisions regarding the approval of medical research in the hands of bureaucrats with considerable expertise, such as the decision-makers at the FDA.

The explicit aim of the FDA and similar agencies is to act in the best interests of the general public. Such proxy roles are coined as agent and principal in the economic literature: The principal (the general population in this case) is the one whose interests should guide decision-making, whereas the agent (the FDA) chooses and acts. Of course, there can be plenty of cases where the incentives of the principal and the incentives of the agent diverge. As the principal has transferred their decision-making power to the agent, it is the agent who ultimately decides—often to the detriment of the principal. Such a situation of diverging incentives has become known as "Principal-Agent Problem."

For example, imagine trying to invest your money, but struggling with finding the right stocks to pick. You ask a stockbroker for help. The stockbroker has a lot of expertise in how to find the right stocks and has no reason to give you bad advice. Quite the opposite, they want you to tell your friends about how good they are at their job! This is a principal-agent situation, but there is no principal-agent *problem*: your incentives are well-aligned with the incentives of your stockbroker. But suppose the stockbroker gets a commission if you buy a particular stock, regardless of the merits of that stock. The situation is different now: what advice is best for you and what advice is best for the stockbroker will diverge. I believe that in the case of Covid-19 HCTs, the incentives of the FDA officials and the general public diverged. If that is true, the absence of early Covid-19 HCTs may be best understood as a principal-agent problem: a difference of interest between FDA decision-makers and the general public.

Why would the interest of FDA officials and the general public diverge when it comes to early Covid-19 HCTs? Let us first inspect the incentives of the public. We have already established that a minimal 5590 deaths could have been averted by Covid-19 HCTs, with the true number likely being one or two orders of magnitude higher. The risk of a Covid-19 HCT fatality for a young, healthy adult is estimated to be around 0.0151% (Manheim et al. 2021). The risk of avoiding any fatality will depend on the number of subjects. The chance of no subject dying in a HCT is $99.9849\%^n$, where n is the number of subjects required by the trial. Even a massive trial using 1,000 subjects, for example, would run only a 14 percent risk of incurring any fatalities. Note that the general public is not asked itself to incur such a risk: rather, the risk is incurred by volunteers, who willingly accept this risk to benefit the general public. Contrast this to the number of deaths occurring daily in the pandemic—as I write this, more than six million individuals have died in total. Earlier in this chapter, I provided a conservative baseline estimate of the lives such an early HCT could have saved, at roughly 5,590 lives. Of course, this number is dependent on information not available to the general public at the moment of decision-making. Yet, it seems clear that a large benefit was foreseeable even from the perspective of 2020—repeated calls for such trials were made because of such foreseeable benefits. Furthermore, each individual member of the public has a significant, vested interested in not dying from Covid-19 themselves. An approved vaccine is a very plausible way to satisfy that interest. Given no direct risk is incurred, and significant benefits are foreseeable, it seems to have been in the interest of the public to support early HCTs during the Covid-19 pandemic. Indeed, polls undertaken during the pandemic in May 2020 underline this: respondents showed broad support for challenge trials (Broockman et al. 2021).

The incentives look different for bureaucratic decision-makers because, unlike the general public, they face outsized individual risks. This risk can be distinguished across three dimensions: legal risks, occupational risks, and first-mover risks. Let us illustrate each in turn.

Legal risks may at first glance strike us as implausible risks for FDA decision-makers to consider, since they are under qualified immunity. It seems unlikely that a fatality during a Covid-19 HCT would be sufficient for successful legal action to be undertaken against the individual decision-maker. Yet, the FDA as an organization is open to legal risks and is generally taken to be quite risk-averse in managing those risks. After all, any successful trial against the FDA sets legal precedents, the consequence of which is a loss of flexibility in decision-making.

The risk-aversion of FDA decision-making is especially prominent in approvals regarding emergency medicine (Schneider 2015, chapter 2), such as the treatment of cardiac arrest, in which it is naturally difficult to ask often unconscious subjects for consent (Kremers et al. 1999; Moler 2004; Ernst and Fish 2005; Biros 2007). While such research was typically conducted using deferred or implied consent, any studies not using prospective consent were forbidden in 1993. This basically halted any progress on emergency medicine—only one research protocol was approved in the three years following the decision. After an outcry by the research community, the blanket ban was relaxed somewhat, but remained excruciatingly difficult to navigate, with only twenty of sixty research proposals accepted in the decade after the ban was relaxed. In the last three decades, the mortality rate of cardiac arrest has *increased*, while treatment options have not seen significant innovations (Nichol et al. 2004; Hiller et al. 2005).

Of course, such risk-aversion that neglects public benefits is rational from a legal point of view. A study which validates a treatment or healthcare innovation does not lead to any legal downsides or benefits, but any study in which something does go wrong imposes a legal risk. So even if the risk for a specific study is extremely low, organizations like the FDA will open themselves to legal risks by having many low-risk studies run (Whitney 2023). The rational response to this risk is to both minimize the individual risk of a study via highly conservative regulations *and* to reduce the number of studies run by increasing the bureaucratic hurdles researchers have to navigate (Infectious Diseases Society of America 2009).

Occupational risks arise from possible consequences to employment that a HCT could bring. If, for example, public opinion on HCTs swung differently after approval for a HCT was given, or if the result of the HCT ended in the unlikely result of a fatality, individual bureaucrats may face occupational consequences. They could be fired, moved to another role, or be overlooked in future promotion rounds. They could also be pushed out of the job by a public backlash, as health officials faced severe public attacks during the pandemic. Such a risk is not just imagined by officials: a survey of the National Association of County and City Health Officials found that 30 percent of health officials leaving their job during the pandemic did so because of conflicts with superiors or the public (Halverson et al. 2021). It is thus plausible for public health officials to recognize the severe occupational consequences that could arise if a HCT went awry. This creates adverse incentives: it is rational for them to be more risk-averse regarding HCTs than a member of the general population, as it is the bureaucrat that faces the occupational risk when things go wrong.

This observation of a systemic shift towards risk-averse decision-making by FDA officials has been made by a variety of authors. Friedman & Friedman articulated the decision officials face as follows:

> Put yourself in the position of an FDA official charged with approving or disapproving a new drug. You can make two very different mistakes:
>
> 1. Approve a drug that turns out to have unanticipated side effects resulting in the death or serious impairment of a sizable number of persons.
> 2. Refuse approval of a drug that is capable of saving many lives or relieving great distress and that has no untoward side effects.
>
> If you make the first mistake (…) your name will be spread over the front page of every newspaper. You will be in deep disgrace. If you make the second mistake, who will know it? (…) The people whose lives might have been saved will not be around to protest. Their families will have no way of knowing that their loved ones lost their lives because of the "caution" of an unknown FDA official (Friedman and Friedman 1980, 208).

Lastly, consider that many countries were involved in vaccine development. The benefits of successful vaccine development and testing, however, were not exclusive to one country but were distributed globally. This leads to a situation in which a possibility of "free-riding" arises: any country that relies on the testing and approval process of another country will be able to reap the benefits of their process without facing the risk. In the concrete case of early Covid-19 HCTs, a likely risk is reputational: If a HCT would have resulted in fatalities or not produced positive results, it is possible that the decision to do a HCT itself would be called into question. Regardless of the merits of such a charge, the reputational risk would only affect the country that first decided to run the HCT. Whoever first approves a HCT will be stuck with a reputational risk, whereas others can avoid that reputational risk while still reaping the benefits of the vaccine approval. Consequently, it is rational for every individual decision-maker to wait and hope for another decision-maker to make the first move.

We just saw three ways in which it was rational for bureaucratic decision-makers to be more risk averse than the general population that they represent, due to the concentrated risks that they face when making decisions. As a result, the incentives of the decision-makers (agents) and the population they represent (principals) came apart: as public choice theory would predict, the decision that ended up materializing favored the risk-averse preferences of the agents, rather than the principals. Early Covid-19 HCTs were never approved, despite widespread popular support and a plausible claim to large societal benefits that may have arisen from them.

Conclusion

I have argued that the failure to approve early Covid-19 HCTs led to the unnecessary loss of at least 5590 lives. This failure, I argued, was not justified by moral concerns, but arose from misaligned incentives of decision-makers vis-à-vis the population whose interests they represent. These incentives were not specific to the Covid-19 virus: unless changes are made, these incentives will again be misaligned if future pandemics require the approval of new vaccines or medicine. What can we do to prevent such failure?

Introducing bureaucracies that decide on behalf of the general population is not just some arbitrary whim imposed by overreaching government agencies. There is a real need for decision-making about new medical innovations that cannot feasibly be done by the general population, as they lack the appropriate expertise and time. I do not seek to undermine the necessity of dedicated experts who can adequately weigh the risks and benefits, yet Covid-19 vaccines were no run-of-the mill medication: they were part of a response to a global crisis that held the world in its grip for years.

Significant media coverage, both regarding the pandemic and vaccine development, was ubiquitous. The general public yearned for information, which both individual experts and the media gladly provided: In such a situation, the overall need for an intermediary decision-maker is reduced, because the public has access to relevant information relating to the Covid-19 virus. At the very least, a broad public debate regarding the desirability or undesirability of early Covid-19 HCTs would have been required. Such a debate would have made clearer the reasons for which an early Covid-19 HCT was not employed. Insofar as the line of argument I presented here was right, these reasons were at the level of individual decision-makers, rather than the general public. A public debate would not have disproportionately factored in the reasons of individual decision-makers but would have revealed the clear public interest in Covid-19 HCTs.

In 2020, calls for early Covid-19 HCTs were largely confined to the scholarly community and were thus easy to ignore. One simple lesson we can learn from the failure of Covid-19 HCTs is that in decisions of significant public import, such as global pandemics, a broad public debate about the risks and benefits of research programs must take place. I think this lesson may be fruitful even outside of pandemic cases: too many decisions on medical research are decided by individual decision makers, ethics boards, and government agencies. Whenever such a decision affects the population at large, it is crucial that the considerations in question should be discussed publicly and openly, to prevent the incentives of the decision-makers from unduly crowding out and undermining the public interest.

Another possible change is at the level of the individual decision-makers. As I have argued, it is not that early Covid-19 HCTs were not used because of angsty or evil bureaucrats. Rather, given the risks individual bureaucrats faced, it would have been irrational for them to approve an early Covid-19 HCT. In a situation as pressing as a global pandemic, it seems especially prudent to reduce these risks to individual decision-makers, so that individual risks do not prevent them from acting in the best interests of the population they represent. This could work by publicly announcing that even a failed HCT will not hold occupational consequences, excluding individual bureaucrats from facing outsized legal risks. Another strategy could be to have multiple actors jointly declare their approval for a HCT attempt before said HCT is run in order to avoid free riding by actors awaiting the results of HCT before lending their approval or disapproval. I believe such steps would be more likely to be undertaken after a public debate had been held, making it prudent to consider both public justification and a reduction of individual incentives towards risk-aversion as a joint strategy to avoid repeating past mistakes during future pandemics.

I believe such changes are no mere fantasy. After a public debate and cooperation between multiple actors, including the NHS, the WHO and the University of Oxford, a Covid-19 HCT was run to study Covid-19 infections (Edwards 2022, Killingley et al. 2022). Subjects were exposed to Covid without any protection from vaccines or previous infections: a higher harm than that of the early Covid-19 HCT we considered here. The British HCT provided valuable information on the kinetics of Covid-19 infections and resulted in no lasting health effects for the volunteer participants. No outsized risk was faced, given the broad support by national and international organizations. But unfortunately, the study was run in 2022, far too late to benefit the development of Covid-19 vaccines. If another pandemic arises, let us hope that it will not take as long to make the right choice: Our failure to approve Covid-19 vaccine HCTs cost thousands of lives, and repeating the same mistake will cost thousands more.

Notes

1 I thank Emil Iftekhar for help in establishing a lower bound for the counterfactual impact of Covid-19 HCT. I thank the editors, as well as all participants of the Mercatus Bastiat Research Sequence, for invaluable feedback on an early draft. Lastly, I thank Danilo Freire, Walker Wright, Jordan Lofthouse, Arielle John, Stefan Kolev, and many others that helped me pursue my PPE interests inside and outside of Mercatus programs.

2 One may object here that using a low-risk experimental group undercuts the scientific aim of a Covid-19 vaccine trial. After all, is it not the most at-risk population, the elderly, which are struck hardest by Covid? Such objections would be misguided. A HCT as discussed here would replace a Phase 3 trial, which tests the efficacy of a vaccine. The efficacy of the vaccine with regard to preventing an infection wholesale in low-risk subjects gives crucial information on its protective effect in elderly populations; even if other studies would have been needed (after approval) regarding the exact magnitude of the effect on other factors, such as the likelihood of severe infections (vis-à-vis mild infections). A regular Phase 2 trial would still have happened and be required to test for side effects that specifically occur with increased frequency in populations that are not included in the HCT. Such data were available early-on for the most promising vaccine candidates and would thus not pose a problem to the counterfactual timeline modeled here.

References

1DaySooner. 2020. "US: Challenge Trials for Covid-19." *1DaySooner*. https://www.1daysooner.org/us-open-letter/.

Arrow, Kenneth J. [1971] 1992. "Insurance, Risk and Resource Allocation." In *Foundations of Insurance Economics*, edited by Georges Dionne and Scott E. Harrington, 220–229. Dordrecht, Netherlands: Springer.

Anderson, Gary M. 1989. "Parasites, Profits, and Politicians: Public Health and Public Choice." *Cato Journal* 9: 557.

Atanasov, Vladimir, Natalia Barreto, Jeff Whittle, John Meurer, Benjamin W. Weston, Qian (Eric) Luo, Lorenzo Franchi, Andy Ye Yuan, Ruohao Zhang, and Bernard Black. 2023. "Understanding Covid-19 Vaccine Effectiveness against Death Using a Novel Measure: Covid Excess Mortality Percentage." *Vaccines* 11 (2): 379.

Broockman, David, Joshua Kalla, Alexander Guerrero, Mark Budolfson, Nir Eyal, Nicholas P. Jewell, Monica Magalhaes, and Jasjeet S. Sekhon. 2021. "Broad Cross-National Public Support for Accelerated Covid-19 Vaccine Trial Designs." *Vaccine* 39 (2): 309–316.

Biros, Michelle. 2007. "Struggling with the Rule: The Exception From Informed Consent in Resuscitation Research." *Academic Emergency Medicine* 14 (4): 344–345.

Buchanan, James M. 1999. *The Logical Foundations of Constitutional Liberty*, Vol. 1. Indianapolis, IN: Liberty Fund.

Calina, Daniela, Thomas Hartung, Anca Oana Docea, Demetrios A. Spandidos, Alex M. Egorov, Michael I. Shtilman, Felix Carvalho, and Aristidis Tsatsakis. 2020. "Covid-19 Vaccines: Ethical Framework Concerning Human Challenge Studies." *DARU Journal of Pharmaceutical Sciences* 28: 807–812.

Centers for Disease Control and Prevention. 2023. "History of Smallpox." https://www.cdc.gov/smallpox/history/history.html (accessed April 13, 2023).

Chappell, Richard Y., and Peter Singer. 2020. "Pandemic Ethics: The Case for Risky Research." *Research Ethics* 16 (3–4): 1–8.

Chappell, Richard Y. 2022. "Pandemic Ethics and Status Quo Risk." *Public Health Ethics* 15 (1): 64–73.

County of San Diego. 2021. "Get Vaccinated for Covid-19." https://www.sandiegocounty.gov/content/dam/sdc/hhsa/programs/phs/Epidemiology/covid19/vaccines/Know%20Your%20Vaccination%20Phase_ENG.pdf (accessed April 13, 2023).

Coyne, Christopher J., Thomas K. Duncan, and Abigail R. Hall. 2021. "The Political Economy of State Responses to Infectious Disease." *Southern Economic Journal* 87 (4): 1119–1137.

Daumann, Frank, and Florian Follert. 2020. "Covid-19 and Rent-Seeking Competition: Some Insights from Germany." *New Perspectives on Political Economy* 16 (1–2): 52–69.

David J. Sencer CDC Museum. n.d. "Covid-19 Timeline." https://www.cdc.gov/museum/timeline/covid19.html (accessed April 13, 2023).

DW. 2021. "German Mayor Suspected of Jumping Vaccine Queue." https://www.dw.com/en/coronavirus-german-mayor-suspected-of-jumping-vaccine-queue/a-56655518 (accessed April 13, 2023).

Edwards, Kathryn M., and Kathleen M. Neuzil. 2022. "Understanding Covid-19 through Human Challenge Models." *Nature Medicine* 28 (5): 903–904.

Ernst, Amy A., and Susan Fish. 2005. "Exception from Informed Consent: Viewpoint of Institutional Review Boards—Balancing Risks to Subjects, Community Consultation, and Future Directions." *Academic Emergency Medicine* 12 (1): 1050–1055.

Evers, David L., Carol B. Fowler, Jeffrey T. Mason, and Rebecca K. Mimnall. 2015. "Deliberate Microbial Infection Research Reveals Limitations to Current Safety Protections of Healthy Human Subjects." *Science and Engineering Ethics* 21: 1049–1064.

Eyal, Nir, Marc Lipsitch, and Peter G. Smith. 2020. "Human Challenge Studies to Accelerate Coronavirus Vaccine Licensure." *The Journal of Infectious Diseases* 221 (11): 1752–1756.

Ferreira, Leonardo Souto, Flavia Maria Darcie Marquitti, Rafael Lopes Paixão da Silva, Marcelo Eduardo Borges, Marcelo Ferreira da Costa Gomes, Oswaldo Gonçalves Cruz, Roberto André Kraenkel, Renato Mendes Coutinho, Paulo Inácio Prado, and Leonardo Soares Bastos. 2023. "Estimating the Impact of Implementation and Timing of the Covid-19 Vaccination Programme in Brazil: A Counterfactual Analysis." *The Lancet Regional Health–Americas* 17: 100397.

Franklin, G. Miller, and Christine Grady. 2001. "The Ethical Challenge of Infection-Inducing Challenge Experiments." *Clinical Infectious Diseases* 33 (7): 1028–1033.

Friedman, Milton, and Rose D. Friedman. 1980. *Free to Choose: A Personal Statement.* New York: Harcourt.

Food and Drug Administration. 2023. "FDA at a Glance." https://www.fda.gov/about-fda/economics-staff/fda-glance.-

Goel, Rajeev K., Michael A. Nelson, and Viraat Y. Goel. 2021. "COVID-19 Vaccine Rollout—Scale and Speed Carry Different Implications for Corruption." *Journal of Policy Modeling* 43 (3): 503–520.

Hafner, Marco, Erez Yerushalmi, Clement Fays, Eliane Dufresne, and Christian Van Stolk. 2022. "Covid-19 and the Cost of Vaccine Nationalism." *Rand Health Quarterly* 9 (4): 1.

Halverson, Paul K., Valerie A. Yeager, Nir Menachemi, Michael R. Fraser, and Lori T. Freeman. 2021. "Public Health Officials and Covid-19: Leadership, Politics, and the Pandemic." *Journal of Public Health Management and Practice* 27 (Supplement 1): S11–S13.

Harris, Sheldon H. 2002. *Factories of Death: Japanese Biological Warfare, 1932–1945, and the American Cover-up*. New York: Routledge.

Heriot, George S., Euzebiusz Jamrozik, and Michael J. Selgelid. 2020. "Tensions between Research and Public Health: Modelling the Risks and Benefits of SARS-CoV-2 Vaccine Field Trials versus Human Infection Challenge Studies." *medRxiv*: 2020–05.

Hiller, Katherine M., Jason S. Haukoos, Kennon Heard, Jonathan S. Tashkin, and Norman A. Paradis. 2005. "Impact of the Final Rule on the Rate of Clinical Cardiac Arrest Research in the United States." *Academic Emergency Medicine* 12 (11): 1091–1098.

Hornblum, Allen M. 1997 "They Were Cheap and Available: Prisoners as Research Subjects in Twentieth Century America." *BMJ* 315 (7120): 1437–1441.

Infectious Diseases Society of America. 2009. "Grinding to a Halt: The Effects of the Increasing Regulatory Burden on Research and Quality Improvement Efforts." *Clinical Infectious Diseases* 49 (3): 328–335.

Jamrozik, Euzebiusz, and Michael J. Selgelid. 2020. "Covid-19 Human Challenge Studies: Ethical Issues." *The Lancet Infectious Diseases* 20 (8): e198–e203.

Karlinsky, Ariel, and Dmitry Kobak. 2021. "Tracking Excess Mortality Across Countries during the Covid-19 Pandemic with the World Mortality Dataset." *Elife* 10: e69336.

Khamsi, R. 2020. "If a Coronavirus Vaccine Arrives, Can the World Make Enough." *Nature* 580 (7805): 578–580.

Killingley, Ben, Alex J. Mann, Mariya Kalinova, Alison Boyers, Niluka Goonawardane, Jie Zhou, Kate Lindsell et al. 2022. "Safety, Tolerability and Viral Kinetics during SARS-CoV-2 Human Challenge in Young Adults." *Nature Medicine* 28 (5): 1031–1041.

Kremers, Mark Stuart, Diane Roe Whisnant, Laurie Silvus Lowder, and Linda Gregg. 1999. "Initial Experience Using the Food and Drug Administration Guidelines for Emergency Research without Consent." *Annals of Emergency Medicine* 33 (2): 224–229.

Leeson, Peter T., and Henry A. Thompson. 2023. "Public Choice and Public Health." *Public Choice* 195: 5–41.

Lerner, Barron H. 2007. "Subjects or Objects? Prisoners and Human Experimentation." *New England Journal of Medicine* 356 (18): 1806–1807.

Levine, Myron M. 1998. "Experimental Challenge Studies in the Development of Vaccines for Infectious Diseases." *Developments in Biological Standardization* 95: 169–174.

Levine, Ruth, Michael Kremer, and Alice Albright. 2005. "Making Markets for Vaccines." Report of the Center for Global Development. https://www.cgdev.org/sites/default/files/archive/doc/books/vaccine/MakingMarkets-complete.pdf.

Manheim, David, Witold Więcek, Virginia Schmit, Josh Morrison, and 1Day Sooner Research Team. 2021. "Exploring Risks of Human Challenge Trials for Covid-19." *Risk Analysis* 41 (5): 710–720.

McCallum, Jan M., Dhananjaya M. Arekere, B. Lee Green, Ralph V. Katz, and Brian M. Rivers. 2006. "Awareness and Knowledge of the US Public Health Service Syphilis

Study at Tuskegee: Implications for Biomedical Research." *Journal of Health Care for the Poor and Underserved* 17 (4): 716.

Metzger, Wolfram G., Hans-Jörg Ehni, Peter G. Kremsner, and Benjamin G. Mordmüller. 2019. "Experimental Infections in Humans—Historical and Ethical Reflections." *Tropical Medicine & International Health* 24 (12): 1384–1390.

Moler, Frank W. 2004. "Resuscitation Research and the Final Rule: Is There an Impasse?" *Pediatrics* 114 (3): 859–861.

Nguyen, Linh Chi, Christopher W. Bakerlee, T. Greg McKelvey, Sophie M. Rose, Alexander J. Norman, Nicholas Joseph, David Manheim et al. 2021. "Evaluating Use Cases for Human Challenge Trials in Accelerating SARS-CoV-2 Vaccine Development." *Clinical Infectious Diseases* 72 (4): 710–715.

Nichol, Graham, Ella Huszti, Jenn Rokosh, A. Dumbrell, Jessie McGowan, and Lance Becker. 2004. "Impact of Informed Consent Requirements on Cardiac Arrest Research in the United States: Exception from Consent or from Research?" *Resuscitation* 62 (1): 3–23.

Pronker, Esther S., Tamar C. Weenen, Harry Commandeur, Eric HJHM Claassen, and Albertus DME Osterhaus. 2013. "Risk in Vaccine Research and Development Quantified." *PLoS One* 8 (3): e57755.

Rose, Sophie M., Virginia L. Schmit, Thomas C. Darton, Nir Eyal, Monica Magalhaes, Josh Morrison, Matthew Peeler, Seema K. Shah, and Abigail A. Marsh. 2021. "Characterizing Altruistic Motivation in Potential Volunteers for SARS-CoV-2 Challenge Trials." *medRxiv*: 2021–03.

Schneider, Carl E. 2015. *The Censor's Hand: The Misregulation of Human-Subject Research*. Cambridge, MA: MIT Press.

Stiglitz, Joseph E. 1989. *Principal and Agent*. London, UK: Palgrave Macmillan.

Storr, Virgil Henry, Stefanie Haeffele, Jordan K. Lofthouse, and Laura E. Grube. 2021. "Essential or Not? Knowledge Problems and Covid-19 Stay-at-Home Orders." *Southern Economic Journal* 87 (4): 1229–1249.

Surprenant, Chris W. and Jason Brennan. 2019. *Injustice for All: How Financial Incentives Corrupted and Can Fix the US Criminal Justice System*. New York: Routledge.

Tollison, Robert D., and Richard E. Wagner. 1991. "Self-Interest, Public Interest, and Public Health." *Public Choice* 69 (3): 323–343.

Weindling, Paul, Anna von Villiez, Aleksandra Loewenau, and Nichola Farron. 2016. "The Victims of Unethical Human Experiments and Coerced Research under National Socialism." *Endeavour* 40 (1): 1–6.

Whitney, Simon N. 2023. *From Oversight to Overkill: Inside the Broken System That Blocks Medical Breakthroughs*. Irvington, NY: Rivertowns Books.

Work in Progress. 2022. "The Story of VaccinateCA." https://worksinprogress.co/issue/the-story-of-vaccinateca/ (accessed April 13, 2023).

World Health Organization. 2023. "WHO Coronavirus (Covid-19) Dashboard." https://covid19.who.int/ (accessed March 27, 2023).

Yamana, Teresa K., Marta Galanti, Sen Pei, Manuela Di Fusco, Frederick J. Angulo, Mary M. Moran, Farid Khan, David L. Swerdlow, Jeffrey Shaman 2023. "The Impact of Covid-19 Vaccination in the US: Averted Burden of SARS-COV-2-Related Cases, Hospitalizations and Deaths." *PLoS One* 18 (4): e0275699.

Yeoh, Ben. 2020. "Regulators Could Allow Early Use of Covid-19 Vaccine or Treatment." Special Edition Policy Brief. Mercatus Center at George Mason University. https://www.mercatus.org/system/files/yeoh_-_policy_brief_-_acceleration_of_regulation_-_v1.pdf.

5

Navigating the Path to Educational Progress

A Public Choice Perspective on Ghana's Reforms

George Agyeah

Numerous economists have acknowledged the pivotal role played by the development of human capital in the advancement of individuals and, by extension, in the progress of nations on a global scale (Becker 2009; Niaz Murshed Chowdhury 2018; Ortigueira and Santos 1997; Jaiyeoba 2015). Delving into Sub-Saharan Africa, some authors have unearthed compelling evidence that underscores the significant impact of human capital development on economic growth, as gauged by gross domestic product (Ogunleye et al. 2017). It comes as no surprise, then, that a multitude of interventions in the developing world have been tirelessly geared toward fostering development by expanding access to educational opportunities.

International powerhouses such as the IMF and the World Bank have channeled substantial resources into numerous developing countries to bolster access to educational facilities. In the context of Ghana, the financial resources provided by these international organizations often synergize with domestic investments (White and Masset 2005). However, evidence shows that there exist numerous cases and scenarios that enhance development gains by optimizing existing community-based approaches to providing common pool resources across the world (McGinnis 2016) as well as in sub-Saharan Africa in the case of Nigeria (Ostrom 1996).

Situated in West Africa, Ghana boasts a strategic geographical position, bordered by the Gulf of Guinea to the south, Togo to the east, the Ivory Coast to the west, and Burkina Faso to the north. Ghana, as a nation, has consistently demonstrated its recognition of the paramount importance of education. Over the course of its history, spanning from its formative years, through the tumultuous eras marked by coup d'états, up to the present democratic establishment, Ghana has undertaken numerous measures to refine and enhance its educational system. Frequently, the more prominent—though not necessarily optimal—reform initiatives have involved the expansion of the existing scope to include new services in the educational domain. Advocates of these reforms, including labor unions in Ghana and international organizations, have argued for the adoption of systems proven effective in other nations to enhance the scope and efficiency of education. Within this chapter, I embark on a comprehensive exploration of educational reform, delving into the realities of its implementation through the lens of public choice theory. My central hypothesis posits that the root causes of inefficiencies within Ghana's educational sector can be attributed to critical issues pertaining to incentives, the knowledge problem, institutional inefficiencies, and contextual challenges.

My analysis spotlights successful instances of policy implementation, offering valuable insights gleaned from the rich reservoir of public choice literature. For the remainder of this chapter, I embark on a journey through the annals of Ghana's educational system, tracing its historical evolution in the subsequent section. This endeavor is crucial in shedding light on the contextual institutions that hold the potential for effective policy implementation. Subsequently, I delve into the framework governing educational policy implementation in Ghana, providing a comprehensive examination of how policies are executed at various government levels. In the following section, I scrutinize the specific circumstances that have contributed to the success of these policies, substantiated by compelling evidence. Finally, in the closing section, I consolidate my findings and propose a roadmap for future research in this domain. This forward-looking approach capitalizes on the incentives inherent in diverse institutions, the cultural context, and the principles of applied public choice to pave the way for the development of a more robust educational system.

History of the Educational Policy Importation in Ghana

The extensive body of literature pertaining to education in Sub-Saharan Africa has frequently delved into the examination of successful cases (Glewwe and Jacoby 1994; Kingdon and Söderbom 2007; Nyarkoh and Intsiful 2018). Nevertheless, it is imperative to embark on a comprehensive exploration of outcomes that have proven less successful. Such an endeavor is essential in order to optimize the delivery and enhancement of educational systems in less developed nations and becomes even more crucial given the inconsistent results yielded by various interventions in the developing world (Boettke et al. 2015).

The concept of educational policy importation is a central theme in the educational landscape. It entails the process of adopting educational policies from foreign countries and applying them to a nation. In the case of Ghana, its history bears witness to the importation of educational policies from a diverse array of sources, including old colonial powers, international organizations, and neighboring countries. Prior to the arrival of Europeans, Ghanaian education predominantly assumed the form of apprenticeships. However, early European settlers in need of local assistance for colony administration and missionary efforts established missionary schools to educate local elites and their offspring. During the colonial period, Ghana (then known as the Gold Coast) was influenced by the British educational system. English was introduced as the medium of instruction, formal examinations were implemented, and the curriculum placed a heavy emphasis on literacy, numeracy, and Christian values. Following independence in 1957, Ghana aspired to create an educational system that would authentically reflect its national identity, culture, and ambitions; yet, it preserved many foundational elements from the pre-independence era.

Remarkably, Ghana has remained reliant on external sources in shaping its educational policies. The country has consistently turned to a wide spectrum of external entities, including UNESCO, the World Bank, USAID, as well as various bilateral and multilateral donors, for financial support, technical expertise, and policy guidance in educational development. This has led to a multitude of policy adaptations derived from other nations. The litany of policies implemented in Ghana encompasses free primary and secondary education, universal basic education, millennium development goals (MDGs), and sustainable development goals (SDGs), as reported by the Ministry of Education of Ghana (*Education strategic plan* 2018). Despite these numerous changes, the Ghanaian education system still shares substantial similarities with other African nations, such as Nigeria and Tanzania, which have undergone comparable processes of decolonization and nation-building. Consequently, these countries often adopt analogous policy approaches (Pinto, 2019). The advantages and challenges faced by the Ghanaian educational system are also echoed across a multitude of nations, largely due to the parallel trajectory of policy implementation.

Educational Policy Implementation in Ghana

The organizational structure of Ghana's executive branch plays a pivotal role in the implementation of policies within the country. This hierarchical arrangement adheres to a traditional model, where each level of government reports to the one above it, ultimately culminating in the president, who occupies the zenith of this administrative pyramid. Immediately beneath the president, a cadre of appointed ministers assumes key positions, responsible for overseeing specific sectors of governance. In the realm of education, the Ministry of Education is entrusted to the stewardship of a minister, a direct appointee of the president. The onus of policy implementation within the education system squarely rests upon the shoulders of this ministry, with the president's appointed minister serving as the chief custodian of this portfolio, directly accountable to the highest office.

Within the Ministry of Education, a multifaceted structure unfolds, with various subsections assuming distinct roles in the complex web of policy implementation. Notably, the Ghana Education Service (GES) emerges as a constitutionally mandated body charged with executing educational policies at the pre-tertiary level. The Ghana Education Service itself operates within a hierarchical framework, featuring regional and district directorates that mirror the overarching bureaucratic structure of the government. This intricate network facilitates the cascading of policies and directives from the national level down to the grassroots.

In addition to this central structure, Ghana's educational landscape also incorporates semi-independent governmental entities that wield significant influence over policy formulation and implementation. Two such quasi-independent bodies, the National Schools Inspectorate Authority and the National Council for Curriculum and Assessment, play pivotal roles in the task of setting, enforcing, and assessing educational standards (National Council for Curriculum and Assessment 2021; National Schools Inspectorate Authority 2020). However, it is essential to note that these semi-independent bodies, despite their distinct functions, remain financially dependent on the Ministry of Education and work in collaboration with the ministry, rather than serving as checks on its performance. Beyond the core policy-oriented bodies, Ghana's educational sphere features a constellation of other entities with diverse functions, such as the National Teaching Council, the National Vocational Training Institute, the National Council for Vocational Education and Training, and the West African Examinations Council. These organizations contribute to the broader educational landscape, albeit without direct involvement in policy formulation and execution.

The implementation of education policies in Ghana commences at the national level through the Ministry of Education. Once a policy is adopted or formulated, it undergoes a meticulous process of dissemination and execution. Initially, policy information is transmitted to the regional directorates, which correspond to the country's sixteen regions. From there, the policies cascade further down the hierarchical ladder to the municipal and district levels. At each tier of this intricate hierarchy, a director assumes leadership and operational responsibilities, reporting to a director at the level immediately above. This centralized approach, while designed to streamline policy execution, is not without its challenges. Scholars have highlighted the inherent limitations of such monocentric systems, citing issues such as information asymmetry, inflexibility, and restricted opportunities for experimentation (Ostrom 1996). These concerns underscore the ongoing need for thoughtful governance reforms within Ghana's educational framework to ensure its continued evolution and adaptability to the dynamic demands of the twenty-first century. A highlight of the issues that need addressing is discussed below.

Policy implementation within Ghana's educational landscape reveals a stark absence of scientific experimentation. At the helm of educational institutions stand school heads, who serve as the chief executives responsible for the day-to-day management of their schools. However, a disheartening reality persists: These educational leaders often find themselves constrained by the rigidity inherent in the prevailing policy approach. This lack of adaptability hampers their ability to apply customized solutions tailored to the unique needs and challenges faced by their institutions. Consequently, inefficiencies permeate multiple levels of the education system, impairing its overall effectiveness. Moreover, recent developments in Ghana's educational system have not only failed to ameliorate these existing issues but have, regrettably, exacerbated them, causing a palpable decline in the quality of education. A noteworthy governmental directive mandating an increase in enrollments has, on the surface, seemingly sought to broaden access to education (Dwomoh et al. 2022). However, this well-intentioned move has inadvertently burdened the system, giving rise to a host of new challenges. Foremost among these challenges is the predicament of overcrowded classrooms, where students and teachers must navigate increasingly crowded learning environments. This overcrowding not only diminishes the quality of education but also strains the resources available to schools. Budgetary constraints loom large, and schools find themselves grappling with the arduous task of remaining financially viable amidst the backdrop of widespread financial difficulties afflicting the government bureaucracy. Furthermore, the education bureaucracy itself has witnessed a significant expansion in its scope and functions as educational services have expanded. This expansion has ushered in a complex array of administrative demands, diverting valuable time and resources away from the core mission of imparting knowledge and nurturing students. Key new functions include managing the school feeding program, managing the funding of free high school programs, as well as a host of other auxiliary functions that are not educationally related. The burgeoning bureaucracy has inadvertently contributed to making the educational system less effective, as educators find themselves navigating a labyrinthine system that often detracts from the pursuit of educational excellence.

Furthermore, the intersection of policy importation and the practical, economic reality in Ghana has unveiled a particularly conspicuous challenge: the knowledge problem (Doing 2011). A recent policy adaptation, namely the free high school policy, which draws inspiration from the American education system's provision of free basic education up to the high school level, is a compelling case study that sheds light on this predicament. While the free high school policy is undoubtedly commendable in its overarching objective of ensuring that every child, irrespective of their parents' economic circumstances, gains access to education, its journey toward realization has been fraught with formidable obstacles. Foremost among these obstacles is the deficiency in essential information necessary for the successful implementation of the policy. Despite its noble intentions, the policy has grappled with the critical issue of inadequate knowledge regarding the specific requirements and challenges faced by individual educational institutions. A glaring illustration of this deficiency manifests in scenarios where students find themselves unable to engage in meaningful study activities due to the sheer lack of desks—a circumstance that has given rise to embarrassing anecdotes (Chanimbe and Dankwah 2021). These anecdotal incidents underscore the profound knowledge gap that has afflicted the policy implementation process from its inception. The knowledge problem has effectively hamstrung the policy's execution from the very outset. Policymakers have found themselves ensnared in a quagmire of uncertainty regarding which students truly require the services envisioned by the policy. Consequently, budgetary concerns have haunted the policy since its inception, with allocations frequently falling short of the actual needs on the ground. This knowledge deficit is not confined solely to the allocation of physical resources but extends to a broader understanding of the diverse needs, aspirations, and challenges faced by students within the educational system. Without a comprehensive grasp of these intricacies, policy framers are ill-equipped to devise strategies that align with the real-world requirements of students. Consequently, a disjunction persists between policy intentions and practical outcomes, exacerbating the challenges faced by the education sector in Ghana.

Another critical challenge that has cast a shadow over the success of policy importation pertains to the oversight of the government bureaucracy tasked with the implementation of educational policies. The prevailing perception of government bureaucracy as an altruistic institution, driven solely by the welfare of society, has, in many instances, overshadowed the reality that it is, fundamentally, an amalgamation of individuals motivated by their own interests. This idealistic view, while well-intentioned, has been scrutinized for its failure to account for the complexities of bureaucratic dynamics, including the influence of individual incentives (Buchanan 1987). This inherent oversight has had far-reaching implications for the effectiveness of educational policy implementation in Ghana. The consequences of this oversight become apparent when examining the various inefficiencies that manifest at different levels of policy execution. Take, for example, the school feeding program, designed with the noble goal of providing meals to needy students. Regrettably, the perception of bureaucracy as an inherently benevolent entity has made it susceptible to political actors seeking to exploit it for personal gain. The program, rather than solely serving its intended purpose, has become a means for political figures to claim rewards and garner support for their respective parties. This diversion of resources and focus has undermined the program's fundamental objective, leaving needy students without the support they require. Furthermore, this blind trust in the innate benevolence of bureaucracy has given rise to the disconcerting phenomenon of rent-seeking behavior (Buchanan and Tullock 1965). A shadowy network of opportunistic entrepreneurs has emerged, capitalizing on their proximity to decision-makers within the bureaucratic machinery. This network thrives by extracting economic rents from the system, often to the detriment of broader educational goals. For example, recent media investigations in Ghana have unveiled an extensive ecosystem of entrepreneurs catering to affluent parents who seek access to elite schools that have remained unscathed by the surge in student populations, despite the glaring absence of a corresponding expansion in infrastructure (Joy News Ghana 2023). It is crucial to emphasize that such opportunistic behavior extends beyond actors external to the education system. Even heads of educational institutions and district directors of education, driven by a desperate desire to demonstrate positive returns on the investments they receive, have been enticed into ethically compromising actions. This includes actively aiding students in cheating, a regrettable consequence of the relentless pressure to produce favorable academic outcomes to justify the immense investments in education (Ghana News Agency 2022). To address these systemic challenges, a paradigm shift is urgently needed in how government bureaucracy is perceived and monitored in the context of educational policy implementation. Recognizing that bureaucratic entities are composed of individuals with their own motivations is essential. It necessitates a recalibration of oversight mechanisms, emphasizing transparency, accountability, and the alignment of individual incentives with broader societal goals. Only through such systemic reforms can Ghana hope to mitigate the adverse effects of these issues and pave the way for a more effective and equitable educational landscape that genuinely serves the needs of its students and society as a whole. The cumulative impact of these challenges has been felt acutely in Ghana's educational landscape, casting a long shadow over well-intentioned policies such as the free high school policy and the school feeding program. These initiatives, designed to enhance educational access and support students in need, have regrettably encountered substantial setbacks due to the intricacies of the issues at hand.

There are clear signals of inefficiencies in the Ghanaian educational system resulting from the centralized, overly hierarchical nature of the system. First and foremost, the knowledge problem has unleashed a domino effect, triggering resource misallocation throughout the education system. This fundamental lack of information regarding the specific needs and conditions of individual institutions has left policymakers in a precarious position. Without a clear understanding of the nuanced challenges faced by schools, allocations of resources have often fallen short of the mark. This misallocation has, in turn, hindered the effective execution of policies and thwarted their potential to deliver intended benefits. Furthermore, the dearth of experimentation within the educational landscape has significantly curtailed the range of solution sets available to address complex challenges. The absence of opportunities to test and refine innovative approaches has left educational institutions ill-prepared to adapt to evolving needs and circumstances. As a result, the educational system has been caught in a cycle of stagnation, unable to harness the full spectrum of creative solutions that could invigorate teaching and learning. This centralization has inadvertently created fertile ground for political actors to exploit the situation for personal gain. The undue benefits reaped by such actors have, regrettably, diverted attention and resources away from the core educational mission, undermining the very essence of these policies.

The consequences of these systemic issues are felt most acutely by the students themselves. Apart from the short-term issues highlighted above, one glaring manifestation of these challenges is the persistent issue of graduate unemployment, which has remained stubbornly high. The disconnect between what students are trained for and the practical demands of the economy is a symptom of the monocentricity inherent in a system where policies are imported and implemented in a top-down manner. There is an urgent need for an educational system that equips students with skills that align with the realities of the job market (Honorati and Johansson DESilva 2016). In the subsequent section, I delve into the characteristics of successful institutions in this setting and the frameworks that underpin the success stories.

Contextual Solutions for a Monocentric System

Addressing the challenges posed by a monocentric system requires a fundamental shift toward adopting a polycentric approach (Ostrom 1996). This shift holds the potential to usher in a new era of innovation, contextual problem-solving, and overall optimization within the Ghanaian education system. A key example of the positive results that can be gained from a polycentric approach can be found in the secondary education setup where institutional changes allow limited control for certain heads of schools. I explore these institutions before discussing the specific setups that make the outcomes of these institutions different.

In the wake of Ghana's independence from the British Empire, it became abundantly clear that the colonial economic framework had prioritized resource exploitation. This left the predominantly arid northern region of the country woefully underdeveloped. In a bold move to rectify this disparity and uplift the northern region, the government instituted one of Sub-Saharan Africa's pioneering free education policies. The cornerstone of this ambitious policy was the establishment of the Northern High Schools program, aimed at ensuring that every qualified child in the north had the opportunity to access secondary school education without imposing a significant financial burden on their parents. This visionary initiative went a step further by incorporating a feeding program, acknowledging that students' ability to benefit fully from their education should not be hindered by the economic circumstances of their families. However, despite the noble intentions underpinning this policy, it has grappled with a multitude of challenges inherent in centralized systems. The perennial issues of insufficient funding, inefficient disbursement mechanisms, and corruption have collectively cast a long shadow over the effective implementation of the program. These issues have, regrettably, left the heads of schools grappling with the daunting task of planning for the feeding of students, often resulting in the closure of northern schools for significant portions of the school year. Nonetheless, amid these challenges, there are invaluable lessons to be gleaned from the institutions that have managed to thrive within this complex environment. These institutions, despite confronting the same universal obstacles, have managed to remain open and provide quality education. One such remarkable institution is Notre Dame Senior High School, located in Navrongo, situated just ten kilometers from the border of Ghana and Burkina Faso. Notre Dame Senior High School has played a pivotal role in the educational landscape of Ghana's northern region. Notre Dame Senior High School also has a unique governance structure. Founded initially by Catholic missionaries, the school's evolution is a testament to the collaboration between religious institutions and the government in fostering quality education. Under this arrangement, the government assumed the responsibility of paying teacher salaries and providing financial contributions on par with other government-run educational institutions. This financial support was crucial in sustaining the school's operations and ensuring the welfare of both students and educators. However, what sets Notre Dame apart from the conventional government-run schools is the unique feature of its governance—the active involvement of the Roman Catholic Diocese of Navrongo–Bolgatanga, the original patron of the institution. This collaborative partnership reflects a deep commitment to preserving the school's mission and values while adapting to the evolving educational landscape.

One of the distinctive roles assumed by the diocese within this collaboration is the nomination of individuals for the prestigious position of headmaster. Notably, these nominations are subject to the stringent requirements and standards established by the government. This dual selection process ensures that the headmaster embodies the educational vision of both the diocese and the government, fostering a harmonious synergy between religious and state interests in education. This cooperation between the church and government in many ways exemplifies the advantages that can be gained from co-production between government agencies and local people who have a stake in the provision of common pool resources (Brady 1993). The involvement of the archdiocese in the selection of the headmaster signifies more than a mere administrative formality. It represents a deeper commitment to maintaining local oversight and accountability within the school's governance structure. This local oversight helps to address issues promptly, ensuring that the school operates smoothly and efficiently, even in the face of external challenges. Moreover, the partnership with the archdiocese extends beyond the administrative realm and touches on the practical aspects of school management. For instance, when the broader education system faces funding shortfalls, as seen in the constraints of the school feeding program, the archdiocese steps in to provide financial support. This intervention ensures that the school can continue to provide meals to its students, promoting their well-being and enabling uninterrupted learning. The collaboration with the archdiocese not only bolsters financial stability but also leverages the institution's unique advantages. For instance, the school can negotiate favorable prices for food items, capitalizing on its ability to purchase when prices are at their lowest, rather than being constrained by sporadic availability of funds.

In essence, Notre Dame's governance structure is a shining example of how partnerships, local oversight, and adaptability can enhance the effectiveness of educational institutions. It demonstrates the potential for religious organizations and the government to work hand in hand to provide quality education while preserving their respective values and principles. This collaborative model serves as an inspiring blueprint for other institutions seeking to navigate the complexities of Ghana's educational landscape and make a lasting impact on the lives of students and communities. This distinctive arrangement offers several advantages. Notably, it enables the diocese to exercise local oversight, ensuring accountability among government employees and addressing some of the inefficiencies that can plague government-run institutions. Additionally, the archdiocese supplements the government's efforts, particularly during challenging times when other schools face closures due to funding shortfalls in the school feeding program. In such instances, the archdiocese steps in to provide financial support for purchasing food, thereby allowing the school to remain open. This confidence in repayment is bolstered by the intimate knowledge the church possesses of the moral character of the headmaster, typically a priest of the diocese nominated by the archdiocese. Furthermore, this collaborative arrangement helps mitigate the knowledge problem. The extensive reach and networks of the diocese facilitate the efficient resolution of questions related to when and what food items to purchase. With this information, Notre Dame is adept at procuring foodstuffs when prices are favorable rather than being constrained by sporadic availability of funds. As a result of these multifaceted advantages, Notre Dame Senior High School stands as one of the best-run institutions in the northern region, exemplifying the potential for innovative and locally tailored solutions within Ghana's educational landscape. These lessons underscore the significance of partnerships, local oversight, and the capacity to adapt to local contexts in addressing the challenges posed by centralized educational policies.

Beyond Notre Dame Senior High School, the Catholic Church has demonstrated a commendable ability to mitigate the inherent inefficiencies of the centralized educational model in various regions across Ghana. One such notable example can be found in the heart of the country, in Sunyani in the Bono Region, where St. James Senior High School has emerged as a beacon of efficiency within the educational landscape of the region. Much like Notre Dame, St. James operates within a governance framework that combines the efforts of the diocese with those of the government. This collaborative approach has yielded remarkable results, underlining the potential for partnership to transform educational outcomes. The results of the effectiveness of coproduction in the provision of education further highlight the effectiveness of this approach. For example, students from these institutions are often the beacons of success in the country.

The National Science and Math Competition is an educational program that pits the best and brightest students across Ghana against one another at the secondary education level. Winners of this competition are often considered the best students in the country (Sulley Lansah 2018). Of the top ten winners of the National Science and Math Quiz in Ghana, eight of the schools are operated under a similar coproduction system. Similarly, of the twenty top high schools in Ghana based on external exam results, ranked by a reputable news agency in Ghana, only three of the schools are distinctly government-run. The remainder are either run with churches or maintain ties with the local stakeholders of churches that are affiliated with them (Murimi 2023). An additional mark of the effectiveness of the coproduction of secondary education is the list of schools classified as Category A. Out of the approximately 1200 secondary schools in the country, fifty-four have earned a Category A rating for their exceptional performance. Among these, approximately thirty (56 percent) are jointly operated with various entities such as churches, mosques, and other groups that actively contribute to the success of these institutions. In the Category B senior schools, 29 percent are co-run, while the lowest-performing Category C institutions show that about 12 percent share a similar structure. Additionally, 16 percent of other lower category institutions are co-run (*List of Senior High Schools in Ghana* 2019). Through the collaborative efforts of different entities, these schools have effectively addressed the challenges associated with the centralized model, achieving notable success by leveraging shared resources and expertise.

This success extends beyond secondary education. The Diocese of Sunyani has extended its reach to encompass primary schools and early childhood education institutions within its network. This holistic approach to education mirrors the collaborative model observed in the higher educational tier. The efficiency gains realized in these lower-level educational institutions illustrate the replicability of success across different educational tiers. A shining example of this efficiency can be found in Sacred Heart School, a pre-high school institution that operates under the auspices of the Sunyani Diocese of the Catholic Church in the Bono Region of Ghana. When compared to government-run pre-high schools in the same diocese, Sacred Heart stands as a clear exemplar of effective governance and educational delivery. This stark contrast highlights the advantages of the partnership between religious organizations and the government in fostering educational excellence. Notably, the success stories are not confined to the Catholic Church alone. Other denominations, such as the Presbyterians and the Anglicans, have adopted similar collaborative arrangements in various regions of Ghana. These arrangements have not only replicated the successes observed within the Catholic Church but have also contributed to the diversification of educational approaches and the spread of excellence across the nation.

The experiences of institutions like St. James and Sacred Heart underscore the transformative potential of collaborative governance models in the educational sector. These models serve as potent illustrations of how partnerships between religious organizations and the government can effectively mitigate the inefficiencies inherent in centralized systems. Moreover, the ability to replicate such successes across various regions and denominations highlights the broader applicability and scalability of these innovative approaches to education. As Ghana seeks to address the challenges facing its educational system, these success stories provide valuable insights and inspiration. They emphasize the importance of adaptability, cooperation, and localized oversight in navigating the complexities of the educational landscape. By drawing upon these examples and fostering a spirit of collaboration, the nation can aspire to cultivate a more efficient, equitable, and responsive educational system that empowers students and communities.

In the realm of policy implementation within the Ghanaian educational landscape, a fascinating pattern emerges. It becomes evident that the institutions that have been most effective in translating government policy changes into tangible outcomes are those that have successfully navigated and overcome the inherent challenges of the monocentric system. These institutions, marked by their remarkable efficiency, have often found innovative ways to address the issues that typically plague centralized systems. A particularly compelling example of this innovative approach can be seen in church-affiliated educational institutions. These institutions have embraced a mixed governance model that combines elements of both public and private involvement. Within this framework, the private churches play a pivotal role in ensuring accountability at the grassroots level of governance. By virtue of their strong presence in local communities, these churches are uniquely positioned to oversee and guide the operations of educational institutions. This localized oversight helps in promptly addressing issues, ensuring that policies are effectively implemented, and students receive the support they require. Moreover, church-affiliated schools leverage the extensive network of church members and their abundant resources to tackle the knowledge problem head-on. The collective wisdom and resources of these church communities prove invaluable in addressing the nuanced challenges that educational institutions encounter. This collaborative spirit fosters a culture of shared responsibility, where the entire community is invested in the success of the school. Crucially, church-affiliated institutions offer a solution that extends beyond the immediate educational sphere—the establishment of property rights. Unlike traditional government-run institutions that may lack a sense of ownership and accountability, these schools operate with a heightened sense of purpose and stewardship. This ensures that they are not run haphazardly but are treated with the same care and diligence as private institutions, ultimately enhancing their efficiency. Beyond the church-affiliated institutions, another category of successful schools emerges. These schools have forged strong alliances and affiliations that mirror the benefits provided by the private sector. For instance, a school like Prempeh College has a long-standing association with the Asante Kingdom. The involvement of kinsmen and chiefs in critical decision-making processes ensures that the institution remains efficient and aligned with the aspirations of the local community. Similarly, other institutions have established robust Parent-Teacher Associations (PTAs) that step in to fill the governance gap. These PTAs are instrumental in ensuring that the school's operations are well-managed, providing essential support and guidance. Perhaps the most compelling evidence of the success of these collaborative approaches lies in the comparative performance of institutions that benefit from these "polycentric additions" versus those that lack decentralized authorities at the implementation levels. Notably, a significant number of the top-performing high schools in Ghana operate in partnership with various private entities, showcasing the transformative power of these cooperative models (Mwendwa and Walubengo 2022).

The evidence shared shows the transformative potential of polycentric models of education. These models, whether based on church affiliations, local associations, or strong community ties, serve as powerful catalysts for efficiency and effectiveness. They provide valuable lessons on the importance of shared responsibility, accountability, and localized oversight in navigating the complexities of education policy implementation. By drawing upon these lessons, Ghana can continue to nurture a dynamic, responsive, and equitable educational system that empowers its students and communities across the nation. By embracing polycentrism, the educational landscape can harness the collective wisdom and diverse strengths of various segments of the system, providing an efficient platform for both experimentation and the implementation of policy initiatives. By tapping into these existing structures, the educational sector can maximize the value derived from its policies and initiatives. One pivotal advantage of polycentrism lies in its capacity to stimulate innovation. Within a polycentric framework, educational institutions, administrative bodies, and other stakeholders are encouraged to explore novel solutions to the myriad challenges they encounter. This newfound freedom to innovate enables the system to adapt more readily to the dynamic and evolving educational landscape, ensuring that policies and practices remain relevant and effective. Contextual problem-solving is another hallmark of polycentrism. By allowing individual institutions and regions to tailor solutions to their specific needs and circumstances, polycentrism promotes a localized approach that recognizes the unique challenges faced by different segments of the education system. This approach contrasts starkly with the one-size-fits-all mentality often associated with monocentric systems. In the Ghanaian context, polycentric organization could mean that schools in different regions have the flexibility to address the specific challenges they face, whether they be resource allocation, infrastructure development, or curriculum design, in a manner that aligns with their unique circumstances. Successful solutions that emerge from various segments of the education landscape can be shared, adapted, and implemented across the system, creating a virtuous cycle of continuous improvement. This cross-pollination of ideas and practices will allow the Ghanaian education system to tap into the collective knowledge and experience of its diverse stakeholders, ultimately enhancing its overall efficiency and effectiveness.

Discussion and Conclusion

The historical trajectory of educational policy in Ghana is characterized by a recurring theme—the importation of policies from a diverse array of sources, including colonial powers, international organizations, and neighboring countries. These imported policies encompass a wide spectrum of educational initiatives, ranging from the noble aspirations of free primary and secondary education to the laudable goals of universal basic education, and the pursuit of millennium development goals. Yet, it is essential to recognize that the mere act of importing policies, while well-intentioned, does not automatically ensure their seamless implementation or the attainment of desired outcomes. Ghana's experience with educational policy importation has, in many ways, been a journey marked by both successes and challenges. These challenges, shaped by the details of policy implementation, have shed light on the need for a more nuanced approach that takes into account the complex realities of the nation's educational landscape. One of the recurring issues that have surfaced in the wake of policy importation is the prudent utilization of resources. Misalignment between policy intent and resource allocation has sometimes led to inefficiencies within the educational system. These inefficiencies manifest in various forms, such as overcrowded classrooms, inadequate infrastructure, and regional disparities in resources. These challenges often stem from the inherent monocentric nature of the educational system, which, by its very design, struggles to adapt to the diverse needs and circumstances of different regions and communities. Inflexibility and a dearth of experimentation within the educational framework have also posed a significant impediment to achieving policy objectives. The rigid adherence to centralized models can stifle innovation and hinder the responsiveness of the system to emerging challenges. A more polycentric approach—one that allows for localized experimentation and tailored solutions—may hold the key to addressing these entrenched issues and optimizing policy outcomes. The knowledge problem looms as another formidable barrier to successful policy implementation in Ghana. Policymakers, often distanced from the on-the-ground realities of individual educational institutions, grapple with a profound lack of understanding regarding the specific needs and nuances of these institutions. This knowledge gap has profound implications for resource allocation, leading to budgetary constraints, inefficiencies, and suboptimal outcomes. Bridging this gap through data-driven decision-making and localized insights is essential to chart a more effective course forward. The challenges extend beyond the educational sphere and into the realm of government bureaucracy. Inefficiencies within the bureaucratic apparatus have given rise to unintended consequences, such as the instrumentalization of the school feeding program for political gain. This departure from the program's original intent has repercussions for its efficacy and, ultimately, the well-being of students who rely on it.

It becomes abundantly clear that the imperative for a comprehensive investigation into best practices for the effective implementation of educational policies in Ghana is often overlooked, to the detriment of the nation's educational landscape. This oversight has far-reaching consequences, significantly impeding concerted efforts to uplift the quality and accessibility of education for the entire population. One of the most glaring and pervasive challenges that must be addressed is the knowledge problem, a persistent obstacle that has hindered the successful execution of educational policies. The lack of comprehensive, granular information regarding the specific needs and circumstances of individual educational institutions has consistently thwarted well-intentioned policy initiatives. Therefore, a critical avenue for research and reform lies in devising strategies to bridge this knowledge gap. By elucidating how policymakers can gain deeper insights into the nuanced requirements of students and institutions, research can catalyze more informed and context-sensitive policy design and implementation. Moreover, the stark absence of experimentation within the educational framework stands as another formidable challenge. The reluctance to explore innovative approaches and experiment with different models has hamstrung the evolution of the educational system. Herein lies an opportunity for scholarly inquiry to uncover pathways to foster a more dynamic and adaptive approach to education. The embrace of a polycentric framework, wherein private entities like the church, traditional rulers, and parents play pivotal roles, holds great potential for mitigating the detrimental effects of this experimentation deficit. Research endeavors could delve into the ways in which these private stakeholders can contribute to a more responsive and flexible educational system. Additionally, it is imperative to recognize the pivotal role of local alternative educational practices, such as apprenticeship programs. These practices offer an unconventional yet potentially powerful pathway to complement formal education. Exploring the integration and feasibility of apprenticeship programs into future educational policy planning and implementation can open doors to a diversified and inclusive educational landscape.

Furthermore, a crucial aspect that deserves careful consideration is the role of local institutions in promoting accountability and providing solutions to the knowledge problem. These institutions, deeply rooted in their respective communities, can serve as vital conduits for enhancing the effectiveness of educational policies. Investigating how these local bodies can be leveraged to inform policy formulation and implementation is a line of inquiry that holds great promise. In closing, the urgent need for a comprehensive examination of educational policy implementation practices in Ghana cannot be overstated. It is imperative that the nation recognize the multifaceted challenges it faces in its pursuit of an equitable and high-quality education system. Through diligent research and a commitment to innovation, Ghana can lay the foundation for a future in which educational policies are informed by a deep understanding of local needs, embraced with flexibility and experimentation, and enriched by the collaborative engagement of private and community-based stakeholders. In doing so, Ghana can aspire to foster a vibrant educational ecosystem that empowers its citizens and fuels the nation's progress.

Given this multifaceted landscape of challenges, it is imperative for policymakers to pause and reconsider context and reality when importing and implementing educational policies. A more holistic approach that combines elements of both centralized and decentralized governance models, places greater emphasis on localized experimentation and innovation, and harnesses the power of data and insights from the grassroots level can pave the way for more effective policy implementation. In essence, Ghana's experience with educational policy importation offers a valuable case study, replete with lessons on the importance of aligning policy objectives with the intricacies of implementation. By heeding these lessons and adopting a more adaptive and context-aware approach, Ghana can chart a more successful trajectory toward achieving its educational aspirations and, in doing so, secure a brighter future for its students and the nation as a whole. The imperative for rigorous research into the effects and implementation processes of imported educational policies in Ghanaian society cannot be overstated. It is evident that there exist critical areas ripe for investigation, each holding the promise of shedding light on pathways to enhance the nation's educational system. First and foremost, there is a compelling need to delve into the viability of adapting the centralized approach to policy implementation in Ghana to a more multi-dimensional model. While the current centralized system has its merits, it is not immune to shortcomings and limitations. Research endeavors could embark on exploring alternative approaches that strike a balance between centralization and decentralization. Such approaches might hold the key to mitigating the challenges posed by a one-size-fits-all policy framework. By investigating the possibilities of devolving certain decision-making powers to local stakeholders, researchers can offer valuable insights into how Ghana's educational system can become more flexible and responsive to the diverse needs of its regions and communities.

Parallel to this is the pervasive knowledge problem. The dearth of information regarding the specific requirements of individual educational institutions has been a recurrent stumbling block in policy implementation. Consequently, research initiatives should focus on illuminating pathways for policymakers to gain a deeper and more nuanced understanding of the unique needs and circumstances of students and institutions. By illuminating how this vital information can be seamlessly integrated into the design and execution of policies, researchers can contribute to the development of more context-sensitive and effective educational initiatives. Furthermore, the role of government bureaucracy charged with the implementation of educational policies warrants meticulous investigation. The conventional view of government bureaucracy as a benevolent and altruistic institution dedicated to the welfare of society merits scrutiny, since, in practice, this perspective has sometimes fallen short of expectations, giving rise to inefficiencies at various levels of policy implementation. Hence, research endeavors could zero in on strategies to incentivize government bureaucrats to operate with greater accountability and efficiency. These investigations may uncover innovative solutions to streamline bureaucratic processes and optimize policy outcomes. Expanding on the above, future research could extend its purview to explore alternative approaches to education that reduce barriers to expanding educational access. One promising avenue that merits consideration is the exploration of local apprenticeship programs. Such programs could potentially offer valuable training opportunities to students while minimizing disruptions to their educational journeys. It's noteworthy that I am currently engaged in a study aimed at exploring the potential of local apprenticeships as a viable pathway to bridging the gap between formal education and practical skills acquisition.

By delving into the nuances of policy implementation, embracing a multi-dimensional approach, tackling the knowledge problem head-on, reevaluating the role of government bureaucracy, and exploring innovative educational alternatives, researchers can pave the way for a brighter educational future for Ghana. This collective endeavor holds the promise of enhancing the nation's capacity to provide quality education that is both inclusive and tailored to the unique needs of its students and communities.

References

Becker, Gary S. 2009. *Human Capital: A Theoretical and Empirical Analysis, with Special Reference to Education*. Chicago, IL: University of Chicago Press.

Boettke, Peter J., Christopher J. Coyne, and Peter T. Leeson. 2015. "Institutional Stickiness and the New Development Economics." In *Culture and Economic Action*, edited by Grube, Laura, and Virgil Henry Storr, 123–146. Cheltenham, UK: Edward Elgar Publishing.

Brady, G. L. 1993. "Governing the Commons: The Evolution of Institutions for Collective Action." *Southern Economic Journal* 60 (1): 249–251.

Buchanan, James M. 1987. "The Constitution of Economic Policy." *Science* 236 (4807): 1433–1436.

Buchanan, James M., and Gordon Tullock. 1965. *The Calculus of Consent: Logical Foundations of Constitutional Democracy (Vol. 10).* Ann Arbor, MI: University of Michigan Press.

Chanimbe, Timothy, and Kwaku Opoku Dankwah. 2021. "The 'New' Free Senior High School Policy in Ghana: Emergent Issues and Challenges of Implementation in Schools." *Interchange* 52 (4): 599–630.

Chowdhury, Md Niaz Murshed, Mohammed Jashim Uddin, Nezum Uddin, and Shamim Uddin. 2018. "Human Capital Development and Economic Growth in Bangladesh." *Journal of World Economic Research* 7 (2): 52–63.

Doing, Park. 2011. "Tacit Knowledge: Discovery by or Topic for Science Studies?" *Social Studies of Science* 41 (2): 301–306.

Dwomoh, Duah, Anthony Godi, John Tetteh, Charles Amoatey, Richard Otoo, Leticia Tornyevah, and Chad Hazlett. 2022. "The Impact of the Free Senior High School

Education Policy and Double-Track System on Quality Education Outcomes: A Quasi-Experimental Policy Evaluation Study in Ghana." *Africa Education Review* 19 (2): 1–24.

Ghana Education Services. 2019. "List of Senior High Schools in Ghana." *Ghana Education Service*, July. https://ges.gov.gh/wp-content/uploads/2020/08/SHSTVET_SCHOOLS.pdf.

Ghana, Ministry of Education. 2018. "Education Strategic Plan." https://www.globalpartnership.org/sites/default/files/2019-05-education-strategic-plan-2018–2030.pdf.

Ghana News Agency. 2022. "Syndicate Cheating, Impersonation in Ongoing WASSCE." *Ghana News Agency*. September 3.

Glewwe, Paul, and Hanan Jacoby. 1994. "Student Achievement and Schooling Choice in Low-Income Countries: Evidence from Ghana." *Journal of Human Resources* 29 (3): 843–864.

Honorati, Maddalena, and Sara Johansson DeSilva. 2016. "Expanding Job Opportunities in Ghana." *World Bank Publications*.

Jaiyeoba, S. V. 2015. "Human Capital Investment and Economic Growth in Nigeria." *African Research Review* 9 (1): 30–46.

Joy News Ghana. 2023. "8 Persons Arrested in 'School Placement for Sale' Exposé." January 30.

Kingdon, Geeta, and Måns Söderbom. 2007. "Education, Skills, and Labour Market Outcomes: Evidence from Pakistan." World Bank education working paper series, no. 11. Washington, DC: World Bank.

McGinnis, Michael D. 2016. "Polycentric Governance in Theory and Practice: Dimensions of Aspiration and Practical Limitations." Available at SSRN: https://ssrn.com/abstract=3812455 or http://dx.doi.org/10.2139/ssrn.3812455

Murimi, Rachael. 2023. "List of Category A Schools in Ghana in Their Respective Locations." *Yen News*. April 10. https://yen.com.gh/facts-lifehacks/study/231083-list-category-a-schools-ghana-respective-locations/.

Mwendwa, V., and P. Walubengo. 2022. "100 best senior high schools in Ghana (WAEC standard) 2022 – YEN.COM.GH." *Yen News*. https://yen.com.gh/107826-best-senior-high-schools-ghana-according-waec.html.

National Council of Curriculum and Assessment. 2021. "National Council of Curriculum and Assessment." https://nacca.gov.gh/who-we-are/.

National Schools Inspectorate Authority. 2020. "National Schools Inspectorate Authority." https://www.nasia.gov.gh/about-us/.

Nyarkoh, Enoch, and Emmanuel Intsiful. 2018. "An Assessment of the Impact of International Aid on Basic Education in Ghana." *American Journal of Educational Research* 6 (1): 43–49.

Ogunleye, Oladipupo O., Oluwarotimi Ayokunnu Owolabi, Oluwafemi Akintunde Sanyaolu, and O. O. Lawl. 2017. "Human Capital Development and Economic Growth in Nigeria." *Journal of Business Management* 3 (8): 17–37.

Ortigueira, Salvador, and Manuel S. Santos. 1997. "On the Speed of Convergence in Endogenous Growth Models." *The American Economic Review* 87 (3): 383–399.

Ostrom, Elinor. 1996. "Crossing the Great Divide: Coproduction, Synergy, and Development." *World Development* 24 (6): 1073–1087.

Pinto, Ransford. 2019. "The Effect of Western Formal Education on the Ghanaian Educational System and Cultural Identity." *Journal of Negro Education* 88 (1): 5–16.

Sulley, Lansah. 2018. "The National Science and Maths Quiz Has Kept Ghanaians Thrilled for 25 Years." *BBC*. July 22.

White, Howard, and Edoardo Masset. 2005. "Books, Buildings and Learning Outcomes: An Impact Evaluation of World Bank Assistance to Basic Education in Ghana (No. 0504013)." University Library of Munich, Germany.

6

Employment Protections and Firm Size Distortion

The Role of Unions

Laura Montenovo

Labor unions are institutions that represent groups of workers and their interests vis-à-vis their employers. The representatives of the workforce, usually in specific sectors, join and organize to advance their common interests as employees in their own sector, trade, or profession. These organized associations are present to some extent in all developed countries, and even in some developing countries, but their influence and power in shaping public policy, influencing the government, and effectively changing the lives of the workers they represent vary greatly by sector, time period, and geographical area.

Employment protections are laws or policies that regulate the costs, pecuniary and non-pecuniary, that firms face after they terminate workers for economic or disciplinary reasons. These regulations are implemented with the stated goal of protecting workers from unfair firings and terminations by their employer. While the strictness and design of these rules vary significantly across countries, these types of laws are quite ubiquitous.

By essentially introducing an implicit tax for dismissing or firing workers, employment protections decrease the ability of firms to freely set the size of their workforce. Through these distorted incentives, employment protection may lead to suboptimally low productivity within firms (Martin and Scarpetta 2012; Berton, Devicienti, and Grubanov-Boskovic 2017; Bratti, Conti, and Sulis 2021; Hijzen, Mondauto, and Scarpetta 2017; Autor, Kerr, and Kugler 2007; Micco and Pagés 2007; Garicano, Lelarge, and Van Reenen 2016; Montenovo 2022). In fact, knowing that it is costly to break employment relationships in case economic conditions change or if the job match turns out to be unproductive or of poor quality, firms may be disincentivized to make hires that would otherwise be profitable to them. Moreover, strict employment protections imply that, due to the high termination costs, firms might find it more desirable to retain low-productivity employees than to face the costs of dismissing them.[1]

The unintended consequences of employment protections may affect workers as well. Since, when making decisions, firms anticipate and account for the consequent potential future costs, one of the main repercussions of employment protection laws is that firms are not only less likely to terminate workers but also less likely to hire them, effectively "freezing" firms' size over time (Boeri and Jimeno 2003; Schivardi and Torrini 2004a; Garibaldi, Pacelli, and Borgarello 2004; Almeida and Carneiro 2009; Bornhäll, Daunfeldt, and Rudholm 2017; Montenovo 2022). Specifically, employment protection decreases permanent hiring (Hijzen, Mondauto, and Scarpetta 2017; Bratti, Conti, and Sulis 2021) and conversion rates from temporary to permanent contracts (Sestito and Viviano 2016). This tendency increases the divide between workers in safe jobs and those stuck in temporary contracts and unstable employment (Martin and Scarpetta 2012). In addition, employment protection may result in lower wages (Leonardi and Pica 2013; Martin and Scarpetta 2012), longer unemployment spells (Gimpelson, Kapelyushnikov, and Lukyanova 2010), and higher youth unemployment (Noelke 2016).

In parallel, the public choice literature discusses the unwanted effects of employment protection legislation. The French economist Frédéric Bastiat laid out the foundations of this literature by writing about the seen and unseen effects of any public policy action and the importance of closely looking for and reflecting on the latter (Bastiat 1883). More recently, public choice economists have specifically considered employment protection legislation and highlighted the chilling effects of such regulations on hiring practices (Mitchell 2016).

The existing evidence on the role that labor union density plays in shaping the relationship between employment protections and firms' size is quite scarce. Broadly, however, the consensus seems to be that unions have been successful at contributing to the passage of protective labor regulations—safety and fairness standards, for example—as well as at facilitating the scrutiny of such standards, and the enforcement of existing regulations. Morantz (2017) provides a comprehensive review of the literature on the topic.

Because employment protections are sets of laws or policies that protect workers in the termination phase of their employment relationships, unions, as institutions that are created with the stated objective of advancing workers' rights, tend to advocate for the tightness of these laws. Consequently, dense unionization in an industry might lead to tighter employment protections in that industry. However, the opposite direction of causality could arise too, in that environments characterized by strict regulations can favor the strengthening of labor unions because the individuals in such environments may increasingly rely on unions to help them tweak the design of these regulations or enforce them via legal counseling. Either way, labor markets associated with high union density are likely to also be characterized by strict employment protections.

By lobbying for these regulations, unions protect workers who are already locked in employment relationships for which employment protections apply. On the side of workers, this implies that dense unionization may result in a labor market divided between workers in stable job trajectories and those stuck in temporary and unprotected employment relationships. If strict employment protections make the labor markets more rigid, such that both hiring and terminations are disincentivized, and if unions are indeed successful at keeping these restrictions in place, then unions might play a non-negligible role in making such negative market outcomes persist among workers, prospective or existing, in that industry. Overall, the literature on the impact of union density on workers' outcomes has found that it decreases wage inequality (Card, Lemieux, and Riddell 2004; Koeniger, Leonardi, and Nunziata 2007), and it is likely to increase unemployment and lower employment (Boeri, Nicoletti, and Scarpetta 1999), especially among the youth, women (Montgomery 1989; Vedder and Gallaway 2002; Bertola, Blau, and Kahn 2007), and older workers.

On the side of firms, dense unionization may exacerbate the size and productivity distortions discussed above, according to which employment protections cause firms to be of suboptimal size and productivity. While there has been substantial work analyzing the impact of union density on the performance of firms (Doucouliagos and Laroche 2003; Addison and Schnabel 2003; Hübler and Jirjahn 2003; DiNardo and Lee 2004; Hirsch 2012; Konings and Vanormelingen 2015), the relevant literature has failed to specifically focus on the empirical estimation of the role that union density plays in shaping the size distribution of firms.

In this chapter, I focus on investigating the extent to which unionization density mediates—alleviates or exacerbates—the impact that employment protections have on the size of firms. If, in economic sectors where unions are stronger, employment protections are more established, salient, or more likely to be enforced, then in these environments the distortions may be stronger.

Because much of the strictness of employment protection laws comes down to their legal enforcement (Güell 2010), it is quite sensible that the constraining potential of these measures may, in turn, depend on the role that unions play in labor courts for that industry. Firms are aware of the level of employment protections that normally applies to their economic sector, and they engage in strategic behavior more or less intensively as a consequence. My understanding is that this work is the first in the literature providing empirical evidence on the role that labor unions play in determining the effects of employment protections on firms' size.

Policy institutions in Italy between 2010 and 2019 provide the ideal setting for this study. Italy has been historically characterized by relatively strict employment protections. Essentially, Italian labor court judges had a great deal of power and agency in setting termination costs; however, in the aftermath of the 2008 financial crisis, a technocratic government was given the responsibility of rescuing the country from potential bankruptcy. The measures adopted included a major structural reform in 2012 that relaxed employment protections restrictions that had applied to firms with at least sixteen employees ever since 1991. The main objective of the reform was to make the Italian labor market more flexible by breaking down the strong market dualism between more protected and less protected workers. Subsequently, in 2015, the Italian prime minister, Matteo Renzi, signed a new labor reform called the Jobs Act that had similar goals as the 2012 Fornero reform, and further reduced the costs of dismissals. The reforms significantly reduced the total costs for terminations deemed unfair, as well as the uncertainty around these costs, by strongly limiting the power of judges and the reliance on courts, and by linking indemnity payments strictly to the seniority of the workers. Both of these reforms were heavily criticized and fought against by the main unions in Italy.

First, this chapter aims at highlighting the differences in the impact of employment protection legislation on firms' size across industries characterized by different levels of unionization density. Second, the objective is to show whether and how the two Italian reforms impacted differences in firm size distributions by unionization density. With these goals in mind, I build descriptive and empirical evidence from a panel dataset on the universe of Italian firms in a time period that covers the pre- and post-reform years. I link information on unionization density in 2013 by industry and geography obtained from the National Statistics Institute in Italy to a firm-level dataset containing detailed information on the Italian firms' size between 2010 and 2019.

My findings show that unionization played a crucial role in shaping the size distortion of firms that was brought about by the employment protections laws. Firms in industries in high unionization density are characterized by a stronger size distortion. That is, they are more likely to behave strategically and remain below the size threshold of sixteen, which is where stricter protections come into play. My second contribution regards the long-lasting effects of unionization density, despite the policy changes. The results suggest that the two reforms were not particularly successful at alleviating such differences in the size distortion across firms in industries with varying levels of unionization density. Hence, the differences by unionization density mostly persist in the post-reforms period.

The evidence in this chapter shows that high unionization density exacerbates the negative effects of employment protection restrictions on the size of firms, because the size distortions deriving from having a sharp increase in terminations costs are much larger in highly unionized industries. Furthermore, results point to the difficulty that public policy may have in attempting to eradicate such undesirable effects. In fact, differences in firms' size across industries with varying levels of unionization density remain, even following two major reforms that have been found to alleviate such distortion on average.

This chapter is organized as follows. Section 2 reviews the relevant literature on employment protection legislation, its impact on size, and the role played by unions in this relationship. Section 3 provides details on employment protection legislation in Italy and the two recent reforms. Section 4 describes the firm-level and industry-level data I use in the analyses. Section 5 discusses the empirical methods, Section 6 reports the descriptive results, Section 7 shows the statistical significance of the model's results, and Section 8 concludes.

Literature Review

Much literature exists on the effects of labor regulations on labor market outcomes, firms, and economic efficiency overall. At the core of the work by public choice scholars is the idea that government representatives are likely not "benevolent agents" who always optimize their decisions solely based on what is best for "society." First, it is quite complicated, often prohibitively so, to identify policies that are beneficial to members of society across the board. Second, and most importantly, public choice theory highlights that policymakers act based on their own individual incentives, which arise from the re-election mechanisms in the democratic process. It is possible, and likely, that such motivations originating from the governmental agents' self-interest do not closely align with what would be the "public good." One potential implication of public choice theory is that regulations are likely to have several consistent, though perhaps delayed and indirect, negative consequences for economic efficiency (Buchanan and Tullock 1962; Tullock 1967; Buchanan 1991). More recently, public choice scholars have investigated the impact of labor regulations like occupation licensing and right-to-work laws on labor market outcomes (Larkin 2016). For example, Kleiner and Kudrle (2000) find that occupational licensing did not raise demand for dentists' services, but it increased prices for consumers and practitioners' earnings. Djankov et al. (2002) find that regulation of entry leads to higher corruption and larger informal economies, with no improvement in the quality of goods, whether private or public. Abraham and Kearney (2020) show that growth in occupational licensing in the United States is a cause of the overall decrease in employment-to-population ratio in the last few decades. Meehan and Benson (2015) provide evidence that the occupations of members of state-level regulatory boards in the United States explain the strictness level of the licensing requirements for private security, with states having licensing boards composed of active private security personnel being associated with stricter licensing requirements for private security personnel. Vedder (2010), Hicks and LaFaive (2013), and Kogan (2017) have found overall positive effects or, at a minimum, strong evidence of a lack of negative effects, of right-to-work laws, which are laws prohibiting agreements between employers and labor unions that force employees to financially contribute to union representation.[2]

However, the literature that is most relevant to this chapter is on how labor unions shape and impact the relationship between employment protection legislations and firms' outcomes. The link between unionization and employment protection is so direct that unionization density has been used as an instrument for employment protection legislation in an instrumental variable study on the effects of employment protection on foreign direct investment (Olney 2013).

Unions may impact the effect of employment protections on firms' outcomes through two main channels. First, unions may impose pressure on policymakers, through lobbying in the policy making phase. Of course, since unions are not equally powerful across all industries, their influence will vary based on the number of workers being represented. Second, unions can mediate the impact of employment protection on firms after the policies are enacted, through their legal enforcement. This is especially likely in a country like Italy, where labor court judges have a lot of power in setting the ex-post costs of termination.

Literature exists on the role that unions play through both of these channels. Weil (1999) recognizes that one of the well-established effects of union density is to increase in the enforcement of government labor policies. Weil (1992) showed that construction sites protected by unions are more likely to be inspected, to solve the irregularities faster and to face higher punishments as a result of such violations compared to the non-union counterparts. Using data from Oregon, Weil (1999) finds that enforcement of OSHA regulations shows patterns of complementarity, rather than substitutability, between mandated safety and health committees and labor unions. Azam and Salmon (2003) show that in Bangladesh the frequency of strike activity increases in pre-election periods, when unions try to extract as much rent as possible knowing that the current governments will increase employment generating-public expenditures in the attempt to remain in power. Ceron, Curini, and Negri (2019) rely on a multivariate time series analysis using Italian data between 1946 and 2015 to estimate the relative impact of political actors, including trade unions, on social expenditures. The results suggest that trade union preferences are important determinants of social expenditures because the government is not successful at retrenching expenditures on public programs when trade unions are cohesive. In fact, the authors point out that a key role of trade unions is to serve their members through the collective support of public good provisioning.

Berglund and Furåker (2016) use survey data on employees from twenty-three European countries and while they find that employment protection legislation and collective bargaining coverage are determinants of tenure—defined as the duration of an employment relationship—surprisingly, union density appears to play a statistically insignificant role. However, in the individual level-analysis, they show that having an employee representative in the workforce is positively and strongly associated with tenure. The role that unions may play after the enactment of employment protection legislation is also discussed in Damiani, Pompei, and Ricci (2020). The authors study the effect of the liberalization of temporary contracts on labor shares in Europe and find that firms pay temporary workers less. As one potential explanation, they suggest that unions are less influential on temporary contracts because temporary workers are less likely to be represented by labor unions. In a descriptive piece, Francesconi and Garcia-Serrano (2004) observe that, while Spain and Britain present very different degrees of employment protection, they are characterized by a similar association of unionization with temporary employment and nonstandard work hours. Essentially, the employment protection strictness is not associated with a different correlation of unionization with temporary work or overtime, implying that unions do not operate differently depending on the strictness of employment protection when it comes to such labor market outcomes (Francesconi and Garcia-Serrano 2004). On a similar note, Wright et al. (2019) argue that the recent trends in labor market outcomes, which include internationalization, the gig economy, nonstandard work, and employment related to online activities and the internet, have undermined the traditional institutions that historically have taken the role of protecting workers. The authors highlight that, in contemporary and future times, the role of unions in representing workers' rights might take a back seat, and they point at the importance for policymakers to come up with creative and innovative solutions that would fill such a role.

Lommerud and Straume (2007) find that the level of employment protection in a unionized firm shapes the union's willingness to welcome technological adoption that is seen as threatening labor as a production input. The authors show that by weakening employment protection *and* increasing the reservation wages in these firms, unions seem more likely to welcome labor-saving technological change. Freeman (2010) writes about the literature on institutions, like labor regulations and unions, on labor markets in the developing countries and concludes that, while unions and collective bargaining appear less important in developing countries compared to developed economies, they still have a clear effect on wage and nonwage outcomes.

Though the literature on the interaction between employment protection and unions agrees on the important roles that unions play, this chapter contributes to filling some obvious and relevant gaps. I use a setting where employment protection regulations sharply jump at a specific firm's size to provide evidence of how such *historical* discontinuity in employment protections interacts with union density to exacerbate or alleviate the effects of the protections on firm size distribution. Moreover, I exploit two policy changes to investigate how "sticky" the employment protection distortions are across industries with different unionization density. To my knowledge, this is the first work providing any kind of evidence on the duration and resilience of the interaction effects of labor unions and employment protections with firms' size outcomes, despite the enactment of two large reforms that weaken such restrictions.

Institutional Background and the Reforms

The evolution of employment protection regulation in Italy is punctuated by several smaller policy changes throughout the past decades, but I focus on three major changes: the "Statute of Workers Rights" (L. May 20, 1970, n. 300), the Fornero Reform (Decree 92/2012), and the Jobs Act (Decree 23/2015). The 1970 law introduced termination costs for firms in all cases of unfair termination, and, by doing that, it implicitly affected their hiring costs. Moreover, it made such costs depend on the size of firms, that is, their number of employees, hence introducing sharp differences across firms as defined by this variable.

Protection Laws Before the Reforms

In 1970, Italy implemented the "Statute of Workers Rights," a major employment protection law which mandated that firms with sixteen or more employees must have a "just cause" for termination. Without a plausible economic reason (e.g., plant closure, closure of a large part of the firm, or the impossibility of relocating a worker within the firm) or disciplinary reason (e.g., worker misbehavior), the judge would deem the termination unfair. By 1990, firms below that size threshold also needed a "just cause" to terminate an employee. However, the consequences of unfair termination depended on the firm's size, as defined by their number of workers. If the worker decided to sue the firm following the termination, and the court, based on the evidence provided by the firm, concluded that the termination was unfair, higher costs would be imposed on firms with at least sixteen employees. For these firms, the worker was entitled to pecuniary compensation corresponding to the wages she forwent during the trial, social security payments, legal expenses, and a choice between reinstatement at the firm or an additional 15 months' worth of salary. For firms with up to 15 employees, the employer could choose to not reinstate the worker in the firm, and the compensation to the worker was fixed between just 2.5 and 6 months of salary, regardless of the duration of the judicial case. Overall, for firms of size 16 and above, termination costs were higher, more uncertain, and varied based on the judge.

There is abundant academic, anecdotal, and news evidence showing that firms above the threshold did in fact experience tighter constraints in their termination decisions. Importantly, while the number of Italian firms with a workforce of more than fifteen employees is low compared to the number of firms beneath that threshold, the number of employees covered by the Statute of Workers' Rights was vast. In 2011, firms above fifteen employees comprised only 2.4 percent of the total number of firms in Italy, but they employed over 57 percent of all workers.[3] Several academic papers (Bratti, Conti, and Sulis 2021; Garibaldi and Violante 2005; Gianfreda and Vallanti 2017; Kugler and Pica 2008; Leonardi and Pica 2013; Schivardi and Torrini 2004b) and news articles (A. Ichino and Pinotti 2012) agree that larger firms were subject to higher and more uncertain termination costs. The uncertainty around the duration of labor trials further complicated things for firms because it directly fed into the pecuniary compensation owed to the worker in the form of foregone wages. Not only did the number of days until the verdict vary greatly, but it varied depending on the geographical areas in Italy (A. Ichino and Pinotti 2012; Gianfreda and Vallanti 2017), with *average* durations of these trials in the South reaching up to 1,500 days. One news report (Tucci 2012) suggests that the judge is a lot more likely to side with the worker, though this strongly varies by Italian macro-region: while in the Center-North the judge favors the firm in about 30 percent of the labor court trials on termination, the number drops to less than 10 percent in the South. Garibaldi and Violante (2005) calculate the ex-ante and ex-post costs of unfairly firing a blue-collar worker with average tenure for a firm above the threshold. Without assuming that the court sides with the worker, the costs are around eighteen months of wages. By contrast, the ex-post costs of terminating a worker, assuming the judge favors the worker, can amount to over 40 months of wages. Overall, the evidence included so far shows that the 1990 law on dismissal has historically been dramatically more vigorous in protecting long-term workers hired at firms with sixteen or more employees.

Background on the Reforms

In the summer of 2011, Italy experienced a sharp decline in its sovereign debt credibility, bringing the country to the verge of an economic crisis that severely affected the entire Eurozone. The concrete risk of a financial breakdown was accompanied by low growth rates and productivity that had characterized the Italian economy for more than two decades.

On November 16, 2011, in the midst of a severe financial crisis, the Minister of Labor, Social Policies, and Gender Equality, Elsa Fornero, in the technocratic government headed by Mario Monti, quickly and unexpectedly designed a large labor market reform that I henceforth call the Fornero Reform. The stated main goal of the reform was to improve the flexibility, dynamism, and productivity of the Italian labor market. In addition, Minister Fornero claimed that a reform was needed that would alleviate the deep labor market divide between the workers in long-term stable employment and those in temporary contracts. In fact, this split in the labor market was not "randomly assigned": Workers protected by the employment protection clauses were disproportionately older and males, while those in unstable job trajectories were more likely to be young and female. The reform aimed at boosting the dynamism of the Italian economy and breaking down the dualism between workers who were more protected (i.e., with long-term contracts) and those who were less protected (i.e., with temporary contracts). In order to achieve such objectives, Minister Fornero made the very controversial decision of loosening up the employment protection restrictions that were implemented by the Statute of Workers Rights in 1970. After the mandate of the technocratic government ended, a new government was elected with Matteo Renzi as Prime Minister. Renzi, in 2015, passed a new labor market reform with goals closely aligned with those of the Fornero Reform. The Jobs Act further weakened employment protection restrictions and reduced the uncertainty around termination costs for employers. The two reforms changed the rules on unfair terminations for disciplinary (subjective) and economic (objective) reasons, as well as on judicial procedures for labor court cases on dismissals that occurred in firms of size sixteen and above.

Next, I will summarize the details of the changes in employment protection restrictions that two reforms introduced.

The Fornero Reform and the Jobs Act

The Fornero Reform applies to all terminations of blue- and white-collar workers and middle-managers in open-ended contracts with firms of size sixteen and above. The changes were put into effect starting on July 18, 2012. The main change introduced by the reform lowers the power of judges to order the reinstatement of the worker within the firm in case they deem their termination unfair. For some types of termination, the reform substituted the option of reinstatement, which previously was always a possibility, with pecuniary compensation to the worker. As a result of the Fornero Reform, reinstatement remains an option only when:

- The disciplinary termination is unfair because the disputed misbehavior of the worker was non-existent.

- The worker did misbehave, but termination is an exaggerated punishment for such wrongful behavior.
- Fair economic reasons for termination, which are completely dependent on the firm, include plant closure, economic insolvency, restructuring of the firm or deep reorganization of it. Unfair termination for economic reasons occurs whenever the judge finds that no such economic issues ever materialized.
- Termination occurred due to the impairment, physical or psychological, of the worker.
- Termination happened during the time period that corresponds to the maximum number of days an employee is allowed to be absent from work due to sickness.

For all other cases, reinstatement was taken off the table, and the unlawful termination could only result in a pecuniary compensation which could range between 12 and 24 months of salary depending on the discretion of the judge, who, in the decision, was supposed to consider the seniority of the worker within the firm.

Given the scope of termination cases where reinstatement was still a potential outcome, and the range within which the pecuniary payments could fall, it is clear that while the Fornero Reform did weaken employment protections, the labor court judges still had strong power in deciding the costs firms would face following termination cases.

To partially alleviate this problem, the Fornero Reform introduced a change in the judicial procedure that lowered the power of judges and the reliance on labor courts in deciding termination cases. The reform introduced a mandatory preliminary conciliation process that workers wanting to sue their employers had to attempt first. While the workers and firms had to try and come up with a friendly agreement first, the reform did not provide the parties with objective guidelines that would have facilitated such a resolution.

The Jobs Act applies to terminations of blue-, white-collar workers or middle-managers, with open-ended contracts, *hired on or after* March 7, 2015, and it continued the dismantling of employment protections started by the Statute of Workers' Rights.

The Jobs Act reduced the discretion of the judges by basing the pecuniary compensation solely on the *seniority* of the workers through a precise formula. Therefore, the Jobs Act made termination costs less uncertain for firms.

Moreover, the Jobs Act eliminated the possibility of reinstatement in *all cases* of termination, with arguably the greatest change being the elimination of the reinstatement option for cases of unfair economic layoffs.

Furthermore, the Jobs Act introduced changes to the judicial procedures available in labor disputes that helped avoid court trials. While it keeps the mandatory conciliation started by the Fornero Reform, it also adds a second venue of conciliation that was voluntary. Importantly, however, as part of this voluntary conciliation the Jobs Act stipulated clear guidelines around the pecuniary compensation that the worker would receive from the firm if they agreed at this stage. A formula for this compensation, strictly determined by the worker's seniority, was published and made promptly available to the parties. This novel change in policy dramatically reduced the uncertainty of firms regarding termination costs.

The Reforms Reduced the Reliance on the Italian Labor Court System

The introduction of the conciliation procedures in cases of terminations appears to have been successful at decreasing the number of cases brought to court. P. Ichino (2022) shows that there was a significant drop in the number of cases in labor courts: between 2012, the year of the first reform, and 2021, courts experienced a 65 percent drop in cases of terminations due to economic reasons and an 80 percent drop in cases of terminations due to disciplinary reasons. This is an important sign that cases of terminations were relying less and less on the often slow, bureaucratic Italian court system, which represented an important determinant of the costs, expected or real, that firms had to face for terminating.

Aftermath of the Reforms: The Interest Groups and Their Reactions

While the Statute of Workers Rights has been on the political agenda for several years (La Repubblica 2012), any proposal to alter it has been blocked by interest groups, mostly political parties, and labor unions. According to public choice theory, outlined in the "Literature Review" section and considering the several findings from the relevant applied research described in that section, it is not surprising that labor unions, which collect fees from their members—the same workers whose employment was protected by the Statute of Workers Rights—would strongly lobby against reforms weakening such protections.

Unions collect rents from workers' membership, and their incentives are based on their membership numbers, which in turn depend on how many workers decide to sign up in a union. Hence, unions are intrinsically incentivized to protect workers. Similarly, it is not surprising that political parties, despite understanding the long-term advantages of the reforms, would be highly hesitant, and indeed would refuse, to enact these reforms given the major backlash that their numerous voters would express about such potential changes. As a reminder, workers protected by the Statute amounted to almost 60 percent of all Italian workers. Because democratic governments, like the Italian one, are interested in their re-election, throughout the years political parties on all sides were disincentivized from taking major employment benefits away from a large portion of their electorate.

The policy window for the Fornero Reform opened because it came from a technocratic government who was in charge of rescuing Italy from a severe financial crisis, and it was relatively unattached to politics. In fact, this government was not elected by the Italian voters nor closely associated with labor unions, rather it was composed of a group of specialized and technical staff appointed by the President of the Republic in a state of emergency. Consequently, this group of technocrats could not be re-elected as a political party, but it represented a temporary measure in an extremely unstable economic and political situation. It is easier for such technocratic governments to be vested with the responsibility of making very deep and unpopular structural changes to the Italian policy realm. Given the incentives of political parties, it is significantly less likely that politicians will undertake such unwanted—but economically necessary—drastic measures like lowering employment protections or sharply increasing retirement age. Renzi was then able to further dismantle the 1970s restrictions because by that point the "ice was broken" and the 1970's Statute was no longer considered untouchable.

These two reforms were not spared from heavy critique. Labor unions, among the main supporters of employment protection laws, were intensively pushing back on both policy changes. Against the Fornero Reform, the three main Italian Labor Unions called CGIL, CISL, and UIL[4] planned over six general strikes between December 2011 and November 2012 (Confederazione Generale Italiana del Lavoro, 2023). The representatives of the labor unions were attacking Minister Fornero and her reform because "the Statute of Workers' Rights says that a worker cannot be fired because he is obnoxious, has political opinions or is a union member. While it doesn't apply to everyone, it is a deterrent to discrimination. A democratic and civilized country cannot give it up." In March 2013, national strikes organized by several labor unions in Italy occurred across all regions and many industries, with a particular focus on the changes made regarding workers' reinstatement for economic reasons (La Repubblica 2012). Labor unions claimed termination laws were not a determinant of the labor market problems that the government was trying to solve (Noemi di Leonardo 2012). In July 2016, the CGIL started raising signatures to call for a referendum with the goal of reinstating the original version of the Statute of Workers' Rights (Il Fatto Quotidiano 2016).

Protests have been continuing for over ten years after the implementation of the Fornero Reform, with CGIL still calling for worker strikes in pushing for its abrogation (Il Manifesto 2022). However, despite the extremely high levels of debate and division these reforms brought for over a decade, the European Union swiftly showed solid support for the changes, which ended up playing a decisive role in their approval (Il Fatto Quotidiano 2012).

Data

For the analysis, I rely on Orbis data, a proprietary firm-level database that the Bureau van Dijk (BvD) provides for economic research. Orbis contains commercial company information on more than 400 million non-farm, mostly private companies in over 200 countries. The BvD gathers data from governments and national business registries in each country. The data are then cleaned and organized in order to facilitate cross-country comparison. The data are collected from the financial and balance sheet data for firms, based on the local reporting requirements.

In Italy, all firms must submit a company registration report at the Business Registry. Some companies must file more detailed accounts with the Registry at the end of each financial year. Small- and medium-sized companies as defined by number of employees and financial criteria are exempt from these standard filing requirements,[5] implying that information on financial performance may be limited for exempt firms.[6]

From the Orbis database, I have downloaded all firms with a workforce between two and eighty employees at any point between the last year of available financial information for each firm and up to nine *available* years of filing prior to that. I exclude public authorities, states, and governments because these are not subject to employment protection laws in Italy. I drop companies with missing information on the key variables I use here. Moreover, I keep firms with size information present in 2011, the pre-policies year, so that I can assign them to a treatment group in the baseline year. To improve the comparability between firms with up to 15 employees and those with more than sixteen workers, I only keep firms that had between 5 and 26 employees during that year.

My analytic dataset is composed of 1,141,301 observations for a varying number of firms over time. For example, in 2011, the pre-reform year, there are 150,541 firms in my sample. Table 6.1 provides details about the composition of my overall sample over time. The differences in the number of firms present in the dataset over the years can be explained by how the Italian data is collected and kept by the BvD. The data are not collected every year, but *every year of financial reporting* for each firm, for up to a maximum of nine years of financial reporting in the past. Hence, even if a firm has decades of financial reporting data available, in Orbis, I only have the last nine. While firms may skip their financial reporting in some years, Orbis provides year-to-year data for most firms, because most firms report their financial information every year. We observe fewer firms in

Table 6.1 Frequency of Italian Firms by Year in the Analytic Sample

Year	Frequency
2005	26
2006	89
2007	203
2008	778
2009	4,666
2010	10,105
2011	150,541
2012	148,773
2013	147,115
2014	145,245
2015	142,680
2016	140,469
2017	138,616
2018	135,586
2019	129,377
2020	119,944
2021	88
Total	1,414,301

Source: Table produced by author using Orbis data.

between 2005 and 2009 because only few firms skipped reporting for enough years to oblige Orbis to use these older records in compiling the nine most recent years of financial reporting. In 2010, we have a small jump in the number of firms because, presumably, these firms have delayed their reporting in 2020, hence 2010 is the ninth year of their most recent financial reporting. Finally, in 2021, we only have eighty-eight firms because, at the time I downloaded the data (spring of 2022), only these eighty-eight firms had reported their financial data for 2021.

While in Table 6.1 I show the entire time composition of the dataset, the empirical analysis in this chapter uses data from 2011 and 2019 and compares information on firm sizes between these two years.

Details on this dataset's characteristics are discussed in Montenovo (2022). Limitations of the Orbis dataset are thoroughly discussed in Ribeiro, Menghinello, De backer (2010), Bajgar et al. (2020), and Kalemli et al. (2022). In this work, I adopt some measures identified in the literature to address such limitations, which broadly regard the sample's heterogeneous coverage, both within and across countries, raising concerns about its ability to represent the entire distribution of Italian firms over time.

Because here I focus on differences in firms' size distortion by unionization density, I need to merge this variable on to the firm-level dataset. The unionization variable is provided, only for the year 2012, by the National Statistics Bureau, as a rate, and more precisely as the number of workers registered in a union divided by the total number of workers in a particular sector or location in 2012. In the National Statistics Bureau report, this information is shown in three different tables. One table shows the average unionization density by industry for seventeen industries, another one by Italian macro-region—specifically for five macro-regions in Italy—and lastly by firms' size classification—that is, for firms of size 10 to 49, 50 to 200, 201 to 500, and over 500. To get the unionization rate as precise as possible for each firm, I consider the average unionization density across the three tables, so that the unionization variable in this paper is computed by economic sector, geographical area, and size of the firm. I obtained a value for unionization density that I merge on to each firm in the Orbis dataset based on their industry, macro-region, and size class. This will be the unionization density value for the firm in question.

In addition to the firm IDs, the variables I use in the analysis are the number of employees and unionization density. Sample statistics for the variable "Number of Employees" are measured in the pre-reform year 2011, and unionization is

Table 6.2 Summary Statistics for Size and Unionization in 2011, the Baseline Year

	Obs.	Mean	SD	Min	Max
Number Employees in 2011	127,761	11.5	4.9	6	25
Unionization Rate	127,761	28.9	3.7	18.8	55.5

Source: Table produced by author using Orbis and ISTAT data.

measured in 2012, the only year for which such information is available. The count, mean, standard deviation, minimum, and maximum of the variables can be found in Table 6.2.

Methods and Computation of Statistical Significance

In the empirical analysis, I exploit the design of these laws in Italy which make employment protections stricter for firms with sixteen or more employees. The idea is that I will observe how the outcome of interest, namely size, varies at that threshold, and how such variation differs among firms in low-unionization density quartiles and those in high-unionization density quartiles. By observing differences in the response of firms based on their size class, region, and industry with varying unionization densities, to the sudden increase in termination costs when it comes to their decision on size, I can draw conclusions on how unionization density mediates the impact that employment protection has on firm size. In other words, by looking at how firms react to the sudden increase in terminations costs through the shape of their size distribution, I observe the extent to which firms are trying to avoid higher terminations costs, and I find how much employment protections distort the behavior of firms.

Moreover, by making time comparisons between years pre and post reform, I observe whether and how unionization density shapes the impact of policy changes that decrease termination costs for firms above a certain size threshold.

The distribution of firms based on their number of employees is useful because it allows me to evaluate whether firms have an incentive to remain undersized and stay below the threshold of sixteen to avoid the higher termination costs that trigger if they pass that threshold. Evidence that firms accumulate beneath the threshold would signal the strategic behavior of firms to avoid hiring and expanding in size if that meant facing higher employment restrictions on their entire workforce. This would constitute a size distortion caused by the design of employment protections, because firms may stay below their optimal size, and not make profitable hires that they would have otherwise made. If such distortion varies between firms of low and high unionization density, then I can conclude that unions play a significant role in exacerbating such unwanted effects of termination costs on firms.

To precisely understand the magnitude of the distortion caused by employment protections, I would ideally compare the observed firm size distribution from the data on Italian firms that are subject to the employment protection laws, to the size distribution of Italian firms in the absence of any protections. The difficulty is that no such counterfactual data exists because the counterfactual has not been a reality in modern Italy. Hence, I use the statistical techniques described next to come up with the best approximation of the counterfactual firm size distributions.

I construct a series of graphs that show the frequency distribution of firms by collapsing, in averages, the number of firms based on the size of their workforce. To enhance the comparability of firms below and above the threshold of sixteen and to address some of the limitations of the Orbis data, I focus on firms of size five to twenty-five. To obtain the *actual* firm size distribution in the presence of employment protections, I compute the average number of Italian firms that have a workforce of five employees, six employees, and so on, until twenty-five employees, divided by the total number of employees. To build the *counterfactual* firm size distribution that we would have observed in the absence of such laws, I use a polynomial prediction by running a regression. In particular, I use a seventh-degree polynomial to estimate the number of firms in each size bin, that is, the number of firms with number of employees from six to twenty-five. Although a higher degree polynomial fits the data better, it may lead to overfitting of the data and to the risk of poor generalization of the inferences over the entire dataset. However, because I am focusing on a smaller part of the firm size distribution (five to twenty-five employees), these concerns are alleviated. For this estimation, the polynomial exploits the count of firms in each size bin *excluding* size thirteen to eighteen, hence it *predicts* the log number of firms of size thirteen, fourteen, fifteen, sixteen, seventeen, and eighteen *using* the actual data on the number of firms of size six to twelve and nineteen to twenty-five. Essentially, I use information on the part of the distribution considered "reliable"—which, being far enough from the threshold, is broadly unaffected by the sharp increase in termination costs—to predict the shape of the distribution that—

being close to the threshold—*is* affected by the cost discontinuity. With this, I can consider the predicted distribution from thirteen through eighteen to be a good approximation of a world where there were there no protections. The reason why I exclude firms of size thirteen to eighteen from the regression and then predict the number of firms in that size range, is that this is range around the size threshold at which termination costs jump, implying that it is the bandwidth where I can expect to have the potential size distortion. In fact, firms further away from that cutoff experience a lower incentive to strategically avoid the jump in termination costs. Those that are smaller than thirteen can still expand by two or three workers without undergoing any changes in costs. Those that are larger than nineteen would need to terminate quite a few workers before they can benefit from smaller termination costs. As a consequence, firms of size thirteen to eighteen are those that have the highest incentive to make strategic hiring and termination decisions as a result of this employment protection design. Hence, the polynomial allows me to use information on the firms least constrained by the employment protection design to predict what the distribution of firms over the entire interval, including the bandwidth around sixteen workers, would look like if *all* firms were less constrained. Differences between the actual distribution of firms and the predicted one likely represent a size distortion, which suggests that firms may engage in strategic behaviors to avoid the higher costs and potentially signals economic inefficiencies.

Because it is expected that we will have *some* deviation between the observed and predicted distributions and I need to figure out whether such deviation is "abnormal," I estimate the statistical significance of deviations. To do that, I first calculate the area of each deviation as a proportion of the total number of firms that each year compose such discrepancy on the left- and right-end sides of the threshold, separately. Then, I compute the standard errors of these areas by using the bootstrapping method of Chetty et al. (2011), which I replicate by randomly sampling the residuals between the observed and predicted counts obtained from running the seventh polynomial regression 1,000 times, with replacement, and re-estimating the binned counts each time. The standard deviation of these counts is the standard error of the distortion I am trying to compute. I perform this estimation strategy for each time I measure the distortion—2011 and 2019—and for low- and high-density unionization industries. This allows me to know the statistical significance of the gaps between the observed and predicted distributions.

Graphical Results

In this section, I show evidence of the response of firms to employment protections legislation by the unionization density of the industry they belong to. Figure 6.1 shows the size distribution of firms of size six to twenty-five in the bottom quintile of unionization density in 2011, the pre-reforms period. Each dot corresponds to the logged total number of firms of that size in 2011. The dashed line is the counterfactual distribution, and it shows us what the size distribution in Italy would have looked like in the absence of the employment protection regulation.

I reproduce this graph for two different sets of information: firms in low-density unionization industries in 2011 (Figure 6.1), firms in high-density unionization industries in 2011 (Figure 6.2), firms in low-density unionization in 2019 (Figure 6.3), and firms in high-density unionization industries in 2019 (Figure 6.4). These allow me to compare how the size distortion varies between firms in high- and low-unionization industries and to check how these potential differences vary between the pre-reform and the post-reform period.

In Figure 6.1, there is no obvious positive gap between the dots and the dashed lines for firms of size thirteen, fourteen, and fifteen, implying that firms in low-unionization industries do not appear to accumulate beneath the threshold to avoid potentially profitable hiring. This is evidence that economic inefficiencies, consisting of firms keeping a suboptimal workforce size to avoid facing hiring

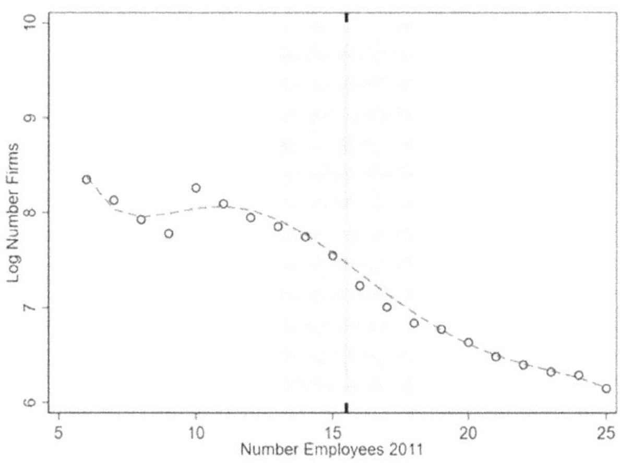

Figure 6.1 Size distribution of firms at the bottom 20 percent for unionization density in 2011. Figure produced by author using Orbis data.

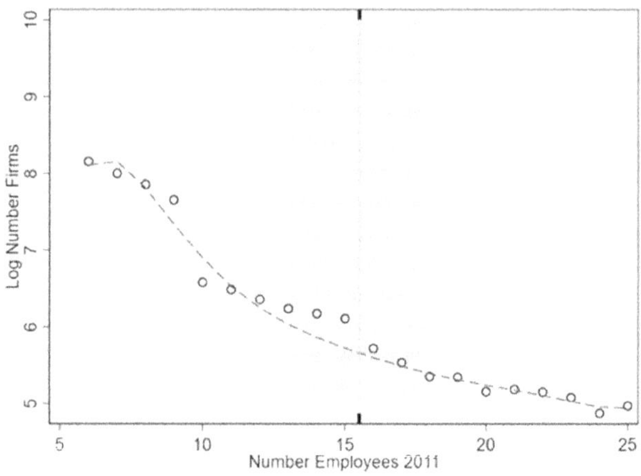

Figure 6.2 Size distribution of firms at the top 20 percent for unionization density in 2011. Figure produced by author using Orbis data.

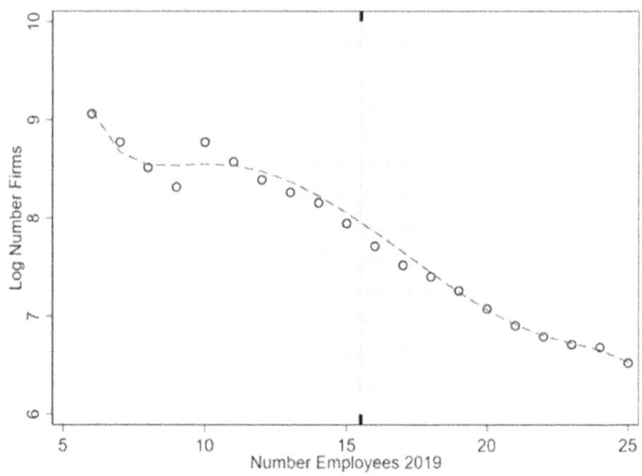

Figure 6.3 Size distribution of firms at the bottom 20 percent for unionization density in 2019. Figure produced by author using Orbis data.

termination costs, may be reduced to a minimum in firms where only a few workers are union members.

By contrast, Figure 6.2, representing firms in high-density unionization industries, shows a stark positive gap between the actual number of firms with thirteen, fourteen, and fifteen workers and the number of firms with thirteen, fourteen, and fifteen workers predicted by the counterfactual. In particular, the discrepancy appears large between the dots and the dashed line on the right-

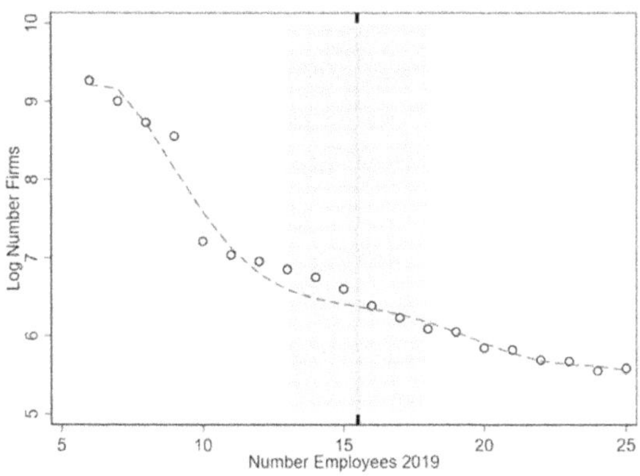

Figure 6.4 Size distribution of firms at the top 20 percent for unionization density in 2019. Figure produced by author using Orbis data.

hand side, close to the threshold, such that in 2011, there are many more firms of size thirteen, fourteen, and fifteen than would be predicted by a regression that ignores the jump in employment protection restrictions. This is explained by the fact that firms accumulate beneath the threshold, where termination costs are lower, and they avoid expanding above it since termination costs would sharply increase. Hence, we observe evidence of strategic behavior of firms in high-unionization industries regarding employment protection restrictions.

The fact that we do not observe a positive size distortion in Figure 6.1, but there is clear evidence of such distortion in Figure 6.2, speaks to the important role that unionization plays in imposing effective constraints on firms when it comes to employment protection regulations or, conversely, that stricter employment protections are more likely to generate an environment characterized by stronger unions. Unions might play a crucial role in helping to pass the laws, enforcing employment protection restrictions in the post-termination phase during the labor court trial, or advising the unemployed worker in this process. Firms learn about these ongoing mechanisms in their own industries, and they react to them by adjusting their hiring and termination behavior.

In cases where firms do not feel threatened by the presence of dense unionization, they are less likely to stay in the part of the size distribution where termination costs are cheaper. In fact, firms in low-unionization density do not engage in any strategic behavior to avoid higher termination costs. This may imply that these firms are aware that such costs are less likely to be enforced on them should they terminate a worker's employment and be sued by them.

By contrast, firms in high-unionization industries show clear patterns of accumulation beneath the threshold, implying that they are avoiding the higher termination costs that likely will be imposed on them in case of termination, given that they are in an industry where unions are well-established and powerful.

Figures 6.3 and 6.4 show the corresponding data exhibited in Figures 6.1 and 6.2, but this time for the year 2019. The objective is to observe how and whether the evidence on the size distortion evolves over the period of the reforms, as the policies have decreased the difference in termination costs between firms with at least sixteen employees and those smaller than that. Because the size distortion was not present in the distribution of firms belonging to low-unionization density industries in 2011, the reforms should, if anything, just leave the graph broadly unchanged, with no positive gap between the dashed lines and scatterplots in 2019. The more interesting question is whether the size discrepancy that emerges in 2011 among firms in high-unionization density industries changes by 2019. Overall, comparing Figures 6.2 and 6.4, it appears that the gap between the dots and the dashed line corresponding to the left-hand side of the bandwidth, that is, for firms with thirteen, fourteen, and fifteen employees, still exists, though only slightly flatter compared to the discrepancy in Figure 6.4. Overall, the reforms appear to have broadly been ineffective at reducing the size distortion among firms in highly unionized industries, though perhaps they represented important steps in the right direction. As a result, unions appear to be such powerful and well-established institutions that they keep shaping the strategic behavior of firms in the industries where they operate and constraining them from reaching their optimal size. However, the analysis of the statistical significance of these discrepancies and their changes over time will help draw more robust conclusions. I turn to that next.

Results on the Statistical Significance of the Discrepancies

On Table 6.3, I report the magnitudes of the discrepancies between the observed distribution and the counterfactual distribution for the first year (2011) and last year (2019) of the data, and separately for firms in the bottom 20 percent and top 20 percent of unionization density. Whenever this discrepancy is positive, it is called excess mass, and whenever it is negative, it is called missing mass. In the graphs, these discrepancies (i.e., excess or missing masses) are the areas

Table 6.3 Estimates of the Gaps between the Actual and Observed Firm Size Distribution as a Proportion of Total Firms and Corresponding Bootstrapped Standard Errors

			Union Density	
			Low Quantile	**High Quantile**
Gap between observed and counterfactual firm distribution	Below threshold	2011	−0.0449***	0.0395**
			(0.007)	(0.043)
		2019	−0.045***	0.0301*
			(0.007)	(0.069)
	Above threshold	2011	-0.039**	0.034*
			(0.018)	(0.068)
		2019	−0.0384**	0.0267
			(0.014)	(0.104)

Source: Table produced by author using Orbis data.
Notes: The top number represents the excess mass, whenever positive, or the missing mass, whenever negative. This number measures the area between the observed and counterfactual distribution computed as the proportion of extra or missing firms causing such discrepancy out of the total number of firms in the year. The standard errors are the bottom numbers, in parentheses. * if p-value is ≤ 0.10, ** if p-value is ≤ 0.05, *** if p-value is ≤ 0.01.

computed as the proportion of firms out of the total number of firms that are in "excess" or "missing" in each year, and unionization density quantiles, separately. Whether they are in "excess" or "missing" is based on the comparison between the observed and counterfactual distributions. These numbers are on the top line of Table 6.3, while the line below, with the numbers in brackets, contains the standard errors computed using the bootstrapping procedure, corresponding to each excess or missing mass above.

Table 6.3 shows that firms at the bottom 20 percent of unionization density display a negative discrepancy around the threshold: that is, the size distribution of firms shows four to 4.5 percent fewer firms below the employment protection threshold than would be expected, given the counterfactual. More precisely, there were about 4.5 percent fewer firms of size thirteen, fourteen, and fifteen, those on the close left-hand side of the threshold, both in 2011 and in 2019 than predicted by the counterfactual that assumes the lack of employment protections. Similarly, there were about 3.9 percent fewer firms of size sixteen, seventeen, and eighteen, those on the close right-hand side of the threshold, than expected. These missing masses are statistically significant at least at the 95 percent confidence level, and they remain broadly unchanged between 2011 and 2019. Missing mass in this context could be explained by firms in low-density unionization industries potentially preferring larger sizes because they may be aware of the low likelihood that stricter employment protections would apply to them if they wanted to shrink in the future, given the low density of unionization. Given how these missing masses are computed, a higher share of firms in the far left end of the size distribution would suggest a higher share on the bandwidth around the threshold, and when comparing this higher share with the observed frequency, a missing mass arises. Moreover, the fact that these missing masses remain mostly identical between 2011 and 2019—the post-reforms year—highlights that low-density unionization industries are broadly unaffected by changes in employment protections.

Firms in high-unionization industries display a statistically significant excess mass below the threshold, confirming the claim that these firms were strategically staying beneath the threshold to avoid the higher termination costs they would face if they went above it. Specifically, in 2011, there were about 4 percent more firms of size thirteen, fourteen, and fifteen than predicted by the counterfactual distribution, with this estimate being statistically significant at the 95 percent level. In 2019, after both reforms were implemented, the excess mass remains, but it is lower and estimated less precisely. In 2019, there were about 3 percent more firms of size thirteen, fourteen, and fifteen than expected. Hence, excess mass on the left-hand side of the legislation threshold (i.e., sixteen employees) among firms in the top 20 percent of union density has decreased by 1 percentage point over the period of the reforms. However, because the 95 percent confidence intervals of the excess masses in 2011 and 2019 overlap, I can conclude that the drop in excess mass following the reforms was not statistically significant.

Importantly, while I can draw conclusions about the statistical significance of the excess and missing masses, I cannot point to any direction of causality between union density and the size distortion because higher unionization rates will strengthen the employment protections, and industries that are more likely to be subject to stricter protections will advocate for stronger unions so as to be better represented when they become actively concerned with such protections. Even though I cannot define the direction of the causality between union density and the stringency of the employment protections generating the distortions, the contribution of this chapter, which consists of evidence of how union density mediates the relationship between employment protection and the size distortions, and how that relationship changes differentially across high- and low-density unionized industries, remains valuable.

Conclusions

In this chapter, I evaluate how labor unions shape the relationship between employment protection laws and the outcomes of firms. Not only will labor unions affect the process of the design and enactment of these laws, they may impact their enforcement as well. I use a particular setting that allows me to produce new and important evidence for this claim. In Italy, employment protection laws have been historically more rigid among firms with sixteen or more employees. This employment protection legislation design introduces incentives for firms to remain below that threshold size, and perhaps to keep unproductive or low-quality employment matches due to the high costs of terminating them. In 2012 and 2015, two reforms were implemented that had the goal of improving the dynamism and productivity of the Italian labor market and economy. I first show evidence that the historical regulations imposing much stricter rules on firms above the threshold size did introduce a size distortion, that is, an accumulation of firms beneath the threshold, specifically among firms in highly unionized industries. Hence, firms in industries characterized by dense unionization are more constrained by the restrictions. On the other hand, firms in low unionization industries experience no such constraints. The most plausible explanation for this is that unions play a role in the aftermath of a termination. Because the employment protection laws are, on paper, the same across industries, such results are unlikely to come from differences in lobbying efforts in the pre-enactment phase of lawmaking. They probably arise from the efforts of labor unions in the aftermath of the termination when the worker looks for legal support as they consider suing their former employer and starting a labor court trial against them. The other important piece of evidence that this chapter contributes involves the durability of the influence of institutions. As the reforms were implemented, the size discrepancy noticeable among firms in high unionization industries in 2011 remains in 2019, although it marginally decreases and loses some statistical significance. The results on the resistance of unions to large structural reforms changing terminations costs highlight how these well-established institutions are able to, in some ways and at least initially, remain a powerful ally of workers who are union members. In fact, the reforms were successful at changing several productivity and size outcomes of firms, on average (Montenovo 2022), and this work shows important heterogeneity of some of those results, based on union density. Moreover, the evidence here might imply that, for unionization density to play a significantly less influential role, we might need to wait longer.

Notes

1 Montenovo (2022) offers a theoretical model deriving such implications.
2 Hence, these laws forbid regulations that provide employees with the freedom to choose to join a union or not.
3 This information is provided by the Association of Artisans and Small Businesses Mestre C.G.I.A.
4 CGIL stands for the Italian General Confederation of Labor, CISL stands for Italian Confederation of Labor Unions, and UIL stands for Italian Labor Union.
5 The criteria on the size of firms and their accounting requirements are defined by Article 2435-bis of the Italian Civil Code and listed here: https://www.pwc.com/it/en/publications/assets/docs/new-financial-statements.pdf
6 These details on the source and quality of the data were provided to me via email correspondence with a representative of Moody's Analytics, which owns BvD, in the Spring of 2022.

References

Abraham, Katharine G., and Melissa S. Kearney. 2020. "Explaining the Decline in the US Employment-to-Population Ratio: A Review of the Evidence." *Journal of Economic Literature* 58 (3): 585–643.

Addison, John T., and Claus Schnabel, eds. 2003. *International Handbook of Trade Unions*. Cheltenham, UK: Edward Elgar.

Almeida, Rita, and Pedro Carneiro. 2009. "Enforcement of Labor Regulation and Firm Size." *Journal of Comparative Economics* 37 (1): 28–46.

Autor, David H., Kerr, William R., and Adriana D. Kugler. 2007. "Does Employment Protection Reduce Productivity? Evidence from US States." *The Economic Journal* 117 (521): F189–F217.

Azam, Jean-Paul, and Claire Salmon. 2003. "Strikes and Political Activism of Trade Unions: Theory and Application to Bangladesh." *Public Choice* 119: 311–334.

Bajgar, Matej, Giuseppe Berlingieri, Sara Calligaris, Chiara Criscuolo, and Jonathan Timmis. 2020. "Coverage and Representativeness of Orbis Data." OECD Science, Technology and Industry Working Papers No. 2020/06.

Bastiat, Frédéric. 1883. "Popular Fallacies Regarding Trade and Foreign Duties: Being the Sophismes Economiques." Adopted to the Present Times by Cassell, Petter, Galpin & Co.: London, Paris & New York.

Berglund, Tomas, and Bengt Furåker. 2016. "Employment Protection Regulation, Trade Unions, and Tenure of Employment: An Analysis in 23 European Countries." *Industrial Relations Journal* 45 (5–6): 492–512.

Bertola, Giuseppe, Francine D. Blau, and Lawrence M. Kahn. 2007. "Labor Market Institutions and Demographic Employment Patterns." *Journal of Population Economics* 20 (4): 833–867.

Berton, Fabio, Devicienti, Francesco, and Sara Grubanov-Boskovic. 2017. "Employment Protection Legislation and Mismatch: Evidence from a Reform." *SSRN Scholarly Paper ID 3029774*, Social Science Research Network, Rochester, NY. https://papers.ssrn.com/sol3/papers.cfm?abstract_id=3029774.

Boeri, Tito, and Juan F. Jimeno. 2003. "The Effects of Employment Protection: Learning from Variable Enforcement." *European Economic Review* 49 (8): 2057–2077.

Boeri, Tito, Nicoletti, Giuseppe, and Stefano Scarpetta. 1999. "Regulation and Labour Market Performance" IGIER Working Paper, 158.

Bornhäll, Anders, Daunfeldt, Sven-Olov, and Niklas Rudholm. 2017. "Employment Protection Legislation and Firm Growth: Evidence from a Natural Experiment." *Industrial and Corporate Change* 26 (1): 169–185.

Bratti, Massimiliano, Maurizio Conti, and Giovanni Sulis. 2021. "Employment Protection and Firm-Provided Training in Dual Labour Markets." *Labour Economics* 69: 101972.

Buchanan, M. James, and Gordon Tullock. 1962. *The Calculus of Consent: Logical Foundations for Constitutional Democracy*. Michigan: The University of Michigan Press.

Buchanan, M. James. 1991. "The Minimal Politics of Market Order." *Cato Journal* 11 (2): 215–232.

Card, David, Lemieux, Thomas, and Craig W. Riddell. 2004. "Unions and Wage Inequality." *Journal of Labor Research* 25: 519–559.

Ceron, Andrea, Luigi Curini, and Fedra Negri. 2019. "Intra-Party Politics and Interest Groups: Missing Links in Explaining Government Effectiveness." *Public Choice* 180: 407–427.

Chetty, Raj, N. John Friedman, Tore Olsen, and Luigi Pistaferri. 2011. "Adjustment Costs, Firm Responses, and Micro vs. Macro Labor Supply Elasticities: Evidence from Danish Tax Records." *The Quarterly Journal of Economics* 126 (2): 749–804.

Confederazione Generale Italiana del Lavoro. 2023. "Ecco Dove Era la CGIL." Last modified April 17, 2023. https://www.cgil.it/campagne-e-iniziative/ecco-dove-era-la-cgil-s6tkl45u.

Damiani, Mirella, Pompei, Fabrizio, and Andrea Ricci. 2020. "Labour Shares, Employment Protection and Unions in European Economies." *Socio-Economic Review* 18 (4): 1001–1038.

di Leonardo, Noemi. 2012. "Presidio CFIL per riforma del lavoro. Gruppi: «Fornero come i templari»" *Bologna Today.*

DiNardo, John, and David S. Lee. 2004. "Economic Impacts of New Unionization on Private Sector Employers: 1984–2001." *The Quarterly Journal of Economics* 119 (4): 1383–1441.

Djankov, Simeon, La Porta Rafael, Lopez-de-Silanes Florencio, and Andrei Shleifer. 2002. "The Regulation of Entry." *The Quarterly Journal of Economics* 117 (1): 1–37.

Doucouliagos, Christos, and Patrice Laroche. 2003. "What Do Unions Do to Productivity? A Meta-Analysis." *Industrial Relations* 42 (4): 650–691.

Francesconi, Marco, and Carlos Garcia-Serrano. 2004. "Unions and Flexible Employment in Britain and Spain: A Descriptive Note." *Industrial Relations: A Journal of Economy and Society* 43 (4): 874–882.

Freeman, B. Richard. 2010. "Chapter 70 – Labor Regulations, Unions, and Social Protection in Developing Countries: Market Distortions or Efficient Institutions?" *Handbook of Development Economics* (5): 4657–4702.

Garibaldi, Pietro, and Giovanni L. Violante. 2005. "The Employment Effects of Several Payments with Wage Rigidities." *The Economic Journal* 506: 799–832.

Garibaldi, Puetri, Pacelli, Lia, and Andrea Borgarello. 2004. "Employment Protection Legislation and the Size of Firms." *SSRN Electronic Journal, IGIER Working Paper* 247. https://papers.ssrn.com/sol3/papers.cfm?abstract_id=472762.

Garicano, Luis, Lelarge, Claire, and John Van Reenen. 2016. "Firm Size Distortions and the Productivity Distribution: Evidence from France." *American Economic Review* 106 (11): 3439–3479.

Gianfreda, Giuseppina, and Giovanna Vallanti. 2017. "Institutions' and Firms' Adjustments: Measuring the Impact of Courts' Delays on Job Flows and Productivity." *The Journal of Law and Economics* 60 (1): 135–172.

Gimpelson, Vladimir, Kapelyushnikov, Rostislav, and Anna Lukyanova. 2010. "Employment Protection Legislation in Russia: Regional Enforcement and Labor Market Outcomes." *Comparative Economic Studies* 52 (4): 611–636.

Güell, Maia. 2010. "Firing Costs, Dismissal Conflicts and Labour Market Outcomes." *Els Opuscles del CREI* 26.

Hicks, Michael, and Michael LaFaive. 2013. "Economic Growth and Right-to-Work Laws." *Mackinac Center for Public Policy.*

Hijzen, Alexander, Mondauto, Leopoldo, and Stefano Scarpetta. 2017. "The Impact of Employment Protection on Temporary Employment." *Labour Economics* 46: 64–76.

Hirsch, T. Barry. 2012. "Chapter 4: Unions, Dynamism, and Economic Performance." In *Research Handbook on the Economics of Labor and Employment Law*, edited by Cynthia L. Estlund and Michael L. Wachter, 107–145. UK: Edward Elgar Publishing.

Hübler, Olaf, and Uwe Jirjahn. 2003. "Work Councils and Collective Bargaining in Germany: The Impact on Productivity and Wages." *Scottish Journal of Political Economy* 50 (4): 471–491.

Ichino, Andrea, and Paolo Pinotti. 2012. "La roulette russa dell'articolo 18." *Lavoce .info.*

Ichino, Pietro. 2022. "Cosa significal la riduzione delle cause del lavoro." *Lavoce.info.*

Il Fatto Quotidiano. 2012. "Articolo 18, la Cgil proclama 8 ore di sciopero. Bersani «Non puo' essere prendere o lasciare»"

Il Fatto Quotidiano. 2016. "Jobs act, Cgil deposita 3,3 milioni di firme per referendum abrogativi: Ripristinare articolo 18 e cancellare i voucher."

Il Manifesto. 2022. "Cgil, oggi in Piazza del Popolo a Roma per rilanciare la questione sociale."

Kalemli-Ozcan, Şebnem, Sørensen, Bent, Villegas-Sanchez, Carolina, Volosovych, Vadym, and Sevcan Yeşiltaş. 2022. "How to Construct Nationally Representative Firm Level Data from the Orbis Global Database: New Facts and Aggregate Implications." NBER Working Paper #21558.

Kleiner M. Morris, and Robert T. Kudrle. 2000. "Does Regulation Affect Economic Outcomes? The Case of Dentistry." *The Journal of Law and Economics* 43(2): 547–582. https://doi-org.proxyiub.uits.iu.edu/10.1086/467465.

Koeniger, Winfried, Leonardi, Marco, and Luca Nunziata. 2007. "Labor Market Institutions and Wage Inequality." *Industrial and Labor Relations Review* 60 (3): 340–356.

Kogan, Vladimir. 2017. "Do Anti-Union Policies Increase Inequality? Evidence from State Adoption of Right-to-Work Laws." *State Politics & Policy Quarterly* 17 (2): 180–200.

Konings, Jozef and Stijn Vanormelingen. 2015. "The Impact of Training on Productivity and Wages: Firm-Level Evidence." *The Review of Economics and Statistics* 97 (2): 485–497.

Kugler, Adriana, and Giovanni Pica. 2008. "Effects of Employment Protection on Worker and Job Flows: Evidence from the 1990 Italian Reform." *Labour Economics* 15 (1): 78–95.

La Repubblica. 2012. "Art. 18, lavoratori in sciopero da Nord a Sud. E dieci anni fa la Cgil invase la Capitale."

Larkin, J. Paul. 2016. "Public Choice Theory and Occupational Licensing." *Harvard Journal of Law & Public Policy* 39 (1): 209–332.

Leonardi, Marco, and Giovanni Pica. 2013. "Who Pays for It? The Heterogeneous Wage Effects of Employment Legislation." *The Economic Journal* 123 (573): 1236–1278.

Lommerud, Kjell Erik, and Odd R. Straume. 2007. "Technology Resistance and Globalization with Trade Unions: The Choice between Employment Protection and Flexicurity." Universidade do Minho. Núcleo de Investigação em Políticas Económicas NIPE Working Paper Series 25.

Martin, John P., and Stefano Scarpetta. 2012. "Setting It Right: Employment Protection, Labour Reallocation and Productivity." *De Economist* 160 (2): 89–116.

Meehan, Brian, and Bruce L. Benson. 2015. "The Occupations of Regulators Influence Occupational Regulation: Evidence from the US Private Security Industry." *Public Choice* 162: 97–117.

Micco, Alejandro and Carmen, Pagés. 2007. "The Economic Effects of Employment Protection: Evidence from International Industry-Level Data." *Inter-American Development Bank Working Papers* #592.

Mitchell, J. Daniel. 2016. "Another Lesson from Bastiat: So-Called Employment Protection Legislation Is Bad News for Workers." Cato Institute. https://policycommons.net/artifacts/1325226/another-lesson-from-bastiat/1928516/.

Montenovo, Laura. 2022. "Employment Protection, Dynamism, and Productivity." Working Paper. www.lauramontenovo.com/research.

Montgomery, Edward. 1989. "Employment and Unemployment Effects of Unions." *Journal of Labor Economics* 7 (2): 170–190.

Morantz, Alison D. 2017. "What Unions do for Regulations." *Annual Review of Law and Social Science* 13 (1): 515–534.

Noelke, Clemens. 2016. "Employment Protection Legislation and the Youth Labour Market." *European Sociological Review* 32 (4): 471–485.

Olney, W. William. 2013. "A Race to the Bottom? Employment Protection and Foreign Direct Investment." *Journal of International Economics* 91: 191–203.

Ribeiro, Samuel Pinto, Menghinello, Stefano, and Koen De Backer. 2010. "The OECD ORBIS Database: Responding to the Need for Firm-Level Micro-Data in the OECD." OECD Statistics Working Papers No. 2010/01.

Schivardi, Fabiano, and Roberto Torrini. 2004a. "Firm Size Distribution and Employment Protection Legislation in Italy." Economic Working Papers, Economic Research and International Relations Area, Bank of Italy 504: 7–48.

Schivardi, Fabiano, and Roberto Torrini. 2004b. "Threshold Effects and Firm Size: the Case of Firing Costs" (Meeting Papers). 445: 1–48. Society for Economic Dynamics.

Sestito, Paolo and Eliana Viviano. 2016. "Hiring Incentives and/or Firing Cost Reduction? Evaluating the Impact of the 2015 Policies on the Italian Labour Market." *Banca d'Italia, Questioni di Economia e Finanza* 325.

Tucci, Claudio. 2012. "Al Sud il licenziamento e' sempre illegittimo." *Il Sole 24 Ore.*

Tullock, Gordon. 1967. "The Welfare Costs of Tariffs, Monopolies, and Theft." *Economic Inquiry* 5 (3): 224–232.

Vedder, Richard, and Lowell Gallaway. 2002. "The Economic Effects of Labor Unions Revisited." *Journal of Labor Research*, 23: 105–130. https://doi.org/10.1007/s12122-002-1021-7.

Vedder, Richard. 2010. "Right-to-Work Laws: Liberty, Prosperity, and Quality of Life." *Cato Journal* 30 (1): 171–180.

Weil, David. 1992. "Building Safety: The Role of Construction Unions in the Enforcement of OSHA." *Journal of Labor Research* 13: 121–132.

Weil, David. 1999. "Are Mandated Health and Safety Committees Substitutes for or Supplements to Labor Unions?" *ILR Review* 52 (3): 339–360.

Wright, Chris F., Alex J Wood, Jonathan Trevor, Colm McLaughlin, Wei Huang, Brian Harney, Torsten Geelan, Barry Colfer, Cheng Chang, and William Brown. 2019. "Towards a New Web of Rules: An International Review of Institutional Experimentation to Strengthen Employment Protections." *Employee Relations: The International Journal* 41 (2): 313–330.

7

Changing Antitrust Law

Cory Jack

In 2017, when Lina M. Khan was just a law student, she penned the now infamous article, "Amazon's Antitrust Paradox," a comprehensive critique of Amazon's seemingly untouchable status in antitrust enforcement (Khan, 2017). Fast forward to September 26, 2023, and Khan, now Chair of the Federal Trade Commission (FTC), has taken a *bold* step: spearheading a lawsuit against Amazon over its alleged anti-competitive practices (*FTC v. Amazon.com, Inc.*, 2024 U.S. Dist. LEXIS 120300). Notably, this decision comes on the heels of a series of losses the FTC suffered in similar antitrust cases.

In the antitrust space, Chair Khan presents herself as a champion of consumer welfare and competition. However, a deeper dive through the lens of public choice theory presents a more nuanced picture. It suggests that her decisions might be influenced by factors beyond pure public interest.

In this chapter, I look at how the goals of the FTC have changed when it comes to ensuring companies compete fairly, especially under the leadership of Chair Khan. I discuss the rules and structures that the FTC uses and examine how its past has played a role in these changes. I also explore how these changes might affect both competition and everyday consumers. By using public choice theory, I attempt to understand the reasons behind this shift and what it means for businesses, consumers, and government officials.

Public choice theory helps us understand why people in government make the choices they do. It looks at the goals of different people involved, like lawmakers, the folks who enforce the laws, and groups that try to influence decisions. When we use public choice theory to look at competition rules, we can get a clear picture of why certain decisions are made and how they might affect businesses and consumers alike.

Chair Khan's rise in the antitrust world has been nothing short of meteoric, but her trajectory has raised eyebrows among groups in the antitrust establishment. After finishing law school, Khan worked at the Open Markets Institute, a think tank known for its critical stance on the monopolistic behavior of major corporations, particularly in the tech industry (FTC, 2024). During her tenure at the Open Markets Institute, Khan was involved in efforts that challenged the market dominance of companies like Google.

Her government tenure began with a stint at the FTC, and by 2019, she was deeply involved in the House Judiciary Committee's Subcommittee on Antitrust, Commercial, and Administrative Law (FTC, 2024). Under her guidance, the subcommittee undertook a broad investigation into digital markets.

Chair Khan's appointment to the FTC in 2021 was met with significant attention and, in some circles, controversy. On March 22, 2021, President Biden announced that he would be nominating Khan for a commissioner role at the FTC. Her nomination was met with bipartisan approval, resulting in a Senate confirmation on June 15, 2021, by a vote of sixty-nine to twenty-eight. This broad support was largely seen as an endorsement of her ability to effectively serve as a commissioner. What caught some off guard was President Biden's subsequent move to appoint Khan as the chair of the FTC. Traditionally, senators are informed in advance if a nominee for commissioner might also be tapped for the chair's role. This deviation from established norms raised eyebrows; perhaps Khan's elevation to the position of chair might have been strategically concealed to ensure smoother passage through the nomination process.

Chair Khan's appointment represented a significant departure from the agency's historical approach to antitrust regulation. While Khan's rapid rise from a law student critical of Amazon's market dominance to the head of a key regulatory body is undoubtedly remarkable, it also raises questions about the direction in which she has steered the FTC. Critics argue that her approach doesn't appreciate the past one hundred-plus years of developments in antitrust law and policy and is more reflective of a theoretical idealism, shaped in academic circles, than of practical enforcement strategies honed through years of regulatory and judicial learning (Abbott 2023).

Since its establishment in 1914, the FTC has been at the forefront of enforcing antitrust laws and ensuring legitimate competition. Over the years, the agency has navigated complex economic landscapes, adapting its policies to changing market conditions and technological advancements. The FTC's historical trajectory has been marked by a careful balance between rigorous enforcement and pragmatic understanding of market dynamics.

However, Chair Khan's focus on big tech companies and aggressive regulatory posture is a shift toward more interventionist policies, possibly at the expense of established legal norms, economic practicalities, and net social welfare.

The skepticism surrounding Chair Khan's approach partly stems from a concern that her policies, while well-intentioned, might not fully account for the complexities and unintended consequences of stringent antitrust enforcement. Critics argue that a more aggressive stance against large corporations, especially in the rapidly evolving tech sector, stifles innovation and economic growth (Portuese, 2022). There is also a worry that such an approach might lead to legal overreach and regulatory burdens that could have far-reaching impacts on the business environment.

As I dive into the historical evolution of the FTC and the antitrust landscape more generally, it becomes imperative to examine how the agency's approach has adapted to various economic challenges and regulatory landscapes. This examination will not only provide a lens to view the historical role of the FTC but will also offer a critical perspective on how Chair Khan might reshape the FTC's legacy. This critical perspective will illuminate whether her strategies align with or diverge from the pragmatic, historically informed approach that has typically characterized the agency's enforcement actions, and what is driving those changes from a public choice perspective.

The Emergence of Antitrust and the Sherman Act

The late nineteenth century in the United States, often characterized by the rise of industrial magnates like John D. Rockefeller's Standard Oil and Andrew Carnegie's Carnegie Steel Company, presents a complex picture. While it is true that these companies and their leaders became synonymous with immense wealth and market dominance, the narrative is more nuanced than a simple tale of unchecked power and anticompetitive practices.

Criticisms of the traditional "robber barons" narrative, such as those presented in "The Myth of the Robber Barons," argue that this period was more about entrepreneurial innovation and the efficient organization of industries than about exploitation and monopoly (Folsom 2018). According to this viewpoint, the success of these industrialists was not simply the result of predatory pricing, mergers, and exclusive deals. Instead, it was also due to their ability to innovate, improve product quality, and reduce costs, which benefited consumers. These entrepreneurs were seen as driving forces in the American economy, contributing to its growth and dynamism.

Regardless of the debate over the methods and merits of the industrial expansion during the late nineteenth century, the era's concentration of economic power in the hands of a few raised concerns among regulators and the public. The massive size and influence of these corporations were viewed with suspicion and led to a growing call for government intervention.

Enter the Sherman Antitrust Act of 1890. The Act was a direct response to the excesses of the corporate giants. Its primary objective was clear: to curb the concentration of economic power and preserve competition. The Sherman Act's language, while broad and ambiguous, was designed to tackle anti-competitive agreements and any monopolistic practices. Although early enforcement of the Sherman Act was spotty and often marred by judicial reluctance, it firmly set the foundation for the federal government's role in regulating competition. Over time, the Act would be fortified by subsequent legislation and court interpretations, giving it more teeth and clarity.

The Era of Structural Antitrust Enforcement

From the passage of the Sherman Act through the 1960s, antitrust enforcement in the United States underwent a transformative phase, known as the era of structural antitrust enforcement. Rooted in the belief that the very structure of the market can either foster or stifle competition, structuralist theories argued that a highly concentrated market, one dominated by a few large corporations, was *prima-facie* anti-competitive.

During this structural era, the emphasis was not just on the behavior of companies, but more so on their size and the share of the market they controlled. The overarching philosophy was straightforward: *big was bad.* If a single company or a handful of companies held a significant portion of the market, it was believed that this could lead to anti-competitive practices, reduce innovation, and harm consumers through higher prices or lower quality products (Libecap, 1991). As a result, antitrust enforcers during this period were extremely aggressive in their approach, frequently moving to break up or heavily regulate dominant firms to ensure market competition. The aim was to prevent excessive concentration of market power and protect the integrity of competitive processes.

This structural approach to antitrust was cemented by significant legislative milestones. The Clayton Act, passed in 1914, was a game-changer. While the Sherman Act had laid the foundation for antitrust policy in the United States, the Clayton Act built upon it by targeting specific behaviors that could lead to market concentration. For instance, the Act tackled price discrimination (charging different customers different prices for the same product), exclusive dealing (where sellers restrict the freedom of buyers to buy from other sellers), and tying arrangements (where a product is sold under the condition that the buyer also purchases another product).

Equally significant was the establishment of the FTC in the same year. The creation of the FTC signaled the government's commitment to active oversight and enforcement of competition laws. Unlike court proceedings, which could be lengthy and complex, the FTC offered a more agile and specialized platform to monitor, investigate, and rectify anti-competitive behaviors. As an administrative body dedicated solely to antitrust matters, the FTC played a pivotal role in shaping and enforcing competition policies during this structural era.

In sum, the era of structural antitrust enforcement reflected a time when the US government was proactive and interventionist in its approach to managing market competition. The belief that market structure directly influenced competitive outcomes ultimately shaped policies, resulting in some of the most significant antitrust actions in US history.

The Adoption of the Consumer Welfare Standard in the 1970s and 1980s

The 1970s and 1980s marked a significant shift in antitrust enforcement, transitioning from the structural approach to the Consumer Welfare Standard. This transformation was largely influenced by the Chicago School of economics, which posited that the primary goal of antitrust enforcement should be to promote consumer welfare, focusing on the effects of business practices on consumer prices, output, and product quality.

The Consumer Welfare Standard has been the dominant paradigm in US antitrust enforcement for over four decades. Its adoption led to a more economically rigorous and targeted approach to enforcement, concentrating on identifying and remedying specific instances of anti-competitive behavior rather than pursuing broad structural changes. This approach resulted in a more lenient attitude towards vertical integration, mergers, and other business practices, as long as they did not demonstrably harm consumer welfare.

Throughout these four decades, the Consumer Welfare Standard has garnered widespread support from economists, legal scholars, and the judiciary. This support stems from the recognition that the Consumer Welfare Standard is rooted in economic knowledge and insights, which provide a solid foundation for analyzing the impact of business practices on competition and consumers. The adoption of the Consumer Welfare Standard by the federal courts has led to more consistent and predictable antitrust jurisprudence, ensuring that enforcement actions are grounded in sound economic principles and focused on promoting consumer welfare.

The shift in antitrust enforcement from a reliance on structural presumptions to the application of the rule of reason and economic analysis represents a fundamental change in the approach to antitrust law. Previously, antitrust enforcement often operated under certain presumptions, where specific market structures, such as high levels of concentration or the presence of large firms, were viewed as being inherently suspect and potentially anticompetitive. Under this paradigm, enforcement actions could be triggered based on these structural indicators without a detailed assessment of the actual market impact.

However, with the adoption of the Consumer Welfare Standard, there was a significant shift toward a more nuanced and analytical approach, encapsulated in the rule of reason (Hovenkamp 2018). This approach requires a thorough examination of the actual or potential competitive harm or benefit of a business practice, rather than relying on assumptions based on market structure alone. The rule of reason does not presume that a particular business practice is harmful solely because it occurs in a concentrated market or involves a large company; instead, it calls for a detailed economic analysis to assess the real-world impact on competition and consumer welfare.

This transformation meant that antitrust authorities and courts began to apply sophisticated economic analyses to evaluate the effects of business conduct. These analyses focus on factors like the impact of a business practice on prices, output, quantity and quality of products or services, innovation, and overall consumer choice. For instance, in merger cases, rather than opposing a merger simply because it leads to increased market concentration, antitrust authorities examined whether the merger could lead to efficiencies that benefit consumers, such as lower prices or improved product quality.

In essence, the rule of reason approach demands a more evidence-based and less strict application of antitrust laws. It moves away from the view that certain market structures or business sizes are inherently problematic, focusing instead on the specific effects of business conduct on market competition and consumer welfare. This shift has made antitrust enforcement more dynamic, context-specific, and aligned with contemporary economic understanding, although it also requires more complex and detailed analysis in each case.

However, the recent changes in the global economy and the rise of technology giants have led certain groups to question the adequacy of the Consumer Welfare Standard in addressing modern antitrust challenges. This has prompted a reexamination and a recent shift in antitrust enforcement goals and methods, sparking a broader conversation about the future of antitrust policy in the twenty-first century.

The Evolving Role of the FTC and DOJ Antitrust Division in Recent Years

Chair Khan's appointment marks a significant shift in a *new* direction, with her leadership signaling a broader interpretation of antitrust laws, a greater emphasis on addressing market power, and a return to structural issues. This change in approach reflects a growing debate over the appropriate goals and methods of antitrust enforcement in the twenty-first century.

However, the rapid changes ushered in by Chair Khan and the Biden Administration more broadly have been met with widespread concern and skepticism. Critics argue that these changes represent a departure from the established consensus around the Consumer Welfare Standard, which has provided a stable and economically grounded foundation for antitrust enforcement for over forty years.

Some stakeholders, including businesses, legal scholars, and economists, express distrust in the new direction of antitrust policy, fearing that it may lead to overzealous enforcement, increased uncertainty, and unintended consequences for innovation and competition. They argue that the Consumer Welfare Standard, despite its potential shortcomings, has been successful in promoting economic efficiency and consumer benefits, and that moving away from this standard without a clear and well-articulated alternative may jeopardize these achievements.

This evolving landscape highlights the importance of carefully examining the underlying assumptions and motivations driving the changes in antitrust enforcement and considering the potential implications for businesses, consumers, and the broader economy.

Interest Groups and Antitrust

The Influence of Interest Groups on the Origins of Antitrust Legislation

From the outset, antitrust legislation in the United States was not purely a product of altruistic ambitions to ensure market fairness and protect consumers. Rather, like most things in politics, it was deeply intertwined with the maneuverings of influential interest groups, each vying to shape policy in a manner conducive to their interests.

The early calls for antitrust measures often came from smaller businesses and agrarian communities. Fearing the overpowering influence and potentially predatory practices of colossal corporations, these groups lobbied fervently for legal safeguards. Their central argument revolved around the idea that, without regulatory intervention, these mammoth entities would be able to crush smaller competitors, monopolizing entire industries in the process.[1]

Labor unions also became prominent actors in the antitrust scene. Their concerns were somewhat different, however. The burgeoning trusts and monopolies of the era were not just economic threats but also powerful entities that could, and often did, wield their influence to suppress wages, hinder unionization efforts, and otherwise deteriorate working conditions. As such, labor unions saw antitrust policy as a potential avenue to curtail corporate overreach and guarantee better conditions for workers.

Yet, as research by authors like DiLorenzo (1985) suggests, the genesis of antitrust legislation was not solely, or even primarily, about maintaining competitive markets or ensuring consumer welfare. Instead, it was significantly about protectionism. A coalition of diverse interest groups, ranging from struggling businesses to powerful industries, often saw antitrust laws as instruments to shield themselves from fiercer competition or to gain an advantageous position in the market.

A notable instance of this is seen in the case of the meatpacking industry. Far from being passive observers, key players in this industry proactively engaged in shaping early antitrust directives. For them, the policy was not just a protective shield but also a weapon: a means to stymie emerging competitors and solidify their dominant positions. Moreover, by supporting and even championing antitrust measures, these firms could project an image of social responsibility, thereby earning goodwill and deflecting public criticism.

In sum, while the historical narrative often presents antitrust legislation as a noble endeavor to ensure market fairness, the deeper examination reveals a more intricate tapestry. A tapestry woven not just by concerns for the public good but also by the strategic interests and machinations of influential interest groups.

Antitrust as a Double-Edged Sword: When Big Companies Use It to Limit Fair Play

Public choice theory provides a useful framework for examining the role of interest groups in shaping antitrust policy. By applying the insights of economics to the analysis of political decision-making, public choice theory highlights the potential for interest groups to capture regulators and influence policy outcomes in ways that serve their own interests rather than the broader public interest.

On the surface, antitrust is about making sure markets stay competitive and consumer welfare is protected. But, like any powerful tool, antitrust can be twisted and turned against its original purpose. As pointed out by Baumol and Ordover (1985), there's a potential dark side to antitrust policies: sometimes they're used by big companies to knock down their competitors, not by competing fairly, but by using the rules against them.

Imagine being a big company and seeing a smaller, innovative rival starting to eat into your profits. Instead of improving your products or lowering your prices, you might be tempted to use your deep pockets to drag this rival into court, accusing them of breaking competition rules. Even if the smaller company has done nothing wrong, the cost and stress of defending itself can slow it down or even push it out of business.

Another similar narrative comes from the recent AI hearings. (Vincent, 2023). Sam Altman, CEO of OpenAI, recently appeared before the Senate Judiciary

Subcommittee on Privacy, Technology, and the Law. During his testimony, he insisted on intense regulation of the AI field. Regardless of Altman's intentions, there's a clear benefit for OpenAI. More regulations mean more barriers for new companies trying to enter the field, leaving established players like OpenAI with a firmer grip on the market. Such action is protected by law. The legal doctrine known as the *Noerr-Pennington* Doctrine stems from two Supreme Court decisions, which grant individuals or businesses immunity from liability when they petition the government or engage in advocacy activities, even if the intent is to eliminate competition (*Eastern Railroad Presidents Conference v. Noerr Motor Freight, Inc.*, 365 US 127 (1961); *United Mine Workers v. Pennington*, 381 US 657 (1965)). Essentially, this doctrine acknowledges the right of any entity, whether an individual or a business, to freely advocate and petition the government, even if their motivations are self-serving. While this can be seen as safeguarding First Amendment rights, it also opens the door for established businesses to use regulatory processes to their advantage while being shielded from antitrust implications.

Sam Altman's advocacy for intense regulation in the AI field, while ostensibly aimed at ensuring safety and ethical standards, inadvertently highlights a broader trend in industry dynamics. Established companies, due to their existing resources and market position, are often more adept at meeting regulatory requirements compared to new entrants. This phenomenon isn't confined to the tech industry but is a pervasive aspect of the business landscape.

Another compelling example of how regulations can be shaped to favor established players at the expense of smaller competitors is the case of the Consumer Product Safety Improvement Act (CPSIA) and Mattel (Carney 2009). Mattel, a toy manufacturing giant, was instrumental in shaping the CPSIA, a law designed to improve toy safety. The irony is that Mattel's lobbying efforts led to a law that exempted them from some of its most burdensome requirements, even though their own safety lapses had prompted the legislation in the first place.

Under the CPSIA, every manufacturer of children's products was required to submit their products for independent testing for lead and other chemicals before selling them. However, Mattel obtained an exemption from this third-party testing requirement, as the law allowed exemptions for companies with in-house testing facilities meeting certain standards. As a result, while smaller businesses and independent craftsmen faced significant new burdens, Mattel was able to use its existing resources to comply with the law more easily and at a lower cost.

This case is a textbook example of regulatory capture, where a company not only influences but also actively shapes the regulations in its industry to its advantage. The Mattel case also illustrates how large firms can use their influence to create barriers to entry and increase the cost of compliance for smaller competitors. Such maneuvers align perfectly with the concerns raised by public choice theory, which posits that interest groups and large corporations can exert disproportionate influence on policymaking, often leading to outcomes that favor their interests over the broader public good (Tullock, 1987).

Existing companies are typically better equipped to meet regulatory requirements than new entrants for many reasons. One of the primary factors is the availability of resources: established companies usually possess greater financial, technical, and human resources, which allow them to invest in necessary compliance infrastructure, employ experts, and adapt to regulatory changes more efficiently. Furthermore, these companies have a wealth of experience with the regulatory frameworks within their industry, giving them a clearer understanding and a strategic advantage in compliance matters.

Additionally, economies of scale and scope play crucial role. Larger companies can distribute the costs of meeting regulatory requirements across a wider range of operations and products, making these expenses more manageable. This is often a challenge for new entrants who face these costs on a smaller operational scale. Established companies also tend to have long-standing relationships with regulatory bodies and may engage in lobbying, providing them with valuable insights and influence in regulatory affairs. This can lead to regulations that are inadvertently more favorable or easier for them to comply with.

In-house expertise is another significant factor. Over time, established companies develop teams specializing in regulatory affairs, making them well-equipped to understand and implement regulatory changes swiftly. Coupled with robust systems for risk management, larger companies are often more adaptable to regulatory changes. These combined attributes—resource availability, experience in regulatory navigation, economies of scale, established relationships, in-house expertise, and effective risk management—give existing companies a distinct advantage in meeting regulatory requirements compared to new market entrants. This advantage not only affects their ability to comply but also influences the competitive landscape, potentially creating higher barriers for new entrants and impacting market competition.

This perspective emphasizes the need for a careful and critical examination of the motivations behind antitrust enforcement actions and policy changes.

It also underscores the importance of institutional safeguards and checks and balances to minimize the risk of regulatory capture and ensure that antitrust policy remains focused on promoting competition and consumer welfare.

By considering the role of interest groups and the potential for regulatory capture, public choice theory offers valuable insights for understanding the dynamics of antitrust policy and the complex interplay of economic, political, and legal factors that shape policy outcomes.

Chair Khan and the FTC

Chair Khan's Background and Her Critique of Traditional Antitrust Enforcement

Chair Khan has emerged as perhaps the most prominent critic of traditional antitrust enforcement and a leading advocate for a more expansive approach to competition policy. Chair Khan first gained prominence with her 2017 article "Amazon's Antitrust Paradox," in which she argued that the Consumer Welfare Standard, with its focus on price effects, fails to adequately address the market power and anti-competitive practices of technology giants like Amazon.

But Chair Khan likely has ulterior motives at play. Under Chair Khan's leadership, the FTC has brought cases against three of the five largest tech firms: Amazon, Meta, and Microsoft. The outcome of the Amazon case is yet to be seen; however, the FTC lost its cases against Meta and Microsoft.

The Biden Administration's Emphasis on Competition Policy

The Biden administration has signaled a renewed emphasis on competition policy and a desire to reinvigorate antitrust enforcement. This is evident in several key events, including Khan's appointment as the chair of the FTC, Tim Wu's appointment to the National Economic Council, and the release of the Executive Order on Promoting Competition in the American Economy. The Executive Order directed federal agencies to adopt a "whole-of-government" approach to promote competition and to review and revise existing regulations and enforcement practices in order to address market concentration and anti-competitive practices (White House 2021).

In President Biden's remarks at the signing of the Executive Order, he somewhat infamously referred to the last 40 years of antitrust policy as a failure (The White House, 2021a).

The Question of Welfare Loss

Chair Khan's ascent at the FTC has been marked by a departure from previous antitrust enforcement paradigms, leading some to question the underlying motivations guiding the Commission's actions. One of the traditional measures of antitrust enforcement, particularly in the context of economic analysis, is the extent to which actions prevent or rectify welfare loss. Welfare loss pertains to a reduction in societal well-being resulting from market inefficiencies, often stemming from monopolistic behaviors. Arguably, the role of the FTC should be to minimize welfare loss. The FTC is the best-positioned agency to do this, as it staffs hundreds of economists who are aptly positioned to determine such loss.

Historical examinations into antitrust enforcement's motivations began with Posner, who initiated statistical examinations of these actions (Posner 1970). Following Posner's groundwork, research by Long, Schramm, and Tollison (L-S-T) revealed a tenuous connection between antitrust activity and the actual prevention of welfare loss (Long, Schramm, and Tollison 1973). Their research suggested that welfare loss played only a minor role in determining antitrust actions. The underlying implication is that other non-economic variables, perhaps political or strategic, exerted greater influence on antitrust enforcement.

Siegfried's subsequent work echoed these findings (Siegfried 1975). Even after adjusting several assumptions made by L-S-T, the link between economic welfare loss and antitrust actions remained weak, leading Siegfried to infer that economic factors were not the principal drivers behind the decisions of the Antitrust Division. Further complicating matters, Asch highlighted the pitfalls of using broad industry data in this context (Asch 1975). Since antitrust actions are levied against individual firms rather than entire sectors, an industry-wide perspective can be misleading. This leaves the reasoning behind such enforcement actions somewhat nebulous.

So, what does this all mean for Chair Khan and the FTC's current direction? While it would be speculative to definitively state the Commission's motives under Chair Khan's leadership, the historical disconnect between welfare loss and antitrust enforcement may lead one to believe that some public choice theory could explain her decisions. Drawing from Coats, Higgins, and Chesney's narrative, one could argue that the FTC, under Chair Khan, might be swayed more by interest groups and political considerations than by genuine concerns over economic welfare loss. Or perhaps Chair Khan may be swayed by some other motivation, perhaps she strongly believes in and makes decisions based upon the idea that *big is bad*. It is not challenging to view the modern FTC as an agency wielding its power to benefit specific, well-organized interests rather than the broader public.

Consider the recently settled Microsoft-Activision decision, where the FTC's decision to *attempt* to block Microsoft's acquisition of Activision was not devoid of external influences, furthering the skepticism surrounding its motives (*FTC v. Microsoft Corp.*, 681 F. Supp. 3d 1069).

While many were speculating about the merits of the deal in terms of competition and market dominance, whispers in the industry corridors suggested that Sony, Microsoft's main competitor in the gaming arena, voiced concerns to the FTC about the merger, especially with respect to Microsoft's ability to create exclusivity for one of the best-selling game franchises, *Call of Duty*. Sony's grievance, if it played a role in influencing the FTC's decision to challenge the merger, offers an illustrative example of how regulatory actions might be swayed by well-organized private interests. Though it is natural for competitors to voice concerns over significant market consolidations, it is crucial for regulatory bodies to ensure their decisions remain rooted in objective analysis rather than succumbing to corporate lobbying or external pressures.

Challenges Faced by the FTC under Chair Khan

Staff Morale, Internal Struggles, and Public Choice Theory Insights

Public choice theory, which seeks to understand the decisions made within public institutions through the lens of individual motivations and incentives, provides a framework to comprehend the turbulence within the FTC during Chair Khan's tenure.

On March 2, 2023, Commissioner Christine Wilson resigned from her position as the sole Republican commissioner at the FTC (Wilson, 2023). In her resignation letter, Commissioner Wilson painted a vivid picture of an agency in disarray, contrasting starkly with the FTC's past reputation. She evoked her earlier tenures at the FTC, praising the agency's enduring commitment to consumer welfare and bipartisan traditions. But her description of the FTC's present state under Chair Khan's leadership is far from this celebrated past. The plummeting morale and sharp departures from the agency, which she notes haven't been witnessed in three decades, can be interpreted through public choice theory as the natural response of individuals to shifting incentives and perceived breaches in institutional integrity.

Commissioner Wilson's reflection on employee satisfaction surveys at the FTC highlights a drastic decline in confidence and respect for senior leadership. In 2020, prior to Khan becoming Chair, the FTC was the highest-ranking agency to work at. However, within just a year of Chair Khan's tenure, the trust and faith vested in the leadership of the FTC took a nosedive. This decline, from a public choice perspective, might be indicative of misaligned incentives, wherein the personal motivations of the staff and the newly implemented institutional direction diverged significantly.

The "brain drain" that Commissioner Wilson alludes to is also symptomatic of the altered incentive structures. When institutional directions shift so abruptly, experienced personnel, who have built their careers and expectations around a particular set of organizational goals, might find themselves in dissonance with the new directives. In public choice terms, they react to these altered incentives by opting out.

Furthermore, the sharp drop in enforcement actions, both in competition and consumer protection spheres, can be viewed as another dimension of the internal struggles within the FTC. Public choice theory would suggest that this is not just a simple matter of policy redirection, but is possibly a result of internal inefficiencies, mismanagement, or a conscious choice to shift the agency's priorities, all leading to a decline in the agency's traditional roles.

Commissioner Wilson's concluding remarks hint at a divergence from the expected "return to normalcy." From a public choice viewpoint, this might suggest that the stated goals of leadership can sometimes be incongruent with the resulting outcomes, influenced as they are by the dynamics of internal politics, interest groups, and shifting power structures within an institution.

In essence, the unfolding narrative at the FTC, as outlined by Commissioner Wilson, underscores the importance of understanding the interplay of individual motivations and institutional goals. Public choice theory offers a lens to dissect these complexities, illuminating the challenges faced by institutions undergoing significant internal change.

Balancing Political, Economic, and Personal Goals in Antitrust Enforcement

One of the key challenges facing the FTC under Chair Khan's leadership seems to be striking the right balance between political, economic, and personal goals in antitrust enforcement. To date, Chair Khan's approach has seemed mostly political. While targeting certain firms may be successful in some realms, antitrust jurisprudence heavily relies on economics. Without economic support for the theories purported under Khan's FTC, successful judicial decisions are, and have proven to be, unlikely.

Incorporating a public choice perspective into the analysis of Chair Khan's leadership at the FTC helps to explain her enforcement paradigm. From the public choice perspective, Chair Khan's shift in antitrust enforcement could be interpreted as aligning with the political objectives of the current administration. This alignment might not only reflect a genuine commitment to a particular regulatory philosophy but also could be strategically aimed at garnering political support. Such support could be crucial for Chair Khan's reappointment or future career prospects within the government. The decision to adopt a more politically charged enforcement strategy could therefore be seen as a way to maintain or increase her influence and standing within the current political landscape.

Furthermore, Chair Khan's past involvement with the Open Markets Institute suggests the possibility of influence by certain interest groups. These groups often advocate for stricter regulation of big tech companies, and their ideologies and support could have shaped Chair Khan's approach at the FTC. This raises questions about whether her enforcement actions are primarily driven by objective economic analysis or by the agendas of these interest groups.

Another aspect worth considering is the phenomenon of the "revolving door." This term refers to the movement of individuals between roles as regulators and positions within the industries they formerly regulated. In the context of the FTC and big tech firms, there is a concern that such revolving door relationships could lead to conflicts of interest or biased enforcement actions. If FTC employees have prospects of future employment in the tech industry, it could influence the agency's decisions and priorities. Conversely, former tech industry employees who join the FTC might bring biases from their previous roles.

Regarding Chair Khan, her personal incentives and career trajectory could also play a role in shaping her enforcement strategy. Public choice theory suggests that individuals in government positions are motivated by factors beyond public interest (Shughart et al., 1985), including career advancement, reputation, and political influence. Chair Khan's approach to antitrust enforcement, particularly her focus on major tech companies, might be influenced by a desire to align with the current political climate, gain favor with influential political figures, or bolster her professional standing and prospects for future appointments. Her actions could be seen as an attempt to establish a legacy or build a reputation as a tough regulator in the tech sector.

Conclusion

This chapter has applied various tools from public choice theory to analyze the motivations and implications behind the recent shift in antitrust goals at the FTC under the leadership of Chair Khan. Public choice theory provides a useful framework for understanding how the actions of regulators, politicians, and individuals are influenced by the incentives and constraints they face, as well as the impact of interest groups and political pressures on the formation of policy and enforcement priorities.

The chapter began by outlining the historical context of antitrust enforcement in the United States, tracing its evolution from the origins of the Sherman Act through the adoption of the Consumer Welfare Standard in the 1970s and 1980s up to the recent changes at the FTC (Stigler, 1985). The role of interest groups in shaping antitrust law and policy was explored, highlighting their influence on the origins of antitrust legislation, as well as their potential to subvert competition using antitrust enforcement.

I examined Chair Khan's background, her critique of traditional antitrust enforcement, and the new direction she has charted for the FTC. This shift in antitrust goals has been met with both support and criticism, with concerns arising about the potential impact on innovation, consumer welfare, and market competition. Through the lens of public choice theory, I analyzed the role of political incentives, interest groups, and the potential for regulatory capture in driving these changes at the FTC.

I also discussed the challenges faced by the FTC under Chair Khan, such as staff morale and internal struggles, critiques of the new approach from various perspectives, and the need to balance political and economic goals in antitrust enforcement. By applying public choice theory to the current shift in antitrust goals at the FTC, this chapter has shed light on the complex interplay of factors likely shaping the direction of antitrust enforcement in the United States.

The new approach to antitrust enforcement under Chair Khan and the FTC could potentially create long-term implications for competition policy, market dynamics, and consumer welfare in the United States. While some argue that this shift could lead to more robust enforcement and a renewed focus on addressing the challenges posed by concentrated market power, others raise concerns about the potential negative consequences.

One potential long-term implication of the new approach is an overall increase in the aggressiveness of antitrust enforcement. This could manifest through more frequent and stringent investigations, increased regulatory scrutiny, and a higher likelihood of enforcement actions against dominant firms. While this may lead to some benefits in terms of curbing anticompetitive behavior, it also carries risks of over-enforcement, which could stifle innovation and potentially discourage pro-competitive conduct.[2]

The FTC's emboldened stance seems to be paving the way for an overhaul of the regulatory blueprint, but whether this overhaul is beneficial or will have any long-term impact remains to be seen. On December 18, 2023, the FTC and DOJ rolled out the final revised version of the merger guidelines (Department of Justice, 2023). These guidelines have historically been the bedrock of antitrust evaluations, having been thoroughly vetted and consistently referenced by courts over the years.

The sudden urge to rewrite these guidelines has raised eyebrows. Is it truly about adapting to a changing economic landscape, or is it an attempt to exert more control over the free market under the banner of consumer welfare and protection? By significantly altering the precedent set by the guidelines, there's a risk of introducing ambiguity into a process that has long benefited from clarity. Historically, federal and state courts have looked to the merger guidelines as a reliable source; however, sudden and drastic changes will likely mean that courts will not be ready to accept the new guidelines.

Perhaps the most important long-term implication of the new approach is for innovation and economic growth. I argue that overzealous enforcement deters investment and stifles the development of new products, services, and technologies, ultimately harming consumers and hindering economic growth. Companies of the size likely to attract antitrust scrutiny are risk-averse and have become increasingly risk-averse in the context of a hawkish antitrust regulatory regime. It is likely that the FTC's over-enforcement has hindered economic growth and innovation in the United States already.

The potential long-term implications of the new approach to antitrust enforcement under Chair Khan and the FTC are complex. While some aspects of this shift may lead to positive outcomes, there are many risks and uncertainties associated with over-enforcement, changes in legal and regulatory frameworks, and the impact on innovation and economic growth. Time will tell whether such changes are beneficial.

Notes

1 This narrative is all too familiar. Recently, Bill Gurley, a venture capitalist, gave a speech discussing regulatory capture and how certain market participants will advocate for regulation to create barriers to entry for potential entrants (https://www.youtube.com/watch?v=F9cO3-MLHOM).

2 This argument is distinct from antitrust enforcement's success rate. Chair Khan has brought many cases that fail to set the legal precedent the FTC hopes for.

References

Abbott, Alden. 2023. "A Consumer-Welfare-Centric Reform Agenda for the Federal Trade Commission." *Truth on the Market.* December 14, 2023. https://truthonthemarket.com/2023/12/14/a-consumer-welfare-centric-reform-agenda-for-the-federal-trade-commission/.

Asch, Peter. 1975. "The Determinants and Effects of Antitrust Activity." *The Journal of Law & Economics* 18 (2): 575–581.

Baumol, William J., and Janusz A. Ordover. 1985. "Use of Antitrust to Subvert Competition." *The Journal of Law & Economics* 28 (2): 247–265.

Carney, Timothy P. 2009. "Timothy P. Carney: Mattel Exempted from Toy Safety Law It Helped Write." *Washington Examiner* (blog). September 3. https://www.washingtonexaminer.com/news/2250656/timothy-p-carney-mattel-exempted-from-toy-safety-law-it-helped-write/.

Dilorenzo, Thomas J. 1985. "The Origins of Antitrust: An Interest-Group Perspective." *International Review of Law and Economics* 5 (1): 73–90.

Eastern Railroad Presidents Conference v. Noerr Motor Freight, Inc., 365 U.S. 127 (1961).

FTC v. Amazon.com, Inc., 2024 U.S. Dist. LEXIS 120300.

FTC v. Microsoft Corp., 681 F. Supp. 3d 1069.

Folsom, Burton. 2018. *The Myth of the Robber Barons: A New Look at the Rise of Big Business in America.* Reston, VA: Young America's Foundation.

Hovenkamp, Herbert. 2018. "The Rule of Reason." *Florida Law Review* 70 (1): 81–167.

Khan, Lina M. 2017. "Amazon's Antitrust Paradox." *Yale Law Journal* 126 (3): 564–907.

Libecap, Gary D. 1991. "The Rise of the Chicago Packers and the Origins of Meat Inspection and Antitrust." National Bureau of Economic Research. Working Paper 29. Historical Working Paper Series.

Long, William F., Richard Schramm, and Robert Tollison. 1973. "The Economic Determinants of Antitrust Activity." *The Journal of Law and Economics* 16 (2): 351–364.

Portuese, Aurelien. 2022. "Biden Antitrust: The Paradox of the New Antitrust Populism." *The George Mason Law Review*, 29 (4): 1087–1134.

Posner, Richard A. 1970. "A Statistical Study of Antitrust Enforcement." *The Journal of Law & Economics* 13 (2): 365–419.

Shughart, Willam F., and Robert D. Tollison. 1985. "The Positive Economics of Antitrust Policy: A Survey Article." *International Review of Law and Economics* 5 (1): 39–57.

Siegfried, John J. 1975. "The Determinants of Antitrust Activity." *The Journal of Law and Economics* 18 (2): 559–574.

Stigler, George J. 1985. "The Origin of the Sherman Act." *The Journal of Legal Studies* 14 (1): 1–12.

The White House. 2021a. "Executive Order on Promoting Competition in the American Economy." *The White House*. July 9. https://www.whitehouse.gov/briefing-room/presidential-actions/2021/07/09/executive-order-on-promoting-competition-in-the-american-economy/.

Tullock, Gordon. 1987. "Concluding Thoughts on the Politics of Regulation." In *Public Choice & Regulation*, 333–343. Hoover Press Publication.

United Mine Workers v. Pennington, 381 U.S. 657 (1965).

United States Department of Justice. 2023. "Antitrust Division | 2023 Merger Guidelines | United States Department of Justice." December 12. https://www.justice.gov/atr/2023-merger-guidelines.

Vincent, James. 2023. "The Senate's Hearing on AI Regulation Was Dangerously Friendly." *The Verge*. May 19. https://www.theverge.com/2023/5/19/23728174/ai-regulation-senate-hearings-regulatory-capture-laws.-

Wilson, Christine S. 2023. Christine S. Wilson to Joseph R. Biden (a letter from the Commissioner of the Federal Trade Commission to the President of the United States. Washington, DC, March 2, 2023. https://www.ftc.gov/system/files/ftc_gov/pdf/p180200wilsonresignationletter.pdf.

8

Public Choice v. Policy

The Implications of Public Choice on the United States Supreme Court

Saige M. Hill

Established through the Judiciary Act of 1789, the purpose of the Supreme Court is to provide legal oversight for court cases at the federal level (United States Courts n.d.a; United States Senate, n.d.b). Touted as the "Highest Court in the Land," the Supreme Court hears cases involving states, government officials, and other dignitaries and appeals for cases decided in lower courts (United States Courts n.d.a). The role of the Supreme Court is to act as a nonpartisan arbitrator that interprets the law; cases heard at this level set legal precedents with the authority to influence policies and practices across states and localities (United States Courts n.d.a; Blazina and Gramlich 2022). Within the bounds of the aforementioned legal interpretation, decisions put forth by the Supreme Court should objectively enforce the law. However, Justices may be inclined to take a stance based on personal ideologies, to receive various incentives—monetary or non-monetary—or due to affiliations with the political party of the executive that nominated them. Exploring this concept, the intended neutrality of the Supreme Court of the United States is analyzed through the lens of public choice theory and investigates the following questions:

1. Are Supreme Court Justices capable of making objective, bias-free court decisions?
2. Can public choice theory be used to overcome challenges associated with maintaining objectivity within the Supreme Court?

Public choice theory explores the role that self-interest and incentives play in decision-making. Developed by James Buchanan, public choice theory challenges the notion that political actors selflessly make decisions for the betterment of their constituency rather than based on their own motivations (Tullock and Buchanan 1962). In the public sector, officials, such as the President of the United States, are expected to make decisions and enact policies based on the needs of the people. However, public choice theory acknowledges the faults of human nature that make it difficult for duties to be fulfilled in a vacuum without self-interest and incentives (Tullock and Buchanan 1962). This concept explores how decision-making is self-interested and how groups experience benefits or burdens through those decisions. Furthermore, individuals, including governmental actors such as Supreme Court Justices, who are expected to be nonpartisan arbitrators, may, if left unchecked, act in ways that favor their own benefits. Public choice theory in the Supreme Court is especially interesting due to the commitment of Justices to make court rulings that are unbiased and nonpartisan. Despite this, the voting records of many Justices show alignment with political parties (Liptak and Kao 2022; Supreme Court Public Opinion Project 2022). Furthermore, "the rise of interest groups influencing the selection of Supreme Court Justices also reflects the increasing role of issue partisanship in the process" (Constitution Annotated n.d.). These facts suggest that public choice theory may be useful in explaining the attitudes and behaviors of Supreme Court Justices, especially when Justices choose to vote in ways that appear to contradict their oath of office.

The Supreme Court in the context of public choice theory is a research area that deserves much consideration. This chapter aims to contribute to the existing scholarship on the significance of public choice in Supreme Court rulings and the relationship of those rulings to the views of constituents. A 1993 article found that overall, Supreme Court decisions fluctuated based on public opinion and presidential leadership at the time of a ruling (Mishler and Sheehan 1993). However, when the Court lacks balance, such as during times when more conservative-leaning Justices serve, Court approval decreases (Mishler and Sheehan 1993). Furthermore, lack of turnover and the increase in term lengths have led to a Supreme Court deficient in diversity and dynamism, or in other words, a court that is too stagnant (Giles et al. 2008). In the Giles et al. article, the authors suggest that instead of Justices being influenced directly by public opinion, they are instead affected by other factors such as the news and other media (Giles et al. 2008). However, in another study using data from the latter half of the twentieth century, researchers found that Justices were influenced by both the public and their own self-interest (McGuire and Stimson 2004).

This analysis will also highlight the Virginia, Austrian, and Bloomington schools of political economy and how they fit into the discussion of judicial decision making. The discussion on the Virginia School will not only focus on self-interested decisions but also on how groups experience benefits and burdens as a result. The Austrian School will be discussed in terms of subjective values, and the Bloomington School will be analyzed as it relates to rational choice. The chapter will conclude with potential solutions to promote accountability within the Supreme Court and to mitigate the future policy impact of high-stakes cases.

History and Politics of Supreme Court Justices

Since its inception, 165 judges have been nominated for the Supreme Court, with 128 (77.58 percent) being appointed (United States Senate n.d.a). Since its inception, the diversity of the Supreme Court has been very limited. The first African American appointed to the Supreme Court was Justice Thurgood Marshall in 1967; the first woman was Sandra Day O'Connor in 1981; the first Hispanic Supreme Court Justice was Justice Sonia Sotomayor in 2009; and Justice Ketanji Brown Jackson was the first African American woman appointed to the Supreme Court in 2022 (Supreme Court of the United States n.d.a). An overwhelming number of Supreme Court Justices have been white males, and minority groups, such as Asian American and openly LGBTQ community have still not been appointed. Supreme Court Justices serve life terms—but may choose to retire, as demonstrated by former Associate Justice Breyer—to alleviate political pressures influencing decisions made by the Court (Blazina and Gramlich 2022), so demographic distribution that more adequately reflects the American population and encompasses a variety of lived experiences and perspectives is paramount.

There is a lot of politicization of the judicial nomination process. In order to maintain a favorable influence on court rulings, parties employ different strategies. In 1912, William Taft was the first president to nominate a Supreme Court Justice during an election year and most recently, Donald Trump nominated Amy Coney Barrett in 2021 (Supreme Court of the United States, n.d.a). Barrett was reported to have one of the fastest confirmations in history at only twenty-seven days (Chang and Freeman 2021), highlighting the urgency exercised by the Republican party. Election year appointments are considered controversial because the president's nominated Justice can have a lasting impact on the Supreme Court and on public policy, even if the president is at the end of their term or does not win re-election. Approximately one-third of presidents, both Democratic and Republican, have appointed Supreme Court Justices despite it being an election year. This is important to note because during the last two election cycles, there has been debate about whether the sitting president should have the authority to nominate a Supreme Court Justice at the end of their term. In fact, the *Washington Post* reported that in 1992, current US president Joe Biden stated that during an election year, a president should not make a nomination and "Senate consideration of a nominee under these circumstances is not fair to the president, to the nominee, or to the Senate itself" (DeBonis 2016). Since then, President Biden has changed his stance.

> Some critics say that one excerpt of my speech is evidence that I oppose filling a Supreme Court vacancy in an election year. This is not an accurate description of my views on the subject. In the same statement critics are pointing to today, I urged the Senate and White House to work together to overcome partisan differences to ensure the Court functions as the Founding Fathers intended. That remains my position today.

Furthermore, in a statement arguing against the nomination of a new Supreme Court Justice by the Obama Administration following the death of Justice Antonin Scalia in 2016, Senate Majority Leader Mitch McConnell stated, "No one disputes the president's authority to nominate a successor to Scalia, but as inconvenient as it may be for this president, Article II, Section 2, of the Constitution grants the Senate the power to provide, or as the case may be, withhold its consent" (McConnell and Grassley 2016).

Another strategy that has been utilized is for Supreme Court Justices to retire at times that would allow the appointment of a new Justice of the same party. For example, Justice Breyer, appointed in 1994 and serving 27 years, retired in 2022 and was replaced by Justice Jackson (Supreme Court of the United States n.d.a). Regarding his impending retirement, an NBC article stated, "Ginsburg's death from cancer at eighty-seven allowed then-President Donald Trump to appoint her successor, Amy Coney Barrett, moving the court further to the right. An appointment by Biden could keep Breyer's seat on the liberal side of the court for years or decades to come" (Williams 2022). This practice has been repeatedly utilized over the years in favor of allowing Justices to be replaced by the opposing party due to untimely deaths. A 2023 The Hill article considers the potential retirement of Justices Thomas and Alito, further emphasizing the importance of the 2024 election:

> [Senator Debbie] Stabenow [Democrat – Michigan] warned that if Republicans flip the White House and Senate and replace Thomas and Alito with younger conservatives, "it would be devastating for anyone who cares about privacy and their own personal freedom," alluding to last year's 6–3 Supreme Court opinion that overturned Roe v. Wade and raised questions about other rights protected by the Fourteenth Amendment.

As President Gerald Ford stated, "few appointments a president makes can have as much impact on the future of the country as those to the Supreme Court" (Perry 2016) which is supported by the fact that Justice Clarence Johnson has served for over 31 years and has played a role in influencing American policy throughout his tenure.

Although the Supreme Court claims nonpartisanship, the aforementioned instances of strategies utilized to maintain control of the Supreme Court support the notion that the Supreme Court has politicized foundations. Currently, three of the nine Supreme Court Justices have been appointed by Democratic presidents as opposed to six who were appointed by Republican presidents (Supreme Court Nominations 2022). Furthermore, according to Pew Research Center, 57 percent of adults who identify as Democrats or lean Democrat state that the Supreme Court votes conservatively, in comparison to 62 percent of adults identifying as or leaning towards Republican who state that it is more neutral (Blazina and Gramlich 2022). Similarly, a poll by Marquette University Law School in Milwaukee, Wisconsin showed that in 2019, 38 percent of respondents stated that the Supreme Court voted conservatively, 50 percent said it was moderate, and 12 percent stated that it voted liberally (Conway 2022). In 2022, 67 percent stated that the Supreme Court rules more conservatively, 21 percent believe it is more neutral, and only 10 percent felt that the Supreme Court votes liberally (Conway 2022).

Before public choice theory can be examined as it relates to the Supreme Court, a deeper look into the history of the Court should be discussed. Article III, Section 1 of the US Constitution mandated the establishment of the Supreme Court and that it act as the government's judiciary body (U.S. Senate Committee on the Judiciary n.d.). The Supreme Court originally consisted of one Chief Justice and five Associate Justices (U.S. Senate Committee on the Judiciary n.d.). A requirement for Supreme Court Justices under the Judiciary Act was that they serve as judges in the circuit court (National Park Service 2022; US Senate Committee on the Judiciary n.d): Supreme Court Justices were assigned to different regions and traveled between municipalities hearing cases, a practice also referred to as "riding the circuit." This was to ensure that Justices maintained familiarity with issues up for debate in the lower courts (National Park Service 2022; US Senate Committee on the Judiciary n.d). The requirement to "ride the circuit" was abolished in 1911, potentially limiting Justices' understanding of issues heard at lower levels of government (National Park Service 2022).

There are two types of cases the Supreme Court hears. Some cases are presented directly to the Supreme Court without being forwarded from a lower court (United States Courts n.d.b); however, cases involving officials, ambassadors, governmental departments or agencies, and states are sent directly to the Supreme Court for ruling. Alternatively, the Supreme Court also operates on an appellate basis. After a ruling from a lower court that a party would like reviewed, the Supreme Court must be petitioned to hear the case (United States Courts n.d.b). Four Supreme Court Justices must decide to accept a case before it can be heard at the federal level (United States Courts n.d.b). The Supreme Court rules on between 100 and 150 cases annually, and Court decisions are based on the votes of the majority of Justices (United States Courts n.d.a).

Since its inception, there have been numerous landmark cases that have shaped not only legislation but also the culture of the United States. A landmark case is defined as "a court decision that establishes an important new legal principle or concept, or which changes the previous interpretation of current law" (World Law Dictionary n.d.). Examples include Brown v. Board of Education (1954), which challenged the 1896 case of Plessy v. Ferguson and determined that segregation in schools is unconstitutional, as well as Roper v. Simmons (2005), which found that sentencing individuals to death for crimes committed before the age of eighteen violates the Eighth Amendment. Another example is the recently overturned Roe v. Wade (1973), which protected women's access to reproductive rights through privacy granted by the Fourteenth Amendment (United States Courts n.d.a). Due to this, it is important to consider the consequences when self-interest or incentives—such as gifts, bribes, political favor, and other monetary and non-monetary personal incentives—influence the ability of Justices to rule objectively and accurately interpret the law.

There are two perspectives through which Justices interpret the Constitution that play a role in how they view cases. The "enduring" versus "living" debate highlights the fact that some Supreme Court Justices interpret the Constitution based on its original intended purposes (enduring), while others view it as a document that is meant to be understood based on the current climate and needs (living). Supreme Court justice Thurgood Marshall delivered an address in 1987 highlighting the benefits of interpreting the Constitution as a living document, noting that many of the issues of today's society did not exist when the Constitution was written, leading to a critique of the enduring perspective (Marshall 1987). It's worth noting that the perspective that Justices use has an influence on how they interpret the law and how they vote.

Importance and Implications

The key question that arises from this analysis is "why is this important?" Maintaining the integrity of the Supreme Court of the United States should be a priority for all Americans due to the significant impact that court proceedings can have on every facet of daily life. According to *CNN*, the Supreme Court "decides if laws and government actions are constitutional and outlines the breadth and limits of government" and furthermore states that "the precedent the majority opinion sets is then the standard by which future laws are measured" (Berman 2022). If the decisions made by Justices poorly interpret the law, the implications can be devastating.

For example, the 2022 Supreme Court decision in New York State Rifle & Pistol Association (NYSRPA) v. Bruen, which determined that it is unconstitutional to require those seeking to apply for concealed firearm licenses to show proper cause for the need, may have major public health implications moving forward (Kapadia 2022). Conversely, the decision could have set a precedent that would limit further intrusions on rights that could be harmful and disproportionately impact those without the resources to defend themselves legally. In proceedings such as these, there is room for Justices to use discretion, which will inevitably be informed by personal ideologies and interests.

In the first nine months of 2022, there were 515 mass shootings, over 15,000 people were killed with a gun and over 18,000 committed suicide by way of firearms (Kapadia 2022). By denying that those seeking concealed carry permits in New York be required to show proper cause, the Supreme Court set a precedent which will further limit gun control in the United States. Considering the staggering number of lives lost to gun violence and the uptick in mass shootings over the past few years, gun control is a key concern. However, not living in or serving a community that has been intimately affected by mass shootings can inhibit one's understanding of the reality of the situation. Decisions made by the Supreme Court not only affect the citizens of today but precedents can have long-term effects that span generations. The NYSRPA v. Bruen case is just one example of why the Supreme Court's business should be everyone's business, especially when the actions of Justices appear to be political in nature.

The Supreme Court's role is to act as an unbiased interpreter of the law, and as such, it has the authority to impact legislation on every level of government. The Supreme Court is essential because it hears federal cases that influence policy across the country and provides checks and balances by ensuring that the legislative and executive branches act within their constitutional bounds. Despite the presumed neutrality of the Supreme Court, acknowledging potential pitfalls of human error is essential. Even when an actor may believe that he or she is performing in the best interests of those they serve, self-interest and personal incentives may influence them.

As much as 25 percent of Marquette University Law School survey respondents stated that they have a lot of confidence in the Supreme Court, while 36 percent stated that they have some confidence and 39 percent of respondents stated they have little-to-no confidence in the Supreme Court (Conway 2023). 26 percent stated that they believed that the Supreme Court Justices display high or very high ethical standards, 39 percent stated that they have an average level, and 35 percent believed that the Justices show low or very low ethical standards (Conway 2023). One thing that was specifically mentioned was Justice Thomas's financial disclosure documents, which showed that a GOP donor paid for trips for the justice (Breuninger 2023). 72 percent of Survey respondents aware of this disclosure rated the ethical standards of Justices as low or very low (Conway 2023). Regarding rent seeking, or ways in which individuals and groups aim to acquire benefits and advantages through manipulation, Shepherd (2011) stated, "Despite the general preference for litigation over legislation, judicial self-interest has been shown to be an important determinant of judicial behavior. Moreover, like legislatures, executives, and bureaucrats, the judiciary is also susceptible to inappropriate rent seeking. The courts simply represent another opportunity for interest groups to shape the law" (Shepherd 2011 p. 102). Judges accepting gifts from partisan donors appears to be a case of rent-seeking that may be influencing interpretation and voting on Supreme Court cases.

Ideologies, Incentives, and Affiliations

Public choice theory is defined as the "[application of] economics to political decision-making and defies the conventional beliefs that politicians act in the best interest of their constituents. It evaluates how incentives and personal gain shape politicians' choices" (Dhir 2023). The public choice framework allows us to consider the implications of self-interested action within the Supreme Court. This section explores how personal ideologies, incentives, and political affiliations impact the ability of Supreme Court Justices to make objective, bias-free court decisions.

Personal Ideologies

Ideology is defined as, "A systematic scheme of ideas, usually relating to politics, economics, or society and forming the basis of action or policy; a set of beliefs governing conduct" (Oxford English Dictionary 2023). Ideologies not only act as a foundation for one's moral compass and affect an individual's personal attitudes and behaviors but also influence how they interact with the world around them. Governmental actors, including Supreme Court Justices, are not exempt from the influence of ideologies. Considering the impact of ideologies within the context of the courts, Cross states, "Empirical data also suggests that bureaucratic action is heavily influenced by ideology" (Cross 1999 p. 370). Cross goes on to say that, "Ample evidence indicates that ideology is a good predictor of congressional voting . . . . A recent study of educational finance reform found decisions explained more by ideology and media influence than by special interest lobbying" (Cross 1999 p. 369–370). In addition to a Justice's personal viewpoints being affected by ideologies, the way they vote in Supreme Court cases may also be swayed by their perspectives, thus highlighting the role of self-interest. "If judges are immune from the pressures of reelection, they are likely to try to satisfy themselves or their close friends . . . . We should expect to see the decisions of judges heavily influenced by the intellectual orientation and political inclinations" (Epstein 1990 p. 838).

A key component to the success of the Supreme Court is the Justices' ability to exercise objective and bias-free decision-making. However, due to the often-controversial nature of cases heard by the Court, it is unrealistic to believe that every Justice can display 100% objectivity and remove themselves from case considerations at all times: "In contrast to all other courts, the majority of the Supreme Court's docket involves cases with politically salient issues. As a result, the policy preferences of the Justices are likely to be the biggest influence on their decision-making" (Shepherd 2011 pp. 103–104). Although a justice inserting their own ideologies into decisions may be unintentional and they may genuinely believe they are fairly adjudicating the law in question, this shortcoming supports the public choice theory tenet that all actors display some level of self-interest, even when it is believed that they are not expected to do so.

Of the 2021 to 2022 term (October 2021 to July 2022), there were many controversial Supreme Court cases through which public choice theory can be analyzed. One of the most notable Supreme Court rulings of the year was Dobbs v. Jackson Women's Health Organization, which overturned Roe v. Wade—the case that guaranteed access to legal and safe abortion (Cornell Law School n.d.). The Supreme Court voted six to three that the Mississippi ban on abortion after the fifteenth week of pregnancy was constitutional based on the interpretation that the Constitution does not protect access to abortion and that states should be able to implement their own laws regarding the medical procedure (Cornell Law School n.d.). The Justices who voted in favor of upholding the ban were the court's conservative justices, Samuel Alito, Jr.; Amy Coney Barrett; Neil Gorsuch; Brett Kavanaugh; John Roberts, Jr.; and Clarence Thomas (Cornell Law School n.d.). In other words, the vote was split along political lines. The question is, did the Justices genuinely believe that Roe v. Wade was unconstitutional based on their interpretation of the law—despite past Justices ruling it constitutional—or did pro-life ideologies come into play? Although a Justice's motivation is difficult to determine without concrete evidence, the political preferences of the nominating party do continue to play a role. Fascinatingly enough, in a 2007 article by Farnsworth, the author found that because the views of Justices are dynamic, their inclinations may change throughout their tenure, along with their voting behaviors. The author concludes that presidents should not necessarily depend on the leanings of a Justice at the time of nomination to hold throughout the duration of their career (Farnsworth 2007).

Incentives

Incentives are one of the most widely researched components of public choice theory. Incentives in government—either positive or negative—can take a variety of forms, including more common incentives such as gifts, donations, career advancement, favors, and others, but the underlying theme is that incentives affect or manipulate behavior and beliefs. A part of the reasoning behind Supreme Court Justices serving life terms is to attempt to prevent the potential influence of incentives related to the election process on judicial decisions: "By conscious design, federal judges are insulated from these electoral sanctions and therefore have far greater ability to ignore short-term public opinion except in the most pressing and important cases" (Epstein 1990 p. 836). Despite this, Justices may still be vulnerable to the pull of incentives, which can affect their voting behaviors. In relation to how incentives may influence Justices, Shepherd states that, "like legislatures, executives, and bureaucrats, the judiciary is also susceptible to inappropriate rent seeking. The courts simply represent another opportunity for interest groups to shape the law" (2011 p. 102–103).

At lower levels of the court, Shepherd found that approximately 75 percent of voters believe that judges are influenced by donations and 52 percent believe that they are affected by lobbyists (2011). Furthermore, funders and voting records have shown a correlation that cannot be ignored, and at all levels, interest groups with more resources and better connections outperform their peers in court: "Throughout the court system, big business wins an overwhelming proportion of its cases, whether as plaintiff or defendants" (Cross 1999 p. 362). Due to the emphasis on "litigation over legislation," this is problematic because better-equipped groups, or those more likely to provide Justices with favorable incentives, are more likely to secure court rulings that impact future legislation. A variety of schemes have been devised to mitigate the negative influence of perverse incentives in a variety of government positions. For example, "Campaign contributions have been regulated, the outside income of legislators has been limited, many gifts have been banned, and terms have even been limited" (Cross 1999 p. 378), all of which are recommendations that may be beneficial within the judiciary. Despite the numerous scholars who have delved into the implications of incentives within the Supreme Court, there have been limited suggestions regarding restructuring the Supreme Court or the lower courts to incentivize judges to maintain objectivity and nonpartisanship (Macey 1996).

One of the most compelling analyses of incentives within government is the distinction between the protective, productive, and predatory roles of the state. In the protective state, "the state is charged with the responsibility of enforcing property rights" (Boettke and Candela 2020 p. 338), and in the productive state, "government becomes a means by which citizens can accomplish jointly desired objectives, including not only the provision of public goods, but also the capacity to finance publicly the creation and administration of such goods"

Boettke and Candela 2020 p. 338). However, the predatory state "[promotes] the private interests of dominant groups inside the state (such as politicians, the army, and bureaucrats) or influential private groups with effective lobbying powers," (Vahabi 2020 p. 234) which means that the minority groups are preyed upon to advance the dominant groups (Buchanan 1975 [2000]). While there may be incentives for Supreme Court Justices to vote in ways that contradict their commitment to be objective and nonpartisan, a completely fair and unbiased judiciary would ensure that each case is argued within the scope of the Constitution and that no entity, whether related to donors, political affiliations, big business, lobbyists, et cetera, is given preferential treatment and furthermore, facilitates predation. "While protection and predation are two faces of the same coin, a predatory state protects only to promote its predation" (Vahabi 2020 p. 235). Instead of influential or preferred actors receiving benefits, thus leading to predation, all cases should be adjudicated in an unbiased and nonpartisan manner, despite the presence of potential incentives to protect the productive state.

Political Affiliations

Political affiliations have the potential to play a significant role in the performance of Supreme Court Justices. Studies not only show that Supreme Court Justices are more likely to vote along party lines consistent with the president who nominated them, but they also often maintain voting records similar to before joining the Court. A chapter discussing the implications of public choice theory on the judicial system highlights how a Justice's party may influence their Court decisions: "there was considerable interest group pressure, but voting patterns were explained well by ideology, party loyalty, and constituent interest" (Cross 1999 p. 370).

A metric that has been used to determine the political leanings of Supreme Court Justices is the Martin-Quinn Score. Developed by Andrew Martin and Kevin Quinn and published in 2002, the purpose of the Martin-Quinn scoring method is to calculate each Supreme Court Justice's voting patterns based on Supreme Court rulings, with higher numerical scores indicating more polarity (Justices with negative scores being more liberal and positive scores being more conservative) and scores closer to zero showing more neutrality. Martin-Quinn Scores have been calculated from 1937 to the present, traditionally showing consistency between Justices' scores and the party under which Justices were nominated (Rubin 2023). For the 2022 to 2023 Supreme Court term, the scores of the Supreme Court were as follows: Justices Sotomayor (−4.09), Kagan (−2.07), and Jackson (−1.70) scored more liberally, while Alito (2.57), Thomas (2.36), Gorsuch (1.08), Barrett (0.82), Kavanaugh (0.45), and Roberts (0.42) obtained more conservative scores (González and Alberti 2023).

Supporting this, Epstein wrote, "Parsimonious attribute models of the voting behavior of Supreme Court judges explain between 70 and 90 percent of the 'liberal' and 'conservative' variance by an appeal to such variables as party identification, appointing president, region of birth, and prior judicial and prosecutorial experience" (1990 p. 839) and "straightforward interpretation in accordance with original intention therefore greases the wheels of politics, and that type of interpretation can only come from independent judges who have no special affiliation with either party to the transaction" (1990 p. 849). In other words, although Justices may aim to exercise nonpartisanship when deciding Supreme Court cases, unless the Justice truly has no party affiliation, it can be difficult for them to completely extract themselves from party loyalties. "In contrast to partisan judges that have a party label to inform voters about their policy preferences, nonpartisan judges communicate their policy positions through their decisions on the bench" (Shepherd 2011 p. 109). That being said, the voting records and affiliations of Justices contribute to their notability and furthermore, initial nomination (Epstein 1990).

Ideologies, incentives, and affiliations are some of the biggest obstacles to overcoming partisanship and bias in the Supreme Court, let alone in the overall government. This is not to say that Supreme Court Justices cannot be objective and bias-free, but human nature, along with various internal and external factors, can significantly affect the performance of the Court when left unchecked. Methods to promote effective judicial decision-making and accountability of the Supreme Court should be explored to mitigate the implications of public choice.

Recommendations and the Schools of Political Economy

Even the most well-intentioned Justice may inadvertently allow their personal values and perceived obligations to leach into their rulings, so methods to hold Supreme Court Justices accountable to the people they serve must be considered. In this final section, three primary recommendations to address the influence of ideological and personal incentives on judicial behavior are discussed.

SCOTUS Elections

The first suggestion for increasing accountability among Supreme Court Justices is to allow constituents to vote to determine who will fill empty seats. The President of the United States has the authority to nominate Supreme Court Justices, who are then questioned through a hearing and confirmed or rejected by the Senate (Supreme Court of the United States n.d.b). Nominated Supreme Court Justices are confirmed through a simple majority vote (Supreme Court of the United States n.d.b). Allowing the president and Senate to have absolute control over who is appointed to the Supreme Court can be problematic if the political leaning of the president and Senate is extremely liberal or conservative or employs an approach that is self-interested. Although Supreme Court Justices are expected to be nonpartisan, studies show that Justices appointed by liberal presidents vote more liberally and vice versa for those appointed by conservative presidents (Epstein 1990; Farnsworth 2007; Zeitz 2022; Conway 2023). This becomes an issue when, rather than having a balanced Supreme Court that represents constituents with differing points of view, seats are repeatedly filled by one political party. Voting on who will fill vacant seats may be one way to make the Court more reflective of the constituency and the public's desires.

There is very limited literature on the justification for why Americans are not permitted to vote for Supreme Court Justices outside of the constitutionality of legislation. Again, preventing the need for Supreme Court Justices to run for office negates the likelihood of succumbing to the pressure associated with the election process. However, a 2022 Politico article discusses the reality of true isolation from these issues. The author articulates how various Supreme Court Justices—for example, former chief justice Salmon Chase—served in elected positions prior to and after being appointed to the Supreme Court (Zeitz 2022). Other Justices, such as former chief justice Roger Taney and Justice Abe Fortas, supported their nominating presidents as advisors (Zeitz 2022). Another article explored how, despite the fact that Justices are not directly elected, voters—especially those identifying as Republican—were more likely to vote for officials that would support Supreme Court Justices of their preferred party and views (Badas and Simas 2022). Considering this, in addition to the current discussion surrounding gifts and bribes within the Court, eliminating the political pressures on the Supreme Court is paramount, and therefore, the current appointment process should be reevaluated.

In the absence of the ability to hold the Supreme Court accountable through methods such as elections, Justices may be more likely to vote based on their personal ideologies or may be more vulnerable to the potential influences of gifts and bribes, such as in the case of Justice Thomas. That being said, public choice scholars acknowledge the potential unintended consequences of electing Supreme Court Justices, including the possibility that Justices will succumb to the pressures associated with campaigning or will align with public opinion to maintain approval ratings, which may compromise their judicial integrity. Shepherd, channeling Justice Anthondy Kennedy, argues that:

> Justices of the U.S. Supreme Court have also recently indicated their concern that judicial self-interest plays a role in the decision-making of elected judges . . . "elections [that] require candidates to conduct campaigns and to raise funds in a system designed to allow for competition among interest groups and political parties . . . is consistent with the perception and the reality of judicial independence and judicial excellence." (2011 p. 111)

She continued, stating: "Judges without permanent tenure have the incentive to vote strategically if they believe it will help them get reappointed, reelected, or otherwise retained. As a result, the judges may decide cases in ways that benefit specific litigants or establish precedents that are favored by the people responsible for retaining judges," further explaining why electing Justices may be problematic (Shepherd 2011 p. 107). This first recommendation aims to address the challenges associated with public choice exhibited in the Supreme Court by providing a method of external checks and balances through the election of Justices, which, if implemented effectively, may limit both the personal benefits to Justices and the undue burdens on the public perpetuated through highly controversial and divisive cases.

SCOTUS Qualifications

A second possible way to reduce the harms of a biased and self-interested judiciary is to introduce stricter eligibility qualifications for nominated Justices. As of now, there are no formal requirements for individuals who are nominated to be Supreme Court Justices: "The Constitution does not specify qualifications for Justices such as age, education, profession, or native-born citizenship. A Justice does not have to be a lawyer or a law school graduate, but all Justices [to date] have been trained in the law." Due to this, a president may appoint any person they see fit as long as they are confirmed by the Senate, but there are no formal requirements regarding judicial education or experience. Strict requirements such as a moderate judicial record (rather than one that leans liberal or conservative), experience working with a variety of populations (i.e., experienced with marginalized or underrepresented communities), and a certain number of years as a lawyer or judge may help ensure that the most qualified candidates are appointed. This suggestion is especially important for maintaining accountability when Justices continue to be appointed by the president to serve life terms. Even the president, who is only permitted to be elected for two four-year terms, must meet certain requirements to serve.

The lack of explicit qualifications for Supreme Court nominees has often been considered political in nature. Vile and Perez-Reilly (2016) offer a few potential reasons why qualifications were not originally outlined in the Constitution and still do not exist—namely, to limit abuse of the system due to unduly filtering out prospective nominees and the lack of standardized legal education. Others suggest that political self-interest and incentives do play a role. For example, nominees such as Justice Robert Bork, who was considered to have exceptional professional experience, were rejected supposedly due to having unfavorable political views, despite the belief that nominations are confirmed in the absence of "ideological bias" or "results orientation" (Kahn 1995 p. 25). Considering political goals, Kahn continues, stating that "the unambiguously political nature of the appointment process is proved finally and irrevocably by the confirmation process . . . which subjects the nominee to the vagaries of a vote by one hundred democratically elected officials, the appointment is inexorably dictated by political considerations, not by professional ones" (1995 p. 35). Furthermore, even informal "requirements" standardized across Supreme Court nominees exemplify the role of self-interest and incentives in the appointment process. Epstein et al. argue that similarities in the career paths of nominees and Supreme Court Justices hinder racial and gender diversity, perpetuating a court that is overwhelmingly white, male, and rather homogenous in lived experiences and perspectives (2003).

Menger's *The Principles of Economics* (1980) examines economy as a function of subjective values, or one's perceived value of a good or service. The discussion on subjective values correlates perfectly with proposals for an amendment involving requirements that individuals must possess in order to qualify for the Supreme Court. Subjective values are a topic of concern because one person's values may differ from those of another, especially when considering which qualifications and accomplishments are most important for high-ranking government officials. Any eligibility requirements would necessarily be subjective in nature because great discrepancies will exist between the level of value both officials and constituents place on the requirements. Additionally, some requirements may be viewed as arbitrary, such as the minimum age required for candidates running for president, or they may be interpreted as a potential barrier to entry. Furthermore, unless a thorough process is developed for determining which requirements should be implemented and how, emphasis on certain requirements (e.g., a recommendation from a sitting Justice), may point to the influences of public choice lingering in the process. This could even undermine the purpose of recommending standardized minimum qualifications for Supreme Court Justices.

SCOTUS Term Limits

A final suggestion for addressing the concerns raised by a public choice analysis of Supreme Court Justices is to impose a limit on how long they may serve. As of now, Justices are eligible to serve life terms. The purpose of this is to limit potential external influences that may arise when seeking re-election (Calabresi and Lindgren 2006; Cooper et al. 2021; Chilton et al. 2022). According to the Supreme Court of the United States website, the average length of service for a Justice is 16 years, and the longest-serving justice held his seat for nearly 37 years (n.d.). Because Justices serve life terms, Justices remain in office unless they retire or are impeached (Calabresi and Lindgren 2006; Cooper et al. 2021; Chilton et al. 2022). Chilton et al. published a 2022 article discussing strategies to implement term limits. The authors state, "judges and Justices serve for life unless they are impeached by the House of Representatives and convicted by a two-thirds vote in favor of removal by the Senate" (Chilton et al. 2022 p. 9). Forty Supreme Court Justices have chosen to retire, one—Associate Justice Samuel Chase— has been impeached, and one has resigned—Associate Justice Abe Fortas—due to threat of impeachment. Considering that there have been 116 Supreme Court Justices to date, the number of Justices serving until death is astounding. This fact begs the question of whether a Justice in the latter part of their life can remain knowledgeable about current issues (Cooper et al. 2021). Given how much greater longevity is in the twenty-first century as compared to the eighteenth, this raises again the question of whether the Constitution should be interpreted as it was originally written or as a living document which should be read based on the needs of the time.

There have been a number of studies on the potential effects of imposing term limits on Supreme Court Justices. Proponents of the current capacity of Justices to serve for life believe that this policy allows Justices to serve independent of external influences, such as politics, bribery, and the need to maintain favor for reelection (Calabresi and Lindgren 2006; Cooper et al. 2021; Chilton et al. 2022). However, without terms, there is limited ability to hold the Supreme Court accountable, and critics argue that too much independence is problematic since serving too long may not only allow the court to lean towards one political pole for extended periods of time, but Justices may continue to serve in old age even when they have limited mental capacity to do so (Cooper et al. 2021). Eighteen-year terms have been the most common suggestion. Terms of this length will help limit strategic turnover based on retirement, limit the amount of time Justices can serve, allow staggered turnover based on the year of appointment, with nominations occurring every two years, and prevent a single president from filling too many vacant positions (Calabresi and Lindgren 2006; Cooper et al. 2021; Chilton et al. 2022). Other studies have also suggested that, although currently, increasing the number of Justices has been often considered with constant threats of parties "packing the courts" to maintain political control, amending the Constitution to maintain a standard of nine Justices should be considered (Calabresi and Lindgren 2006). If presidents are able to simply appoint additional justices when desired, the recommendations to maintain the legitimacy of the Court will be undermined. These suggestions to promote accountability in the court through term limits could potentially promote a more effective judicial process, leading to a more evenly ideologically distributed Supreme Court and ensure that the Supreme Court Justices are regularly replaced.

The Bloomington School, developed by Elinor and Vincent Ostrom, builds on public choice theory and discusses how the intersection of institutions and rules influence decision-making and outcomes (Duhnea and Martin 2021). One of the most notable foundations of the Bloomington School is the role of collective action, or people working together to achieve a common goal. Referencing collective action problems, Elinor Ostrom stated: "Collective-action problems occur when individuals choose actions . . . in an interdependent situation. If each individual in such situations selects strategies based on a calculus that maximizes short-term benefits to self, individuals will take actions that generate lower joint outcomes" (2010, p. 155). To avoid falling into this trap, Ostrom emphasized that "an important task for all social scientists is achieving a more coherent synthesis of theoretical work that posits variables affecting the likelihood of undertaking diverse forms of collective action. We must be able to explain success as well as failure of efforts to achieve collective action" (Ostrom 2010, p. 156). This applies to the problem of selecting appropriate terms for Supreme Court Justices since a common goal of both Democratic and Republican officials is to maintain control over the Supreme Court by securing a majority of seats with party-nominated justices. In essence, political representatives act independently for the benefit of themselves and their constituents, despite the fact that the maintenance of a neutral, high-quality Supreme Court is a collective benefit that requires interdependent cooperation. In the spirit of Elinor Ostrom, it is worth thinking creatively about how collective action could take a different form in order to avoid this collective action problem. Many strategies have been considered to prevent parties from acquiring extensive control over the Supreme Court, with the proposed eighteen-year term limit being one of the most common and well-developed solutions. Imposing term limits on Supreme Court Justices addresses many of the concerns associated with maintaining Court integrity, especially in relation to dissuading calculated and self-interested turnover of Justices executed to preserve political power.

In concert, public choice economics, the Bloomington School, and the Austrian school of economics provide an overview of how political economy influences human beliefs and behaviors. Moreover, this analysis shows how a thorough understanding of the tenets of public choice and the manner in which they interact with judicial decision-making can address longstanding obstacles within the American judicial system and promote more effective Supreme Court processes in the future.

Conclusion

The Supreme Court of the United States plays a vital role in upholding the Constitution. Despite the commitment of Supreme Court Justices to remain unbiased and nonpartisan in decision-making, the complexities of human nature may influence Court rulings. The two following questions were addressed in this analysis:

1. Are Supreme Court Justices capable of making objective, bias-free court decisions?
2. Can public choice theory be used to overcome challenges associated with maintaining objectivity within the Supreme Court?

Public choice theory challenges the ability of the Supreme Court to remain neutral in the presence of self-interest and incentivization. In light of the potentially devastating implications of internal and external influences, checks, and balances are necessary to hold Justices accountable and ensure they are able and willing to perform their duties, considering the high stakes of their position and the reach and longevity of decisions made by the Court.

Implementing judicial elections, eligibility requirements, or term limits may promote better judicial decision-making and, by extension, more positive public policy outcomes. By allowing constituents to take part in the voting process, selected Justices will be more representative of the population rather than receiving appointments solely based on the president's nomination. This practice will prevent some of the critiques associated with election year appointments and the president's nominating of Justices with more polarized views. Secondly, guaranteeing that candidates are highly experienced and nonpartisan will prevent unqualified persons from being nominated, especially in the absence of voting requirements or term limits for Justices. This suggestion is especially important because only the most qualified judges with proven track records of effective rulings should be promoted to such a distinguished position, particularly considering the long-term implications their work will have on future precedents. Lastly, limiting the amount of time each Justice serves and the number of terms for which they are permitted to maintain their positions will ensure that Supreme Court Justices are regularly replaced, remain knowledgeable about current issues and public opinion, and are more accountable to the American people. All of the preceding recommendations have the potential to positively impact policy by ensuring that Justices are able to perform their duties to the best of their ability and with the needs of the country in mind—rather than in favor of their own personal preferences, potential incentives, and political affiliation.

The present analysis opens the door for future research on public choice considerations in the judicial process. A more thorough analysis of the implications of public choice that spans from the inception of the Supreme Court to the present day can be conducted to examine the influence of incentives on Supreme Court decisions through the decades. Research can also be expanded to include the exploration of public choice theory among other government officials or departments, or to compare how public choice theory is presented in American culture versus abroad. Research on how bias and self-interested decision-making can be overcome in the judiciary should be explored to promote more effective public policy, especially when it comes to courts as influential and significant as the United States Supreme Court.

References

Badas, Alex, and Elizabeth Simas. 2022. "The Supreme Court as an Electoral Issue: Evidence from Three Studies." *Political Science Research and Methods* 10 (1): 49–67.

Berman, Dan. 2022. "What Is the Supreme Court and Why Does It Have So Much Power?" CNN. July 2, 2022. https://www.cnn.com/2022/07/01/politics/what-is-the-supreme-court-how-does-it-work

Blazina, Carrie, and John Gramlich. 2022. "5 Facts about the Supreme Court." *Pew Research Center*. February 25. https://www.pewresearch.org/fact-tank/2022/02/25/5-facts-about-the-supreme-court/.

Boettke, Peter J., and Rosolino A. Candela. 2020. "Productive Specialization, Peaceful Cooperation and the Problem of the Predatory State: Lessons from Comparative Historical Political Economy." *Public Choice* 182 (3–4): 331–352.

Breuninger, Kevin. 2023. "Supreme Court Adopts Ethics Code as Justices Face Criticism over Financial Disclosures." CNBC. November 13, 2023. https://www.nbcconnecticut.com/news/business/money-report/supreme-court-adopts-ethics-code-as-justices-face-criticism-over-financial-disclosures/3147578/?os=vbkandrefa_2&ref=app

Buchanan, James M. [1975] 2000. *The Limits of Liberty: Between Anarchy and Leviathan.* Indianapolis: Liberty Fund.

Calabresi, Steven G., and James Lindgren. 2006. "Term Limits for the Supreme Court: Life Tenure Reconsidered." *Harvard Journal of Law and Public Policy* 29 (3): 769–877.

Chang, Connie, and Josh Freeman. 2021. "Supreme Court Confirmation of Amy Coney Barrett: A Blatant Act of Bad Faith?" *Dttp (College Park, Md.)* 49 (3–4): 30.

Chilton, Adam, Daniel Epps, Kyle Rozema, and Maya Sen. 2022. "Designing Supreme Court Term Limits." *Southern California Law Review* 95 (1): 1.

Conway, Kevin. 2022. "New Marquette Law School Poll Finds National Approval of U.S. Supreme Court's Work Continues to Be Lower Than in 2020." *Marquette University Law School.* https://www.marquette.edu/news-center/2022/new-marquette-law-school-poll-finds-national-approval-of-scotus-work-continues-to-be-lower.php.

Conway, Kevin. 2023. "New Marquette Law School Poll National Survey Finds Continuing Decline in Approval of the Way the U.S. Supreme Court Is Doing Its Job, With Amount Varying According to Respondents' Partisanship." Marquette University Law School. https://www.marquette.edu/news-center/2023/marquette-law-poll-finds-continuing-decline-in-approval-how-supreme-court-does-its-job.php.

Cooper, Tyler, Amanda Dworkin, Dylan Hosmer-Quint, and Amanda Pescovitz. 2021. "Retiring Life Tenure: On Term Limits and Regular Appointments at the Supreme Court." *Cardozo Law Review* 42: 2763–2776.

Cornell Law School. n.d. "Supreme Court: Most Recent Decisions." *Cornell Law School.* https://www.law.cornell.edu/supremecourt/text.

Cross, Frank B. 1999. "The Judiciary and Public Choice." *Hastings Law Journal* 50: 355.

DeBonis, Mike. 2016. "In 1992, Biden Called for an Election-Year Blockade of Supreme Court Nominations." *The Washington Post.* https://www.washingtonpost.com/news/powerpost/wp/2016/02/22/in-1992-joe-biden-called-for-an-election-year-blockade-of-supreme-court-nominations/.

Dhir, Rajeev. 2023. "James M. Buchanan: Early Life, Education, Works." *Investopedia.* https://www.investopedia.com/terms/j/james-m-buchanan-jr.asp.

Duhnea, Emil, and Adam Martin. 2021. "Public Choice Theory: Reuniting Virginia and Bloomington." In *Elinor Ostrom and the Bloomington School: Building a New Approach to Policy and the Social Sciences*, 7–24, edited by Jayme Lemke and Vlad Tarko. Newcastle upon Tyne: McGill-Queen's University Press.

Epstein, Lee, Jack Knight, and Andrew D. Martin. 2003. "The Norm of Prior Judicial Experience and Its Consequences for Career Diversity on the U.S. Supreme Court." *California Law Review* 91 (4): 903–965.

Epstein, Richard A. 1990. "The Independence of Judges: The Uses and Limitations of Public Choice Theory." *Brigham Young University Law Review* 1990: 827–855.

Farnsworth, Ward. 2007. "The Use and Limits of Martin-Quinn Scores to Assess Supreme Court Justices, with Special Attention to the Problem of Ideological Drift." *Northwestern University Law Review* 101 (4): 1891.

González, Oriana, and Daniella Alberti. 2023. "The Political Leanings of the Supreme Court Justices." *Axios.* https://www.axios.com/2019/06/01/supreme-court-justices-ideology.

Giles, Micheal W., Bethany Blackstone, and Richard L. Vining Jr. 2008. "The Supreme Court in American Democracy: Unraveling the Linkages between Public Opinion and Judicial Decision Making." *The Journal of Politics* 70 (2): 293–306.

Kahn, Michael A. 1995. "The Appointment of A Supreme Court Justice: A Political Process from Beginning to End." *Presidential Studies Quarterly* 25 (1): 25–41.

Kapadia, Farzana. 2022. "Gun Control for Health: A Public Health of Consequence, December 2022." *American Journal of Public Health* 112 (12): 1710–1712.

Liptak, Adam, and Jason Kao. 2022. "The Major Supreme Court Decisions in 2022." *The New York Times*. June 30, 2022. https://www.nytimes.com/interactive/2022/06/21/us/major-supreme-court-cases-2022.html.

Macey, Johnathan R. 1996. "Public Choice, Public Opinion, and the Fuller Court." *Vanderbilt Law Review* 49: 373.

Marshall, Thurgood. 1987. "The Constitution: A Living Document." *Howard LJ* 30: 915.

McConnell, Mitch, and Chuck Grassley. 2016. "Democrats Shouldn't Rob Voters of Chance to Replace Scalia." Opinions, *Washington Post*. February 18. https://www.washingtonpost.com/opinios/mcconnell-and-grassley-democrats-shouldnt-rob-voters-of-chance-to-replace-scalia/2016/02/18/e5ae9bdc-d68a-11e5-be55-2cc3c1e4b76b_story.html.

McGuire, Kevin T., and James A. Stimson. 2004. "The Least Dangerous Branch Revisited: New Evidence on Supreme Court Responsiveness to Public Preferences." *The Journal of Politics* 66 (4): 1018–1035.

Menger, Carl. [1890] 1950. *Principles of Economics*. United States: Ludwig von Mises Institute.

Mishler, William, and Reginald S. Sheehan. 1993. "The Supreme Court as a Countermajoritarian Institution? The Impact of Public Opinion on Supreme Court Decisions." *American Political Science Review* 87 (1): 87–101.

National Park Service. 2022. "Early Supreme Court Justices Ride the Circuit." *National Park Service,* August 15. https://www.nps.gov/articles/000/riding-circuit.htm.

Ostrom, Elinor. 2010. "Analyzing collective action." *Agricultural Economics* 41: 155–166.

Oxford English Dictionary, s.v. 2023. "ideology (n.), sense 4." July 2023. https://doi.org/10.1093/OED/3067572701.

Perry, Barbara A. 2016. "One-Third of all U.S. Presidents Appointed a Supreme Court Justice in an Election Year." *The Washington Post*. https://www.washingtonpost.com/news/monkey-cage/wp/2016/02/29/one-third-of-all-u-s-presidents-appointed-a-supreme-court-justice-in-an-election-year/.

Rubin, April. 2023. "Supreme Court Ideology Continues to Lean Conservative, New Data Shows." *Axios*. https://www.axios.com/2023/07/03/supreme-court-justices-political-ideology-chart.

Shepherd, Joanna. 2011. "Measuring Maximizing Judges: Empirical Legal Studies, Public Choice Theory, and Judicial Behavior." *U. Ill. L. Rev.* 2011 (5): 1753.

Supreme Court of the United States. n.d.a. "Justices." *Supreme Court of the United States.* https://www.supremecourt.gov/about/justices.aspx.

Supreme Court of the United States. n.d.b. "FAQs – General Information." *Supreme Court of the United States*. https://www.supremecourt.gov/about/faq_general.aspx.

Supreme Court Public Opinion Project. "2022 Survey Results." *Supreme Court Public Opinion Project*. https://projects.iq.harvard.edu/scotus-poll/2022-survey-results.

Tullock, Gordon, and James Buchanan. 1962. *The Calculus of Consent, Logical Foundations of Constitutional Democracy*. Ann Arbor, MI: University of Michigan Press.

United States Constitution. n.d. "ArtII.S2.C2.3.5 Appointments of Justices to the Supreme Court." *Constitution Annotated: Analysis and Interpretation of the U.S. Constitution*. https://constitution.congress.gov/browse/essay/artII-S2-C2-3-5/ALDE_00013096/.

United States Courts. n.d.a. "About the Supreme Court." United States Courts. https://www.uscourts.gov/about-federal-courts/educational-resources/about-educational-outreach/activity-resources/about.

United States Courts. n.d.b. "Supreme Court Procedures." *United States Courts*. https://www.uscourts.gov/about-federal-courts/educational-resources/about-educational-outreach/activity-resources/supreme-1.

United States Senate. n.d.a. "Supreme Court Nominations (1789-Present)." *United States Senate*. https://www.senate.gov/legislative/nominations/SupremeCourtNominations1789present.htm.

United States Senate. n.d.b. "Judiciary." *United States Senate*. https://www.senate.gov/reference/reference_index_subjects/Judicial_Branch_vrd.htm#:~:text=The%20Supreme%20Court%20consists%20of,and%20consent%20of%20the%20Senate.

United States Senate Committee on the Judiciary. n.d. "The History of the Supreme Court of the United States." *U.S. Senate Committee on the Judiciary*. https://www.judiciary.senate.gov/nominations/supreme-court/history/.

Vahabi, Mehrdad. 2020. "Introduction: A Symposium on the Predatory State." *Public Choice* 182 (3–4): 233–242.

Vile, Jone R., and Mario Perez-Reilly. 2016. "The US Constitutional and Judicial Qualifications: A Curious Omission." *Judicature* 100: 65.

World Law Dictionary. n.d. "Landmark Case." *World Law Dictionary*. https://dictionary.translegal.com/en/landmark-case/noun.

Williams, Pete. 2022. "Justice Stephen Breyer to Retire from Supreme Court, Paving Way for Biden Appointment." NBC News. January 26, 2022. http://nbcnews.com/politics/supreme-court/justice-stephen-breyer-retire-supreme-court-paving-way-biden-appointment-n1288042

Zeitz, Joshua. 2022. "The Supreme Court Has Never Been Apolitical." *Politico*. April 3, 2022. https://www.politico.com/news/magazine/2022/04/03/the-supreme-court-has-never-been-apolitical-00022482

9

Can Public Choice Theory Explain the Judicialization of Politics in Brazil?

Jean Vilbert

Judges in the Political Spotlight

On January 8, 2023, thousands of demonstrators stormed the Presidential Palace, Congress, and the Supreme Court in Brasilia, the capital of Brazil. The popular signal was clear: those unsatisfied with the political scenario targeted politicians and justices alike. In the ordinary order of things, this could cause surprise: The judiciary is typically thought to lie in some space outside the political game (Hart and Sacks 1994). How did judges become a focus of social unrest?

In recent decades, the judiciary in Brazil has emerged as an arena for citizens and social movements seeking to assert their rights and secure public goods. While courts were once detached from social demands, they are now an important battlefield for political claims. This change is especially evident in the Supreme Court of Brazil (STF), which has taken on a range of cases that illustrate this conjuncture. For example, after suspending the enforcement of eviction orders during the Covid-19 pandemic, whenever the squatters were multiple families, the court conditioned the resumption of the writs to the reallocation of the families living in the area, asserting the effectiveness of housing as a social right (ADPF 828/DF 2022). In a less consequential but not less demonstrative case, the court ruled that brothers have the constitutional right to study in the same public school (ADI 7149/RJ 2022). The court also acknowledged that every citizen holds a justiciable right to health, meaning that federal and local governments have a shared obligation to provide medical care, including hospitalization, outpatient services, and medications to plaintiffs (RE 855.178/SE 2019). Indeed, at least since 2004, the STF has signaled the judiciary's willingness to take on public policy affairs:

> While it is typically not the role of the Judiciary to formulate and implement public policies, as this responsibility lies primarily with the Legislative and Executive Powers, in certain circumstances the Judiciary may be called upon to perform such a task. This is particularly true when other branches of government fail to meet their political and legal obligations, thereby jeopardizing the protection of constitutional rights, whether individual or collective, even those with programmatic content. In these exceptional cases, the Judiciary may assume the responsibility of ensuring the integrity and effectiveness of such rights. (ADPF 45 MC/DF 2004, Justice Celso de Mello)

Some view the process of the judicialization of politics as a beneficial sign of the enforcement of fundamental rights and a potential remedy for poor governance (Botero, 2022). Others are less sanguine, cautioning that the perception of judicial activism as a force outside or even above politics neglects the political foundations of such activism, its limitations, and its unintended consequences (Hirschl 2009). While the literature has investigated multiple positive and negative aspects of the judicialization of politics both in Latin America and elsewhere, there remains a scarcity of studies that delve into the mechanisms that give rise to it. This piece intends to address this gap by examining why judges accept the task of dealing with thorny political issues. Undoubtedly, by doing so, the judiciary expands its powers. Yet, as the events in Brasilia have made clear, such an activist approach comes at a cost. Despite possible differences, judicial politics, the judicialization of politics, and judicial activism are here treated as interchangeable terms, since all refer to the intention of producing social change via judicial rulings (see Kmiec 2004).

It might be the case that part of the motivation for judicial activism stems from self-interest, as judges seek to maximize their authority, influence, and prestige. If so, public choice theory (PCT) could provide insight into this phenomenon. Interestingly, though, public choice authors have long recognized that the institutional constraints that regulate the judiciary may not fully align with the premises underlying PCT (Mitchell and Simmons 1990), thereby reducing the theory's explanatory power in understanding judicial behavior (see Epstein 1990). In fact, many public choice analysts prefer the judiciary over other branches of government. Given the lack of direct career and financial interests, judges are typically thought to be less susceptible to rent-seeking at the expense of the collective welfare (see Skeel 1997). In this sense, judicial intervention could offer a remedy for the deficiencies of electoral politics (Siegan 1984; Rose-Ackerman 1992; Grofman 1991).

Justice Roberto Barroso, a member of the STF, is a vocal proponent of this line of thought. According to Barroso, states are constantly at risk of being captured by special interests. What is more, this threat is not a temporary aspect of legislative democracies but rather a persistent one, particularly in cases of low state capacity. If institutional failure is prevalent in the political branches, then the judiciary remains the only institution that is unaffected by political distortions. This, in turn, justifies judicial activism as a means of preventing private interests from prevailing over the public good (Barroso 2016; Barroso 2019).

Against this background, this chapter aims to make two contributions. Firstly, it reinforces the applicability of PCT to judicial politics. Just like elected officials and bureaucrats, judges are rational actors who are influenced by tangible and intangible interests when making decisions. These interests may include individual beliefs, career aspirations, the need to uphold the legitimacy of the judiciary as an institution, and the preservation of personal reputation. Secondly, I propose an explanation for the functional form of the supply curve for judicial policy change, integrating subjective (incentive) and environmental (institutional) factors to argue that this curve has shifted in Brazil. To do this, I draw on my experience of nearly a decade working as a judicial clerk and judge in the Brazilian judiciary.

It is important to note that, while the empirical focus of this piece is on Brazil, the discussion at hand is not geographically limited. Judicial politics is a contentious issue across Latin America, Europe, and the United States—particularly in light of the recent US Supreme Court decision to overturn Roe v. Wade (1973), which has given states the power to restrict legal abortion. The matter of whether, when, and how courts can effect social change is a present-day topic of global relevance. Moreover, the premises and conclusions offered in this chapter can be adjusted and externalized (or serve as a warning and lesson) to other countries.

The rest of this chapter is organized as follows: the following section reviews the existing theoretical and empirical literature on the judicialization of politics in Latin America, which presents both optimistic and cautious perspectives on the effects of judicial politics. Moving on to the third section, I develop the main argument of this piece, employing PCT to contend that social and personal incentives and institutional design impels judges to embrace judicial activism in Brazil. The final section concludes that judges are influenced by a variety of factors, including their personal preferences, the legal culture, and the institutional context in which they operate, besides the political and social pressures they face. These elements, together with the cost structure of producing social change through courts, determine the level of judicial politics in a political system. The closing remarks raise a series of questions that can orient future research.

Judicial Politics in Brazil: The Rise of the Judiciary

Beginning in the 1980s, a wave of democratization swept through Latin America as many nations, including Brazil, broke free from the dictatorships that had long controlled the region. In order to anchor the new democratic rules, policymakers proceed to implement radical institutional changes; although democratic rules cannot be permanently set in stone, they can be enshrined in laws. Following this recipe, in 1988 Brazil enacted a new constitution, whose text listed a long catalog of fundamental rights, including "education, health, food, work, housing, transportation, leisure, security, social security, protection of motherhood and childhood, and assistance to the destitute," all of which were recognized as social rights (Article 6).

To safeguard these newly established rights, the Brazilian constitution significantly strengthened the judiciary. Policymakers entrusted Brazilian judges with the mission of preventing democratic backsliding, as stated in the slogan "dictatorship never again" (*ditadura nunca mais*), by monitoring government behavior and protecting fundamental rights (Domingo 1999; Nunes 2010). The implicit premise was that "legislatures cannot be relied upon to protect citizens' rights in any area" (Riker and Weingast 1988, p. 375). Nearly four decades into the arrangement, the judiciary has consolidated its position as the enforcer of the social contract, with judges taking on the responsibility of ensuring that constitutional rights will live up to their expectations and be fully enforced.

Litigants, in turn, have responded to this call by increasingly petitioning courts through individual or class action lawsuits. As a result, courts have become battlegrounds for political disputes, and judges have become prominent political figures with a hand in shaping policies that were previously the sole purview of presidents and legislators (Helmke and Figueroa 2011). As Justice Gilmar Mendes (2009) of the STF contends, in countries where poverty is rampant and millions of people have no access to basic conditions necessary for a dignified life, judges should shoulder greater political responsibility. Seen in this context, the judicialization of politics reflects the failure of traditional political mechanisms to address these challenges.

The political literature describes the *judicialization of politics* as the judiciary asserting its authority over questions that were classically reserved for the political decision-making process (Gauri and Brinks 2008; Wilson 2009; Botero, Brinks, and Gonzalez-Ocantos, 2022). This expression should not be confused with the *politicization of the judiciary*, which refers to judges making decisions under political pressure or based on ideological, or attitudinal (extralegal) factors related to partisanship. This latter phenomenon is most often considered detrimental to the democratic system, as it could compromise judicial independence, the separation of powers, and the rationality of the legal system (see Friedman 1998; Domingo 2004; Ciencia 2002; Martin 2019). The judicialization of politics, on the other hand, is a much more complex issue, and its positive and negative effects are still subject to wide debate and controversy.

In 1957, Robert Dahl published a seminal paper arguing that the Supreme Court of the United States is not a neutral legal institution, but rather a key player in the democratic game. The court plays a crucial role in shaping policies by interpreting the Constitution and making decisions on cases that have broad implications for society and the political process (Dahl, 1957). Examples of such decisions in the United States include those that ended racial segregation in public schools (Brown v. Board of Education of Topeka, 347 US 483 1954) or granted and revoked the right to abortion (Roe v. Wade, 410 US 113 1973 and Dobbs v. Jackson Women's Health Organization, n. 19–1392, 597 US 2022). In Brazil, this phenomenon is even more pervasive, spanning from the Supreme Court down to the lower courts, all of which have become relevant political actors, for better and for worse (Kapiszewski 2008).

Focusing on the positive aspects, case studies across Latin America reveal that the judiciary can provide visibility for human rights, as legal activists and human rights organizations can use the courts to challenge abuses of power and hold states accountable for their actions and omissions (González-Ocantos 2016). If this is the case, by safeguarding rights and providing an effective check on the other branches of government, judicialization may have helped ensure the pre-conditions for effective democratic rule in the region (Nunes 2010, Roa Roa 2019, Antía and Vairo 2019).

Conversely, judicial intervention in political issues may generate a host of problems. The nature of such intervention remains highly controversial, with extensive scholarship warning of the risks of transforming democracies into "government by judges" (Berger 2012). It is conceivable that in situations of bad or unfair government, where political forces are overly responsive to an uneven distribution of powers—allowing elites to dominate the political process—or where bureaucratic inertia impedes progress, courts may provide an avenue for correcting political pathologies. However, courts can also bring about significant social change that exceeds what elected officials are willing to undertake or what public opinion supports (Rosenberg 2008). Moreover, once judicial activism is unleashed, courts may be tempted to replace democratic institutions (executive and legislative branches) with their own judicial authority (Issacharoff 2019).

To give a concrete example of the scenario raised above, in Argentina, regardless of the cultural dominance of Roman Catholicism and its status as the state's official religion, lawmakers have gradually separated the institution of marriage from its religious connotations. In 2010, a legal reform was passed to grant same-sex couples the right to marry, marking a significant milestone in the movement for sexual diversity (Vaggione 2010). In Brazil, Congress consistently rejected bills seeking to extend marriage protection to partners of the same sex. Then, in 2011, the Brazilian Supreme Court declared unconstitutional any interpretation of the Civil Code (Article 1.723) that limited civil unions to only heterosexual couples (ADI 4.277/DF 2011 and ADPF 132/RJ 2011). A noteworthy aspect of the decision is that the constitution itself reads: "For purposes of protection by the State, the civil union between a *man* and a *woman* is recognized as a family" (Article 226, Paragraph 3). Soon after the landmark decision, polls revealed that 55 percent of Brazilians disagreed with the ruling (G1 2011).

The substance of the judicial ruling on gay marriage is commendable. Nevertheless, it brings forth an essential discussion concerning the role and limits of the judiciary in a democratic society. At the heart of the concern is a methodological approach that leans significantly on hermeneutics when adjudicating, venturing into areas where the explicit text of the constitution does not provide clear grounds. This approach, while offering depth and nuance to the juridical review, potentially blurs the lines between constitutional interpretation and policymaking—courts might be perceived as making rather than interpreting laws. Therefore, while the ruling permitting gay marriages holds substantial merit, it invites a broader conversation on the checks and balances that ensure each branch of government can operate within its designated domain. Besides posing a possible challenge to democracy, the judicialization of politics may lack the necessary linkage between social demands and mass politics (Sieder, Schjolden, and Angell 2005). This is relevant because if legal-based mobilization occurs in the absence of a political base and social roots to shore up decisions, unpopular rulings may be met with effective resistance and low levels of compliance (Brinks and Gonzalez-Ocantos 2022). In other words, without public trust and support, particularly in instances where state capacity is insufficient to uphold the rule of law, the impact of judicial politics is limited (Helmke and Figueroa 2011). A related issue is that as judicialization progresses, political actors can exploit more activist courts to further their political goals. Consequently, courts may become closely intertwined with politics, to the point where the conventional notion of the judiciary as an impartial and non-partisan arm of the government becomes inaccurate (Kapiszewski 2008). In other words, even though the judicialization of politics and the politicization of the judiciary are diverse phenomena, the first can lead to the second.

Therefore, when considering the role of courts in producing social change, there is a normative point to be made from a democratic and institutional perspective: whether courts *ought* to shape public policy at all. In a political system where the popular will holds sovereignty, it may not be immediately clear why courts should have the authority to dictate political outcomes (Rosenberg 2008). Yet, given the reality that courts in Brazil do produce social change, it is crucial to understand how and why this happens. The following section will apply public choice theory to address these questions.

Judicial Activism: Demand and Supply

Public choice theory is an analytical approach that applies economic analysis to public decision-making. It assumes that individuals involved in the political process act as utility maximizers, being motivated by factors similar to those that drive their behavior in other aspects of their lives: while businesspeople are driven by profits, politicians pursue power and reelection, and bureaucrats seek better wages and influence (see Olson 1971; Buchanan 1987; Buchanan and Tullock 1999). As one can see, PCT posits that elected officials and bureaucrats are rational actors who act for their own benefit when making decisions on public affairs. The theory implies that this self-interested behavior leads institutions to produce outcomes that are not in the public interest.

Extensive research supports the assertion that legislators often cater to narrow special interests, as interest groups seek to purchase rents from them, which are often sold by the legislators in exchange for votes (see Landes and Posner 1975; Eskridge and Frickey 1990). Bureaucrats, in their turn, are not affected by the pressure of re-election but may still seek to maximize their agency's power and budget or aim for lucrative future employment opportunities (Stigler 1971). Unlike legislators and bureaucrats, judges are not as clearly influenced by private interests. As judges hold life tenure, they do not have to worry about re-election, and their salaries cannot be reduced during their terms, as guaranteed by the constitution (Article 95, I and III). Due to these differences, the nature of judges' self-interest is still not fully understood (Cross 1999). Perhaps James Madison is in the right, after all, and the judiciary is the "least dangerous" branch of government (Federalist 78), which may make it best suited to pursue the public interest.

Addressing the controversy on whether PCT justifies judicial activism (see Epstein 1985; Komesar 2001), Thomas Merrill developed an economic model centered on a *market for law change*, where the legislature and the courts are the two sellers. According to Merrill (1997), PCT can justify judicial activism to some extent, as it expands the number of players in the market for social change. This allows under-represented groups, who may have limited resources (see Elhauge 1991), to gain traction and add some "spice" to the political system by bringing up dormant issues that would otherwise remain unaddressed, such as gay marriage and racial discrimination (see also Flemming, Bohte, and Wood 1997). By slightly adapting Merrill's model, we can obtain the structure shown in Figure 9.1a.

The graph depicts the relationship between the quantity (Q) of policy change achievable through legislative or judicial action and the associated price (P), which encompasses both the costs for the buyer and the benefits for the supplier. While assigning a monetary value would simplify the illustration, a broader unit is used here to account for the various types of costs and benefits, including financial and political costs, as well as tangible and intangible benefits. It's worth noting that assigning monetary values to the thresholds would be arbitrary, as there are numerous costs and benefits that are not purely financial. For example, lobbying is not a legal activity in Brazil, and thus, interest groups employ more subtle means to influence public policy.

To better understand the model, we need to delve into the demand and supply curves, which are crucial components. Since Mancur Olson's seminal work "The

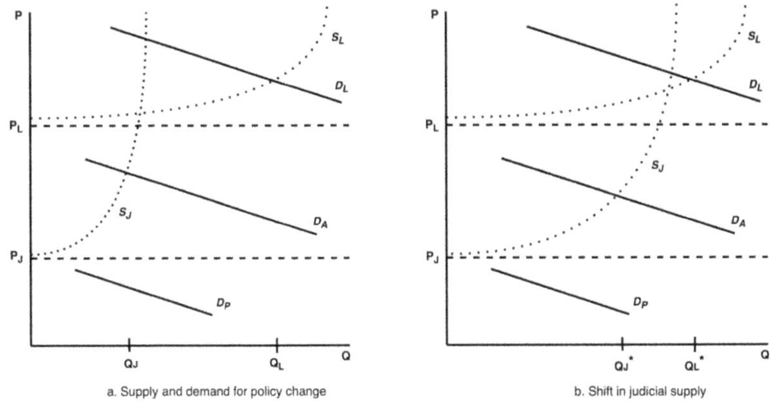

Figure 9.1 Supply and demand for policy change and shift in judicial supply. Author's illustration adapted from Merrill (1997).

Logic of Collective Action," we know that PCT provides a useful framework for comprehending the "logic underlying processes of collective action" (Lemke and Storr 2021). Specifically, the *demand* side denotes the extent to which a group is capable of mobilizing for collective action. This capability depends on factors that include the personal stakes of each individual in the group and whether the group has the resources to cover the costs of mobilization (Olson 1971).

Following this theoretical framework, Figure 1a indicates that there is a minimum price threshold below which no policy change is achieved, whether through legislative or judicial action. In the judiciary, the price of litigation (P_J) involves hiring lawyers, filing petitions in lower courts, and employing amicus briefs (see e.g., Bradley and Gardner 1985). In the legislative process, raising awareness about the issue, utilizing the media, and mobilizing unions, associations, and other interest groups are necessary steps that entail costs as well (P_L). In any case, the minimum price for litigation is usually much lower than that for legislative change (Merrill 1997). Facing this cost structure, certain powerless groups will transmit only a weak demand (D_P), failing to reach the threshold to induce policy change. Other groups with strong lobbying efforts (D_L) can successfully bring about legal change (S_L). Advocacy groups (D_A) may not have the resources to entice legislators, but they often have enough in the tank to get the judiciary on board (S_J).

The intuition behind the model is supported by empirical evidence, particularly in Brazil, where the third sector experienced significant growth in the 1990s, shortly after the Constitution of 1988 expanded the catalog of justiciable rights (Calegare and Silva Junior 2009). In the 1980s, the number of non-governmental organizations (NGOs) in the country was approximately 90,000, but by 2016, this figure had increased tenfold to nearly 900,000, with advocacy groups comprising roughly one-third of the total (IBGE 2019; Costa 2017). Due in large part to the work of these groups, the STF has consistently received around 100,000 law cases annually since the 2000s (STF 2023). Taking into account only the rulings made by the plenary (as most decisions are made in-chambers, where a single justice or small groups of justices issue opinions), the STF issued an average of 2.6 thousand opinions per year between 2010 and 2021, with a peak of 5,829 in 2021 (Matias-Pereira, 2021). For comparison, during the same period, the US Supreme Court issued 203 opinions (SCOTUS 2022).

Even though the model provides a compelling explanation for the rise of judicial activism in Brazil, it still does not explain why Brazilian judges tend to be more activist than their American or German counterparts. The missing piece in the puzzle lies in the elusive supply side of the equation, which remains a topic of much debate in the literature. Specifically, what motivates judges to engage in policymaking and produce social change, despite the backlash and controversy that may ensue? While public choice scholars have shed light on the demand side of the phenomenon, this chapter goes one step further and explores the various incentives that drive judges to become activists, thus providing a comprehensive analysis of the supply of social change via judicial rulings.

In an effort to address what motivates a self-interested judge to maximize their personal gains from public office, Epstein (1990) proposes a distinction between two judicial functions. The first pertains to the adjudication of cases, while the second, which is less procedural in nature, involves judicial administration, lecturing, participating in conferences and organizations, and speaking to the media. Both functions may be influenced by various public and private factors, many of which are intangible.

Regarding the ordinary duties of issuing opinions, public factors such as media attention and public opinion can make judges eager to make the "right" decision, and sometimes this can result in yielding to social pressure. Like any other human beings, judges also seek to maintain their self-esteem, which they can do by validating their decisions with the approval of audiences important to them (Baum, 2009). Likewise, private factors such as personal relationships, professional networks, and career ambitions can shape judges' decision-making. In the case of judges appointed by politicians—as the justices of the Supreme

Court are—outright political factors can come into play, as judges may be influenced by the preferences of the political actor who appointed them to their positions (see Sunstein et al. 2007). A recent study found that justices recently appointed to the Brazilian Supreme Court are more likely to be responsive to the president that appointed them (Medina, Pellegrina, and Garoupa 2022).

In a second level of analysis, judges may use their decision-making to empower their non-clerical roles. In order to maintain the legitimacy of the judiciary as an institution, as well as their own reputations, judges are likely to consider the potential impact of their decisions on their status and influence (Garoupa and Ginsburg 2015). Ambitious judges may endeavor to maximize their "influence" or prestige through their arguments and writing. Judges care about whether their opinions are cited, followed, and included in casebooks, as well as whether they are discussed in popular legal journals and law reviews (Epstein 1990). The behavior of the STF justices is a clear illustration of this scenario. Since the live broadcast of STF deliberations began in 2002, the length of opinions has more than tripled. "STF justices behave as politicians: when given free television time, they act to maximize their individual exposure" (Lopes 2018). Today, STF justices are more active than ever outside of the court, often giving interviews and using social media to express their thoughts. In extreme cases, this inclination towards public life can give rise to a phenomenon we can call the "judge hero"—a magistrate who seeks to fulfill the expectations of popular culture by being a powerful and charismatic figure willing to take on corrupt or oppressive systems, protect the vulnerable, and help those in need (see Gava, 2001).

Contemplating this setup, Figure 1a above offers a plausible representation of the judiciary's behavior in the United States. At the outset, the supply curve shows a willingness to engage in judicial activism, but once the (reasonably low) equilibrium quantity (Q_J) is reached, any further incentives (P) have little effect on the quantity of activism (Q), as the judicial supply curve (S_J) becomes perfectly inelastic. This reluctance to supply more activism can stem from several factors, such as self-imposed limits due to institutional constraints, a conviction about the respective roles of the branches of government, cultural norms, and concerns about potential negative repercussions.

For example, during his first term as President, Roosevelt became increasingly frustrated as the Supreme Court struck down a series of measures central to his New Deal agenda. Following his resounding reelection victory, emboldened by the demonstration of public support, Roosevelt proposed a bill to Congress that would "reorganize" the federal judiciary, including a provision to increase the number of justices on the Supreme Court. Although the court-packing plan ultimately did not become law, the controversy did apply significant pressure on the judiciary and arguably influenced the Supreme Court in their decision to back down (Shesol 2011; Carson and Kleinerman 2002; Cushman 2013).

The judiciary in Brazil works under a diverse set of incentives and an institutional design whose practical effect is to shift the judicial supply curve, as described in Figure 1b above. The new equilibrium quantity for policy change through the judiciary (Q_J*) is much higher than before (Q_J), bringing it closer to the legislative supply (Q_L). This means that using the judiciary as a venue for political claims is now even cheaper relative to pursuing legislative change. Although there is still a point where further increases in incentives do not yield additional expected payouts, this inelasticity is situated at higher levels of activism. In essence, Brazil's "market structure" for policy change encourages the judicialization of politics. This elucidates the prevalence of judicial politics, but we still need to reveal the underlying reasons for this phenomenon.

To begin with, the legal culture in Brazil fosters a higher likelihood of judges engaging in political matters, as illustrated by the nearly horizontal shape of the judicial supply curve (S_J) at low levels of incentives (P). As Couso, Hunneus, and Sieder (2010) assert, there is a prevailing "culture of legality" in Latin America that emphasizes a *language of rights*, meaning that political claims are inherently treated as legal claims. For sure, the United States crafted a robust lexicon of individual rights, which significantly influenced the "foundational period" of Brazilian constitutionalism: the American emphasis on personal liberties and freedoms became a guiding light for many emerging democratic nations, including Brazil, as they endeavored to develop legal frameworks that safeguarded the rights of their citizens. Still, the evolution of rights in Latin America has been characterized by a more profound process, with a trajectory marked by the increasing incorporation of social and economic rights (Gargarella 2014). Beginning in the early twentieth century and continuing into the dawn of the twenty-first, many Latin American nations embarked on a journey to integrate a broader spectrum of entitlements as legal claims—citizens are legally entitled and culturally encouraged to demand housing, healthcare, transport, or childcare from the state. By contrast, in the United States, while there is a safety net to assist those in need, the general expectation is that the government is not primarily responsible for attending to people's material needs. This dichotomy in the understanding and expression of rights manifests not only in policy and governance but also profoundly influences the social fabric, shaping the aspirations, expectations, and viewpoints of respective populations.

Even if we consider that certain segments of US society do talk about public benefits as a right to government assistance, this language is barely visible in judicial records (Tani 2012). In Brazil, however, the popular and judicial vocabularies reflect each other. From a critical perspective, Rosenberg (2008, p. 2–3) highlights the influence that law schools have in shaping students' perceptions of the judiciary, often imbuing them with a sense that a rights-based approach can solve social problems via judicial rulings, which may overstate the judiciary's importance, role, and influence in civic life. Consequently, judges are more likely to view themselves as relevant players in political issues. In this context, the judicialization of political matters appears almost "natural" and uncontroversial, lacking significant social debate.

Legal cultures that place a high value on legal rights certainly have their benefits. Still, one potential drawback is that they tend to produce judges who view their role as that of a guardian of all rights, which can result in an overreliance on judicial activism. This is particularly evident in regions like Latin America, where neo-constitutionalism has shifted the balance of power from the legislative branch to the constitution, resulting in an expansion of the judicial supply curve (see Barroso 2006; Hirschl 2009). Conversely, judges who are socialized in more formal legal cultures tend to demonstrate greater judicial restraint. For example, legal traditions that prioritize the separation of powers and a legicentric approach, where the legislative branch represents popular will, such as those found in the United States and Britain, tend to have lower levels of judicial activism.

It is worth noting that although legal values associated with a liberal legal culture, such as a commitment to fundamental rights or deference to social policy, are expected to serve the public interest, there are circumstances in which coordinating individual interests within the judiciary can pose a collective challenge. For example, with the reduction in costs to litigate, individuals seeking public goods have incentives to claim rights, regardless of the costs imposed on society. One such example is universal access to healthcare, with a recent report revealing over 800,000 legal cases filed in Brazilian courts requesting health-related goods and services (CNJ 2019). In a share of these cases, plaintiffs refuse more economic treatments offered in the public health system and instead seek to compel the state to provide them with more expensive drugs. From a collective perspective, the marginal increase in utility for these citizens may not justify the increase in shared costs. For a particular plaintiff, as long as the individual cost to litigate is lower than the marginal increment in utility, they rationally prefer litigation.

Moreover, when a commitment to rights becomes a specific type of public policy, judges may become more susceptible to ideologies, intellectual orientations, or political leanings. This may lead them to prioritize abstract rights over social costs or even disregard established legal precedents and laws in favor of their policy preferences. Judges who hold stronger ideological views are more likely to engage in judicial activism than those with more moderate views; as Epstein (1990, p. 838) notes, "the lack of short-term financial incentives necessarily increases the relative importance of a judge's world view." Empirically, studies on the ethos of the Brazilian judiciary reveal that many judges see themselves as "social activists" or "service providers" (Gomes, Guimaraes, and Lucas de Souza 2016).

Of course, as courts' interference in political affairs increases, the likelihood of political resistance also rises (Keck 2009; Voeten 2020). Backlash is not an anomaly but a fundamental aspect of the movements and counter-movements that characterize the political process (Lehoucq 2021). Therefore, if the judiciary is willing to engage in political affairs, it must be prepared to play the entire game. However, when faced with backlash, judges may exceed the equilibrium quantity of activism to protect themselves or the judiciary's position. In response to fierce opposition, the STF fought back by launching its own investigation allegedly to investigate fake news (ADPF 572 MC/DF 2020). This move represented a drastic self-expansion of its jurisdiction, which allowed the court to order pretrial detentions, authorize search and seizures, and block social media accounts and posts (Nicas 2023). It is difficult to find a parallel to this situation anywhere else in the world.

Furthermore, institutional design in Brazil also contributes to the judicialization of politics. Unlike in the United States where Congress can potentially regulate the Supreme Court, in Brazil the attributions of the STF are set in the constitution, and any attempt to restrict them would face judicial review. This means that the court itself could strike down any reform by declaring it unconstitutional. As a result, threats from the executive branch to pack the court or from the legislative branch to regulate what topics the court can adjudicate do not hold weight in Brazil.

Such allocation of prerogatives has a unique feature that overturns the traditional balance of power. As Merrill (1997) points out, in the United States "legislative action can trump a judicial outcome," but in Brazil the judiciary has the final say. This explains why, if a sizeable amount of resources is invested or if the stakes are high enough, the quantity of policy change in the judiciary can be enormous—very close to that in the legislature— as the point of intersection between S_J and D_L indicates in Figure 1b. Recently, this scenario materialized during the Covid-19 pandemic, when politicians and advocates turned to the Supreme Court to decide nearly every question related to the pandemic. Between the first quarter of 2020 and the first quarter of 2023, the STF issued 15,564 opinions (in 11,616 cases) related to the pandemic. According to the court, 6,236 of these opinions were of "high complexity and great impact and repercussion" (STF 2023).

Not only has the Brazilian Supreme Court produced a stunning quantity of opinions, but the nature of the decisions is also noteworthy. Some of the court's rulings go so deep into political issues that judges around the world would be left blushing. For instance, in two recent criminal policy cases, the court ruled in favor of the Brazilian Socialist Party's request to halt police operations in Rio de Janeiro's slums during the Covid-19 pandemic and to forbid the use of helicopters and armored vehicles during police operations (ADPF 635/RJ 2019). The court then went on to declare that homophobia and transphobia should be classified as transgressions in the same category as racism, despite the Constitution explicitly stating that "there is no crime without a previous law to define it, nor a punishment without a previous legal commination" (Article five, XXXIX). The STF argued that since Congress had failed to criminalize such acts, it was up to the judiciary to take action (ADO 26/DF 2019 and MI 4733/DF 2019).

One might wonder why Brazilian legislators do not resist judicial activism. The evidence shows that politicians themselves have embraced judicial politics in Brazil, transforming courts into a battlefield for political claims. In this regard, Olson's (1971) theory of collective action illuminates the issue again. The size of a group is a crucial factor in determining its ability to mobilize and act collectively. Larger groups tend to transmit demands very weakly, since the benefits to each individual are too small to provide an incentive for action. Consider the size of the Brazilian legislative chambers, which comprise of 512 representatives and 81 senators at the federal level: There is no guarantee that any member would be able to gain significant power by curbing judicial activism. In fact, it may be advantageous for members of political minorities to have an additional avenue to pursue their goals. It is no surprise that between 1988 and 2008, 25.5 percent of constitutional challenges were filed by state governors, and 19 percent were filed by political parties or state legislative houses, adding up to a total of 44.5 percent of cases brought before the Supreme Court being cases where politicians themselves were trying to overturn legislation (STF, 2008). That is, only half of constitutional challenges are proposed by external actors—the federal Attorney General or national associations. The data indicate that politicians have adapted to the cost structure of the policy change market and have become consumers of judicial politics by exploiting the judicialization process.

Implications: Why Judicial Activism May be a Problem

Once the applicability of PCT is established, one can utilize its framework to scrutinize the potential implications of judicial activism, taking into account the existing (a) incentives, (b) accessible information, and (c) the institutions that establish the boundaries under which each decision is made.

Commencing the analysis with the institutional settings that delineate the context wherein decisions are formulated, Buchanan (1987) notices that formal and informal rules generate an environment where outcomes may either align with or diverge from the intended objectives of the decision-makers. In this regard, even a strong set of justiciable rights, which empower citizens to legally challenge government behavior, coupled with judges willing to act, may still allow for substantial variations in executive enforcement (Jung, Hirschl, and Rosevear 2014; Sadurski 2005). Empirical studies have underscored a significant gap between the legal promises and the actual practices of governments. Disturbingly, the correlation appears to be negative (Fraser 1998).

Indeed, evidence indicates a level of comfort amongst office-holding politicians with the judicialization of public policymaking, possibly due to the potential reduction in political costs. Rather than countering the trend of judicialization, politicians seem to welcome the shift in responsibility for the delivery of public goods over to the judiciary. This scenario introduces a paradox where, on one hand, window dressing laws become costly because courts will actually enforce those rights, but on the other hand, necessary structural changes to enhance the provision of public goods are neglected (Brinks, Levitsky, and Murillo 2019). For a long time, dating back to when Scheingold (1974) elucidated the "myth of rights," it has been acknowledged that the simple existence of rights can potentially conceal the political and social dynamics that dictate the extent to which these rights are brought to fruition.

Furthermore, within the realm of judicial proceedings, institutional design predominantly directs courts to concentrate on individual cases brought before them—a scenario that can make them overlook the aggregate societal costs their rulings might impose. This focus, largely guided by single-case interpretations rather than a comprehensive cost-benefit analysis (Anderson, 1992), may make courts not only neglect budgetary constraints but also disrupt political priorities. The atomized enforcement of rights via judicialization may thus undermine social policies aimed at enhancing the welfare of a broader segment of the population. For example, in São Paulo, Brazil's wealthiest state, the funds allocated for individual healthcare lawsuits equate to the cost of building a new hospital every month (Ribeiro and Hartmann, 2016).

In this context, a staggering increase in government expenditure on healthcare lawsuits—a rise from US$ 38.25 million in 2008 to US$ 2.13 billion in 2016 (a 5500% increase)—signals a concerning trend, with the judiciary absorbing nearly 6 percent of the 2016 health budget (BRASIL, 2016)—a development that threatens to destabilize governmental ability to streamline its long-term initiatives and policies, which is a fundamental goal for any administration (Comparato, 1990). As noted by Brinks and Gauri (2014), attempting to produce socioeconomic welfare through judicialization, without addressing the deep roots of social inequality observed in developing nations, might ironically undermine the very goals that judicial activism intends to fulfill.

The second facet of analyzing judicialization through the lens of PCT pertains to the inherent question of knowledge. In the context of judicial decision-making, judges typically operate under situations of incomplete information. When their responsibilities extend to shaping broader aspects of political life, the intricacy and the scope of the "knowledge problem" expand exponentially. This shift in role is critical because it not only amplifies the complexity of the information required but also makes the interpretative process more prone to errors and misalignments, as the legal guidelines (if there are any) are much less clear in political issues. Moreover, being less accustomed to the political games, judges may fall prey to interest groups, which might be able to exploit the judiciary's inability to identify and curb these influences adequately, thereby compromising the democratic ethos of representation (Farber and Frickey 1991).

Another pivotal aspect of judicial politics is the disparity in awareness levels among citizens about their rights and the means available to exercise them.

This informational asymmetry prevalent across diverse social groups can potentially fuel existing socioeconomic inequalities. For example, empirical research has demonstrated that the judicialization of economic and social rights has not been beneficial to the most vulnerable sectors of society in Latin America. On the contrary, it seems to foster resource concentration in regions with better socioeconomic backgrounds, where individuals are better equipped with both the knowledge and resources necessary to initiate and sustain litigation processes (Lopes 2019). Therefore, even when the judicial political structure functions optimally, the actual results can deviate considerably due to prevailing socioeconomic disparities. The existing barriers, which preclude the economically weaker sections of the population from accessing the courts, hint at a system where judicialization privileges are disproportionately accrued by wealthier segments of society. These groups, with their substantial resources, are better positioned to navigate and benefit from litigation processes, thus potentially skewing justice in their favor (Galanter 1974).

Under PCT, it is argued that judges, like other public officials, are motivated by personal incentives and disincentives, which can significantly influence the decisions they make. The challenge of making decisions under incomplete or inaccurate information—and little legal directive—may well increase the incidence of rulings that align more closely with the judges' individual biases or the influences of powerful interest groups, as opposed to adhering to the legal canon or catering to the broader welfare of society (Rizzo and Whitman, 2009).

I agree with Lemke and Storr (2021) that there is no a priori justification for a pattern of judicial deference to legislators on matters of constitutionality. Indeed, as a society, we are better served by an institutional structure centered around multiple veto powers, seeking balance through processes of competition, cooperation, and contestation. However, Lemke and Storr's assessment that "*legislators have no direct access to the will of the people that would justify them holding a unique position as the final arbiter*" deserves some qualification. First, there is a qualitative difference between elected officials and unelected officials, and judges are not elected in most of the world. In the sphere where electoral results matter, there are at least minimal incentives toward collective-choice processes, including those in which citizens are directly involved in making the choices that create and enforce law (Buchanan, 1999). Nothing like this happens in the judiciary. For sure, history unveils several instances in which certain groups were marginalized and excluded from the political debate—women, Native Americans, and enslaved individuals, just to mention the most evident examples. Still, in the judicial realm, the complexities are manifold; the legitimacy of litigation rights is an intricate labyrinth and the criteria to define who possesses authority is often muddled by layers of legal intricacy. In other words, the average individual citizen still has inexpensive ways to influence legislators: by voting and voicing their needs. Yet, the average citizen has no way to change judges' minds (Cross 1999).

There remains the question of instances where we expect judges to counter majorities, particularly when tasked with protecting minorities and upholding fundamental rights. Komesar (2001) references scholarship which suggests that judicialization is a positive step towards safeguarding the essence of legal rights. While this perspective has its merits, there are two essential considerations. Firstly, it overlooks supply-side issues like judicial biases or errors, which may arise from incomplete information. This can disrupt legitimate social choices, impede social programs due to unplanned reallocation of limited resources, and cause a regressive redistribution of benefits from poorer to richer segments of society. Secondly, the optimistic stance perceives the judicial enforcement of rights as an isolated force that does not provoke reactions from other political entities. In reality, politicians are (and should be) expected to adjust in the face of court-mandated policy alterations. If judges are assertive in social regulation, politicians might become more hesitant to debate and enact costly social reforms, opting instead to wait for the judiciary's decisions. When judges set social policy from their chambers, politicians might preemptively cut public investments to accumulate reserves for contingency purposes—saving resources to accommodate judicial mandates, and so forth.

The underlying assertion is that reality, particularly in the context of sociopolitical environments, cannot be captured fully in a static, unchanging representation, akin to a snapshot or a photograph. Instead, it embodies a constantly shifting and evolving entity that is influenced by a multitude of factors, including the actions and reactions of various stakeholders, such as policymakers, bureaucrats, and the judiciary. In the complex interplay of judicial politics, once judges initiate moves to implement certain policies or enforce rights through judicial mechanisms, it naturally prompts responses from other sectors of the government. This process can be visualized as a strategic game where each move is met with a countermove, adjusting the state of play and potentially altering the outcomes in unforeseen ways. There is a cautionary note here against an excessive reliance on judicial mechanisms to address and resolve deep-seated socioeconomic issues. What could be perceived as a "romantic view" of judicial action fails to appreciate the complexity and nuance of the political game.

Conclusion: The Two Faces of Judicialization

PCT offers an insightful framework for understanding judges' behavior, explaining why judges in Brazil are more likely to engage in judicial activism. Judges are influenced by a multitude of factors, such as their personal preferences and the legal culture of their country, as well as the political and social pressures they encounter. These factors, combined with the cost structure of producing social change, determine the level of judicial politics in a political system. In Brazil, these factors are organized in such a way that the supply curve for political change has shifted to the right, inducing judges to adopt a more proactive approach to policy than in countries with more formalistic legal cultures, lower incentives for judicial policy change, and institutional designs that limit the judiciary's authority.

The implications of PCT's findings related to judicial politics are still open to debate. According to Merrill (1997), judicial politics expands the pool of groups capable of promoting social change and facilitates greater change. Eliminating judicial activism could limit the scope of groups capable of influencing public policy, thus skewing the legal change market in favor of the wealthy and organized groups. However, acknowledging judges' status as rational actors who respond to incentives requires us to scrutinize the institutional and sociopolitical context in which judges function and how it may divert their behavior away from the public interest (Cross 1999). Regardless of which view one adopts, the development of a better understanding of the supply curve for judicial politics opens a series of opportunities for future research.

The first such opportunity is to scrutinize whether judges get financial benefits from judicial activism, via invitations to conferences and to author books for example, and double checking the possibility of direct financial benefits to activism. Along similar lines, there is still little research on the possible impacts of activism on judges' influence and prestige. On a macro level, it is critical to explore whether judicialization diverts blame attribution towards the atomized enforcement of rights, thereby alleviating political pressure, or if activist courts hinder the achievement of structural changes that necessitate political capital and grassroots support.

By examining these issues, we can deepen our understanding of judicial politics and recognize its dynamic and contentious nature. As the rules of the political game increasingly embrace judicialization, judges will rationally adapt to benefit from the evolving landscape, while policymakers and bureaucrats are expected to countermove accordingly. Through an exploration of the subjective and institutional structures that govern these movements, we can gain crucial insights into their historical underpinnings, current trends, and future implications.

References

Anderson, Gerard F. 1992. "The Courts and Health Policy: Strengths and Limitations." *Health Affairs* 11 (4): 95–110.

Antía, Florencia, and Daniela Vairo. 2019. "Política y justicia en Uruguay: el poder de la Suprema Corte de Justicia (1990–2018)." *Revista Uruguaya de Ciencia Política* 28 (2): 61–86.

Barroso, Luís Roberto. 2006. "Neoconstitucionalismo e Constitucionalização do Direito (o Triunfo Tardio do Direito Constitucional no Brasil)."*Themis: Revista da ESMEC* 4 (2): 13–100.

Barroso, Luís Roberto. 2019. "Countermajoritarian, Representative, and Enlightened: The Roles of Constitutional Courts in Democracies." *The American Journal of Comparative Law* 67 (1): 109–143.

Barroso, Luís Roberto. 2016. "Reason without Vote: The Representative and Majoritarian Function of Constitutional Courts." In *Democratizing Constitutional Law: Perspectives on Legal Theory and the Legitimacy of Constitutionalism*, edited by Thomas Bustamante, 71–90. New York: Springer.

Barroso, Luís Roberto. 2019. "Countermajoritarian, Representative, and Enlightened: The Roles of Constitutional Courts in Democracies." *The American Journal of Comparative Law* 67 (1): 109–143.

Baum, Lawrence. 2009. *Judges and Their Audiences: A Perspective on Judicial Behavior.* Princeton: Princeton University Press.

Belov, Martin, ed. 2019. *Courts, Politics and Constitutional Law: Judicialization of Politics and Politicization of the Judiciary.* New York: Routledge.

Berger, Raoul. 2012. *Government by Judiciary.* Indianapolis, IN: Liberty Fund.

Botero, Sandra, Daniel M. Brinks, and Ezequiel A. Gonzalez-Ocantos. 2022. "Working in New Political Spaces: The Checkered History of Latin American Judicialization." In *The Limits of Judicialization: From Progress to Backlash in Latin America,* edited by Botero, Sandra, Daniel Brinks and Ezequiel Gonzalez-Ocantos, 1–38. Cambridge: Cambridge University Press.

Bradley, Robert C., and Paul Gardner. 1985. "Underdogs, Upperdogs and the Use of the Amicus Brief: Trends and Explanations." *The Justice System Journal* 10 (1): 78–96.

Brasil, Portal da Transparência. 2016. Controladoria Geral da União. http://www.portaltransparencia.gov.br/funcoes/10-saude?ano=2016.

Brinks, Daniel M., and Varun Gauri. 2014. "The Law's Majestic Equality? The Distributive Impact of Judicializing Social and Economic Rights." *Perspectives on Politics* 12 (2): 375–393.

Brinks, Daniel M., Steven Levitsky, and Maria Victoria Murillo. 2019. *Understanding Institutional Weakness: Power and Design in Latin American Institutions.* Cambridge: Cambridge University Press.

Buchanan, James M. 1987. "The Constitution of Economic Policy." *Science* 236 (4807): 1433–1436.

Buchanan, James M. 1999. *The Collected Works of James M. Buchanan Volume* 6, 41–42. Indianapolis, IN: Liberty Fund.

Buchanan, James, and Gordon Tullock. 1999. *The Calculus of Consent: Logical Foundations of Constitutional Democracy.* Indianapolis: Liberty Fund.

Calegare, Marcelo Gustavo Aguilar, and Nelson da Silva Junior. 2009. "A 'Construção' do Terceiro Setor no Brasil: da Questão Social à Organizacional." *Revista Psicologia Política* 9 (17): 129–148.

Carson, Jamie L., and Benjamin A. Kleinerman. 2002. "A Switch in Time Saves Nine: Institutions, Strategic Actors, and FDR's Court-Packing Plan." *Public Choice* 113 (3–4): 301–324.

Ciencia, Alejandro N. 2002. "From Judicialization to Politicization of the Judiciary: The Philippine Case." In *The Judicialization of Politics in Asia*, edited by Bjorn Dressel, 117–138. New York: Routledge.

Comparato, Fábio Konder. 1990. "The Economic Order in the Brazilian Constitution of 1988." *The American Journal of Comparative Law* 38 (4): 759.

Conselho Nacional de Justiça. 2019. "Judicialização da Saúde no Brasil: Perfil das Demandas, Causas e Propostas de Solução." https://rb.gy/c5uf.

Costa, Marcelo Marchesini da. 2017. "Análise de Colaborações Entre Governo e ONGs e da Densidade de ONGs no Brasil." *Revista de Administração Pública* 51: 330–347.

Couso, Javier, Alexandra Huneeus, and Rachel Sieder, eds. 2010. *Cultures of Legality: Judicialization and Political Activism in Latin America.* Cambridge: Cambridge University Press.

Cross, Frank B. 1999. "The Judiciary and Public Choice." *Hastings Law Journal* 50: 355.

Cushman, Barry. 2013. "Court-Packing and Compromise." *Const. Comment* 29: 1.

Dahl, Robert. 1957. "Decision-Making in a Democracy: The Supreme Court as a National Policy-Maker." *Journal of Public Law* 6 (2): 279–295.

Domingo, Pilar. 1999. "Judicial Independence and Judicial Reform in Latin America." In *The Self-Restraining State: Power and Accountability in New Democracies,* edited by Schedler, Andreas, Larry Jay Diamond and Marc F. Plattner, 151–176. London: Lynne Rienner Publishers.

Domingo, Pilar. 2004. "Judicialization of Politics or Politicization of the Judiciary? Recent Trends in Latin America." *Democratization* 11 (1): 104–126.

Elhauge, Einer R. 1991. "Does Interest Group Theory Justify More Intrusive Judicial Review?" *Yale Law Journal*, 101 (1): 31–110.

Epstein, Richard A. 1990. "The Independence of Judges: The Uses and Limitations of Public Choice Theory." *Brigham Young University Law Review*, 1990 (3): 827–855.

Epstein, Richard A. 1985. *Takings: Private Property and the Power of Eminent Domain.* Cambridge: Harvard University Press.

Eskridge Jr, William N., and Philip P. Frickey. 1990. "Statutory Interpretation as Practical Reasoning." *Stanford Law Review* 42 (2): 321–384.

Farber, Daniel A., and Philip P. Frickey. 1991. *Law and Public Choice: A Critical Introduction.* Chicago, IL: University of Chicago Press.

Flemming, Roy B., John Bohte, and B. Dan Wood. 1997. "One Voice among Many: The Supreme Court's Influence on Attentiveness to Issues in the United States, 1947–92." *American Journal of Political Science* 41 (4): 1224–1250.

Fraser, Elvis E. 1998. "The Dimensions of Human Rights: A Confirmatory Factor Analysis of Human Rights Provisions." *International Journal of Sociology*, Winter, 2003/2004, 33 (4): 11–40, 15, 25–28.

Friedman, Terry B. 1998. "The Politicization of the Judiciary." *Judicature* 82: 6.

G1. 2011. "55% Das Pessoas São Contra União Estável Gay, Diz Pesquisa do Ibope." Globo.com. July 28. http://j.mp/oyN2s1.

Galanter, Marc. 1974. "Why the Haves Come out Ahead: Speculations on the Limits of Legal Change." *Law & Society Review* 9: 95.

Gargarella, Roberto. 2014 "Latin American Constitutionalism: Social Rights and the 'Engine Room' of the Constitution." In *Law and Society in Latin America*, edited by Sieder, Rachel, Karina Ansolabehere, and Tatiana Alfonson, 83–92. New York: Routledge.

Garoupa, Nuno, and Tom Ginsburg. 2015. *Judicial Reputation.* Chicago, IL: University of Chicago Press.

Gauri, Varun, and Daniel M. Brinks. 2008. *Courting Social Justice: Judicial Enforcement of Social and Economic Rights in the Developing World.* Cambridge: Cambridge University Press.

Gava, John. 2001. "The Rise of the Hero Judge." *The University of New South Wales Law Journal* 24 (3): 747–759.

Gomes, Adalmir Oliveira, Tomas Aquino Guimaraes, and Eda Castro Lucas de Souza. 2016. "Judicial Work and Judges' Motivation: The Perceptions of Brazilian State Judges." *Law & Policy* 38 (2): 162–176.

González-Ocantos, Ezequiel A. 2016. *Shifting Legal Visions: Judicial Change and Human Rights Trials in Latin America.* Cambridge: Cambridge University Press.

Grofman, Bernard. 1991. "Public Choice, Civic Republicanism, and American Politics: Perspectives of a Reasonable Choice Modeler." *Texas Law Review* 71: 1541.

Hart, Henry Melvin, and Albert Martin Sacks. 1994. "The Legal Process: Basic Problems in the Making and Application of Law." Goleta, CA: Foundation Press.

Helmke, Gretchen, and Julio Ríos Figueroa, eds. 2011. *Courts in Latin America.* Cambridge, UK: Cambridge University Press.

Hirschl, Ran. 2009. *Towards Juristocracy: The Origins and Consequences of the New Constitutionalism.* Cambridge: Harvard University Press.

Instituto Brasileiro de Geografia e Estatística. 2019. "As Fundações Privadas e Associações sem Fins Lucrativos no Brasil 2016."

Issacharoff, Samuel. 2019. "Judicial Review in Troubled Times: Stabilizing Democracy in a Second-Best World." *North Carolina Law Review* 98: 1.

Jung, Courtney; Ran Hirschl, and Evan Rosevear. 2014. "Economic and Social Rights in National Constitutions." *The American Journal of Comparative Law* 62 (4): 1043–1093.

Kapiszewski, D., and Taylor, M. 2008. *Doing Courts Justice? Studying Judicial Politics in Latin America. Perspectives on Politics* 6 (4): 741–767.

Keck, Thomas M. 2009. "Beyond Backlash: Assessing the Impact of Judicial Decisions on LGBT Rights." *Law & Society Review* 43 (1): 151–186.

Kmiec, Keenan D. 2004. "The Origin and Current Meanings of 'judicial activism.'" *California Law Review* 92 (5): 1441–1477.

Komesar, Neil K. 2001. *Law's Limits: The Rule of Law and the Supply and Demand of Rights.* Cambridge: Cambridge University Press.

Landes, William M., and Richard A. Posner. 1975. "The Independent Judiciary in an Interest-Group Perspective." *The Journal of Law and Economics* 18 (3): 875–901.

Lehoucq, Emilio. 2021. "Legal Threats and the Emergence of Legal Mobilization: Conservative Mobilization in Colombia." *Law & Social Inquiry* 46 (2): 299–330.

Lemke, Jayme, and Virgil Henry Storr. 2021. "Defending the Weak Will of the People: An Economic Perspective on Collective Will in Democratic Societies." *George Mason Law Review* 29: 471.

Lopes, Felipe de Mendonça. 2018. "Television and Judicial Behavior: Lessons from the Brazilian Supreme Court." *Economic Analysis of Law Review* 9 (1): 41–71.

Lopes, Luciana de Melo Nunes, et al. 2019. "(Un)Equitable Distribution of Health Resources and the Judicialization of Healthcare: 10 years of Experience in Brazil." *International Journal for Equity in Health* 18 (1): article 10.

Matias-Pereira, José. 2021. "Impactos da Judicialização da Política e Ativismo Judicial no Brasil." *Brazilian Journal of Development* 7 (3): 29286–29316.

Medina, Damares, Lucia dalla Pellegrina, and Nuno Garoupa. 2022. "Unfolding Judicial Ideology: A Data-Generating Priors Approach with an Application to the Brazilian Supreme Court." *Review of Law & Economics* 18 (1): 1–54.

Mendes, Gilmar. 2009. "The Adjudication of Socio-Economic Rights in Brazil." *STF.* September 13. http://www.stf.jus.br/arquivo/cms/noticiaArtigoDiscurso/anexo/londres.pdf.

Merrill, Thomas W. 1997. "Does Public Choice Theory Justify Judicial Activism after All." *Harvard Journal of Law & Public Policy* 21: 219.

Mitchell, William C., and Randy T. Simmons. 1990. "Public Choice and the Judiciary: Introductory Notes." *Brigham Young University Law Review* 1990: 729–744.

Nicas, Jack. 2023. "He Is Brazil's Defender of Democracy. Is He Actually Good for Democracy?" *The New York Times.* January 22. https://www.nytimes.com/2023/01/22/world/americas/brazil-alexandre-de-moraes.html.

Nunes, Rodrigo M. 2010. "Ideational Origins of Progressive Judicial Activism: The Colombian Constitutional Court and the Right to Health." *Latin American Politics and Society* 52 (3): 67–97.

Olson, Mancur. 1971. *The Logic of Collective Action: Public Goods and the Theory of Groups*, Cambridge: Harvard University Press.

Ribeiro, Leandro M., and Ivar A. Hartmann. 2016. "Judicialization of the Right to Health and Institutional Changes in Brazil." *Journal of Constitutional Research.* Curitiba, 3 (3): 35–52.

Riker William H., and Barry R. Weingast. 1988. "Constitutional Regulation of Legislative Choice: The Political Consequences of Judicial Deference to Legislatures." *Va. Law Review* 74: 373.

Rizzo, Mario J., and Douglas Glen Whitman. 2009. "The Knowledge Problem of New Paternalism." *Brigham Young University Law Review* 905: 922–931.

Roa Roa, Jorge Ernesto. 2019. "Justicia Constitucional, Deliberación y Democracia en Colombia: Jeremy Waldron Reflexivo en Bogotá." *Revista Derecho del Estado* 44: 57–98.

Rose-Ackerman, Susan. 1992. "Judicial Review and the Power of the Purse." *International Review of Law and Economics* 12 (2): 191–208.

Rosenberg, Gerald N. 2008. *The Hollow Hope: Can Courts Bring about Social Change?* Chicago, IL: University of Chicago Press.

Sadurski, Wojciech. 2005. *Rights before Courts: A Study of Constitutional Courts in Post-Communist States of Central and Eastern Europe,* 183. Dordrecht: Springer.

Scheingold, Stuart A. 1974. *The Politics of Rights: Lawyers, Public Policy, and Political Change.* New Haven, CT: Yale University Press.

Shesol, Jeff. 2011. *Supreme Power: Franklin Roosevelt vs. the Supreme Court.* New York: WW Norton & Company.

Sieder, Rachel, Line Schjolden, and Alan Angell (eds). 2005. *The Judicialization of Politics in Latin America.* New York: Palgrave Macmillan.

Siegan, Bernard H. 1984. "Economic Liberties and the Constitution: Protection at the State Level." *Cato Journal* 4: 689.

Skeel Jr, David A. 1997. "Public Choice and the Future of Public-Choice-Influenced Legal Scholarship." *Vanderbilt Law Review*, 50 (4): 647.

Stigler, George J. 1971. "The Theory of Economic Regulation." *The Bell Journal of Economics and Management Science* 2 (1): 3–21.

Sunstein, Cass R., David Schkade, Lisa M. Ellman, and Andres Sawicki. 2007. *Are Judges Political? An Empirical Analysis of the Federal Judiciary*. Washington: Brookings Institution Press.

Supreme Court of the United States. 2022. "Opinions of the Court." https://www.supremecourt.gov/opinions/slipopinion/22.

Supreme Federal Tribunal. 2008. "1988–2008: Vinte Anos de Ações Diretas de Inconstitucionalidade." https://rb.gy/kv7n.

Supreme Federal Tribunal. 2023. "Painel de Ações Covid-19." https://transparencia.stf.jus.br/extensions/corte_aberta/corte_aberta.html.

Tani, Karen M. 2012. "Welfare and Rights before the Movement: Rights as a Language of the State." *Yale Law Journal* 122: 314.

Vaggione, Juan Marco. 2010. "Sexual Rights and Religion: Same-Sex Marriage and Lawmakers' Catholic Identity in Argentina." *University of Miami Law Review* 65: 935.

Voeten, Erik. 2020. "Populism and Backlashes against International Courts." *Perspectives on Politics* 18 (2): 407–422.

Wilson, Bruce. 2009. "Rights Revolutions in Unlikely Places: Costa Rica and Colombia." *Journal of Politics in Latin America* 1 (2): 59–85.

10

Time Taxes and Avoidable Structural Injustice

Gah-Kai Leung

Consider the following three paradigmatic cases:[1]

> *Pandemic Redundancy*: A New York City data analyst is laid off just after the start of the Covid-19 pandemic. She files for unemployment benefits accordingly. She then spends the next six months pressing New York State's Labor Department over the phone, over email and via social media to give her the money she is rightfully owed.
>
> *Access to Tax Credits*: A disabled mother in Philadelphia cares for her daughter, who is also disabled. Because she lives below the poverty line, she does not regularly file taxes. Furthermore, she does not have regular access to a computer. In the end, she has to seek help from a legal aid group to ensure she receives the correct child-tax-credit payments.
>
> *Job Switch*: A Colorado systems administrator, with a chronic medical condition, switches jobs. The job switch leads to an accidental lapse in the administrator's health insurance coverage. This results in an extremely large amount of paperwork concerning the responsibility for a medical bill. The systems administrator spends about 100 hours, by his own estimates, trying to fix the problem (Lowrey 2021).

The protagonists in all three cases face a barrage of administrative hoops and bureaucratic obstacles to receiving the social assistance that they are duly owed. Each individual spends dozens, if not hundreds, of hours negotiating the maze of state bureaucracy to resolve their issues. Each of those hours represents lost time that they could have spent doing something more productive, had they not been forced to engage with the administrative state. Indeed, these experiences of being "a cog in the administrative machine" (Lovell 2022, 118) or of being "lost in the system" will resonate with many ordinary Americans and citizens of other well-developed states.

As the above three cases illustrate, administrative and paperwork burdens impose enormous costs on rank-and-file citizens. In the United States alone, for example, individuals spend almost 9 billion hours a year ensuring their tax returns are IRS compliant; this costs the American economy over $400 billion annually (Hodge 2016). The UK's Behavioral Insights Team estimates that Britons spend about 3 billion hours of their personal lives every year dealing with public services (Halpern 2022). These burdens have been referred to as "sludge" (Sunstein 2019), a term which suggests the creak and friction that arises when administrative processes don't work as smoothly or efficiently as one would like. I, however, will follow Annie Lowrey's terminology and call them "time taxes" (2021), which captures perhaps one of the most important features of this phenomenon: a colossal investment of man-hours often with very little visible return. As David Halpern of the Behavioral Insights Team puts it: "This tax on our time is a *hidden cost of living* that needs to be taken seriously and treated as the economic drag that it is" (2022; my emphasis).

As should be evident from my remarks up until this point, time taxes can and should be considered a genuine problem, but I want to go deeper than that here and elucidate precisely what is wrong with time taxes. My core claim in this chapter is that time taxes constitute a kind of *avoidable structural injustice.* Put simply, structural injustices are those injustices which arise due to the interactions of a wide range of actors within the large-scale social processes that make up the overarching social and political structure (Young 2006; Young 2011). The injustices are *avoidable* when powerful agents are capable of changing the system but signally fail to do so (McKeown 2021; McKeown 2024). One reason for this failure may have to do with the *incentives* produced by the socio-political structure, which occasion the structural injustice. Having identified time taxes as a product of avoidable structural injustice, we open opportunities for policy reform, especially on the part of powerful actors within the social system. Further, the lens of avoidable structural injustice allows us to add moral force to a policy issue that is usually framed in economic terms—i.e., the financial costs of administration.

The rest of the chapter proceeds as follows. I begin by clarifying the definition of time taxes and discuss their problematic features. I then introduce the notion of structural injustice and apply it to the problem of time taxes. Next, I consider the issue of avoidability by elaborating on the incentives that make time taxes a type of avoidable structural injustice (rather than structural injustice *simpliciter*), drawing on the public choice literature within political economy.

Here, I also comment on what we gain, normatively speaking, by calling time taxes an avoidable structural injustice. Finally, I suggest some ways to reduce the problem of time taxes from a policy standpoint, building on the arguments up to this point, and making some brief concluding remarks.

This chapter makes four main scholarly contributions. First, it contributes to the public choice literature by identifying the incentives that encourage the creation of structural injustice, using time taxes as a case study. Second, it shows how the burgeoning literature on administrative burdens[2] can benefit from a consideration of the normative issues at stake, with reference to the literature on structural injustice. Third, it contributes to the literature on structural injustice by showing how time taxes can be interpreted as a case of avoidable structural injustice. Fourth, in combining the public choice literature with the normative literature on structural injustice, the chapter arrives at a novel synthesis of these two literatures, using the case study of time taxes.

Three clarificatory points are worth noting at the outset. First, my argument is only meant to apply to liberal democracies with well-established bureaucracies, such as those in North America and Western Europe (though most of my examples will be drawn from Britain and the United States). Developing, middle-income, and transitional economies will raise different political economy considerations and so are excluded, in principle, from this analysis. At the same time, the conclusions I draw may serve as a cautionary tale for developing countries before their bureaucratic systems become as deeply entrenched as those in wealthier nation-states.

Second, I will only be concerned here with the administrative burdens faced by everyday citizens when interacting with public services, such as the UK's National Health Service or the USA's Social Security Administration. While administrative burdens are also a feature of business-government and business-citizen relationships (e.g., Petersen et al. 2024; Halpern 2022), I will set these aside for the sake of argument. However, what I say may have applicability to these other cases.

Finally, while I draw attention to the injustices imposed by administrative work, my argument should not be interpreted as a call for the total abolition of bureaucratic systems. We may concede that citizens will inevitably have to interact with the administrative state on some level, given that social security policies often enjoy popular support (cf. Tabellini 2000) and that modern liberal democracies are complex beasts that require administrative mechanisms (cf. Weber 1946), making it impossible to completely remove time taxes. I grant that not all time taxes are created equal: they may be justifiable in certain circumstances, for instance when they create genuine public value and prevent abuse of the public purse (Nisar and Masood 2023). My interest here is when time taxes are *pernicious* and pose a threat of serious injustice. So, my overall claim is more modest: a call for *smarter* governance of bureaucracies and a more conscious effort among policymakers to consider the severe costs that social welfare programs can place upon service users in certain circumstances.

Time Taxes and Their Problematic Features

I treat time taxes as synonymous with administrative burdens. Therefore, I follow Pamela Herd and Donald Moynihan's definition of administrative burdens, which are "an individual's experience of a policy's implementation as onerous" (2018, 22). This synchronizes with Annie Lowrey's definition of a time tax: "a levy of paperwork, aggravation, and mental effort imposed on citizens in exchange for benefits" (2021). It is worth noting that state actions by themselves do not constitute administrative burdens. A law requiring people to fill out a certain form is an example of a state action, but it is not an administrative burden until someone must actually fill out that form (Christensen et al. 2020, 128).

Herd and Moynihan further break down administrative burdens into three types of costs experienced by government service users: learning, compliance, and psychological costs (ibid.). Learning costs are those which the user undergoes to ascertain the nature of the program or service, the extent to which one is eligible, the kinds of benefits offered, any conditions that must be met, and how to gain access (ibid., 23). Compliance costs concern the extent to which citizens must produce information and documentation to prove eligibility, the financial costs involved in accessing services (e.g., legal representation), and the extent to which citizens avoid or respond to discretionary demands for compliance by administrators (ibid., 23). Psychological costs comprise the stigma associated with participating in a program or service that is perceived to be unpopular, the loss of autonomy from administrative intrusion, frustration at dealing with learning or compliance costs or unfair procedures, and the stress from uncertainty at whether negotiating processes or compliance costs will produce tangible benefits for the service user (ibid., 23). Demarcating costs can be useful as a diagnostic tool for policymakers: rather than trying to eliminate all burdens, they can direct their interventions towards which types of costs are most likely to arise in a particular case, and which ones are the most problematic (Madsen et al. 2022b, 387).

Time taxes can be conceptualized as a kind of transaction cost, in that they are costs required for an action to happen that do not themselves create value (Shahab and Lades 2021, 9). In his discussion of transaction costs, the economist Carl Dahlman pointed to three types of such costs: search and information costs, bargaining and decision costs, and policing and enforcement costs (1979, 148). Search and information costs and policing and enforcement costs correspond well to Herd and Moynihan's categories of learning and compliance costs, respectively. Additionally, the decision costs in Dahlman's analysis are well represented by administrative burdens: if the subjective experience of a burden is high, this will increase the cost of the decision to engage with further administrative processes (Martin et al. 2022, 8). But the psychological costs identified by Herd and Moynihan arguably represent an important extension of the original transaction-cost analysis.

Time taxes, as administrative burdens, can be usefully distinguished from neighboring concepts such as sludge, red tape, and ordeals, in at least four relevant ways. For one, while the other three concepts largely concern *objective* measures of burdens, time taxes emphasize the end-user's *subjective* experience of burdens (which can still often be captured in objective ways). Consider, for example Amrita and Ben, who are both forced to spend one hour waiting in an office. Amrita's subjective experience of the wait might entail a considerably larger burden than Ben's, because Amrita has to look after two hyperactive small children, while Ben is childless (Madsen et al. 2022b, 379). Secondly, time taxes are thought to *worsen inequality*, unlike ordeals, which are conceptualized as minimizing inequality, and red tape, which does not really consider the notion of inequality at all. On the ordeals approach, burdens are supposed to be a socially efficient mechanism for rationing scarce resources because well-resourced individuals will choose not to undergo them for the sake of benefits. However, it is actually the poorest and most vulnerable who are often targeted by administrative burdens. Thus, the ordeals approach fails to consider the regressive effects of burdens (ibid., 379–381; cf. Thomas 2019), which I discuss in more detail below. Thirdly, time taxes may be *deliberately imposed* to the overall detriment of service users—as Herd and Moynihan put it, they can be interpreted as "policymaking by other means" (2018)—rather than, as the ordeals literature would have it, by rational policymakers seeking to maximize the general welfare given scarce resources (Madsen et al. 2022b,

382–383). While I grant that time taxes may be deliberately enforced in some circumstances, I only make the minimal claim that time taxes are a source of *avoidable* rather than *deliberate* injustice. Focusing on avoidability is more likely to capture all the relevant burdens and may be more politically productive in terms of identifying areas for social change rather than assigning blame, fault, or liability (cf. Young 2011, ch. 4), especially as it might be hard in many cases to determine that an injustice has occurred deliberately rather than accidentally or avoidably. A final point is that while a neighboring concept like sludge is meant to capture burdens imposed by the private sector as well as the public sector, I will restrict my discussion here to public sector burdens (cf. Madsen et al. 2022b, 379; ibid. 381–382), though it is worth noting that administrative burdens are a feature of commerce as well as public government.

Time taxes are criticized from various angles in the literature. They (i) produce regressive welfare effects; (ii) shift the burdens of administration onto service users rather than the administrators themselves; (iii) discriminate against people with low human capital; (iv) prevent citizens from accessing life-changing goods or enjoying important constitutional rights; (v) induce stigmatization and shame among service users and a consequent loss of self-respect; and (vi) violate citizens' rights to discretionary time. While this list is not meant to be exhaustive, it illustrates key problematic features of time taxes. Let me comment on each of these in turn.

Regressive Welfare Effects

Time taxes often impose disproportionate costs on disadvantaged groups such as the poor or racial minorities. Empirical evidence from the United Kingdom shows that those with ill health or low incomes may spend more time dealing with administrative burdens and are particularly likely to engage in costlier types of burden—i.e. government services—simply because it is demanded by the nature of their situation. They also experience higher emotional costs from administrative tasks (Martin et al. 2022, 25). In the United States, social programs that are used disproportionately by Black or Hispanic Americans impose a larger time tax burden than those programs which are overwhelmingly used by white Americans (Lowrey 2021). For example, most users of the Temporary Assistance for Needy Families (TANF) program are either Black or Hispanic (Falk 2016, 5). TANF comes with invasive compliance requirements, such as drug screening (e.g., WVDHHR 2017) and work mandates (CBPP 2022, 5).

TANF beneficiaries who are single, poorly educated, and in profound poverty are statistically more likely to lose their benefits because they are unable to meet procedural costs (Brodkin and Majmundar 2010, 841). Meanwhile, setting up a 529 higher education savings plan has no such strings attached (Lowrey 2021) and its user base tends to be white and wealthier (GAO 2012, 16; ibid., 18–19). Indeed, American states' implementation of TANF has been predicated on racist and sexist stereotypes about parenting (CBPP 2022, 4). In a similar vein, access barriers in the Medicaid system arguably reflect systemic racism, especially as these barriers are disproportionately faced by people of color (Wikle et al. 2022, 1–2). Even when technology is introduced to ostensibly remove bureaucratic clerical errors, racial minorities are more likely to have welfare claims wrongfully underpaid or even wrongfully denied compared to whites (Compton et al. 2023). Historically, there was significant opposition to the creation of European-style welfare programs in the United States, again due to racial animus against the poor, who were predominantly Black (Alesina et al. 2001). The role of time taxes in amplifying racial, class, and gender disparities is clear.

The public choice literature on regulation can help us see why time taxes might be regressive in this way. In the domain of risk regulation, for example, Diana Thomas has suggested that even well-intentioned regulation can reflect the preferences of the wealthy, insofar as it fetishizes negligible risks and crowds out expenditure on more salient risks that are more likely to adversely affect low-income people. As a result, regulation arguably forces low-income individuals to protect themselves against insignificant risks where they would not have otherwise chosen to do so (2019). This fetishization of trivial risks occurs in the US Army, for example, with respect to the radiological risk posed by the chemical tritium. Even though tritium has been declared safe for use in wireless exit signs and is a very minor health risk even by the Army's own lights, Army commanders must appoint two radiological safety officers, have them undergo online training, and ensure that military personnel are trained every year in radiological risk (Lipsky 2022). This may seem an innocuous procedure by itself, but it can compound existing administrative burdens within the military bureaucracy.

More generally, time taxes can similarly reflect the preferences of the wealthy even in cases where the underlying political economy dynamics do not involve issues of risk. This can happen in three kinds of ways. First, administrative burdens tend to appear in regulatory schemes that do not impact wealthy people *because they are wealthy*, such as in the case of unemployment benefits or food stamps. Second, high-income individuals can afford to pay *somebody else* to experience the administrative burdens for them instead, such as an accountant to manage their tax affairs or an attorney to deal with legal issues. Thus, wealthy people can effectively escape the burdens of administration that often come with time taxes (see the following subsection). Third, wealthy people have the political power to push for policies to ensure that time taxes do not apply to them. For example, as of late 2022, the US Internal Revenue Service now requires transactions of at least $600 made through "third-party" apps like Venmo or PayPal to be reported for tax purposes. Importantly, there is an exemption for rent payments (Zilber 2022), which suggests that landlords captured the policy process to ensure that this regulatory burden did not apply to them.[3] I say more about capture by special interests later in this chapter. The fact that time taxes frequently favor the preferences of wealthy individuals, in the manner predicted by public choice theory, gives us further reason to worry about their regressive nature.

Shifted Burdens of Administration

Time taxes shift the burdens of administration away from bureaucrats themselves and onto service users, who possess no expertise in the relevant policy domains. Attempts to automate compliance processes in higher education, for example, have magnified the burdens placed on researchers, yet they have resulted in few productivity or efficiency gains for university administrators (Bozeman and Youtie 2020, 158). Automated bureaucracy tends to overestimate the extent to which the user is familiar with administrative systems; equally, automated processes cannot assume that the user already understands new knowledge or new rules (ibid., 161). In Denmark, mandatory digital self-service has had similar effects, forcing service users to become "their own, sometimes accidental, caseworkers" (Madsen et al. 2022a, 10). This trend toward placing the burdens of administration onto citizens is replicated elsewhere. Matthew Cortland, a disabled lawyer with experience of the American social security system, writes: "You shouldn't have to be a lawyer to keep Medicaid coverage, understand Medicare drug plans, get your insurance company to cover your prescriptions [. . .] or get reasonable accommodations at work or school" (quoted in Schweitzer et al. 2022). Or as Annie Lowrey succinctly puts it: "Getting hit by a car means becoming your own hospital-billing expert" (2021).

Service users consequently end up having to invest significant mental energy in familiarizing themselves with the relevant policy domain, which is often full of technical terms, legalese, and jargon. Navigating time taxes thus requires *administrative capital*: "explicit or tacit knowledge of bureaucratic rules, processes, and behaviors," which is distinct from economic, social, or cultural capital because it requires repeated socialization into bureaucratic norms (Masood and Nisar 2021, 57) or specialized training. Therefore, to successfully reduce their administrative burden, citizens have to learn not just the routines and workarounds but also the euphemisms and technical language (ibid., 66). Of course, this comes with certain costs, such as the costs of learning which behavior or strategy is most likely to be effective depending on the bureaucratic context (ibid., 61). The fact that individuals must be *socialized* into the bureaucratic process to navigate it implies the existence of knowledge problems within the bureaucracy (cf. Hayek 1945). One way of putting the point is to ask the question: "How can an economic system mobilize knowledge that exists in dispersed bits throughout society such that individuals can use such knowledge to coordinate with each other?" (Rizzo and Whitman 2023, 199–200). The "insider" understanding of bureaucratic procedures inherent in administrative capital is not immediately available to service users at first sight and entails an ongoing process of acculturation (Masood and Nisar 2021, 65–67).

Discrimination against People with Reduced Human Capital

Administrative capital, discussed above, can be thought of as one type of human capital. The latter can be generally defined as the knowledge, skills, abilities, habits, characteristics, and dispositions which contribute to a person's income and well-being over time (Becker 1994; Christensen et al. 2020, 127; cf. Schultz 1961). Time taxes discriminate against citizens with reduced human capital in this administrative sense, to the extent that they are less familiar with the unspoken rules of the bureaucratic game and are thus less able to play the rules to get the benefits they need.

Time taxes are also biased against those who lack other types of human capital, such as the ability to overcome cognitive biases. One relevant bias concerns the extent to which individuals discount the future. People may (irrationally) discount for reasons of time, wealth, or risk (Caney 2009). They may engage in pure time discounting, such that they will sacrifice the substantial long-term benefits of social welfare programs in the face of administrative burdens in the here and now (Moynihan et al. 2015, 46; cf. Frederick et al. 2002). They may discount for wealth: if they believe they will become wealthier in the future, they may choose to avoid engaging with social insurance programs because they think such programs are only reserved for hard times. And they may discount for risk: if they believe they are unlikely to fall ill, for example, they will be less likely to endure the burdens of taking out health insurance (Moynihan et al. 2015, 46).

Cognitive failures can also come about due to choice overload or decisional conflict. If an administrative procedure allows for too many choices at once, service users may become so overwhelmed that they either fail to make a choice, make a poor one, or simply fall back on the default (Christensen et al. 2020, 129). An example from the author's own experience concerns wayfinding in public transportation systems (see also Kelly 2016). On the London Underground, there is usually only one decision point at each level of any given Underground station. First, customers must decide at the concourse level which *line* they wish to take; it is only when they descend to the platform level that they choose which *direction* they are heading in along that line. A traveler on the New York City Subway, by contrast, must handle all of these decisions simultaneously: Which line? Uptown or downtown? Local or express train? It is quite easy in New York to erroneously catch an express train (when one meant to catch a local train) and therefore miss one's stop. In London, the local/express distinction generally does not exist, so British users do not have to deal with this psychological pinch point. By analogy, administrative procedures that present users with many decision points simultaneously are likely to demand more cognitive resources from users, disproportionately affecting those who are less able to process such complex choice situations effectively.

Another cognitive aspect of citizens' ability to navigate time taxes concerns their executive functioning: their psychological capacity "to engage in purposeful, goal-directed, and future-oriented behavior" (Suchy 2009, 106). Poor executive functioning can entail the inability to plan and prioritize tasks, stay on task, delay gratification, or meet a deadline. Thus, it can amplify learning costs, in the sense that citizens will fail to follow through on cumbersome processes even if they manage to identify and learn about the relevant state benefit (Christensen et al. 2020, 130). Executive dysfunction can also contribute to compliance costs, to the extent that poor task monitoring can cause paperwork errors and the failure to manage tasks systematically can lead to missed deadlines. As a result, people with low executive functioning are more likely to be excluded from public services and suffer sanctions related to noncompliance (ibid.). It is worth noting that executive functioning is cognitively demanding and energy-intensive; it is only triggered when a task is not automatic or routine (Suchy 2009, 106). Since administrative work does not come naturally to most people—consider how much mental effort it takes to compose the typical grant application, even when one is accustomed to the process—a person's executive functioning capabilities will affect the extent to which they can deal with such burdens successfully.

Moreover, citizens' executive functioning abilities vary due to life circumstances such as poverty, health, or age. Indeed, it is often the poor, the sick, and the elderly who are among the most vulnerable groups in society and so most in need of state assistance. At the same time, their ability to access state benefits in an effective manner is often undermined by executive dysfunction. Consequently, these marginalized groups face a "human capital catch-22" (Christensen et al. 2020, 127). Either they seek government support, in which case they cannot do so successfully due to their lack of executive function, or they attempt to repair their executive functioning, which presupposes their ability to overcome poverty, sickness, or age-related cognitive decline (see also Herd 2015). In this way, administrative burdens place severe constraints on the well-being of marginalized groups.

Reduced Access to Important Sociopolitical Goods or Constitutional Rights

Time taxes can affect citizens' ability to participate in civic life or enjoy fundamental goods that matter for their life prospects. A notable example in this regard concerns voter eligibility (Sunstein 2019; cf. Herd and Moynihan 2018, ch. 2). Suppose that American law requires proof of English fluency to be able to vote. This would put up a significant administrative barrier to non-native English speakers, to the extent that they presumably would have to pay for and sit through a language exam to certify their English competence. It would also arguably discriminate against racial minorities, by using language as a proxy for excluding (for example) Hispanic/Latino or Chinese people from the democratic process (Boso 2017, 1171).

Real-life voter identification requirements can have similarly consequential impacts. As of 2023, the UK government's *Elections Act 2022* demands that individuals show photographic ID at polling stations. Not all types of photo ID are accepted: university student ID cards and young people's travelcards cannot be used. Thus, critics have charged that the new law discriminates against young people, by forcing them to acquire other acceptable forms of ID if they only carry a university card (Mortimer 2022; Garland 2022). Citizens may apply for a free electoral ID document in lieu of, say, a passport, but applicants must provide a National Insurance number (the British equivalent of a US Social Security number) and the address where they are registered to vote. These administrative barriers effectively deter transient people from voting (Stanford 2022). A House of Commons report calculated that over a million people altogether will be disenfranchised due to the voter ID reforms (House of Commons 2021, 25). The suggestion is that these new administrative procedures are not a form of enlightened rationing, but politically motivated and thus a kind of "gerrymandering" (Mortimer 2022).

More generally, time taxes can interrupt citizens' ability to engage actively with the political process. Effective political participation is not just a matter of being able to vote: it is also a matter of being able to pay attention to current affairs, learn about the policy stances of various public officials, evaluate those policy stances, consider relevant alternatives, make up one's mind, express agreement or dissent, and so on. It therefore requires that citizens commit adequate *time* and *attention* to the political realm. If citizens are not attentive enough to politics, political equality will be jeopardized (Elliott 2018). As Julie Rose has suggested, free time (understood as time not spent on meeting one's basic needs) should be considered a scarce resource (2016, ch. 3). So, if citizens are spending too much time dealing with very onerous administrative procedures—such as waiting their turn to see a Social Security caseworker or filling out paperwork for health insurance claims—they will experience an important opportunity cost, in the form of reduced free time available for conscientious political engagement. Consequently, time taxes can impede citizens' right to effective political participation and therefore damage their status as political equals (cf. Elliott 2018; ibid. 2023).

Administrative burdens may also exclude access to other goods that can influence prospects in society, such as education. In their study of the Oklahoma's Promise student financial aid program, for example, Elizabeth Bell and Kylie Smith suggest that inequalities in administrative capacity can affect local agencies' ability to deal with burdens imposed from above at the state level. In other words, the least-resourced agencies, which often serve the poorest in society, are least equipped to implement Oklahoma's Promise, therefore undermining the program's goal of eliminating inequalities in higher education (2022, 196). Education can be thought of as a strongly *positional* good: its absolute value depends on how much education individuals have relative to others (Brighouse and Swift 2006, 472). The value of one's place in the educational hierarchy depends on how many people are above or below you in that hierarchy. Insofar as education has instrumental value,[4] it is valuable from a positional standpoint to the extent that better-educated individuals can move up the hierarchy and thus secure better life prospects.

The positionality of education is significant in terms of access to it: the more education is hoarded by some, the less is available for others. Consequently, "[t]he superiority of a better-off person's share is part of what makes a worse-off person's share inferior" (Halliday 2016, 153). There is stiff competition for access to elite universities, for example, precisely because of the positional advantages conferred on elite university students when they enter. When administrative burdens restrict access to education, they reinforce the inequalities in life prospects that flow from the strongly positional nature of education. Furthermore, competition for access to positional advantage can itself impose significant non-financial burdens. This can be seen in the rates of sleep deprivation, caffeine addiction, and even suicide among students in South Korea, which is known for its highly competitive educational culture (ibid., 155; cf. Seth 2002). We might think that the search, learning, and compliance costs of time taxes have the potential to exacerbate these existing burdens in education.

Stigmatization, Shame, and the Loss of Self-Respect

The political philosopher John Rawls includes what he calls "the social bases of self-respect" (1999, 54) among his list of primary goods. In other words, the social foundations of self-respect are among those goods that people need to participate as free, equal, and fully cooperating members of the political community over time (ibid., xiii). For Rawls, shame undermines self-respect (ibid., 389–391). Similarly, feelings of stigmatization can also lead to a loss of self-worth and therefore impugn self-respect (Quinn and De Hert 2014, 20). We can understand stigmatization as treating a person as though she were a pollutant, to be wiped from public view (Sangiovanni 2017, 74). When time taxes induce feelings of stigmatization or shame, they destroy people's self-respect and attack people's sense of being valued appropriately as free and equal members of society.

Such feelings of stigmatization, shame, or damaged self-respect are well documented among citizens in their dealings with public administration. The following vignettes paint a vivid picture of the experiences of ordinary Americans (quoted in Schweitzer et al. 2022; emphases added):

> In the Social Security office, it feels like they're treating you as if you're trying to rip them off. Like, *the default is they don't trust you*. (Anonymous, California)
>
> I felt from the beginning, and just continue to feel from Social Security, *the constant presumption that I'm committing fraud*, in spite of my doctors making strong written statements that I am unable to work. (Anonymous, California)
>
> You start adding *all these shames* on top of it, and then, society makes you feel like you're leeching off of the system. (Marcos Castillo, Arizona)
>
> All of the systems are set up to really dehumanize disabled people and not to help us. (Debra Guckenheimer, California)

The Khawaja Sira people—a type of gender nonconforming identity in Pakistan—face stigma and shame from their own families, as well as harassment from the general public. Long queues are a routine in Pakistan, but queuing to get an official ID card is particularly onerous for the Khawaja Sira because there is no separate queue for them in government offices. As a result, Khawaja Sira are routinely harassed and shamed in public: "The women start laughing at us while the men start teasing us" (Nisar 2018, 111). This is compounded by interactions with frontline ID registration workers, who openly mock Khawaja Sira applicants, refuse to "read" them as gender nonconforming and engage in cisnormative gender policing. As one such individual recalled:

> We have to pass through so many hurdles to register as a Khawaja Sira. [The frontline workers say that] You should grow mustaches [because you are actually men] . . . . Your face doesn't look like that of a woman. Your face looks like that of a man. [They said] You should not abandon your parents' name. (ibid., 112)

Because being Khawaja Sira is thought to bring shame upon the rest of the family, claiming it as an official identity is seen as akin to abandoning one's family. Hence, the frontline workers' exhortation not to "abandon your parents' name" (ibid.). This, in turn damages the Khawaja Sira's sense of self-worth: "I don't go home anymore. When someone is not respected at a place, why would s/he go there?" (ibid., 111). For Khawaja Sira individuals, as for Americans in the

Social Security system, time taxes expose these already-marginalized people to opportunities for further stigmatization and abuse.

Violation of Citizens' Rights to Discretionary Time

Time taxes may threaten an arguably overlooked sociopolitical right: the right to free time itself. As Julie Rose has argued, all citizens in liberal societies are entitled to their fair share of discretionary time, in order that they can exercise their formal civil liberties and opportunities (2016, especially ch. 4). When citizens suffer heavy administrative burdens, this eats into their fair share of free time and therefore impinges upon their ability to exercise their civil liberties, which in turn hinders their capacity to participate fully in civil society. The case of Nick, a food stamps user from Missouri, is illustrative: "Anytime I have an issue [with food stamps], they only let you call one number here in Missouri [and] usually, it's at least a *three-hour wait* every time you have to call—if you're lucky, if you even get someone" (quoted in Schweitzer et al. 2022; emphasis added).

Perhaps more significantly, the discretionary time sacrificed for administrative burdens is not adequately compensated, as is the case with "standard" waged labor. One useful way of thinking about wages in this respect is as a form of compensation for losses in access to, the quantity of, and the experience of free time. Citizens may be forced to sell their time (through labor) to meet their financial expenses (Lau 2023; cf. Thompson 1967, 61), in the absence of a universal basic income. In the case of time taxes, people may be forced to surrender months or even years' worth of their free time, with no guarantee that they will receive the desired benefit. Applicants for Social Security Disability Insurance (SSDI) in the United States have reported spending several years on little or no income waiting for their case to be heard, only to experience rejection and then a lengthy and arduous appeals process (Schweitzer et al. 2022). One such applicant (interviewed anonymously) said: "Almost everyone, from what I hear, is rejected on the first time they apply. It's almost as if they just wanted to see if you're really serious about it" (quoted in ibid.). Nearly two-thirds of SSDI applications between 2014 and 2016 were denied (ibid.). Even if they do receive the benefit, the time expenditure may not be fully compensated and certainly cannot be refunded (Rose 2021, 60).

Since time taxes constitute an important source of unpaid labor (Martin et al. 2022, 24), one might surmise that the extraction of discretionary time from citizens is a kind of *exploitation* by the bureaucrat (cf. Swidler 2017, 51), where the bureaucrat takes unfair advantage of the citizen by demanding time and energy for which the citizen is not duly compensated. From a public choice perspective, it could also be viewed as a form of *rent-seeking*. As Gordon Tullock defines it, rent-seeking "is the use of resources for the purpose of obtaining rents for people where the rents themselves come from some activity that has [zero or] negative social value" (Tullock et al. 2002, 43). In rent-seeking, scarce resources are wasted rather than used productively, which leads to allocative inefficiency. Tullock uses the example of the American car industry lobbying the government to impose a tariff on Korean cars, which leaves American people as a whole worse off even though the car companies themselves experience a net gain (ibid.). In the time tax case, bureaucrats force citizens to expend their discretionary time on complex, lengthy, and often redundant bureaucratic procedures, when that time could have been spent on more productive economic activities such as, for example, entrepreneurship or consumption. The bureaucrat appears to leverage their monopoly power to arrive at an inefficient distribution of the scarce resource of discretionary time,[5] which would suggest that substantial rent-seeking occurs in the imposition of time taxes.

While each of these problematic features clearly merits attention, I argue that a significant dimension of the injustice of time taxes has been overlooked: an adequate explanation for *why* governments impose time taxes in the first place. I want to suggest that a structural injustice approach can offer such an explanation. In the next section, I introduce the notion of structural injustice and show how it applies in the case of time taxes.

Structural Injustice

The notion of structural injustice was coined by the philosopher and social theorist, Iris Marion Young (2011). Structural injustices can be thought of as those injustices which arise due to the interactions of a wide range of actors within the social processes that make up the overarching social and political structure. For Young, "structures denote the confluence of institutional rules and interactive routines, mobilization of resources, as well as physical structures such as buildings and roads" (2006, 111). They "serve as background conditions for individual actions by presenting actors with options; they provide "channels" that both enable action and constrain it" (ibid., 112). The metaphor of "channels" is helpful because it suggests ways in which structures guide actors into certain decisions by opening or foreclosing opportunities for action and by attaching incentives or costs to certain options (Wolff n.d., 3). Structures can persist over time, to the extent that they incentivize actions which reinforce that structure, and punish others which undermine it; thus, structures can endure even when injustices arise from them and even when they continue to perpetuate those injustices (ibid.). Philosophers have applied the concept of structural injustice to a wide range of cases, such as colonialism (Lu 2011), private debt markets (Herzog 2017), and even the norms of beauty and appearance that pervade modern society (Widdows 2021).

Young uses the fictional but powerful example of Sandy to illustrate her account. Sandy is a single mother of two who is about to be evicted from her crumbling apartment block because a developer wants to convert it into (presumably more upscale) condominiums. Sandy searches for a new home as the eviction deadline approaches, but soaring rents mean she can find nothing suitable close to her work or on her bus route. The waiting list for a housing subsidy is very long, so she and her children take their chances on a spartan, one-bedroom apartment, a forty-five-minute drive away from work when the traffic is light. Sandy plows her savings into a down payment on a car so she can avoid the arduous bus commute, but the down payment means she cannot afford the deposit on the apartment. As a result, Sandy and her children are threatened with homelessness (2011, 43–44).

Young comments on four features of the Sandy example that make it a structural injustice.[6] First, Sandy's case is not a matter of personal failing or a character flaw: "She is largely a victim of circumstances beyond her control" (ibid., 45). The social structure determines Sandy's *social position*, which is the cumulative result of the opportunities and constraints available to her (ibid., 45). Second, the people with whom Sandy interacts are generally decent individuals who "act within the law and according to accepted norms and rules," even if their well-meaning actions lead to Sandy's precarious position (ibid., 46). For example, suppose Sandy's landlord is himself in financial difficulty, even though he has multiple properties, and sells Sandy's apartment block to the developer so that he can keep the rents on his *other* properties affordable. On Young's account, the landlord "is doing the best thing [he can] considering the constraints under which he operates" (ibid., 46). Third, Sandy's injustice cannot "be attributed to some particular unjust law or policy" (ibid., 47). To be sure, there are regulations and policies, such as municipal zoning laws, which contribute to Sandy's vulnerable social position, as Young admits. Yet she maintains that "none can be singled out as the major cause" (ibid., 47). Fourth, Sandy's circumstances do not come about because of dumb luck: "on the contrary, it is *predictable* and explainable that there will be an insufficient supply of decent affordable housing in an urban area" (ibid., 47; emphasis added). Because a social structure is a self-sustaining and self-reinforcing institution that persists over time, predictable patterns within the social structure can be discerned, which make it the case that a certain injustice will arise due to those very same patterns.

One further point is worth noting about Young's more generalized account, which is not quite captured by Sandy's case: for Young, structural injustice "exists when social processes put large groups of persons under systemic threat of domination or deprivation of the means to develop and exercise their capacities" (2011, 52). Structural injustice is systematic to the extent that it affects many victims simultaneously and affords them few opportunities to participate meaningfully in the whole of civic life. At the same time, it gives others the chance to dominate or it opens many possibilities for community participation (ibid., 52). Structural injustice can therefore be thought of as a kind of systemic *civic exclusion*.

Each of these characteristics can be found in the case of time taxes; together they paint a vivid picture of the nature of time taxes as a structural injustice. First, it is difficult to see how the burdens of administration could be the product of choices on the part of service users or how the wrongs of time taxes are reducible to recipients' individual character flaws. It is precisely because the government bureaucracy is the monopoly supplier of public services that service users are *forced* to engage with it and must experience whatever burdens are imposed by public programs in order to receive the benefits they need. The extent to which these burdens will be imposed is, at least in part, a result of bureaucrats' discretionary power over the degree to which administrative burdens will be confusing, cumbersome, or otherwise invasive.

Second, time taxes arise within the bounds of accepted norms and rules. Bureaucrats are usually not acting unlawfully when they impose substantial administrative burdens on citizens. They may not even be seen as violating public decorum. Time taxes are generally accepted as a necessary evil, a "cost of doing business." Regulators' preoccupation with procedural obstacles can be seen as a way of alleviating public anxieties about state power because they supposedly secure the legitimacy of an otherwise fragile administrative state and also ensure some measure of public accountability by shielding the state from capture (Bagley 2019, 348–349). In this way, administrative procedures do not invite public disapprobation because they are consistent with deep-rooted suspicions of the state, *even if* those procedures become pernicious time taxes.

Third, administrative burdens may not be reducible to a single causal factor. The design of TANF, for example, may be predicated on racist and sexist assumptions about certain kinds of parents (CBPP 2022, 4), but then we must ask ourselves where those assumptions originate. Racism and sexism may themselves be due to structural factors that cannot be easily traced to any one individual, as the literature on these phenomena has shown (see e.g. Bailey et al. 2017; Homan 2019; cf. Widdows 2021).

Fourth, the burdens of administration come about through predictable patterns within the larger social structure. Indeed, for the sociologist Max Weber, the idealized modern bureaucracy is an example of a predictable pattern *par excellence*. One of its virtues is precisely the fact that it generates regularized, repeatable, and scheduled outputs (Newman et al. 2022, 8; cf. Weber 1946, 228–230). These patterns become so embedded within the bureaucratic system that they are difficult to dislodge, which increases the cost of reforming anodyne or counterproductive administrative processes.

Finally, we can notice how time taxes can lead to systematic exclusion from civic life, particularly when fundamental sociopolitical goods or constitutional rights are at stake, such as in the cases of education or voting rights. When administrative burdens are imposed in these domains of life, they will seriously affect people's ability to participate meaningfully in the political community or to exercise their civil liberties. Time taxes can therefore worsen the prospect that people will achieve positive freedom, which is to say, the freedom to enjoy specific life projects and opportunities (cf. Berlin 1969) or what Philippe Van Parijs calls "real freedom" (1997).

Avoidability and the Problem of Incentives

The idea that time taxes are a structural injustice is a powerful insight. But this claim suffers from at least one significant defect: the concept, insofar as Young theorizes it, fails to account for the ways in which powerful agents can be complicit in, prop up, or even deliberately perpetuate structural injustice. This brings us to Maeve McKeown's revision of Young's account. McKeown proposes that we should draw a three-way distinction between:

(a) *Pure* structural injustice: the classic Youngian case;
(b) *Avoidable* structural injustice: when powerful agents can *change* unjust structures but singularly *fail to do so*;
(c) *Deliberate* structural injustice: when powerful agents deliberately perpetuate unjust structures which they could change (2021; see also McKeown 2024, esp. ch. 3).

I want to suggest that time taxes can properly be understood as an *avoidable* kind of structural injustice. That is, the existence of time taxes is maintained through an unjust social structure, where powerful agents within bureaucracies have the power at their disposal to reduce the burden of time taxes on citizens, but they demonstrably fail to do so.

One reason for this failure concerns the *incentives* facing powerful actors within the unjust bureaucratic system. Here is where the public choice literature from political economy can be helpful. Drawing on this literature, I argue that time taxes arise due to three kinds of pernicious incentives: internal incentives, external incentives, and regulatory capture. Internal incentives motivate powerful actors within bureaucracies for personal gain, external incentives motivate politicians to impose policies for optics reasons, and regulatory capture results in welfare administrators being beholden to special interest groups, while service users themselves are underrepresented in policy design. Let me elaborate on each of these types of incentives.

Internal Incentives

In his seminal study of bureaucracy, William Niskanen argued that bureaucrats are self-interested officials who seek to maximize their own budgets to consolidate power and status, and as a result, the public sector exhibits significant inefficiencies (1971). In the context of the time tax problem, bureaucrats are incentivized to devise complex social assistance programs that require large amounts of paperwork in order to justify their ever-expanding budgets. Since bureaucrats are in a position of power relative to citizens (because they dictate the terms on which citizens will engage with the agency), they could avoid submitting to this rational imperative, but this would limit their opportunities to maximize their own welfare, and so they choose not to do so. It is worth noting that while Niskanen's view of bureaucracy has been empirically contested (Dunleavy 2013, chs. 7–8), it still provides a powerful *theoretical* explanation for the incentives faced by bureaucrats, which can tell us why time taxes remain in place even if policymakers possess the ability to reduce them in principle.

External Incentives

Policymakers may be motivated by self-interest in a different sense, to the extent that they create policies which make them look good, but which impose considerable harm through administrative burdens. A clear example of this can be found in the widespread use of mandatory drug testing as a condition for welfare benefits in the United States. This routine administrative barrier has been criticized for invading citizens' privacy (Pérez-Muñoz 2017). It is also unjustifiable from a fiscal standpoint (Walker and Franklin 2018, 324; Cunha 2014). In Tennessee for instance, only sixty-five applicants to the Families First program tested positive out of nearly 40,000: a hit rate of lower than 1 percent. The drug screening cost the state over $23,000 or about $363 per positive test (Wadhwani 2016). Despite both the principled and the practical objections to drug testing, it is often conducted anyway for optics reasons, as it has historically been popular with the American public (Carey 1998, 283–284) and remains so. According to a 2013 YouGov study, 64 percent of Americans favor random drug testing of welfare recipients; Democrats overall support the proposal by a margin of 22 percentage points, Republicans by 78 percentage points, and independents by 48 percentage points (Moore 2013). Given the strength of popular opinion, rational self-interested policymakers are incentivized to impose drug testing on welfare recipients, even if they harbor moral or pragmatic reservations.

Regulatory Capture by Special Interests

Administrators of (for example) disability welfare programs may claim to be experts in the disability domain and may therefore claim to be acting in the "best interests" of disability welfare claimants. But as David Levy and Sandra Peart suggest, experts are not necessarily infallible: they can be just as prone to capture (through bias, conflicts of interest, or motivated reasoning) as non-experts. Levy and Peart cite the infamous case of the (now-discredited) *Lancet* study on the supposed link between the measles, mumps, and rubella (MMR) vaccine and autism, where the author failed to disclose his financial interests and was also found to have used biased estimation methods (2017, ch. 1). In a similar vein, the designers and administrators of public services may end up beholden to special interests, such as lawyers and technocrats (who may indeed themselves be beholden to even more special interests). The application form for Michigan's assistance programs offers an instructive example. In 2015, the state's Department of Health and Human Services contracted the non-profit firm Civilla to simplify the form, which at the time ran to forty-two pages and 18,000 words. As Michael Brennan from Civilla put it: "[The form] was designed around lawsuits. It was designed around technology. It was not designed around people" (quoted in Lowrey 2021). Some social security programs are so complex that an entire legal industry has sprung up to help citizens navigate them and appeal unfavorable decisions (Hoynes et al. 2022). In the words of Debra Guckenheimer, an SSDI recipient from California: "The fact that I needed a lawyer [to help me], it took me a long time to wrap my head around. Because what other federal benefits do people receive that *you need to hire a lawyer for?* I thought, 'This doesn't make any sense'" (quoted in Schweitzer et al. 2022; emphasis added). We may surmise that such complicated social programs are designed for the benefit of these elite groups rather than the socially disadvantaged people whose interests they are supposed to serve.

This problem is compounded by the fact that marginalized groups are severely underrepresented in decision-making around the design, testing, and implementation of administrative procedures. Personal interactions with the state can be considered opportunities for policy learning; thus, policymakers who have first-hand experience of administrative burdens will be more likely to draw attention to such burdens and the threats they pose to participation rates (Baekgaard et al. 2021, 187–188). This is seen in experimental evidence from Denmark (ibid.: 193). When stakeholders with relevant knowledge, such as service users, are unfairly excluded from the decision-making process, such exclusion is a type of epistemic injustice (Byskov 2021, 123–126): an injustice that occurs when people are not given equal credence as knowers in the public sphere (Fricker 2007). It can also be seen as a category of Hayekian knowledge problem, to the extent that knowledge is *unfairly excluded* rather than widely dispersed and unreachable (cf. Hayek 1945). Moreover, these epistemic injustices are structural injustices to the extent that structural inequalities give rise to epistemic inequalities, and in turn, the epistemic inequalities entrench structural inequalities (Byskov 2021, 126). The larger point is that the structural incentive towards regulatory capture has come at the expense of service user representation, with consequent epistemic problems for sound policy design.

What do we gain from calling time taxes an avoidable structural injustice? Since time taxes are procedural by nature, a popular impression exists that administrative burdens are not truly policy decisions and are therefore not imposing real costs on people. Moreover, the costs of administrative processes are frequently hidden and not immediately obvious to service users (Brodkin and Majmundar 2010). When service users do find themselves disadvantaged by time taxes (as in the case of racial minorities, for example), they may see their oppression as natural due to the routine nature of administrative work. As the behavioral economics literature on adaptive preferences suggests, oppressed groups may "adapt" to their oppression and revise their preferences to "fit" the oppression rather than trying to resist it (see e.g. Cudd 2014). One reason this occurs is that existing dysfunctional institutions come to function as mental reference points, which limit any attempt to imagine a counterfactual (Hoff and Walsh 2018, 22). By labeling time taxes as an *injustice*, we bring the counterfactual back into the picture: we make it clear that such "due diligence" measures—which initially appear innocuous—can turn out to impose genuine and systematic harm, as the preceding sections have shown.

Furthermore, by labeling time taxes as an *avoidable structural injustice*, we emphasize the incentives within the social structure (as evidenced by the public choice analysis) that result in these harms and therefore illuminate opportunities for change by powerful agents. As Herd and Moynihan (2018) propose in their work, time taxes need to be reconceived as "policymaking by other means," i.e., as *intended consequences* of policy design that shape the interactions of citizens with the state, as opposed to neutral or benign instruments of administration. Powerful agents have the capacity to shape the policy environment so that time taxes become obstructionist malign influences, rather than tools that serve the public interest. The idea of *intended* consequences may suggest that the injustice is *deliberately inflicted*, rather than merely avoidable (see McKeown 2021; McKeown 2024). Indeed, the empirical literature often suggests that burdens are deliberately targeted at certain marginalized groups (e.g., Chudnovsky and Peeters 2021; Moynihan et al. 2015). I only make the more modest claim that the structural injustice of time taxes is *avoidable*, insofar as powerful actors possess the capacity for policy reform; I leave open the stronger possibility that the injustice is *deliberate*. As I mentioned earlier, focusing on avoidability may be more likely to capture all the relevant burdens, and may be more politically productive in terms of identifying areas for social change, rather than trying to assign blame, fault, or liability (cf. Young 2011, ch. 4) for deliberate injustice.

In emphasizing the role of incentives, I want to draw attention to the public choice insight that policymakers are often not motivated by moral conscience so much as by particular incentive structures, just like consumers, firms, and other economic agents. Rather than "politics with romance," which implies a clear alignment between public and private interests, public choice tells us that public and private interests can often diverge, to the extent that human beings will pursue private interests at the expense of the public good (cf. Buchanan 2003). If the policy environment is set up in such a way as to promote internal incentives, external incentives, and regulatory capture, public officials will accordingly respond to these incentives. In the time tax case, these incentives will ensure that administrative burdens will continue to be perpetuated, despite their clear deleterious effects on the general welfare.

Ways Forward? Some Suggestions for Policy Reform

Thus far, I have tried to make good on the claim that time taxes can be productively seen as an avoidable structural injustice. Given that the injustice is avoidable, what opportunities are there for policy change and reform? In this concluding section, I briefly sketch out some very tentative and non-exhaustive answers to this question. While I do not have the space to defend any of these proposals at length, I hope they provide some useful ideas for policymakers to combat the structural injustice of time taxes.

Implement the Once Only Principle

One solution may come from this principle, which forms the basis for the European Union's Single Digital Gateway Regulation for the Digital Single Market. As the name implies, the principle states that citizens should hand over relevant information "once only" to authorities (Krimmer et al. 2021, 1). The real-life experiences of welfare beneficiaries testify to the burden of repeatedly producing the same information to agencies. An anonymous SSDI recipient from California says: "Every time I fill out paperwork [. . .] They always ask some kind of the same questions over and over again" (quoted in Schweitzer et al. 2022). The primary virtue of the Once Only Principle (TOOP) is that it prevents unnecessary duplication of information, thus reducing administrative burden, increasing efficiency, and allowing for faster data processing. At the same time, it may also increase trust in administrative bureaus, since the right data can be provided at the right time and there is a smaller risk of complaints or lawsuits due to clerical errors (Prentza et al. 2021, 198).

There are at least two challenges with this principle. The first is that successfully implementing TOOP requires coordinating and harmonizing data registries, especially where information is shared across borders (Leosk et al. 2021). The second is that data sharing and portability between agencies may raise worries about privacy and security (ibid.). One way to overcome the second problem might be to demand a strong justificatory test for data sharing since the principle specifies the handing over of *relevant* information. The criteria of *necessity* and *proportionality*, which are mentioned in the *International Principles on the Application of Human Rights to Communications Surveillance 2014*, may be helpful in this respect (UN Human Rights Council 2014). Further, we may demand that such information should only be shared with the explicit consent of the data subject.

Design Administrative Processes with the End User in Mind

As we saw in the previous section, an important failure in existing practice concerns administrative agencies' preoccupation with satisfying the interests of groups such as lawyers and technocrats, rather than the citizens who actually use public services on an everyday basis. To combat this, questions to service users should be kept relevant, comprehensible, and straightforward to answer: this was clearly not the case with the now-defunct Michigan benefits form, which requested arcane information such as the date of conception of one's children (Lowrey 2021). Questionnaire designers should be made to experience filling out the form from the service user's perspective. Again, the Michigan experience is instructive: it was only when agency leaders had to complete the benefits form themselves, as if they were the end user, that they realized the extent of the administrative burden (ibid.).

Increase Responsiveness and Accountability to Marginalized Groups

Simulating the experience of the service user is an indirect way of ensuring that administrative bureaus remain responsive and accountable to citizens. A more direct way would be to increase the representation of service users themselves through deliberative fora or "mystery shopper" style activities, for example, where real-life service users are hired to experience the administrative process (without the knowledge of frontline staff) and then offer anonymized feedback to the agency. This aligns well with Levy and Peart's suggestion that public policy should aim to foster *government by discussion*: scrutiny and discussion of administrative procedures can both improve public trust in expertise and enable citizens to cast a healthy critical eye on the motivations of experts (2017, ch. 1). Increasing the representation of marginalized groups in these ways would help to tackle stakeholder exclusion and thereby plug the knowledge gaps identified in the third section of this chapter. Furthermore, it would reduce the problem of opaqueness that leaves the administrative state prone to capture by special interests.

It is possible that this policy response is vulnerable to C. Thi Nguyen's *epistemic intrusion objection* to public transparency (2022, 340).[7] The objection suggests that this policy solution may over-account for non-bureaucrats' preferences: in other words, bureaucrats with special expertise may come to seek or even prefer the public's preferences over their own. Experts may abandon their skilled perception and trained intuition in favor of some publicly justifiable criteria of accountability, which diminishes the value of the bureaucrats' expertise in the first place (ibid., 343). This objection exposes a deep problem at the heart of the tension between trust and transparency: when experts act in ways out of reach of our understanding, it is often unclear whether they are acting from corruption or responding to subtle good faith reasons that only they can see (ibid., 343–344). I do not have the space here for a fully satisfactory answer to this important objection: indeed, as Nguyen himself suggests, the only way out may be "painful compromise" (ibid., 332). But we can say that responding to this worry will require a complex process of negotiating how at-risk stakeholders can collaborate with bureaucrats to design less cumbersome administrative procedures.

Create Civil Society Institutions to Advocate for Service Users and Help Them Navigate Administrative Burdens

With this proposal, I have in mind institutional models such as the Citizens' Advice Bureau (CAB) in the United Kingdom, which is a free, non-judgmental, and independent universal advice service for anyone in the UK, distinct from government agencies. Trained volunteer caseworkers provide assistance with a wide range of issues, such as employment disputes, housing and consumer matters, discrimination problems, and dealing with debt and welfare benefits. Some clients may be referred to other agencies, but many problems (such as personal budgeting) may be handled directly by CAB caseworkers (Farr et al. 2014, 7–8). In effect, CAB acts as a clearinghouse and interface between service users and the administrative state, helping users to navigate agencies and services (such as debt collection and benefits management) that they would not otherwise be otherwise familiar with. The fact that CAB caseworkers are specifically trained to deal with administrative burdens on their clients' behalf removes many of the costs and burdens for the clients themselves.

The advantage of a universal advice service is that clients' issues are dealt with holistically, recognizing that the needs of vulnerable people are often complex and interrelated: for example, expulsion from a house due to a family dispute may also impact debt, employment, taxation, finding emergency accommodation, mental health, and other personal affairs (ibid., 5). An empirical study from southwest England suggests that CAB delivers substantial tangible benefits for clients, such as prevented homelessness, social services savings, avoided in-patient psychiatric care, prevented depression and alleviated mental health issues, debts managed and rescheduled, and reduced poverty. All these gains are incurred in a highly cost-effective way (ibid., 5). Furthermore, CAB provides information about benefits, services, rights, and entitlements that service users might not even be aware of (Sloviter 1979), thus removing Hayekian knowledge problems in the interaction between citizens and the administrative state. The impartial and non-judgmental nature of the service means that clients receive relevant advice without any undue governmental interference, while also ensuring that all citizens are equally able to access information that governmental caseworkers or bureaucrats may not be able to provide directly, given the complexities of modern bureaucracies (ibid., 567). While the CAB model has been influential in countries as diverse as Australia, Canada, India, and Kenya (Zucker 1965, 91), it is notable that no equivalent institution exists in the United States (Sloviter 1979; Zucker 1965). An independent universal advice service designed specifically to help citizens manage administrative burdens would alleviate many of the extensive injustices associated with such burdens in the American context.

Replace Burdensome Programs with Unconditional Cash Transfers

As the TANF experience shows, for example, many of the pernicious time taxes in social welfare programs occur because welfare payments are made conditional on meeting strict and invasive performance requirements. One solution, therefore, would be to replace burdensome programs with unconditional cash transfers. This policy measure would remove the stigma, shame, and privacy intrusions that frequently accompany administrative procedures. This argument parallels the civic republican justification for universal basic income, as a basic income affords citizens the possibility of escaping from the clutches of arbitrary interference by others (Raventós 2007, 68; see also van Parijs 1997, ch. 2). If the state gave citizens an unconditional cash transfer rather than forcing them to comply with a burdensome welfare program, it would eliminate the arbitrary interference that arises when citizens are subject to strict performance or compliance requirements.

Change the Incentive Structures Faced by Powerful Agents

Since the definition of avoidable structural injustice implies that powerful actors are an important locus for reform, we need to consider the pernicious incentives faced by those actors which obstruct positive change. One possibility is to exploit cognitive biases such as loss aversion (Kahneman and Tversky 1979) and framing effects (Tversky and Kahneman 1981), by making the severe costs of administrative burdens more salient than the purported benefits. For example, the substantial normative and empirical case against mandatory drug testing could be presented to policymakers *before* acknowledging its popular support, rather than the reverse. Such psychological tricks might help to overcome the internal and external incentives elaborated earlier in this chapter.

Conclusion

Max Weber observed, “Once it is fully established, bureaucracy is among those social structures which are the hardest to destroy” (1946, 228). In this chapter, I have argued that well-developed bureaucracies in liberal democracies impose major administrative burdens on the users of public services and that such burdens—or time taxes—can constitute an avoidable structural injustice. I first delineated the problematic features of time taxes before going on to introduce the notion of structural injustice and applying this to time taxes. I further suggested that time taxes can be classified as an avoidable kind of structural injustice because of the incentives that guide policymakers towards perpetuating bad policy design in public administration. In light of this analysis, I closed by providing tentative suggestions for enacting positive change. My overall argument, therefore, reveals the need to: (i) take greater account of the incentives that produce structural injustice and (ii) consider the obstacles to and opportunities for policy reform in the administrative domain. Even if bureaucracy is hard to destroy, it can certainly be governed more smartly.

Notes

1 Special thanks to Tim O'Shea for planting the seed from which this research grew. Versions of this chapter were delivered at the 2023 University of Warwick Graduate Conference in Political and Legal Theory, the 2023 University of Oxford Graduate Conference in Political Theory, the 2023 LSE Graduate Conference in Political Theory, the 2023 Midlands Graduate School ESRC Conference at Aston University, and the Sixth International Conference on Public Policy held at Toronto Metropolitan University. The author would like to thank audiences at all these events for their questions, comments, and feedback.

2 I use "administrative burdens" interchangeably with "time taxes," here and throughout the rest of this chapter.

3 I thank Tim O'Shea for drawing my attention to this case.

4 Education, of course, may also have intrinsic value (Halliday 2016, 152), but I will set that aside here.

5 On discretionary time as a scarce resource, see also Rose 2016, ch. 3.

6 I draw here in part on Heather Widdows' (2021, 257) very helpful reconstruction of Young's case.

7 I thank Matteo Cardarelli for bringing this point to my attention.

References

Alesina, Alberto, Edward Glaeser, and Bruce Sacerdote. 2001. "Why Doesn't the US Have a European-Style Welfare System?" NBER Working Paper 8524. Cambridge, MA: National Bureau of Economic Research.

Baekgaard, Martin, Donald P. Moynihan, and Mette Kjærgaard Thomsen. 2021. "Why Do Policymakers Support Administrative Burdens? The Roles of Deservingness, Political Ideology, and Personal Experience." *Journal of Public Administration Research and Theory* 31 (1): 184–200.

Bagley, Nicholas. 2019. "The Procedure Fetish." *Michigan Law Review* 118: 345–401.

Bailey, Zinzi D., Nancy Krieger, Madina Agénor, Jasmine Graves, Natalia Linos, and Mary Bassett. 2017. "Structural Racism and Health Inequities in the USA: Evidence and Interventions." *The Lancet* 389 (10077): 1453–1463.

Becker, Gary. 1994. *Human Capital: A Theoretical and Empirical Analysis, with Special Reference to Education*, 3rd ed. Chicago, IL: The University of Chicago Press.

Bell, Elizabeth, and Kylie Smith. 2022. "Working Within a System of Administrative Burden: How Street-Level Bureaucrats' Role Perceptions Shape Access to the Promise of Higher Education." *Administration & Society* 54 (2): 167–211.

Berlin, Isaiah. 1969. "Two Concepts of Liberty." In *Four Essays on Liberty*, 118–172. Oxford: Oxford University Press.

Buchanan, James. 2003. "Public Choice: Politics without Romance." *Policy* 19 (3): 13–18.

Boso, Luke. 2017. "Dignity, Inequality and Stereotypes." *Washington Law Review* 92 (3): 1119–1183.

Bozeman, Barry, and Jan Youtie. 2020. "Robotic Bureaucracy: Administrative Burden and Red Tape in University Research." *Public Administration Review* 80 (1): 157–162.

Brighouse, Harry, and Adam Swift. 2006. "Equality, Priority, and Positional Goods." *Ethics* 116 (3): 471–497.

Brodkin, Evelyn Z., and Malay Majmundar. 2010. "Administrative Exclusion: Organizations and the Hidden Costs of Welfare Claiming." *Journal of Public Administration Research and Theory* 20 (4): 827–848.

Byskov, Morten F. 2021. "What Makes Structural Injustice an 'Injustice'?" *Journal of Social Philosophy* 52 (1): 116–133.

Caney, Simon. 2009. "Climate Change and the Future: Discounting for Time, Wealth, and Risk." *Journal of Social Philosophy* 40 (2): 163–186.

Carey, Corinne A. 1998. "Crafting a Challenge to the Practice of Drug Testing Welfare Recipients: Federal Welfare Reform and State Response as the Most Recent Chapter in the War on Drugs." *Buffalo Law Review* 46 (1): 281–345.

Center on Budget and Policy Priorities (CBPP). 2022. *Policy Basics: Temporary Assistance for Needy Families.* Washington, DC: Center on Budget and Policy Priorities. https://www.cbpp.org/sites/default/files/atoms/files/7-22-10tanf2.pdf

Christensen, Julian, Lene Aarøe, Martin Baekgaard, Pamela Herd, and Donald P. Moynihan. 2020. "Human Capital and Administrative Burden: The Role of Cognitive Resources in Citizen-State Interactions." *Public Administration Review* 80 (1): 127–136.

Chudnovsky, Mariana, and Rik Peeters. 2021. "The Unequal Distribution of Administrative Burden: A Framework and an Illustrative Case Study for

Understanding Variation in People's Experience of Burdens." *Social & Policy Administration* 55 (4): 527–542.
Compton, Mallory E., Matthew M. Young, Justin B. Bullock, and Robert Greer. 2023. "Administrative Errors and Race: Can Technology Mitigate Inequitable Administrative Outcomes?" *Journal of Public Administration Research and Theory* 33 (3): 512–528.
Cudd, Ann E. 2014. "Adaptations to Oppression: Preference, Autonomy, and Resistance." In *Personal Autonomy and Social Oppression: Philosophical Perspectives*, 142–160, edited by Marina A. L. Oshana. New York: Routledge.
Cunha, Darlena. 2014. "Why Drug Testing Welfare Recipients is a Waste of Taxpayer Money." *TIME*. 15 August. https://time.com/3117361/welfare-recipients-drug-testing/.
Dahlman, Carl. 1979. "The Problem of Externality." *The Journal of Law and Economics* 22 (1): 141–162.
Dunleavy, Patrick. 2013 [1991]. *Democracy, Bureaucracy and Public Choice: Economic Explanations in Political Science*. Abingdon and New York: Routledge.
Elliott, Kevin J. 2018. "Making Attentive Citizens: The Ethics of Democratic Engagement, Political Equality, and Social Justice." *Res Publica* 24 (1): 73–91.
Elliott, Kevin J. 2023. *Democracy for Busy People*. Chicago: University of Chicago Press.
Falk, Gene. 2016. *Temporary Assistance for Needy Families (TANF): Size and Characteristics of the Cash Assistance Caseload*. Washington, DC: Congressional Research Service.
Farr, Michelle, Peter Cressey, Susan Milner, Nick Abercrombie, and Beth Jaynes. 2014. *Proving the Value of Advice: A Study of the Impact of Citizens' Advice Bureau services*. Exeter: South West Forum.
Frederick, Shane, George Loewenstein, and Ted O'Donoghue. 2002. "Time Discounting and Time Preference: A Critical Review." *Journal of Economic Literature* 40 (2): 351–401.
Fricker, Miranda. 2007. *Epistemic Injustice: Power and the Ethics of Knowing*. Oxford: Oxford University Press.
Garland, Jessica. 2022. "Voter ID List Gives Few Options for Young Voters." *Electoral Reform Society Blog*. November 11. https://www.electoral-reform.org.uk/voter-id-list-gives-few-options-for-younger-voters/.
Government Accountability Office (GAO). 2012. *Higher Education: A Small Percentage of Families Save in 529 Plans*. Washington, DC: U.S. Government Accountability Office.
Halliday, Daniel. 2016. "Private Education, Positional Goods, and the Arms Race Problem." *Politics, Philosophy & Economics* 15 (2): 150–169.
Halpern, David. 2022. "Time taxes." *Behavioural Insights Team Blog*. June 9. https://www.bi.team/blogs/time-taxes/.

Hayek, Friedrich A. 1945. "The Use of Knowledge in Society." *The American Economic Review* 35 (4): 519–530.

Herd, Pamela. 2015. "How Administrative Burdens Are Preventing Access to Critical Income Supports for Older Adults: The Case of the Supplemental Nutrition Assistance Program." *Public Policy & Aging Report* 25 (2): 52–55.

Herd, Pamela, and Donald P. Moynihan. 2018. *Administrative Burden: Policymaking by Other Means*. New York: Russell Sage Foundation.

Herzog, Lisa. 2017. "What Could Be Wrong with a Mortgage? Private Debt Markets from a Perspective of Structural Injustice." *The Journal of Political Philosophy* 25 (4): 411–434.

Hodge, Scott. 2016. *The Compliance Costs of IRS Regulations*. Washington, DC: Tax Foundation.

Hoff, Karla, and James Walsh. 2018. "The Whys of Social Exclusion: Insights from Behavioral Economics." *The World Bank Research Observer* 33 (1): 1–33.

Homan, Patricia. 2019. "Structural Sexism and Health in the United States: A New Perspective on Health Inequality and the Gender System." *American Sociological Review* 84 (3): 486–516.

House of Commons. 2021. *The Elections Bill: Fifth Report of Session 2021–22*. London: House of Commons Public Administration and Constitutional Affairs Committee.

Hoynes, Hilary W., Nicole Maestas, and Alexander Strand. 2022. *Legal Representation in Disability Claims*. Cambridge, MA: National Bureau of Economic Research.

Kahneman, Daniel and Amos Tversky. 1979. "Prospect Theory: An Analysis of Decision Under Risk". *Econometrica* 47 (2): 263–292.

Kelly, Liz. 2016. "Wayfinding in Underground Transit Systems - London Underground v New York City Subway System." https://asisignage.com/2016/08/23/wayfinding-in-underground-transit-systems/.

Krimmer, Robert, Andriana Prentza, Szymon Mamrot, and Carsten Schmidt. 2021. "The Once-Only Principle: A Matter of Trust." In *The Once-Only Principle: The TOOP Project*, 1–8, edited by Robert Krimmer, Andriana Prentza and Szymon Mamrot. Cham: Springer.

Lau, Taylor. 2023. "The Political Phenomenology of Wages." Graduate Conference in Political & Legal Theory, University of Warwick, February 18.

Leosk, Nele, Irma Poder, Carsten Schmidt, Tarmo Kalvet, and Robert Krimmer. 2021. "Drivers for and Barriers to Implementation of the Once-Only Principle." In *The Once-Only Principle: The TOOP Project*, 38–60, edited by Robert Krimmer, Andriana Prentza and Szymon Mamrot. Cham: Springer.

Levy, David M., and Sandra J. Peart. 2017. *Escape from Democracy: The Role of Experts and the Public in Economic Policy*. Cambridge: Cambridge University Press.

Lipsky, Theo. 2022. "The Burden of Command: Checklists, Inspections, and Bureaucracy." *Modern War Institute Blog*, West Point Military Academy. https://mwi.westpoint.edu/the-burden-of-command-checklists-inspections-and-bureaucracy/.

Lovell, Darrell. 2022. "Administrative Burden in the Classroom: An Embedded Mixed Methods Study of How External Pressure Impacts the Burden of Student Success at the Community College Level." *Texas Education Review* 10 (2): 101–127.

Lowrey, Annie. 2021. "The Time Tax." *The Atlantic*. July 27. https://www.theatlantic.com/politics/archive/2021/07/how-government-learned-waste-your-time-tax/619568/.

Lu, Catherine. 2011. "Colonialism as Structural Injustice: Historical Responsibility and Contemporary Redress." *The Journal of Political Philosophy* 19 (3): 261–281.

Madsen, Christian Østergaard, Ida Lindgren, and Ulf Melin. 2022a. "The Accidental Caseworker – How Digital Self-Service Influences Citizens' Administrative Burden." *Government Information Quarterly* 39 (1): 101653.

Madsen, Jonas K., Kim S. Mikkelsen, and Donald P. Moynihan. 2022b. "Burdens, Sludge, Ordeals, Red tape, Oh My!: A User's Guide to the Study of Frictions." *Public Administration* 100: 375–393.

Martin, Lucie, Liam Delaney, and Orla Doyle. 2022. "Everyday Administrative Burdens and Inequality." *UCD Geary Institute for Public Policy Discussion Paper Series*. Dublin: University College Dublin.

Masood, Ayesha, and Muhammad Azfar Nisar. 2021. "Administrative Capital and Responses to Administrative Burden." *Journal of Public Administration Research and Theory* 31 (1): 56–72.

McKeown, Maeve. 2021. "Structural Injustice." *Philosophy Compass* 16 (7): e12757.

McKeown, Maeve. 2024. *With Power Comes Responsibility: The Politics of Structural Injustice*. London: Bloomsbury Academic.

Moore, Peter. 2013. "78% of Americans want Congress to Take Mandatory Drug Tests." *YouGovAmerica*, December 3. https://today.yougov.com/topics/politics/articles-reports/2013/12/03/78-of-Americans-want-Congress.

Mortimer, Josiah. 2022. "Voter ID: 'It's Far Worse Than Any US State." *Byline Times*. November 7. https://bylinetimes.com/2022/11/07/voter-id-its-far-worse-than-any-us-state/.

Moynihan, Donald, Pamela Herd, and Hope Harvey. 2015. "Administrative Burden: Learning, Psychological, and Compliance Costs in Citizen-State Interactions." *Journal of Public Administration Research and Theory* 25 (1): 43–69.

Newman, Joshua, Michael Mintrom, and Deirdre O'Neill. 2022. "Digital Technologies, Artificial Intelligence, and Bureaucratic Transformation." *Futures* 136, article 102886.

Nguyen, C. Thi. 2022. "Transparency Is Surveillance." *Philosophy & Phenomenological Research* 105 (2): 331–361.

Nisar, Muhammed Azfar. 2018. "Children of a Lesser God: Administrative Burden and Social Equity in Citizen-State Interactions." *Journal of Public Administration Research and Theory* 28 (1): 104–119.

Nisar, Muhammad Azfar, and Ayesha Masood. 2023. "Are All Burdens Bad? Disentangling Illegitimate Administrative Burdens through Public Value Accounting." *Asia Pacific Journal of Public Administration* 45 (4): 385–403.

Niskanen, William A. 1971. *Bureaucracy and Representative Government.* New York: Routledge.

Pérez-Muñoz, Cristian. 2017. "What Is Wrong with Testing Welfare Recipients for Drug Use?" *Political Studies* 65 (4): 912–929.

Petersen, Ole Helby, Jesper Rosenberg Hansen, and Kurt Houlberg. 2024. "The Administrative Burden of Doing Business with the Government: Learning and Compliance Costs in Business-Government Interactions." *Public Administration* 102 (1): 188–206.

Prentza, Andriana, David Mitzman, Madis Ehastu, and Lefteris Leontaridis. 2021. "TOOP Pilot Experiences: Challenges and Achievements in Implementing Once-Only in Different Domains and Member States." In *The Once-Only Principle: The TOOP Project*, 191–207, edited by Robert Krimmer, Andriana Prentza and Szymon Mamrot. Cham: Springer.

Quinn, Paul, and Paul De Hert. 2014. "Self-Respect—A 'Rawlsian Primary Good' Unprotected by the European Convention on Human Rights and Its Lack of a Coherent Approach to Stigmatization?" *International Journal of Discrimination and the Law* 14 (1): 19–53.

Raventós, Daniel. 2007. *Basic Income: The Material Conditions of Freedom*, trans. Julie Wark. London and Ann Arbor, MI: Pluto Press.

Rawls, John. 1999. *A Theory of Justice*, revised edition. Cambridge, MA: Belknap Press of Harvard University Press.

Rizzo, Mario J., and Glen Whitman. 2023. "The Unsolved Hayekian Knowledge Problem in Behavioral Economics." *Behavioural Public Policy* 7: 199–211.

Rose, Julie L. 2016. *Free Time.* Princeton, NJ: Princeton University Press.

Rose, Julie L. 2021. "Rationing with Time: Time-Cost Ordeals' Burdens and Distributive Effects." *Economics and Philosophy* 37: 50–63.

Sangiovanni, Andrea. 2017. *Humanity without Dignity: Moral Equality, Respect and Human Rights.* Cambridge, MA: Harvard University Press.

Schultz, Theodore W. 1961. "Investment in Human Capital." *The American Economic Review* 51 (1): 1–17.

Schweitzer, Justin, Emily DiMatteo, Nick Buffie, and Mia Ives-Rublee. 2022. *How Dehumanizing Administrative Burdens Harm Disabled People.* Washington, DC: Center for American Progress. https://www.americanprogress.org/article/how-dehumanizing-administrative-burdens-harm-disabled-people/.

Seth, Michael J. 2002. *Education Fever: Society, Politics, and the Pursuit of Schooling in South Korea.* Honolulu, HI: University of Hawai'i Press.

Shahab, Sina, and Leonard K. Lades. 2021. "Sludge and Transaction Costs." *Behavioural Public Policy.* cambridge.org/core/journals/behavioural-public-policy/article/sludge-and-transaction-costs/D09206BF9B36C129F40A27A9E749074B.

Sloviter, Dolores Korman. 1979. "Let's Look at Citizens Advice Bureaux." *American Bar Association Journal* 65 (4): 567–569.

Suchy, Yana. 2009. “Executive Functioning: Overview, Assessment, and Research Issues for Non-Neuropsychologists.” *Annals of Behavioral Medicine* 37 (2): 106–116.

Stanford, Ben. 2022. “No ID? No Vote! Voter ID comes to Great Britain.” *LSE British Politics and Policy Blog.* November 23. https://blogs.lse.ac.uk/politicsandpolicy/no-id-no-vote-voter-id-comes-to-great-britain/.

Sunstein, Cass. 2019. “Sludge and Ordeals.” *Duke Law Journal* 68: 1843–1883.

Swidler, Eva-Maria. 2017. “Marxism beyond the Economy and Exploitation Beyond the Wage.” *Capitalism Nature Socialism* 29 (2): 43–60.

Tabellini, Guido. 2000. “A Positive Theory of Social Security.” *Scandinavian Journal of Economics* 102 (3): 523–545.

Thomas, Diana. 2019. “Regressive Effects of Regulation.” *Public Choice* 180 (1–2): 1–10.

Thompson, E. P. 1967. “Time, Work-Discipline, and Industrial Capitalism.” *Past & Present* 38: 56–97.

Tullock, Gordon, Arthur Seldon, and Gordon L. Brady. 2002. *Government Failure: A Primer in Public Choice.* Washington, DC: Cato Institute.

Tversky, Amos, and Daniel Kahneman. 1981. “The Framing of Decisions and the Psychology of Choice.” *Science* 211 (4481): 453–458.

UN Human Rights Council. 2014. *International Principles on the Application of Human Rights to Communications Surveillance.*Geneva, Switzerland.

van Parijs, Philippe. 1997. *Real Freedom for All: What (if Anything) Can Justify Capitalism?* Oxford: Oxford University Press.

Wadhwani, Anita. 2016. “Drug Testing for Benefits in Tennessee Yields Only 65 Positives.” *The Tennessean.* February 7. https://eu.tennessean.com/story/news/politics/2016/02/07/drug-testing-benefits-tennessee-yields-only-65-positives/79776756/.

Walker, Mary Jean, and James Franklin. 2018. “An Argument Against Drug Testing Welfare Recipients.” *Kennedy Institute of Ethics Journal* 28 (3): 309–340.

Weber, Max. 1946. *From Max Weber: Essays in Sociology.* Translated, edited and with an introduction by H. H. Gerth and C. Wright Mills. New York: Oxford University Press.

West Virginia Department of Health and Human Resources (WVDHHR). 2017. “DHHR Implements Drug Screening Requirements for TANF Applicants.” Charleston, WV: West Virginia Department of Health and Human Resources. https://dhhr.wv.gov/News/2017/Pages/DHHR-Implements-Drug-Screening-Requirements-for-TANF-Applicants-.aspx?.

Widdows, Heather. 2021. “Structural Injustice and the Requirements of Beauty.” *Journal of Social Philosophy* 52 (2): 251–269.

Wikle, Suzanne, Jennifer Wagner, Farah Erzouki, and Jennifer Sullivan. 2022. *States Can Reduce Medicaid's Administrative Burdens to Advance Health and Racial Equity.* Washington, DC: Center on Budget and Policy Priorities. https://www.cbpp.org/

research/health/states-can-reduce-medicaids-administrative-burdens-to-advance-health-and-racial.

Wolff, Jonathan. n.d. "Structural Harm, Structural Injustice, Structural Repair." Unpublished manuscript.

Young, Iris Marion. 2006. "Responsibility and Global Justice: A Social Connection Model." *Social Philosophy & Policy* 23 (1): 102–130.

Young, Iris Marion. 2011. *Responsibility for Justice*. Oxford: Oxford University Press.

Zilber, Ariel. 2022. "IRS warns Americans over $600 threshold to report Venmo, PayPal payments." *The New York Post*. November 25. https://nypost.com/2022/11/25/irs-warns-americans-over-600-threshold-to-report-venmo-paypal-payments/.

Zucker, Mildred. 1965. "Citizens Advice Bureaus: The British Way." *Social Work* 10 (4): 85–91.

11

AI and Governance

Leading the Future Together

Agostina Lorenzini

AI can build a smart house, but not a home.

Agostina Lorenzini

The rise and pervasive use of Large-Scale Inference, commonly known as Big Data, with its accompanying computational power, has not only increased our ability to compute and store massive amounts of data but has also given birth to many technologies, including both blockchain as well as a new wave of artificial intelligence. The Oxford English Dictionary defines Artificial Intelligence (AI) as:

> The theory and development of computer systems able to perform tasks that normally require human intelligence, such as visual perception, speech recognition, decision-making, and translation between languages. (Knowles, 2006)

The most common definition of AI is "computational intelligence," and beyond that simple definition hides a myriad of different kinds of AI based on such attributes as strength, breadth, and application, each presenting slightly different risks or challenges. No country or supranational entity has yet implemented AI-specific legislation, as some primary questions remain unanswered: who would be the experts to interpret and enforce the law regarding AI, and how would any legislation on AI be implemented?

In this chapter, we will define what AI is and its risks. Although regulations in AI are changing every day, we will analyze the bills currently under consideration and what public choice theory tells us about the roles of experts in public policies. In conclusion, we will propose an AI governance procedure, considering already proposed legislation.

AI Definition and Uses

There are as many definitions of AI as there are papers on the subject—changing and evolving over the years as much as the technology itself. IBM defines AI as anything that makes machines act more intelligently; for them, the "A" in AI stands for *augmented* (2024). They believe that AI should not attempt to replace human experts but should rather extend human capabilities and accomplish tasks that humans and machines could not do independently. MIT, on the other hand, defines AI as *artificial* intelligence, emphasizing the ability of computers to imitate human cognitive functions such as learning and problem-solving (2024).

The internet has given us access to information faster than many of us can process said information. Both distributed computing and the IoT, or the Internet of Things, have generated massive amounts of data, and social networking has encouraged most of that data to be unstructured. For the purposes of this chapter, we will define AI as a set of simulations of mathematical and statistical processes fed by large amounts of data that give AI protocols the ability to adapt and integrate a wide range of problem-solving techniques, including search and mathematical optimization, formal logic, artificial neural networks, as well as methods based on statistics, probability, and economics.

With some initial definitions in mind, it is important to note just how many fields of study seem to converge around the topic. To start, computer science and electrical engineering are fundamental, determining how AI is implemented in software and hardware, while mathematics and statistics provide viable models and can measure performance. Zooming out, psychology and linguistics play an essential role in understanding how AI might work because it is modeled on how we believe the brain works. Perhaps most important of all, philosophy provides guidance on intelligence and—critically—ethical considerations.

While several fields seem to intersect to both create and comprehend it, AI itself can also be subdivided into types reflective of relative strength, breadth, and application. Here are a few:

- *Weak or Narrow* AI is applied to a specific domain. Some examples include language translators, virtual assistants, self-driving cars, AI-powered web searches, recommendation engines, and intelligent spam filters. This kind of *applied* AI can perform specific tasks but not learn new ones, making decisions based on programmed algorithms and training data.

- *Strong or Generalized* AI can operate various independent and unrelated tasks, learning new tasks to solve new problems, and doing so by teaching itself new strategies.
- *Generalized Intelligence* combines many AI strategies that learn from experience, performing at a seemingly human intelligence level.
- *Super or Conscious.* Here, human-level consciousness would require the AI to be self-aware; given the difficulty of defining human consciousness, the likelihood that we will develop such an AI in the near future is minimal.

As intimated previously, AI works differently than the human brain, basing its decisions on inputs we give it and the outputs we set. It can only understand numbers and mathematical operations. For instance, by using machine learning technology, we can use mathematics to understand patterns in vast amounts of structured and unstructured human data. The only difference here is that while humans would manually construct these patterns and conditions, with machine learning it is done automatically, or mostly automatically, by techniques like gradient descent theory[1] and calculus.

AI does not simulate a human mind but rather opens up new doors for computers, enabling them to understand specific data they could not have understood before. For example, as humans, we have both emotions and intuition and are highly adept at processing natural language. We are also made for processing raw auditory data: put crudely, our brain is, in essence taking vibrations of air molecules and converting them to thoughts. We are also great at processing visual data: when we look at someone's face, we can instantly recognize them. These are things that computers cannot do because, fundamentally, they are limited to mathematics.

AI is about pattern recognition, which is at play when AI tools seem to comprehend natural language and understand speech. This becomes that with which we have all become quite familiar: a tool that uses computer power to complete a task automatically with very little human intervention. Underneath the hood, so to speak, AI is a complex series of algorithms that do something with the information coming into them, making them into a set of technologies that allow us to extract information from data. Simply put, AI is any system that learns or understands patterns within data, can identify those patterns, and then reproduce them using new information.

The critical question follows: How does AI learn? The only "intelligence" that machines have is what we give them. We provide machines with the ability to examine examples and create machine-learning models based on the inputs and desired outputs. We do this in different ways, such as Supervised Learning, Unsupervised Learning, and Reinforcement Learning.[2]

According to a study by PwC, $16 trillion worth of value attributed to the growth of AI technologies will be added to the world GDP between now and 2030 (2017). It is a never-before-seen scale of economic impact, and it should be noted that this extends well beyond the IT industry. It impacts virtually every industry and aspect of our lives.

Let's take a moment to explore how AI can mean different things to different people. For a video game designer, AI could help write the code that affects how bots play and how the environment reacts to the player. A screenwriter, on the other hand, may use AI to envision a humanoid character—around which a film or television show could be scripted—or use it as a tool for writing that very screenplay. For a data scientist, AI might provide a method for exploring and classifying data to meet specific goals.

Relevant for several industries, the natural language processing and natural language generation capabilities of AI are not only enabling machines and humans to understand and interact with each other, but they are also creating new opportunities and new ways of doing business. AI algorithms which learn by example are why we can talk to Watson, Alexa, Siri, Cortana, and Google Assistant, and why they can also talk back to us. Chatbots powered by natural language processing capabilities are used in healthcare to question patients and run primary diagnoses like the ones real doctors would otherwise be tasked with doing. In education, chatbots provide students with easy-to-understand conversational interfaces and on-demand online tutors. Perhaps the most pervasive use of AI is with customer service chatbots that improve customer experience by resolving queries on the spot and freeing agents for conversations that add value. AI-powered advances in speech-to-text technology have made real-time transcription a reality. Advances in speech synthesis enable companies to use an AI-powered voice to enhance customer experience and give their brand a unique voice. In medicine, such advances are helping patients with Lou Gehrig's disease, for example, to regain their natural voice instead of using a computerized voice. Due to advances in AI, the field of computer vision has surpassed humans in tasks related to detecting and labeling objects. Computer vision is one of the reasons why self-driving cars can steer their way on streets and highways and avoid hitting obstacles. Computer vision algorithms detect facial features and images and compare them with face profile databases, allowing consumer devices to authenticate the identities of their owners through facial recognition, social media apps to detect and tag users, and law enforcement agencies to identify criminals in video feeds. Computer vision algorithms are helping automate tasks, such as detecting cancerous moles in skin images or finding symptoms in X-ray and MRI scans.

Computer vision can be a highly applicable technology in perhaps unexpected industries. The Abu Dhabi National Oil Company used AI to address a common problem in their industry: Where is the best place to drill for oil? Part of their work involves using variations in rock samples to determine the optimal drilling locations. Such work had historically been done exclusively by highly skilled geologists. Rather than continuing to train geologists to classify the sheets of rock correctly, which could be tricky, time-consuming, and expensive, they used an AI-empowered computer vision system to classify said rock samples, which in turn helped to identify which locations were the most promising for future drilling (ADNOC 2020).

Generative Artificial Intelligence, or GenAI, presents a potentially concerning type of AI for many, if not all, industries. GenAI uses a technique capable of creating new and unique data, ranging from images and music to text and entire virtual worlds. Unlike conventional AI models, which rely on predefined rules and patterns, Generative AI models use deep learning techniques and rely on vast datasets to generate entirely new data with various applications. A Generative AI model can also use an LLM, or Large Language Model, which is a type of artificial intelligence based on deep learning techniques designed to process and generate natural language. For instance, Generative AI can develop new and more powerful LLM algorithms or architectures, resulting in more accurate or efficient natural language processing and generation capabilities. Alternatively, Generative AI can design and incorporate LLMs into a more extensive, advanced AI system to perform various complex tasks, such as decision-making, problem-solving, and creative work. While the ramifications and knock-on effects of Generative AI are unfolding and will continue to unfold in the years ahead, some of its demonstrated uses suggest it is already becoming a strategic technology, improving processes on the margins of creativity and innovation, cost and time savings, personalization, scalability, and robustness. Let us look at some diverse use cases of Generative AI.

In healthcare and precision medicine, Generative AI can support physicians in identifying genetic mutations responsible for patients' illnesses and providing customized treatments. It can also produce medical images, simulate surgeries, and predict new drug properties to aid doctors in practicing procedures and developing treatments. In agriculture, Generative AI can optimize crop yields and create more robust plant varieties that can withstand environmental stressors, pests, and diseases. In biotechnology, Generative AI can aid in developing new therapies and drugs by identifying potential drug targets, simulating drug interactions, and forecasting drug efficacy. In forensics, Generative AI may help solve crimes by analyzing DNA evidence and identifying suspects. In environmental conservation, it could support the protection of endangered species by analyzing their genetic data and suggesting breeding and conservation strategies. In creative fields, Generative AI can produce unique digital art, music, and video content for advertising and marketing campaigns, and generate soundtracks for films or video games. Generative AI can create interactive worlds in gaming by generating new levels, characters, and objects that adapt to player behavior. In fashion, Generative AI can design and produce virtual try-on experiences for customers and recommend personalized fashion choices based on customer behavior and preferences. In robotics, Generative AI can design and adapt new robot movements to changing environments, enabling them to perform complex tasks. In education, Generative AI can create customized learning materials and interactive learning environments that adjust to students' learning styles and pace. Generative AI can also produce new training data for machine learning models in data augmentation, enhancing their accuracy and performance.

Generative AI has emerged as a powerful technology that enables software applications to create, generate, and simulate new content, enhancing their capabilities and providing unique experiences. Unlike traditional software that follows predefined rules and algorithms, Generative AI leverages machine learning and deep learning techniques to learn patterns and generate original content based on the knowledge acquired during training. Due to its potential to create new, personalized content that would have been impossible to create otherwise, Generative AI has been used in various fields, leading to the development of numerous engaging and well-liked applications.

Some popular applications of Generative AI in action include:

1. A Generative Pre-trained Transformer, or GPT, is a family of large language models developed by OpenAI and capable of producing human-like text. GPT-3.5 and GPT-4 are iterations in this family of models, with additional ones under development. They have many

applications, including chatbots powered by GPT like ChatGPT, automated journalism, and creative writing.

2. ChatGPT is a chatbot or conversational AI tool developed by OpenAI that enables users to have text-based conversations with the underlying language model, GPT. Trained on diverse internet text, it generates human-like responses, provides information, answers questions, assists with tasks, engages in creative writing, and offers suggestions across various subjects.
3. Bard is an AI-powered writing assistant from Google that aims to assist users in producing high-quality writing for communicational documents like emails and social media posts. Bard generates text using a large language model called LaMDA (Language Model for Dialogue Applications) and can adjust to the user's preferences for style and tone.
4. Watsonx.ai from IBM is an AI and data platform for model development which helps build, deploy, and manage AI applications at scale, enhancing the impact of AI across an organization.
5. DeepDream is a generative model that can generate surreal and psychedelic images from real-life images. It has been used in art and entertainment, producing unique and visually stunning images.
6. StyleGAN is a generative model capable of producing high-quality images of faces that do not exist in reality. It has been used in various applications, including creating realistic video game avatars and simulating human faces for medical research.
7. AlphaFold is a generative model that can predict protein structure. It has the potential to transform drug discovery and make it possible to develop more effective treatments for diseases.
8. Magenta is a Google project that creates music and art using Generative AI. It has yielded some intriguing and impressive results, such as a piano duet performed by a human and an AI-generated piano.
9. Google AI's PaLM 2 is a powerful LLM trained on a dataset ten times larger than PaLM 1. It excels in understanding nuances, generating coherent text and code, translating, and answering questions.
10. GitHub Copilot is an AI-powered coding assistant developed by OpenAI and GitHub, designed to help developers write code more efficiently. It uses a deep learning algorithm to analyze code and generate suggestions for the developer, such as auto-completing code snippets or suggesting functions based on the context of the code.

Ongoing development promises to revolutionize human-computer interactions, enhancing accuracy, efficiency, creativity, and communication.

Generative AI is rapidly evolving and is expected to grow dramatically in the coming years; however, there are undoubtedly ethical concerns about Generative AI, including potential misuse of AI-generated content, privacy issues, and implications for intellectual property and copyright laws.

AI and Risks: Algorithmic Bias

We begin with a statistical risk: overfitting. Many AI models, such as neural networks,[3] can easily overfit data, meaning they tend to fit the historical data almost too well but fail in realistic situations. This happens because these models often have too many parameters that can fit very complex layers of the network, but they only generalize within the historical data. We need to understand what is helping the model to perform well because this poses a significant risk when we deploy these models in the real world. There are many operational risks from using models that overfit data. For example, a trading algorithm based on AI makes stock trading decisions that could make mistakes by over-relying on historical data.

There are also consumer perceptions, as well as reputational risks. For example, a poor-performing chatbot or a poorly designed personalization algorithm may serve as deterrents or irritants to consumers rather than as the useful tools they were intended to be. This, in turn, hurts customer perception and retention over the long run. Many of these potential risks can be mitigated by thorough testing, which explains why machine learning models must go through significant stress testing exercises, including validation.

Social and ethical risks pose serious concerns as well. In Kartik Hosanagar's book *A Human's Guide to Machine Intelligence* (2019), the Wharton professor explored a couple of case studies. First, he analyzed two chatbots, one in China and the other in the United States. "Xiaobing" was a chat bot that simulated a teenage girl who had 40 million followers in China, and "she" could engage in fun and innocent conversations. It was created by Microsoft Research and was very successful in China. The same company launched the same chatbot in the United States called "Tay." Unfortunately, Tay engaged in sexist, racist, and fascist conversations with many people and had to be shut down within twenty-four hours of being launched.

Another example concerns resume screening. Big companies might receive hundreds of thousands or even millions of resumes in any given year; they must sift through these and select a subset of the applicants to invite for a job interview. It is tough to do this at scale with human beings. So, many big companies are using AI technology to do CV screenings. However, it was reported that Amazon discovered their initial CV screening algorithms had a gender bias. Fortunately, said bias was discovered by employees at Amazon, and the algorithm was summarily replaced.

Nevertheless, it is noteworthy that even a large company like Amazon found itself reliant upon a tool which, though designed based on cutting-edge advanced machine learning algorithms, still contained a gender bias. A few years ago, ProPublica reported problems with algorithms used in US courtrooms, designed to help judges and parole officers make bail, sentencing, and parole decisions (Angwin 2016). These algorithms were designed to look at defendants' histories and predict the likelihood that a defendant would re-offend. Based on these predictions, judges could then make sentencing decisions. The investigation found that the algorithm was twice as likely to falsely predict future criminality in black defendants than in white defendants. This is an example where the algorithm developed a racial bias even though no developer programmed such a bias.

The question that arises is how these kinds of biases are emerging. Why are some CV screening algorithms showing gender bias? Why are some sentencing algorithms racist? Why are some chatbots racist? Traditional software is entirely rule-based, but AI adds data to traditional software rule-based,[4] learning from the data we give it. If we look at what drives the behavior of AI systems, we observe that they are partly driven by the logic that the programmer has when he creates the algorithm, and those algorithms are mostly rule-based or traditional software. Then there is also data: much of what AI learns is learned from this data.

Analogue—nature and nurture determine human behavior. Nature is our genetic code, and nurture is our environment, and we learn from that environment. In AI, nature can be thought of as the rules the programmer has created for the AI, whereas nurture is essentially the data from which it learns. If there are biases in the data, then the AI system can also pick them up. A lot of these biases might exist in the data. When we say a resume screening algorithm has a gender bias, what is in practice happening is that the algorithm is learning from past data and applying it to its decision-making. This past data is based on decisions made previously by human beings: in years past, people decided who to invite for job interviews, who got a job offer, and afterward, who got promoted. An AI system is designed to invite precisely these kinds of people for job interviews, so if there was a gender bias in the past, then that might have been captured in the data, and, in turn, captured in the AI as well.

If AI-based decisions' faults are often rooted in biases in the data, then what are some of the associated risks, particularly when operational biases initially go unnoticed? There are societal risks, especially when AI-based system decisions serve to reinforce existing barriers to already disadvantaged minorities.

Humans are prone to stereotypes, implicit biases, and even explicit discrimination, and an AI system looks at and processes data created by humans. Ergo, it is dangerous and misleading to think AI is inherently objective. It can replicate or even reinforce human biases and produce deep unfairness. Algorithmic bias is ethically wrong, and it is potentially harmful to marginalized populations. It can lead to backlash from employees, customers, and other stakeholders, and it may even lead to legal consequences.

The AI Now Institute classifies these risks into two groups:

1. Harms of allocation: This refers to situations where a scarce resource must be allocated to people by an AI. For example, loan approval decisions involve multiple people, as does applying for a job; however, only a few people will get anything, and in both cases, an algorithm decides which applicants will be allocated that scarce resource.
2. Harms of representation. This refers to situations where a system represents a group unfavorably. For example, suppose we have an airport screening system that looks at people's facial expressions and other factors to figure out who needs to be screened. If it has a bias against minorities, then it is a harm of representation (Whittaker 2018).

As we've established previously, data can hold embedded human prejudice. If women repeatedly fail to get promoted or enjoy long careers at a company because of sexism in the past, an AI system will associate being female with poor outcomes. In the healthcare example cited previously, the primary problem was that the algorithm used previous treatment costs as a proxy for how sick a patient was. The difficulty was that black people, on average, received worse care, meaning less was spent on them even when they are equally sick or sicker than white patients. In many cases, like those mentioned previously, the data itself is biased. Additionally, there may be fewer examples of minority populations in a training dataset, resulting in less accurate models. That is part of what happened with facial recognition systems. Sometimes, even when classifications such as race and gender are not in the dataset, they influence models through proxies. For instance, a zip code is just an address marker, but it can be strongly correlated with race or socioeconomic status.

We should be aware of and concerned by both types of harm as defined above. They present societal risks on a macro level, while also creating reputational, legal, and regulatory risks for the companies and organizations that may be associated with them. The reputational risk comes from being perceived as a biased or prejudiced company, which could mean the loss of a customer base. The legal risk comes from being sued by customers or others for discriminatory practices. Lastly, regulatory risks arise when regulators feel that the algorithms are actually discriminating or creating social risks.

Data Protection

As AI has taken off, so too have worldwide concerns about digital privacy since AI depends on data. Ever since databases were widely applied in business in the 1960s, there have been concerns about how that power might be abused or could violate fundamental rights, and big data and machine learning now raise novel data protection issues. First of all, they require immense quantities of data since the value of AI often comes from the ability to employ massive datasets. More data means more information needs to be collected from more people, as well as finding opportunities to integrate different datasets and pieces of information, the latter of which may be individually of little concern, but when aggregated can easily paint a comprehensive profile of an individual. A second issue concerns the possibility of inferential privacy violations. Simply put, with AI and other data analysis techniques, sometimes there is no need to explicitly ask someone for a piece of personally identifiable or sensitive information to figure out their identity. The third new issue with AI and machine learning is that models often require significant data transfers to be updated. When data are collected from many users, for example, from activity on phones, and then aggregated in the Cloud and centrally processed there, huge sums of personal data must transfer across a network or find storage in the Cloud. However, some new techniques are being developed to moderate this problem, especially one called federated privacy, which allows for models to be updated without necessarily transferring all the personal information from end-user devices.

There are five stages of what is called the privacy lifecycle, and each is important to consider in developing AI solutions.

1. The first stage is collection. This is perhaps the most self-evident one, referring to the gathering of information from users.
2. The second stage is aggregation and analysis. At this stage, one considers the next logical step: what is done with the collected data. Sometimes, users may only provide a small amount of information, but that dataset is integrated with other datasets collected elsewhere. Further data analysis and feature engineering[5] can raise privacy concerns.
3. The third step is storage, which needs to be addressed. If we use a large dataset to derive machine learning algorithms, then that dataset becomes a considerable security risk. We usually think of security as different from privacy, but the more private data we have, the more concerned we should be about security. Even if we are not doing something illegal or unethical, if our data gets hacked and the private data gets exfiltrated, then that becomes a huge problem, not only in terms of financial security (like personal banking information), but also in terms of personal security (threats from hackers), and even federal security, if strategic decisions are publicized. Storage, maintenance, and decisions about what data we store and keep become critically important as a matter of privacy.
4. The fourth stage is the use of the data. Sometimes, the data collection is fine, but the data gets used for reasons about which users may rightfully have concerns. If, for example, a medical practice collects sensitive health data, patients may fully understand its immediate relevance as it would be necessary for their medical treatment. If, however, that data is then sold for profit to an aggregator that uses it to market other products, those same patients might be concerned—if not alarmed. Patients would likely find this to be an inappropriate use of their data.
5. The final stage of the privacy lifecycle is distribution. Where does the data go if companies transfer it or resell it? Reselling data is the foundation of a vast economy of data brokers. It is not generally illegal if it is authorized under the relevant contracts or agreements to collect and transfer data; nevertheless, it is an issue that users are often very concerned about, and it is an issue that raises additional security concerns. What if a company is excellent at what it does with data, but then transfers it to a third party that is not? Here, problems arise.

The EU's GDPR (General Data Protection Regulation), which is focused primarily on privacy, does have some clauses that relate to automated decisions, like a right to explanation,[6] which is a primary right that consumers can and should have. Moreover, the GDPR legislation includes an anti-bias provision in the sections dealing with fully automated processing, though these provisions are limited. In the United States, there have been proposals for what is called the Algorithmic Accountability Act, both rejected, which would require bias-checking techniques.

Existing AI Policy

To create AI algorithms, it is crucial to have specific mathematical and computing knowledge, but what must be known in order to regulate AI? There is a clear intention from governments the world over to launch a legal framework to mitigate the risks of AI, and, as has been established above, there is a clear need for it. The same questions persist: "How does one do that?" and "Where might attempts to mitigate the risks begin to disincentivize innovation?" This section will summarize the rough framework of proposed legislation in both Europe and the United States, and how these proposals attempt to find a sweet spot between innovation and regulation.

Let us start with the United States, where no such AI-specific legislation exists at the federal level. A bill was proposed and rejected by the US Congress twice: The Algorithmic Accountability Act of 2019/2022 (US Congress 2022). The bill provided a baseline requirement that companies assess the impacts of automating critical decision-making, including decision processes that have already been automated. It requested transparency from companies to the clients when an AI algorithm was being used. Also, it required that the FTC (Federal Trade Commission) hire fifty staff members and create the Bureau of Technology to enforce the act: They would have needed to create guidelines for reporting and assessment to publish anonymized aggregate reports where the customers and advocates would have reviewed which critical decisions had been automated by companies along with information on things like data sources, high-level metrics, and how to contest decisions.

On the other side of the Atlantic, the European AI Act is yet to be approved[7]; however, European officials claim that theirs will be the first regulatory framework on AI once fully approved—a prospect which seems hopeful, as negotiations with the EU Council on the law's final form began last June. Based on the GDPR, the rules will follow a risk-based approach and establish obligations for providers and those deploying AI systems, depending on the level of risk the AI can generate. AI systems with an unacceptable level of risk to people's safety would, therefore, be prohibited. It bans the use of AI for biometric surveillance, emotion recognition, and predictive policing, as well as "real-time" remote biometric identification systems in publicly accessible spaces and "post" remote biometric identification systems, with an exception for law enforcement for the prosecution of serious crimes, and only after judicial authorization. It would also prohibit biometric categorization systems using sensitive characteristics (e.g., gender, race, ethnicity, citizenship status, religion, political orientation), predictive policing systems (based on profiling, location or past criminal behavior), emotion recognition systems in law enforcement, border management, the workplace, and educational institutions, and untargeted scraping of facial images from the internet or CCTV footage to create facial recognition databases (as doing so would be violating human rights and the right to privacy).

Generative AI systems would have to comply with transparency requirements, disclosing that the content was AI-generated, helping to distinguish so-called deep-fake images from real ones, and ensuring safeguards against generating illegal content. Detailed summaries of the copyrighted data used for their training must also be publicly available. Also, AI systems that influence voters in elections, like ANALITICA, would be considered high risk.

While yet to be fully approved, it seems that Europe is leading the way in AI regulatory frameworks. How it will be implemented in concrete terms, and its impact on innovation, remain open question.

The Public Choice Problem of AI: The Role of Experts in Government

As previously stated, to create AI algorithms, specific mathematical and computing knowledge is crucial, but the regulation of such algorithms requires input from an even wider audience of experts, from business to the social sciences to philosophy. Proposed legislation on AI is well-intended attempts to rein in a novel technology's biggest risks, but the salient question is: how would such legislation be implemented? Who will be the experts (with what background?) who are asked by politicians to help craft and later implement any given AI-related legislation—especially when the use of AI creates such intense social reactions as it does? On the one hand, some view AI as the best invention in the world; on the other hand, some believe quite strongly that by implementing AI so swiftly, some societies may inadvertently be digging their own graves. Subsequently, much of the current debate has been dominated by two groups: the "apocalyptic" view, led by Elon Musk, Bill Gates, and Stephen Hawking, the latter of whom said in 2014 that AI could even end humanity, and the "techno-optimists," led by Mark Zuckerberg and Larry Page, who emphasize the power of innovation and its positive impact on our quality of life, business opportunities, and medical care.

Such disagreements could be constructive when discussing how any proposed AI regulation framework should be applied. In this section, we will analyze public choice theory's insights on the role of experts in government, and then we will try to apply them to the AI regulation framework.

Nowadays, there exists a primarily self-regulated AI market, *primarily* because the big tech companies are pioneering AI development by signing AI ethics codes or sponsoring AI projects. What would happen if the situation changed, and a governmental agency regulated the AI market? In other words, what should the government do, and would that be better than what we are doing currently?

The role of experts in public policy and the economy of bureaucracy needs to be referenced at this point.

Every person has incentives, including experts, bureaucrats, and public policymakers. The AI market is not an exception. In the book *Escape from Democracy*, professors David M. Levy and Sandra J. Peart introduce us to several points where the role of experts in public policy should be analyzed.

The authors explain many points from which we choose the four that are the most relevant to our topic. The first is discussion: an expert is constrained by discussion. Discussion ensures that results can be elaborated and checked, leading to trustworthy results being published. Discussing results among different groups of experts helps foster a healthy amount of skepticism, and cooperation flourishes. The problem arises when a policy is treated as a linear policy instead of a cyclical one. Experts are asked to find optimal solutions to achieve a specific end: in our case, this would entail weighing AI opportunities and threats. Ignoring that AI is not static, but continuously evolving, could lead to obsolete rules. Therefore, those "optimal solutions" and ends must be reviewed and discussed constantly. Unfortunately, experience shows that once the decision is made, the discussion is minimal. In the process of implementing policy, there is temptation for those experts to avoid continuous review and discussion. After all, this might put their position in the government at risk. This problem is known as "regulatory capture". After the goals are agreed on, those who implement them may use their authority to achieve their own private goals.

> Discussion as a correction to bias and a means by which society's goals are endogenously determined and constantly checked and revised. People come to appreciate the goals of others through discussion with them. Through discussion, they come to appreciate differences and points of view. Discussion is part and parcel of a healthy skepticism of expert recommendations and policy formulations that presume exogenous goals. (Levy and Peart, 2017)

Second is transparency. Transparency is normally considered a binary state: either we are transparent (stage one) or not (stage zero). The authors argue that transparency is a fuzzier concept since it is impossible to have a situation of full transparency. It is more realistic to be aware of a non-transparent situation than to try to create a fully transparent one. In our case, it would be impossible to make AI 100% transparent. On the one hand, AI models are too complicated to be understood by most people, but there will always be a learning curve that even experts will not be able to follow.

Third, Sympathetic Bias: Since experts are part of a group that shares methods, affinities, and also some ideology, they could be motivated to obtain results consistent with those of their group and to render their methods nontransparent to those outside the group. Fourth, Exogenous vs. Endogenous Goals: Exogenous goals put the experts as outsiders of the policy instead of participants of it; the incentive is clear, and exogenous goals offer tractability.

> If a group of goals are taken to be exogenous, the implementation of the policy is fundamentally an engineering calculus. But once the goals are taken as endogenous in an ill-understood process . . . the implementation is contingent on the shifting goals and ambiguity pours into analysis. (Levy and Peart 2017)

The authors recommend better aligning the incentives associated with expertise: "Instead of 'better people watching worse people,' we suggest that people must watch each other."

Multiple combinations of experts will decrease the potential failures associated with uncritical acceptance of expertise, since an "open, competition-rich, scientific environment has a better chance of offering the community of experts, and the public competing views."

In the case of the public sector, the policymakers and the experts are participants in AI, either in the industry or the development itself.

When Elon Musk withdrew his signature from the open letter requesting a halt on AI for six months at the Future of Life Institute, his main argument was that it was unrealistic to pause for six months. He launched his own AI company called xAI, under the argument that if everyone has access to AI, it is less likely we will use it to attack each other (Reuters 2023).

Suppose experts in private and public sectors, from different backgrounds and nations, work together on an AI regulation framework that weighs opportunities with risks: We may get a framework that protects us from the risks but lets us continue enjoying the benefits.

We are at a very strategic point, where regulations are not implemented yet, but AI keeps developing. Regulations always follow behind innovation. It may be time for a new opportunity where policymakers and big tech companies work together, with neither having power over the other.

We also need to address the role of bureaucracy. The theory of the economics of bureaucracy shows us that without profit and loss signals to indicate the success or failure of their decisions, bureaucratic agencies must measure achievement differently. In the private sector, entrepreneurs fight to get more customers, whereas bureaucrats fight against each other for government resources. This dynamic implies that bureaucracies will engage in intense rent-seeking behavior to increase their budgets and expand their personnel. In the case of AI, the EU, and USA Acts requesting the opening of new specialized governmental AI agencies could be seen as examples of such rent-seeking.

The incentives of these new agencies will be to stay alive in the government or even increase their size, alleging that AI needs more regulations when, in reality, we do not know if that will be the case. For example, assume an agency demonstrates to the government that some of its programs are successful. In that case, it can claim it could achieve more significant results with more resources, especially if the public is demanding regulation, like in the case of AI. This rent-seeking behavior has further implications for the government's allocation of resources.

Entrepreneurs or tech companies can quickly adapt to new information and changing conditions. In the case of AI, for instance, they would lose the trust of their clients and face a significant market loss that could even take them out of the market. A clear example of this was the aforementioned case of Microsoft's "TAY" chatbot, which had to be removed twenty-four hours after they launched it. Making changes like that in a bureaucracy is much more difficult because all the incentives of bureaucracy push people to be protective, cautious, and slow with their budgets.

People assume that bureaucrats work exclusively in the "public interest," which implies that our experts will put aside their own private or selfish purposes to protect the public, instead of particular groups, especially regarding AI, where it is challenging to understand what would be "the best public interest" at all. James M. Buchanan noted that this public interest framework ignores the bureaucratic context in which government and other agencies operate. Failing to extend the behavioral assumptions of rational self-interest across all contexts leads to a poor understanding of policy. While not denying that bureaucratic actors may value the well-being of others, public choice theory points out that those in positions to influence the trajectory of policy do not look solely to maximize the welfare of others. Instead, they suggest that, just like private actors, they respond to the incentives created by the institutions, or the "rules of the game" in which they operate (Buchanan 1999; North 1990).

An AI Governance Proposal

The three principles of user control, transparency, and audits could ensure the benefits of AI without experiencing some of the discussed risks (Hosanagar 2019). What are these principles?

First: User control. This is the idea of giving users some control over how algorithms make decisions for or about them—in other words, keeping a human in the loop.

A study by Wharton University evaluated the impact of user control on trust (Hosanagar 2019). In their experiment, users were asked to predict high school students' scores in standardized tests based on information about these high school students. Users were allowed to consult algorithms. These users or subjects in the experiment were divided into four groups. Group 1 had no control over the algorithm: They had to decide whether or not they wanted to use the algorithm, but if they decided to use it, then whatever the algorithm suggested would be their choice. Groups 2 and 3 had minimal control over the algorithm. Group 2 was able to overrule the algorithm or AI in a few instances, and Group 3 was allowed to overrule the model by changing the algorithm's predictions by a small amount. Group 4 had complete control over the algorithm. Finally, they evaluated how much users trusted the algorithm—how often they wanted to use the algorithm and what percentage of these users wanted to use the algorithm. They found that users with no control had low trust and were less willing to use the algorithm, while users with even a little bit of control had very high trust and were willing to use the algorithm much more.

Interestingly, they found that the amount of control did not matter. Whether users had little control or a lot of control, the trust levels remained high. In short, a little control goes a long way in establishing user trust, but we do not necessarily need a lot of control.

The idea of user control is to give users enough options in the product design and the user interface to guide the algorithm's performance and even overrule it when they notice something is going wrong.

Second: Transparency. We can find three different interpretations in cases of transparency in AI. First, technical transparency is the idea of revealing the algorithm's source code. After the crash of 2010 in the US stock market, an investigation suggested that automated algorithms played a primary role. In 2015, the CFTC (Commodity Future Trading Commission) proposed that the Department of Justice force traders to reveal the source code of the algorithms. Traders and industry professionals resisted this because it would cause them to reveal their proprietary IP. Furthermore, it would allow hackers to evaluate their code, identify vulnerabilities in the code, and attack it. For these reasons, the CFTC proposal was rejected. Full transparency could lead us to more significant problems. The kind of transparency needed is for end-users to understand how the algorithm works. Was an algorithm used to make a decision? What kinds of data are being used by the algorithm? What variables were considered and were most important for this decision?

Another study that supports this argument was done by a researcher named Rene Kizilcec (Lee 2020). He evaluated how user trust of an algorithm changes with transparency. In the experiment that the researcher ran, students were given a grade for an assignment, which was determined algorithmically. Some students received no information about how the algorithm decided their grades; their trust was very low. Another group of students got some minimal information on how the algorithm decided grades—high-level information on the factors that the algorithm weighed and some basic explanations that provided them with an intuition of the algorithm's design. Trust went up dramatically when this kind of transparency was provided. A third group received a very high amount of transparency, where they were given detailed formulae that were used in the algorithm and very detailed specifics. Trust remained low with this group. This is partly because these users could not evaluate the complex information provided and make use of it. All of this suggests that for end-users, we do not need much transparency; we need basic information such as variables, data information, and the outcome.

We mentioned before that the EU has a regulation called GDPR, which gives consumers a right to an explanation: if companies are using advanced machine learning such as neural networks or random forests, then they need to provide explanations to consumers. The field of interpretable machine learning will become relevant because it allows high-level explanations to consumers about the factors driving the model's predictions, or decisions. Transparency has another exciting aspect to it: data scientists. Today, when a data scientist uses a very complex model, like a neural network, to make a decision, such as loan approval, even the data scientist might need to learn the factors driving the model's performance. Interpretable machine learning is not only relevant for the end-user but also for the data scientists or managers who are deploying these algorithms. Here again, global interpretability and local interpretability matter. Global interpretability is when we can explain at a high level the essential variables driving a model's predictions. For a loan approval decision, feedback may be that the loan approval is determined primarily by the applicant's income, second by their credit history, third by some other variable, etc. Local interpretability is about getting feedback on the most critical variables driving a decision. If our loan application were not approved, local interpretability would involve explaining the factors resulting in the loan application being denied. This is becoming an increasingly important field within machine learning, with many open-source tools and third-party vendors offering solutions that help companies offer interpretability as part of their machine-learning activities. This can not only provide explanations to consumers and increase trust, but it can also increase trust among managers trying to deploy these systems. They are also valuable tools for debugging.

The third principle is the idea of auditing algorithms, especially in high-stakes settings. Companies often audit their high-risk automated decision systems, such as machine learning models used to make high-risk decisions like loan approvals or resume screening, to evaluate them evaluated for accuracy and fairness. The EU regulation has yet to be passed, and it is unclear whether it will be passed in its original form. Nevertheless, forward-looking companies should not wait for regulation; they should take proactive steps to win consumer trust, prevent problems with the algorithms, and ensure that their systems are robust in the long term. An audit process begins by first creating an inventory of all machine learning models used by an organization. Next, for each model, we identify all use cases, whether oriented around a complex or simple decision. We identify the use cases, who is the developer of the model, who is the owner of the model, which division owns it, and which individual in the division is responsible for it. Each model might be given a risk rating, assessing the social and financial risks if the model goes wrong. This might be the basis of a decision on whether an audit is needed: if the risk rating of a model is relatively low or moderate, we may not need an audit process for that model. An audit would be needed for any high-risk model, however. Such an audit can be conducted by an internal or an external expert who is an outsider and would look at several factors. For example, they would start by looking at the inputs into the model: What is the data quality? Are there biases in the training data? They would look at the model itself, benchmarking it against alternative models and confirming that it performs better than the alternatives. They would also stress test the model against simulated data and confirm that the model works well even when it relies on data other than the training data. Lastly, they would look at the decisions or predictions made by the model, evaluate them, and look at explanations or interpretations to understand if the model is weighing the right factors appropriately. They could also look at outliers in the predictions. This is all collectively part of the audit process.

A growing number of organizations are creating official AI ethics frameworks. A Harvard report in 2020 evaluated thirty-six major AI ethics frameworks from big companies like Microsoft, Telefonica, and Tencent, from standards bodies, industry coalitions, and governments worldwide (Fjeld 2020). It identified eight common categories that appeared again and again. These are privacy, accountability, safety and security, transparency and explainability, fairness and non-discrimination, human control and professional responsibility—which entails infusing ethical and legal concerns throughout the process and the organization—and finally, the promotion of human values, which means asking whether our actions are ultimately in service of human flourishing. An essential finding of the Harvard report was that these principles converge. Companies, organizations, and governments are considering existing frameworks, and the principles are becoming understood as the general foundation for most frameworks.

Conclusion

There are some points we need to consider before we start implementing AI regulation frameworks: first, regulation tends to slow down innovation; second, we need a group of diverse experts who are in constant contact with each other. Experts should come from both the public and private sector to work on a worldwide AI regulation framework. Even after the first laws are implemented, they should remain attentive to AI development: this requires having a framework that is flexible enough to evolve as AI does, to avoid becoming obsolete and harmful. On the other hand, consumers need to be aware of the risks of AI algorithms in order to confidently use AI in their private lives.

Notes

1 Gradient Descent in mathematics is an optimization algorithm for finding a local minimum of a differentiable function. There are three types of gradient descent learning algorithms: Batch gradient descent, Stochastic gradient descent, and mini-batch gradient descent. BGD sums the error for each point in a training set. SGD runs a training epoch for each example within the dataset and it updates each training example's parameters one at a time. Mini-batch gradient descent combines concepts from both.

2 Supervised Machine Learning learns from using labeled data; the algorithms used are linear regression and logistic regression. The problems to be solved are regression and classification. Unsupervised Machine Learning trains using unlabeled data without any guidance; the algorithm used are K-Means, and the problems to be solved are by association or clustering. Reinforcement ML works by interacting with the environment. The algorithms used are Q-learning and SARSA.

3 Artificial neural networks (ANNs) are composed of a node layer, containing an input layer, one or more hidden layers, and an output layer. Each node, or artificial neuron, connects to another and has an associated weight and threshold. If the output of any individual node is above the specified threshold value, that node is activated, sending data to the next layer of the network. Otherwise, no data are passed along to the next layer of the network. Neural networks rely on training data to learn and improve their accuracy over time.

4 A traditional software rule-based system is a system that applies human-made rules to store, sort, and manipulate data; it executes instructions from a starting set of data and rules.

5 Feature engineering is the process of selecting, manipulating, and transforming raw data into features that can be used in supervised learning.

6 A right to be given an explanation for the output of the algorithm.

7 On June 14, 2023, Members of the European Parliament adopted Parliament's negotiating position on the AI Act. The talks will begin with EU countries in the Council on the final form of the law. https://www.europarl.europa.eu/news/en/press-room/20230609IPR96212/meps-ready-to-negotiate-first-ever-rules-for-safe-and-transparent-ai

References

Abu Dhabi National Oil Company (ADNOC). 2020. "ADNOC Completes First Phase of Artificial Intelligence Predictive Maintenance Project." *ADNOC*. https://www.adnoc.ae/en/news-and-media/press-releases/2020/adnoc-completes-first-phase-of-artificial-intelligence-predictive-maintenance-project/.

Angwin, Julia, Jeff Larson, Surya Mattu, and Lauren Kirchner. 2016. "Machine Bias." ProPublica. https://www.propublica.org/article/machine-bias-risk-assessments-in-criminal-sentencing.

Buchanan, James M. 1999. *The Logical Foundations of Constitutional Liberty*. Indianapolis, IN: Liberty Fund.

Fjeld, Jessica. 2020. "Principled Artificial Intelligence: Mapping Consensus in Ethical and Rights-Based Approaches to Principles for AI." Harvard University. January 15. http://nrs.harvard.edu/urn-3:HUL.InstRepos:42160420.

Hawking, Stephen. 2014. "Artificial Intelligence Could Spell End of Human Race" *The Guardian*. https://www.theguardian.com/science/2014/dec/02/stephen-hawking-intel-communication-system-astrophysicist-software-predictive-text-type.

International Business Machines (IBM). 2024. "What Is AI?" *IBM*. https://www.ibm.com/topics/artificial-intelligence.

Hosanagar, Kartik. 2019. "Who Made That Decision: You or an Algorithm?" Knowledge at Wharton. https://knowledge.wharton.upenn.edu/article/algorithms-decision-making/.

Knowles, Elizabeth. 2006. *The Oxford Dictionary of Phrase and Fable*. Oxford: Oxford University Press.

Lee, Hansol. 2020. "Evaluation of Fairness Trade-Offs in Predicting Student Success." June 30. https://arxiv.org/abs/2007.00088.

Levy, David M., and Sandra J. Peart. 2017. *Escape from Democracy*. Cambridge, UK: Cambridge University Press.

North, Douglass C. 1990. *Institutions, Institutional Change and Economic Performance*. Cambridge, UK: Cambridge University Press.

PwC. 2017. "Sizing the Prize: What's the Real Value of AI for Your Business and How Can You Capitalize?" PwC. https://www.pwc.com/gx/en/issues/analytics/assets/pwc-ai-analysis-sizing-the-prize-report.pdf.

Reuters. 2023. "Elon Musk Launches AI Firm xAI as he Looks to Take on OpenAI." *Reuters*. https://www.reuters.com/technology/elon-musks-ai-firm-xai-launches-website-2023-07-12/.

United States Congress. 2022. "Algorithmic Accountability Act of 2022." United States Congress. https://www.congress.gov/bill/117th-congress/house-bill/6580/related-bills.

Whittaker, Meredith, et al. 2018. "AI Now Report 2018." AI Now Institute. https://ainowinstitute.org/wp-content/uploads/2023/04/AI_Now_2018_Report.pdf.

Index

About the Editors and Contributors

About the Editors

Paul Dragos Aligica, Senior Fellow with the F. A. Hayek Program for Advanced Study in Philosophy, Politics, and Economics at the Mercatus Center at George Mason University and KPMG Professor of Governance at the University of Bucharest.

Jayme S. Lemke, Senior Fellow with the F. A. Hayek Program for Advanced Study in Philosophy, Politics, and Economics at the Mercatus Center at George Mason University.

Brian Meehan, Associate Professor of Economics at Berry College.

About the Contributors

George Agyeah, Data scientist at Walmart Global Tech.

Brittany K. Giles-Jones, PhD student in humanities (history concentration) at Clark Atlanta University.

Malte Hendrickx, PhD student in philosophy at University of Michigan, Ann Arbor.

Saige M. Hill, Assistant Director of the Monarch Internship and Co-Op Office at Old Dominion University.

Cory Jack, Associate at Patomak Global Partners.

Gah-Kai Leung, PhD student in politics and international studies at the University of Warwick.

Agostina Lorenzini, Chief Operating Officer at Exibhu.

Laura Montenovo, Assistant Professor in the Department of Agricultural Economics at Purdue University.

Dallin Overstreet, PhD student in public policy and administration at Arizona State University.

Jean Vilbert, PhD student in government at Harvard University.

www.ingramcontent.com/pod-product-compliance
Ingram Content Group UK Ltd.
Pitfield, Milton Keynes, MK11 3LW, UK
UKHW020219290926
15470UKWH00001B/278